LEVINASIAN MEDITATIONS

Levinasian Meditations

Ethics,

Philosophy,

and

Religion

Richard A. Cohen

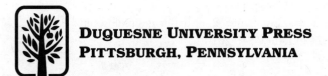
DUQUESNE UNIVERSITY PRESS
PITTSBURGH, PENNSYLVANIA

Published in the United States of America by
Duquesne University Press
600 Forbes Avenue
Pittsburgh, Pennsylvania 15282

Library of Congress Cataloging-in-Publication Data

Cohen, Richard A., 1950–
    Levinasian meditations : ethics, philosophy, and religion /
Richard A. Cohen.
        p. cm.
    Includes bibliographical references and index.
    ISBN 978-0-8207-0432-6 (acid-free paper) — ISBN 978-0-8207-0433-3
(pbk. : acid-free paper)
    1. Lévinas, Emmanuel. 2. Judaism and philosophy. I. Title.
    B2430.L484C645 2010
    194—dc22

                                                              2010005353

∞ Printed on acid-free paper

In memory of Edith Wyschogrod,
first in American Levinas studies,

Sidney S. Cohen,
exemplary in all his ways,

to encourage the "humanity that adorns the world."

CONTENTS

ACKNOWLEDGMENTS

Earlier versions of essays in this volume were previously published in the following:

"The End of the World: Heidegger, Kant and Levinas," in *Responsibility, God and Society: Theological Ethics in Dialogue (Festschrift Roger Burggraeve)*, ed. J. De Tavernier, J. A. Selling, J. Verstraeten, and P. Schotsmans, 49–68. Leuven: Bibliotheca Ephermeridum Theologicarum Lovaniensium 217, 2008.

"Being, Time and the Ethical Body," in *The Body in Human Inquiry: Interdisciplinary Explorations of Embodiment*, ed. V. Berdayes, L. Esposito and J. W. Murphy. Cresskill, N.J.: Hampton Press, 2004; 87–104.

"Thinking Least about Death—Contra Heidegger," in *International Journal for Philosophy of Religion*, ed. E. Long, vol. 60 (2006): 21–39. Reprinted in *Phenomenology 2005*, vol. 5, ed. L. Embree, 163–98. New York: Zeta Books, 2008.

"Buber and Levinas—and Heidegger," in *Levinas and Buber: Dialogue and Difference*, ed. P. Atterton, M. Calarco, and M. Friedman, 235–49. Pittsburgh: Duquesne University Press, 2004.

"Levinas, Plato, and Ethical Exegesis," in *Levinas Studies: An Annual Review*, vol. 1, ed. J. Bloechl and J. L. Kosky, 37–50. Pittsburgh: Duquesne University Press, 2006.

"Uncovering the 'Difficult Universality' of the Face-to-Face," *Cahiers d'Etudes Levinassiennes*, no. 6 (2006): 93–115.

"Some Notes on the Title of Levinas's *Totality and Infinity* and Its First Sentence," in *Studia Phaenomenologica: Romanian Journal for Phenomenology* 6 (2006): 117–37.

"Choosing and the Chosen: Levinas and Sartre," in *Cahiers d'Etudes Levinassiennes*, no. 5 (2006): 55–82.

"Some Reflections on Levinas and Shakespeare," in *Ethics and Literature*, ed. D. Gelhard, 107–34. Cambridge, Mass.: Galda und Wilch Verlag, 2001.

"Defending Levinas: An Interview by Raymond Lai (Chung-Hsiung Lai)," trans. Yu-Wen Liu, *Chung-Wai Literary Quarterly* 36, no. 4, ed. Chung-Hsiung Lai (2007): 267–306.

An earlier version of "Levinas, Judaism and the Primacy of the Ethical," appeared in *Cambridge Companion to Modern Jewish Philosophy*, ed. M. L. Morgan and P. E. Gordon, 234–55. Cambridge: Cambridge University Press, 2007.

"Emmanuel Levinas: Philosopher and Jew," in *Revista Portugesa de filosofia* (Braga, Portugal), special issue, *Entre Razao e Revelacao* 62, nos. 2–4, ed. Jao J. Vila-Cha (2006): 481–91.

"Singularity: The Universality of Jewish Particularism — Benamozegh and Levinas," in *Religious Experience and the End of Metaphysics*, ed. J. Bloechl, 135–52. Bloomington, Ind.: Indiana University Press, 2003.

"Virtue Embodied: Brit Mila, Desire and Levinas," *Shofar: An Interdisciplinary Journal of Jewish Studies* 16, no. 3 (Spring 1998): 63–70.

"Against Theology," in *The Exorbitant: Emmanuel Levinas between Jews and Christians*, ed. Kevin Hart and Michael A. Signer, 74–89. New York: Fordham University Press, 2010.

"Theodicy after the Shoah: Levinas on Suffering and Evil," revision of chap. 8, R. A. Cohen, *Ethics, Exegesis and Philosophy: Interpretation after Levinas*, 266–82. Cambridge: Cambridge University Press, 2001.

ABBREVIATIONS

(All text by Levinas unless otherwise noted)

AT   *Alterity and Transcendence*
BPW   *Basic Philosophical Writings*
BV   *Beyond the Verse*
CPP   *Collected Philosophical Papers*
DEH   *Discovering Existence with Husserl*
DF   *Difficult Freedom*
EE   *Existence and Existents*
EI   *Ethics and Infinity*
EN   *Entre Nous*
GCM   *Of God Who Comes to Mind*
GDT   *God, Death, and Time*
HO   *Humanism of the Other*
IRB   *Is it Righteous to Be?*
ITN   *In the Time of the Nations*
LR   *The Levinas Reader*
NT   *Nine Talmudic Readings*
NTR   *New Talmudic Readings*
OB   *Otherwise than Being or Beyond Essence*
OE   *On Escape*
OS   *Outside the Subject*
PN   *Proper Names*
SE   *"Le scandale du mal"*
TI   *Totality and Infinity*
TTI   *The Theory of Intuition in Husserl's Phenomenology*
TO   *Time and the Other*
UH   *Unforeseen History*
US   *"Useless Suffering"*

BT   *Being and Time* (Martin Heidegger)

PART ONE

Ethics as First Philosophy

Part One

Terms such as "science," "ethics, and "aesthetics," which refer to
actions and judgments and to the intellectual disciplines which produce and reflect on them, are less inspiring and evocative than "the
true, the good, and the beautiful." The latter refer to ideals, to the
heights to which these actions, judgments, and disciplines aim. But
is not all this finished? For these ideals have become questionable,
are considered archaic, "essentialist," ideological constructions made
obsolete by the more sophisticated judgments of the self-appointed
cultural elite of our day. Nevertheless, the traditional terms, outdated
or not, better convey the lineage and nobility of all three registers of
signification, and by doing so they better suggest that lacking any one
of them human life would surely be less full. Whatever the significance
and standing of these three ideals or of the disciplines which reflect
upon them, whether traditional or postmodern, their import is more
than sufficient to obligate us to ask what is at stake in the claim central to Emmanuel Levinas's thought that "ethics is first philosophy."

We hesitate before the question itself. Are we inclined today to
think it worthwhile, let alone possible, to resolve the perennial struggle between the good, the true, and the beautiful, or between ethics,
science, and aesthetics? Can we really say that one comes first? Will
not poets, artists, and their cultivated followers always favor the beautiful, the ugly, the strong, or the fantastic, that is to say, the aesthetic?
Will not intellectuals, great minds, and their fastidious students forever seek knowledge, truth, and science, or their inverted shadow
images in sophistry, skepticism, and politics? And will not others,
no doubt the vast majority, with Levinas among them, good and
upright people, give greatest praise to the noble heights of kindness

and fairness, of morality and justice, love of the neighbor, no matter how simple or plain or even lowly such desiderata may appear to
the ostensibly more discriminating eyes of artists and intellectuals? Is
there any sense, then, to establishing a hierarchy? Or does not this
very hesitation, this felt reluctance to establish a hierarchy, *paradoxically* indicate the unacknowledged *priority* of one or another of these
three registers of meaning, a priority whose primacy precisely includes
the enforcement—gentle or rough, insinuated or violent—of a leveling of hierarchy?

Levinas will answer in the affirmative. Science, in its quest for
knowledge, would level all playing fields, the entire universe, including this grand debate itself, reducing all and everything to the true
and the false, to knowledge and nothing but knowledge. Levinas will
oppose such leveling—which he will name "totality" and "totalitarianism"—with the "infinity" of ethics, the good, the good above evil,
justice above injustice, *ethical orientation*. And Levinas's answer, like
that of science, occurs in the face of the *fact* that the debate between
these grand projects with their great aims—the good, the true, and
the beautiful—is a perennial one. But Levinas's answer is one that
accounts for and respects the debate itself, while science—and in its
own way aesthetics too—would put an end to it.

One thing is certain: in the precincts of *philosophy,* the birthplace
and home of the reflexive and reasoned deliberations which have
given rise to the very names and disciplines of "ethics," "science,"
and "aesthetics," it is *science* that has reigned supreme for two and
half millennia. And the supreme result of this supremacy is *modern*
science, methodical, constructive, and mathematical knowledge of
the real. Modern science represents the most demanding, the most
powerful, and the most successful form that the quest for truth has
ever taken on the planet. Perhaps Edmund Husserl—mathematician,
founder of the modern science of phenomenology, and Levinas's
teacher—expressed this best in an appropriately titled article,
"Philosophy as Rigorous Science" (1911). "There is, perhaps, in all
modern life no more powerfully, more irresistibly progressing idea
than that of science. Nothing will hinder its victorious advance. In
fact, with regard to its legitimate aims, it is all-embracing. Looked
upon in its ideal perfection, it would be reason itself, which could
have no other authority equal or superior to itself."[1]

As if in testimony to Husserl's paean to the triumph of science, when we speak today of "the West" or of what is "Western," we no longer refer to a geographic region, nor even do we think of the hallowed discipline of "philosophy," but rather we have in mind a spiritual discipline, philosophy's greatest progeny: modern science and the technologies integral to it. So successful has been modern science, the triumph of objective truth, that philosophy itself has been forgotten by and within it. Now it seems as if philosophy with its quest for truth were but another quaint and obsolete tradition superseded and properly dismissed by the appearance of "the real thing," modern scientific knowledge. Science was always first philosophy—and now more than ever.

It is by keeping the above perspective in mind, and at the same time without in the least diminishing the greatness of science, that we must understand and acknowledge the momentous revolution in Western thought that Levinas accomplishes by conceiving ethics as first philosophy. It is not, however, a revolution in morality or justice. Kant once remarked that ethics is never so foolish as to invent a new morality, but rather gives a novel explanation for the same old morality. The old and tried imperatives are the only ones, at all times, in all places: Do not murder; do not steal; do not lie; do not covet; and the like. Only a mad or evil person would invent new tablets. What ethics does is give an account—a philosophical account—of morality and justice. This is the first sense in which ethics is first philosophy. Levinas does not dispute the philosophical character of ethics; what he does dispute is its status. Contrary to the main thrust of the long history of philosophy, which has been its noble struggle for truth, and in the face of the present triumph of science which is the brilliant result of that long history and struggle, for Levinas ethics is not second to science. It is first philosophy. Socrates was mistaken: one must not first *know* the good in order to do the good. Doing the good comes first. Morality comes first, and philosophical reflection as knowledge, as science, or as truth, comes second.

But we must be careful to appreciate the meaning and manner in which ethics is first philosophy. We shall make our approach by way of Kant. This is because Kant, who was perhaps, the greatest philosopher of science Western philosophy has ever known (equaled only by Aristotle before him and Husserl after him), also affirms the primacy

of ethics, or in his terminology, "the primacy of practical reason."
It is because they agree on this all-important point that Levinas's
difference from Kant is so instructive. By contrast, Spinoza, another
philosopher of science, but one who more typically affirms science as
first philosophy, and is indeed the first philosopher to affirm *modern*
science as first philosophy and by so doing *reduces* the good and the
beautiful to the true, stands at the "antipodes" from Levinas. Thus
Levinas's differences from Spinoza while far greater than his differences from Kant are for the same reason less instructive regarding
the significance of recognizing the primacy of ethics as first philosophy. What makes the contrast with Kant illuminating, then, is that
despite his good intention, as it were, despite the primacy he intends
to accord to ethics, Kant nevertheless succumbs in his ethical account
of morality and justice to the primacy of science, knowledge, and
truth. The rationality explicated in the *Critique of Pure Reason* not
only "makes room" for the freedom of will which is the condition
of the morality Kant explicates in the *Critique of Practical Reason*, it
continues to determine the form, the parameters, the "autonomy"
of the latter. As a result, Kant's ethics is a rational ethics in the sense
that it presents a morality conforming to and subordinate to the standards of science. Once again, as with Socrates, one must *know* the
good—determine maxims of behavior in conformity to the principle
of noncontradiction and universal law—before doing the good. And
once again, ethics is in this way made subordinate to the standards
of science.

Must Levinas's ethics in contrast therefore be *irrational?* Not at
all, or not in the sense that his ethics opposes science by taking sides
with antiscience, with the irrational, the mythical, the dark, and the
like, which would not and could not produce an ethics at all. What
follows from the irrational is, as every logician knows, everything,
neither good nor evil but both and all, all things possible and impossible, anything, and hence evil. That Levinas succeeds where Kant
fails does not come at the price of a turn to the irrational (even, and
perhaps especially, under the name of "faith"), a turn which apparently seduced such thinkers as Jacobi, Hamann, Schelling, and the
German Romantics. Rather, what Levinas does, in contrast to Kant,
is to understand ethics not rationally but ethically. That is to say, his

ethics is not based on the deficiency of reason but on the surplus of morality. Levinas's philosophy is an account of morality faithful to morality rather than to the rational standards of account giving. It is a much more troubling difference and approach than may strike the reader at first glance.

To conceive ethics ethically involves neither a "vicious circle" nor the famous "hermeneutic" circle, but rather the difficult passage and hyperbole of the ethical. It makes Levinas's philosophy difficult, his language strange, even strained, but this difficulty and strangeness are, in one sense, brought on by and designed to break the hegemony hitherto exerted by truth and knowledge, by the rule of an episte-mologically minded philosophy, philosophy in the service of science. On the other hand, the difficulty is not simply relative to science but comes from elsewhere, from the very difficulty of morality. The difficulty of science is that it requires great mental power and con-centration, cleverness, mathematical ability, and like cognitive skills, combined with a long training in the current complexity of a scientific discipline. The difficulty of morality, in contrast, comes from a dis-tracting counter movement against my natural inclinations, from the disturbing and vexing demands that I respond to the other's needs which are imposed—without my permission—on me. Very simply, it is difficult to be good, to care for the other before oneself. Or as Levinas has said: "No one is good voluntarily" (*OB* 11). Morality is an interruption of enjoyment, a check on vital energies, a restraint of the will, not to mention our resources. This strain or difficulty, as well as the linguistic strain or difficulty for ethical philosophy to break free from the usual standards of knowledge, are both expressions of the primacy which is the very elevation of moral imperatives.

It is well known that in *Totality and Infinity* and elsewhere, Levinas speaks of morality in terms of "infinity"—"infinite responsibilities." Such infinity not only contrasts with but bursts the self-presence or "totality" of science, its tendency to construct a closed system of signs, even if that closure is deferred as Husserl understood (or deferred and celebrated as such as in Derrida). Moral obligations rupture knowing by their greater exigency. It is more important to help others. And, as we shall see, it is this overriding exigency which at the same time drives sci-ence and without which science could neither function nor make sense.

If philosophy has the task of "defining" the human, or if more precisely it is a reflection of the truly human, then Levinas conceives philosophy and the human not by a questing for knowledge, "love of wisdom" as love of knowledge, as is usual, but in terms of the greatest imperatives, the highest obligations and responsibilities, as did Plotinus who asked "What is philosophy?" and answered: "Philosophy is the supremely precious."[2] Thus for Levinas, both philosophy and the human are constituted not as a "love of wisdom," but rather as the "wisdom of love"—love of the neighbor (*OB* 162). The human, for Levinas, arises as a responsibility to and for the other person, for the other's suffering, a responsibility always and only taken up in the first person singular, but nevertheless no less universal, in its own way, than the universality of knowledge. The "universal" we call the human arises not in a proposition or a concept, however rational, but across the imposition of a disproportion, an asymmetry, an inordinateness wherein the other person stands higher than the self, in a moral height, which obligates me before all others, including my for-itself.

One's original obligation is not, therefore, and contrary to Kant, to the *law* in another, a law whereby the singularity, the other's otherness, is dismissed as mere particularity and bias. Such is the path of knowledge. Rather, the moral self is directly, immediately, hyperbolically obligated to the other person in his or her singularity, the unique other, the neighbor, with his or her particular needs, in a relation Levinas calls the "face-to-face" or "proximity." Morality thus does not first arise as a consciousness of responsibility, but as responsibility itself, "proximity and not the truth of proximity" (*OB* 120). Responsibility, a being beholden to the other beyond one's own being, hostage to the other in an immediacy or passivity greater, more important, and more pressing than the intentionality of consciousness. "Do not murder!"—It is a command, but one first traced not in stone but in the very face of the other as the incomparable face of the other in whose elevation discourse itself opens up and communication becomes possible.

First philosophy, then, is moral responsibility for the other. Such a responsibility is a "diachrony" of the self for-the-other before itself, the other-in-the-self, the self not questioning but "put in question," a shattering of the self's self-presence, unity and identity overloaded, pregnant with the surplus of another's needs, a turning of the self inside-out for-the-other, "giving to the other of the bread out of one's own mouth" (*OB* 142; 64, 74), a saying elicited by the other, a going forth to the other which never comes back and never reaches a destination. Always goaded to go farther still, "in the measure that responsibilities are taken up they multiply" (12)—infinite responsibility. This is the "relation without relation" Levinas's ethics puts first because its exigency—responsibility for the other—comes first. It is first philosophy, the wisdom of love that first makes the love of wisdom possible and, as we shall see, necessary.

Clearly from such a perspective certain commonplaces of academic life will be called into question, indeed challenged and overturned. For instance, consider the superior snobbery which looks down on ethics as a kind of narrow-mindedness or "preaching," the sneering dismissive use of the term "moralist" whenever ethical issues are taken seriously, i.e., when they demand a response and not merely an intellectualization (We recall here Heidegger's ponderous debasement of morality as "ontic.").[3] No doubt, like everything else, one can overdo morality, help where it is not needed or invade the privacy of others, but is this a greater fault than dismissing morality altogether? To care about morality, to be moved by moral obligations, this is not simply "bad form," even if it is disturbing. To mock or dismiss morality is no criticism; it is flight. To conceive ethics as first philosophy, as does Levinas, means no longer misrepresenting moral agency or fleeing from moral obligations and responsibilities as if they were forms of ignorance, stupidity, naivete, lack of sophistication, and various other failures of knowledge. Knowledge is not the proper judge, for moral issues cannot be decided true or false; facts are not adequate to valuations, the "ought" does not derive from the "is." To conceive ethics as first philosophy is to no longer place philosophical questioning first, but to question philosophy. It is to hold the question of worthiness and unworthiness more worthy than that of success or failure.

The matter is deeper *for science* than getting its priorities straight. The issue, for philosophers, for scientists, for everyone, given the value of science, is to properly grasp the nature and meaning of science itself. A scientific understanding of science is not enough: one must understand the ethics of science, the ethics that constitute science. Far from glorifying irrationality, and far from attacking science, the ethics of Levinas for the first time, by recognizing the ethical dimension that science on its own would otherwise mask, enables us to grasp (1) how science is possible, that is, the ethics which from the very interior makes science possible, and (2) the true vocation and grandeur, indeed the justification for science, i.e., what science is good for.

If the mind were pure, in a strictly spiritualist sense, without any attachment to body or materiality, then thoughts would commune with thoughts. That is to say, intellection would be monologue, or really silence, pure transparency, the mind in communion with itself. Such was the image of thought advanced by Plato and Aristotle despite their differences. In their vision, language would be a garb or a cloak (metaphors always seem unavoidable at just this point) blurring, but nonetheless at its best, pointing beyond itself to pure ideas or essences. Thus there is always a moment at the high point of the greatest of Plato's dialogues where a myth intervenes to suggest an absolute transcendence of unalloyed ideas, indeed the Idea of the Good, whether it is somehow shining outside a cave or somehow driving a chariot. In Aristotle, this desire to discard the bodily and material for the sake of absolutely pure intellection manifests itself in an ambiguity or unresolved debate as to whether friends are or are not necessary to the best life, the life of thought thinking itself. If friends aim for the best for their friends, and if the best of all is thought thinking itself, purely active intellection, then would not the very best friend have to end friendship for the sake of the intellectual autonomy of each thinker's purely active intellect? It would seem so. Such would be the lonely gnostic world—or worlds—of monadic intellects, above good and evil.

But Levinas answers radically differently, siding not with friendship over truth, but with friendship, as it were, sociality, intersubjectivity, the face-to-face, as the irreducible path to truth. In this profound insight he also sides with what is perhaps Plato's most profound insight, and certainly his most brilliant creative achievement: dialogue, as the philosophical form par excellence, the very manner of doing philosophy. Even if this form contrasts with the famous "Theory of Forms" attributed to Plato, in truth that theory itself is always articulated by one or another interlocutor within Plato's dialogues and never by Plato himself. To be sure, Levinas's insight does not derive from a critical exegesis of Plato or Aristotle. To recognize language, the body, time, and history not merely as garments, cloaks, shadows, or degradations of pure mind and pure thought but as the very medium of signification, that without which there would be no meaning at all, is the basic insight which inaugurates contemporary philosophy as a whole.

Contemporary philosophy begins with Henri Bergson's notion of temporal duration and creative mind, is refined and fleshed out by the phenomenology of Edmund Husserl, and his numerous disciples, regardless of the extent to which they diverge from his specific methodological directives. It is the basis of all subsequent philosophy, whether pragmatic, analytic, ontological, metaphysical, aesthetic, or ethical. Who is still perturbed or seriously concerned with pure mind or pure body, these abstract constructs of ancient gnosticism or modern rationalism, or with the impossible task of joining them together? Rather, the starting point today is their integral unity, and the issue today is determining the proper sense of their divergence, the meaning of mind and mental constructions for an embodied being, or of body and embodiment for a mindful being. It is within this context that one must now understand science, as a theory and practice grounded in the human situation, incarnate, in language, time, and history.

The old questions regarding science, of how truth is possible, the question of epistemology, of how we know truth in contrast to opinion, reality in contrast to appearance, however, do not go away. But the answers for philosophers have changed. What is the significance for epistemology of Levinas's claim that ethics is first philosophy? Levinas's claim is that truth is certainly not a function of pure mind conversing silently, transparently, and simultaneously with itself, as in the ancient model. But neither must truth be teased from the alternative of causal necessity (or probability) in the material world and deductive necessity in the world of ideas, as if mind-body dualism were still the ruling model for the philosophy of science, as it was in the modern period. Rather, contemporary epistemology must come to recognize that for there to be truth—objective, scientific knowledge—the notion of truth-value by itself, or truth-value bound to coherence and correspondence theories alone, is not enough. Knowledge does not come out of a vacuum. Another dimension must be acknowledged: the role of human communication in the constitution of meaning and the validation of truth. For propositions to be true they must be communicated, confirmed or disconfirmed, just as they must be articulated over time and within a historically constituted symbolic network of signifiers, which is to say, a language. The fulcrum of this whole complex, for Levinas, is not the intrarelationship of signs to one another within a language, but rather the manner in which language itself, whatever is *said,* whatever meanings are proposed within a social arena as possible candidates for truth, begin in a *saying.* And saying, speaking one to another, conversation, is originally made possible as a moral relation.

So the very possibility of verifying the evidential basis of statements proposed as true propositions, that is to say, "knowledge interests," are inextricably linked to "human" and "emancipatory interests."[4] Levinas's ethics starts with an ethics of communication, which is not a situation but the responsibility of one for another, a sensitivity and responsiveness of one singular flesh and blood human being to and for another singular flesh and blood human being. The face of the other I face breaks from its historical and linguistic context, and breaks into the self with obligations shattering the circuits of its self-identity. Thus the first "word" which makes communication possible is a word not spoken, but a significance that makes itself felt without being uttered, a word prior to all words but which nevertheless makes them possible as meaningful speech, communicative discourse. This word is *listen.*[5]

Hear!

The pacific force of the other as other, singular, obligating the self in an uplifted and uplifting proximity, "the ethical event of communication which is presupposed by every transmission of messages" (CPP 125), is the unspoken imperative—*Listen to me! Hear me! Do not murder me!*—which makes meaningful speech possible. It is, as I have already cited, "proximity and not the truth of proximity." A signifying prior to whatever may be signified, the "saying of the said": to listen to, to hear, to be able to respond to the other as other, singular, communication initiates meaning, and begins as my moral *responsibility* before and for the other. Prior to anything said, including the propositions of scientific knowledge with all its methodological cautions and formulaic and quantitative precision, as the very possibility of meaningfulness, what is said is said *by someone to someone.*

Communication begins in the accusative, not as an intentional contract but as an obligation undergone, as covenant.[6]

It is this latter relation, the condition—or "uncondition," as Levinas would say, or "unconditional," we would add—for the possibility of communication, the "face-to-face," which arises for Levinas through the "accusative" dimension of meaning, the "to" and "for" the other that are responsibility and moral obligation. The otherness of the other, the other's expressivity coming from an irreducible, unknowable, and unpredictable interiority, the other's singularity as a concrete being, whether that expressivity be manifest through words, sounds, gestures, movements, or actions, is thus already an accusation of and an obligation put upon the self. The otherness of the other "puts into question" the self "despite itself," prior to its own synthetic self-identifications, whether pragmatic or representational. Freedom is thus not a choosing but a being chosen. Such is the "difficult freedom" of responsibility which in turn makes possible and indeed requires the "freedom of thought" which constitutes science, as it makes possible all registers of signification.

All of the above, the inner moral character of science as a communicative enterprise, reinforces the first sense in which science is ethical: that it too, like all human registers of signification, is subject to the demands of morality. Science is not above, but rather, is also subject to the moral constraints that guide humans in their humanity, e.g., to not be cruel to animal or human subjects of scientific experimentation, to conscientiously avoid toxic contaminations of laboratory personnel and society at large, to consider that research projects can (though certainly all do not have to) be aimed at solving pressing problems of human suffering: diseases, deformities, hunger, pollution, energy shortages, and the like. Here the ethical demands on scientists in their scientific work are the same as those demanded everywhere else.

But for Levinas the role of science in ethics or, rather, the ethical role of science, is even greater. Science is a region of signification not simply on the same plane as others, as sports, or fashion, or landscaping for instance. *The knowledge and technology which produce and which are produced by science are essential to the creation of a just society.* So it is not enough to recognize that scientists should perform their work ethically or that science is made possible by morality. Rather, the role of science in ethics is greater: scientific knowledge, objective truth, exact measurement and calculation, and the technologies that produce and are produced by rigorous science, all these make contributions essential to the creation and maintenance of a just society. *Justice requires measure.*

Assuming I possess a limited amount of food, to the one I face who is hungry, I can give to him or her all my food. But there is a problem: what about all the others who are also hungry but who are absent? If I give all the available food to the person I face, in an act seemingly so moral, then at the same time and by the very same act I commit a terrible injustice to all the others who now will go hungry because there is no food for them. Justice precisely *rectifies* the injustice that follows from morality alone. To be sure, justice by itself, separated from the morality that is its source and its goal, also becomes unjust, abstract, inhuman, and tyrannical. But that, like morality without justice, is an aberration, for it should be evident that here we are linking justice to morality. What is required by morality, and what we are calling "justice," is a demand for equality, for equal measure, and hence a demand for law.

While morality is a relation of inequality—a for-the-other before oneself—justice, in contrast, is a relation of equality, indeed, of law—no person above the law or beneath it. One must treat others equally, give food to all who are hungry. Or, more broadly, one must also distribute finite resources to all who are in need of them and who suffer without them. But to give food equally to all who are hungry, and not merely to the one who happens to be in closest proximity, one needs scientific knowledge and technology. One needs these to evenly distribute goods—by shipping them by boat or plane, or to protect from theft or exploitation—but also to maximize the production of needed goods and their efficient and equitable distribution. Science is required by the justice that is required by morality. Science thus has an imperative higher than truth: it serves the justice that serves morality.

Thus ethics as first philosophy means that ethics is the very *justification of philosophy*. Philosophy is not justified, as it has too often taught, because its truth-claims are justified. The justification of truth-claims is found in appropriate *evidence,* as Husserl taught. But this does not answer the larger and more pressing question: What is the purpose of true scientific knowledge? What justifies the quest for propositions grounded in evidence? Ethics as first philosophy is the final answer to these questions. Levinas articulates the *reason* for philosophy, the reason for science, the purpose of truth, the *raison d'être* of knowledge: to serve justice. Science, knowledge, and advanced technology, thus do not corrode human dignity, stripping life of its meaning, as Spinoza, Nietzsche, and Heidegger thought, but rather are great and necessary contributing agents for the construction of a just society. "Justice," Levinas writes, "requires contemporaneousness of representation. It is thus that the neighbor becomes visible and, looked at, presents himself, and there is also justice for me. The saying is fixed in a said, is written, becomes a book, law and science" (*OB* 159).

Or, to invoke a citation from a lecture, which as an undergraduate I heard Levinas give 38 years ago: "It is not always true that not-to-philosophize is still to philosophize! The interrupting force of ethics does not attest to a simple relaxing of reason, but to placing in question the *act of philosophizing*, which cannot fall back into philosophy" (GCM 4).

Richard A. Cohen
March 20, 2010

ONE

The End of the World
Heidegger, Kant, and Levinas

HEIDEGGER: BEING BEING

When Aristotle thought of the end of the world he had in mind its *telos*, asking whether man's purpose was one or many, and whether our highest goal was an achievement of contemplation or moral action, and how the two were related. Today when we think of the end of the world we are more likely to think of its destruction, the devastation of a nuclear holocaust, global incineration in a solar supernova, or the planetary disruptions resulting from rapid climate change.

One also thinks of the end of the world as the disappearance of certain styles of living and outlook, the passing of a *Zeitgeist*, a social "paradigm shift," as when historians speak of the end of the Victorian era, or the end of community, or even the end of nation-states in the face of globalization and the unprecedented financial power of trans-national corporations.

It is in the latter historical sense that Heidegger thinks of the character of worldliness, human being-in-the-world enmeshed in the spirit of the times, a spirit determined historically, and of the passing of such "epochs" of being. Hegel and Comte similarly divided history into epochs, as did Judaism and Christianity, but Heidegger sees the source of such epochs not in the unfolding of a rational logic or a divine providence, but in the "generosity" of being itself. In *Being and Time*, Heidegger delineated the character and structure of worldliness itself and of human and mortal Dasein, from the first "being there" in the world. Human being was no longer conceived as the Cartesian subject in opposition to an objective world, but as a prior "there" already spread out in an "ecstatic" or relational being-in-the-world. The human, above all in its self-understanding and language, would be a reflection of its historical situation, and history itself would be the dispensation of being. Heidegger distinguishes "inauthentic" Dasein as someone who gets lost in the historical situation, wrapped up in a concern for beings, while "authentic" Dasein, in contrast, opens itself up to the be-ing of beings, to the generative dispensation of its epochal world of meaning.

What is the *telos*, the end or goal, of the be-ing of beings? What one discovers in reading Heidegger is that he has a great deal to say about what the be-ing of beings is *not*, or how it has gone awry in the present historical epoch, but little, indeed nothing to say about what it is. The latter failure derives precisely from Heidegger's specific determination of the former. The present historical epoch is "technological." Technology, for Heidegger, represents endless instrumentality. Technology is endless because it has no end, no goal. It is always a means to further means, an exaltation of efficiency for its own sake. In this way it occludes any appreciation for the wholly alternative structure, or what Heidegger calls the "ontological difference" or the "essence," of its own birth from out of the be-ing of beings. "The essence of technology," Heidegger famously declared, "is by no means anything technological."[1] Technology is only one historical dispensation, indeed the current dispensation of be-ing, but not its only dispensation. More lies in store. But that "more" is prevented from coming because technology is the endless dispensation. It is for this reason that Heidegger characterizes the current technological world—our world—as "the greatest danger." It blocks be-ing's world creativity as did no dispensation ever before.

Thus we can understand Heidegger's problem with true ends. Having freed be-ing from rational and theological glosses, its world-giving becomes an aesthetic-artistic function, a matter of its unpredictable creativity. The coming of new future worlds is entirely left up to being, being's move, and not up to humans. Heidegger endlessly complains about human imposition of meaning on being when the role of humans is to sensitively await be-ing's next world gift. There is no gradualism, or continuity, or development in world-giving, because being gives whole worlds, one replacing the other according to no rational or theological order. The present world is entirely corrupted, entirely technological, so no resources taken from it can advance or even intimate be-ing's next move. Indeed, all resources taken from the present world precisely eclipse such a possibility. Thus the very structure of Heidegger's thinking is blocked and apocalyptic, a character of which Heidegger himself may have become conscious in his reliance, in his late writings, on theological language, as when he suggests that a proper attentiveness to be-ing would be the "piety of thought,"[2] and even more obviously when, with evident resignation, he declared: "Only a god can save us."[3]

Heidegger suffers from more than a writer's block; he suffers from a God complex: in the name of be-ing he demands to be a creator of worlds—and the latter is what makes the former a matter of principle rather than accident. Just as Marx's historicism forced him to say everything about capitalism but nothing about communism, Heidegger's historicism forces him to say everything about technology but nothing about thinking. Marx, however, engaged in revolutionary activity to overthrow capitalism. Heidegger, in contrast, was an intellectual and academic mandarin, having radically deconstructed the entire history of Western philosophy and spirituality in a series of lectures, books and articles, he awaited be-ing's next move with vague philological and poetic musings. From the very start of his public intellectual career, already in *Being and Time,* he had ruled out the possibility of a genuinely ethical critique of the present as merely "ontic" and thus thoroughly technologically tainted. Heidegger was, we might say, too pure for this world, but unfortunately his exquisite fastidiousness, as we all know only too well, came with reprehensible ethical consequences.[4]

Since Dasein's "purpose," its "reason to be," is to hearken to the new dispensation of the be-ing of beings, it is natural to then ask what is the purpose, goal, or end of the be-ing of beings. Having unmasked and rejected the orientations of rational development, as in Hegel or Comte, and of providential unfolding, as in Judaism or Christianity, what does Heidegger teach regarding the unfolding, the so-called generosity of be-ing? Indeed, although "being gives" (*Es gibt*), in what sense is it "generous"? Already in the 1920s Cassirer criticized Heidegger's "fundamental ontology" for lacking standards. Later Levinas will ask if the Holocaust was a gift. Rejecting theory, Heidegger's ontology naturally rejects coherence or correspondence theories of truth, which are said to only distract the thinker from the one genuine question, the question of being. "Being gives," but it gives whatever it gives. This is the tautology of all philosophies which worship success.

Being gave the classical world of ancient Greece; it gave the medieval world of Christian piety; and now it gives the modern world of technology. To what end are these given? No answer. Nor does Heidegger's philosophy provide or want to provide answers. Heidegger's goal, his end, is abstract and formal: to keep the door open for the next revelation of epochal being. He never wonders, because he cannot, if being's next dispensation will be better or worse than the present one. Ethical determinations are not, in any event, "essential" determinations of being. Being gives, we receive. End of story. But it is childish and we are reduced to children by it. However, the emperor is not wearing any clothes after all; or in this case, there are only clothes, but no emperor. Calling it "the simple," as Heidegger in the end does, is no revelation either, but rather should be heard as the admission of failure.

Why, then, does Heidegger end in the morass? Final answer: the "purpose" of being is being, which is another way of saying that being has no purpose. This is what Spinoza means, and freely admits, when he gives to all beings the basic character of *conatus,* "perseverance in being." This is what Nietzsche, a post-Darwinian, means by "will to power." Being wants nothing more than itself, more being, to stay in being, to persist. It is inertial. Heidegger wants to glorify this inertia, to transfigure it poetically, to bask in its aura of its inevitability, but his thinking, for all its delicacy, always and eventually sinks back mired in an empty abstraction.

More radically, both Kant and Levinas challenge the adequacy of being unto itself. Both thinkers question being's sufficiency not with an aesthetic anticipation of more being, but through the moral imperative of an "otherwise than being." Being is not enough not because it fails to bring yet more being, but because by itself it is unworthy. Being is not enough because it is not good enough. Aristophanes championed the inarticulate wholeness of being, but Socrates understood more profoundly that the only wholeness worth pursuing lies beyond being in the Good. The real challenge to being is not to be more real but to rise upward in an elevation toward the good, for it lies not in ontology but in ethics.

KANT: AIMING FOR THE GOOD, BEING HAPPY

The distinction between "appearances," the subject matter of scientific knowledge, and the "thing-in-itself," exterior to such knowledge, constitutes the innovative core of the "transcendental idealism" which Kant elaborated in the "Dialectic" of the *Critique of Pure Reason*. By limiting the realm of knowledge, it "makes room,"[5] as Kant modestly puts it, for the freedom of will which, while inscrutable to knowledge, is no longer dogmatically asserted but transcendentally deduced as the possible unconditional ground of morality. Morality, which Kant calls "practical reason," is elaborated in the *Foundations of the Metaphysics of Morals* and the *Critique of Practical Reason*, and elsewhere in Kant's corpus. By this means Kant is able to defend the legitimacy and rationality of morality, and its *telos*, which is freedom itself. Negatively, moral freedom cannot be refuted by knowledge without contradiction or dogmatism. Positively, it is autonomy, respect for self-legislated law. All this is well known.

But Kant goes farther. He relates the *highest end* of morality, which is rational respect for moral law, to the supreme end of religion, pious conformity to divine command. In the *Critique of Judgment*, Kant examines teleology, but there he considers it primarily with regard to standards of aesthetic taste and the evaluation of beauty, though also in terms of its role in biology and its contribution to the achievement of human happiness before God. It is later, however, after having completed his three critiques, in a book which might well be called his fourth critique, titled *Religion within the Limits of Reason Alone* that Kant offers a sustained discussion of the question of ends in relation to God and organized religion. The book begins, however, with a renewed elaboration of the ethics of his second critique. Indeed, most of *Religion within the Limits of Reason Alone* is devoted to that ethics, and in its entirety it remains based in that ethics. This is because, as we shall see, Kant in the eighteenth century, like Levinas in the twentieth century, argues that enlightened, mature or adult religion, in contrast to fantastic, fanatic, and infantile religion, necessarily begins and ends within the orbit of morality.

Indeed, in a gesture that seems to defy the book's very title, but which in fact states the true meaning of its restricting clause, "within the limits of reason alone," in the very first sentence of the preface to the first edition, Kant boldly declares that morality is in absolutely no need of God, or of the rewards, punishments, immortality of soul, rituals, figurations, and all the various consolations taught by religions. "So far as morality is based upon the conception of man as a free agent who, just because he is free, binds himself through his reason to unconditioned laws, it stands in need neither of the idea of another Being over him, for him to apprehend his duty, nor of an incentive other than the law itself, for him to do his duty."[6] Respect for the moral law is humanity's highest end, and it stands as such with or without religion. What then is the role of religion?

Negatively, in this book Kant wants to show the failings of religion conceived outside of the limits of reason alone. This is why, like his earlier books, it is a *critique*. Kant also called his transcendental idealism a "critical philosophy." Religion heedless of reason—unenlightened religion—turns into its opposite: mythology, fanaticism, and superstition. Kant believes that reason, that binding religion not to pure reason, as Spinoza tried and failed, but to practical reason, can prevent this eventuality. But for Kant there is also the possibility and the actuality of enlightened religion, religion which has a positive role to play. And the role it plays, which is also its very maturity and enlightenment, is to support and to bolster humanity's highest aim, moral freedom. How, then, does Kant conceive the supreme end of religion bound to the highest end of morality?

Crucial to his account of this binding of ethics and religion is the distinction between rational moral agency as such and the rational moral agency of finite human beings. Religion, as we shall see, is something that helps human beings, even if rational moral agents as such may not be in need of it. To be sure, humans seem to be the only rational moral agents on the planet earth, and when we speak of practical reason on this planet we mean the moral agency of humans, even if in principle there can be nonhuman rational moral agents. Now, what we know of human rational moral agents—what we know about ourselves—is that in addition to pure respect for rational law as our highest end, we also want to be happy, and thus we also hold happiness to be a legitimate end. Thus there are two ends for human agents: duty and happiness.[7]

Why do humans aim for happiness? Because this is to be human! The specific sensibility of finite human embodiment is such that, beyond purely rational considerations, humans are ridden with inclinations and aversions, desires for pleasure, fame, prestige, glory, wealth, power, material success, love, and the like, and desires to avoid their opposites. In his earlier ethical work, *Foundations of the Metaphysics of Morals,* Kant expresses this point as follows: "happiness is an ideal not of reason but of imagination."[8] Practical reason (moral agency) wants freedom; human sensibility, through the imagination, wants happiness.

What I want to call to attention here is the Cartesian mind-body dualism that haunts Kant's philosophy. The rational mind wants freedom; the human body wants happiness. But this difference is not actually the proper reflection of the Cartesian mind-body dualism. The actual dualism occurs not between mind and body, but between mind and matter. This is the dualism that lies at the root of Kant's transcendental idealism. Because matter is strictly caused and necessary, freedom is completely free and pure. But human sensibility, then, with its desire for happiness, is therefore neither pure matter nor pure mind. It is not simply a cog in an unbreakable causal chain because it has its own ends, and its own ends are not purely rational: humans want happiness. But neither is it, strictly speaking, purely rational, because freedom can only be free when it is autonomous, obeying self-legislated rational moral law, doing its duty completely regardless of happiness. Human sensibility with its desire for happiness is neither strictly determined nor purely free.

How does Kant extricate himself from this conundrum? How can he speak of sensibility and its desire for happiness outside of the confines of the necessity and freedom that structure and are demanded by his transcendental idealism? We have already heard Kant's answer: "happiness is an ideal not of reason but of imagination." Let us recall that in the *Critique of Pure Reason* Kant located the imagination (as schematization) between sensible intuition and categorical understanding (*Verstand*) in order to bridge and join them, lending order to sensations and giving flesh to the categories. Here, however, in *Religion within the Limits of Reason Alone,* it seems to me that Kant locates the imagination between sensibility and reason (*Vernunft*), lending order and direction to sensations (desires) and giving flesh to reason's need for absolute unity and coherence.[9] The ideal of happiness, then, originating in the imagination, is a demand for wholeness made by humans as humans and not by pure reason itself.

And thus the "answer" to the demand for happiness, namely religion, is also a set of significations made by humans, or, to put this point more delicately, it is a set of significations made for humans to help humans do their duty as humans. God and religion promise humans happiness for doing their duty, even though the imperative to respect the moral law is and can be nothing other than a pure duty, unaffected in its purity by the imagination or any other inclination. Perhaps, we can muse, there are other moral agents in the universe who do their duty without the consolations of religion, but humans—we ourselves—are apparently not among them. But let us note also that for Kant the consolations of God and religion to aid humans have the very specific task of aiding humans to do their duty. Religion serves morality or it becomes irreligious. The supreme end of enlightened religion, in other words, is to facilitate humans in achieving the highest end of morality. Who, then, is God, and what, then, is religion "within the limits of reason alone"?

For their *moral happiness,* humans want two additional and related desires satisfied which rational moral agency (duty) by itself cannot in principle supply them. First, despite the impossibility of empirical proof for freedom and hence for the morality of actions, humans want to believe that moral actions are not merely subjective but are in fact effective in the world. Humans as moral agents want to believe that their actions make a real difference, that they change the world for the better. Accordingly, they want to believe that goodness is rewarded and evil is punished and that the soul is immortal and will reach perfection. Good people should be rewarded with happiness and evil people should be punished with suffering. Second, human moral agents want also to believe that individual moral acts are not isolated and haphazard occurrences but add up and contribute to the creation of a coherent moral world, a moral world consistent with all other moral actions, whether one's own or another's, or whether past, present, or future.

The idea of God and religious organizations provide answers to the above two wishes, providing assurances that moral action is not in vain, that it has real consequences, and that a coherent world of morality can result. They answer to the human hope that good is rewarded and evil is punished and that by behaving morally, with the numerous sacrifices such behavior exacts from human happiness, that humans are indeed making the real world a better place and that eventually their souls will reach perfection. God and religion are thus functional consolations or encouragements for an embodied humanity otherwise likely to feel overburdened and discouraged by the self-sacrifice demanded by the purity of its moral obligations, and therefore likely to shirk its duty, give in to its self-love, and hence succumb to evil. God and religion are thus both instrumental and supplemental, concessions to human self-love, in relation to the rational end, moral freedom, which remains in its purity unaffected by them and which they only serve. Or, to invoke Kant's terminology: moral freedom is a "categorical imperative," binding without exception, while "God and religion" create only "hypothetical imperatives," whose worth derives exclusively from their service to the unconditional moral categorical imperative.

Let us note that just as scientific knowledge cannot refute the possibility of freedom, so, too, it cannot refute the possibility of God and religion. But there is a difference. Freedom is a necessary transcendental condition for morality. God and religion, however, are only hypothetical transcendental conditions for the satisfaction of human self-love. Morality, obedience to self-legislated moral law, is the only manner in which freedom makes rational sense. God and religion, in contrast, only answer to a specifically human desire, the desire to be happy, and hence are not necessary requirements of pure rationality. Accordingly, freedom is an ideal of reason without which morality cannot be rational, while God and religion are but ideas, without which humans presumably would be unhappy, but lacking which humans might very well still be fully moral and rational—and perhaps even happy. "Within the limits of reason alone," God and religion are imaginative bulwarks or compensations for human weakness, or, human self-love, rather than fully rational constituents of the true end of human moral agency, which remains freedom as respect for moral law (duty).

In the second half of *Religion within the Limits of Reason Alone* Kant makes two more relevant distinctions. He first distinguishes "natural religion" or the "invisible church," which postulates a God guaranteeing the efficacy of moral action as indicated above: knowing and rewarding good, knowing and punishing evil, and offering the prospect of a final Kingdom of Ends. This he distinguishes from

"ecclesiastical faith" or the "visible church," which is a concrete historical organization which by means of particular scriptures, symbols,
rituals, prayers, community gatherings, exegesis and the like, is the
contingent but *public* manifestation of natural religion. Though the
idea of natural religion comes into being to satisfy human self-love,
in relation to the concrete churches of ecclesiastical faith it functions—or should function—as a regulative ideal. Ecclesiastical faiths,
in other words, should strive to bring their congregants to a faith
consistent with the moral truths elaborated in Kant's second critique.
They should, in other words, be taught to see their religious beliefs
and practices as serving to achieve fuller adherence to the categorical
imperative as such.

Thus, the second distinction: between ecclesiastical faiths which
conscientiously do facilitate the establishment of natural religion—which convert religion (self-love) into morality (duty)—and
ecclesiastical faiths which do not, but instead promote their particular
and contingent scriptures, rituals, symbols, doctrines, and beliefs as
if they were ends (indeed universal ends) rather than means. In
today's parlance, the former faiths are called "liberal" and the latter
"fundamentalist."

Interestingly enough, though historically excusable, Kant claims
that there is only one ecclesiastical faith in the service of natural religion, namely, Christianity. So, too, while there are many ecclesiastical
faiths working in the opposite direction, exalting as universal what is
only particular, he writes about only one, namely, Judaism. Judaism
is thus made up of a "perfunctory worship" which is "at bottom
merely statutory."[10] This is a double bias. It seems to me that it once
again reflects Kant's fundamental attachment to mind-body dualism
(though which of the two, Cartesian dualism or Christian faith, is the
cause and which is the effect is not quite so obvious).

In any event, for Kant the "final purpose" of *ecclesiastical faith
as of natural religion* is, as Kant declares, "to make men better."[11]
Morality, the highest end, remains untouched by God or religion,
such that "the moral improvement of men constitutes the real end
of all religion of reason."[12] It is clear that Kant's answer is the same
as Socrates' answer to the classic question in this regard which was
asked in Plato's *Euthyphro*: "Do the gods love piety because it is
pious, or is it pious because they love it."[13] The reverse produces only

superstition, fanaticism, violence and evil.[14] "*Whatever,*" Kant writes emphatically, "*over and above good life-conduct, man fancies that he can do to become well-pleasing to God is mere religious illusion.*"[15] "[T]he highest goal of moral perfection of finite creatures—a goal to which man can never completely attain—is love of the law."[16] God and religion, natural or ecclesiastical, are thus useful fictions serving at their best to aid humanity to achieve its one and only rational and moral end. Or as Kant famously writes and as we can now fully appreciate: "Religion is (subjectively regarded) the recognition of all duties as divine commands."[17]

LEVINAS: THE ELEVATION OF HOLINESS

When we read in Kant "that when they fulfill their duties to men (themselves and others) they are, by these very acts, performing God's commands…and that it is absolutely impossible to serve God more directly in any other way,"[18] it is natural to recall the striking and similar sentences in *Totality and Infinity* where Levinas declares that: "Everything that cannot be restored to an interhuman relation represents not the superior form but the forever primitive form of religion" (*TI* 79);[19] and that "God rises to his supreme and ultimate presence as correlative to the justice rendered unto men" (78). Both Kant and Levinas agree in affirming the primacy of *morality* over *knowledge,* *ethics* over *science,* without rejecting or demeaning knowledge and science. And both thinkers agree that moral goodness coupled with justice is the highest end of *ethics* and of *religion,* the *summum bonum.* Thus Levinas and Kant are in these two ways kindred spirits.

And yet while agreeing with Kant about the *status* of ethics,[20] Levinas disagrees with him over its *nature,* because, so Levinas writes, "Kantian philosophy…was misled by a traditional logic accepted as fixed, and needed a phenomenology" (*OS* 31). In this demand for a phenomenological correction to replace Kant's Cartesian rationalism, Levinas stands in a long line of post-Kantian thinkers such as Fichte, Schelling, Schleiermacher, Hegel and Heidegger. But unlike his post-Kantian predecessors, Levinas's solution for overcoming Kant's rationalist dualism (material necessity/intelligible freedom) is not a phenomenological ontology (of self-negation, existence, sentiment,

Geist or Dasein) but rather—and in greater conformity to Kant him-self—an ethics, but now an ethics conceived starting from sensibility and intersubjectivity.

In contrast to Kantian freedom that is pure, for Levinas freedom is "difficult." Kant, as we know, rescued freedom from causality, but both strict causal necessity and pure freedom are dialectical partners necessitated by the rationalist framing of Kant's thought. The only freedom capable of escaping absolute necessity is a completely pure freedom, a "supersensible" or purely "intelligible" freedom. Levinas, in contrast, as a post-Darwinian, post-Bergsonian and post-Husser-lian philosopher, that is to say, as a phenomenologist, is no longer beholden to Kant's rationalist presuppositions and hence no longer required or able to deduce a pure freedom. That freedom is *difficult* rather than *pure* indicates that from the start it is enmeshed in an embodied subjectivity.

Freedom is difficult because humans are neither necessarily deter-mined nor necessarily free. Mind and body, the world and ideals, the true, the good, and the beautiful, in other words, are interconnected from the start. Heidegger locates this root in Dasein's existence and its source in the self-understanding of historical be-ing. But the price of this essentially aesthetic worldview is a quiescence helpless before the upsurge of be-ing, that is to say, the loss of standards of knowl-edge and of ethics. This price, as we have seen, is too high. Freedom may not be pure, but for all that humans remain free and goodness remains their highest vocation. Human freedom is difficult because being good rather than evil is difficult, to be sure, but more pro-foundly it is difficult precisely because freedom is not pure and hence never guaranteed. Freedom, for Levinas, is not found in autonomy but in responsibility, responsibility in the face of the other person. And such responsibility is not intelligible but sensible: a giving based in a "suffering for the suffering of the other."

Levinas's phenomenological account of human embodiment leads him to an ethics based in what he calls the "face-to-face," the encounter of two flesh and blood human beings in their vulnerabil-ity and mortality, rather than the Kantian "respect for law" which sees in the human body only an impediment to righteousness, only a countervailing force ("inclination"), rather than the very thing—the suffering of the other person—that elicits moral responsibility in the first place and enables one person to materially help another person with material needs. Purely rational beings conform to law, and when they do not, for whatever finite reasons, they "ought" to insofar as they are by definition rational agents; but finite or flesh and blood human beings are mortal and suffer, and to aid one another, to alleviate suffering and to promote well-being in all the registers of their being-in-the-world, is a human being's highest obligation. Duty, we can say, is elicited by the suffering other person and is a response to that suffering, and not simply a conformity to law.

In contrast to Heidegger's phenomenological account of subjectivity which locates the self's originary constitution in the world as instrumentality, for Levinas subjectivity emerges in the independence of self-sensing, in what he calls an "enjoyment" of elemental sensations. While Heidegger's "fundamental ontology" effects an ontological revision of Kant's epistemological account of the imagination in the *Critique of Pure Reason*,[21] Levinas's intersubjective ethics effects a revision and a unification of Kant's account of the ethical subject in the *Critique of Practical Reason* and the role of religion in *Religion within the Limits of Reason Alone*. If freedom is difficult rather than pure, in other words, then religion is no longer a supplement to ethics but an integral component of it. Levinas does not separate and evaluate "ecclesiastical faith" and "natural religion" according to prior rational suppositions, ones that separate mind and matter, soul and body, spirit and letter, as did Kant. For Levinas, Judaism—the Judaism of the rabbis, distinguishes but does not radically divorce the pure from the impure, soul from body, or spirit from letter, and as such is a genuinely ethical religion and not merely, as Kant put it, a "mechanical worship."[22] From this perspective we understand both why Kant is led to criticize Judaism for its absence of pure spirit and why, in return, Levinas would criticize Kant's Christianity ("natural religion") for its Manichaeism.

In view of Levinas's radical phenomenological revision of Kant's ethics, and because I elsewhere examine the role of sensibility and the body in Levinas's ethics,[23] here I simply give an abbreviated summary of Levinas's conception of ethics in four theses. Then I turn in greater detail to his account of ethics in terms of its relation to religion and how this relation differs, as I have already indicated, from the Kantian conception:

(1) The constitution of subjectivity begins with the body. Embodied selfhood, phenomenologically explicated, occurs across three types of syntheses of identification, each of which is ecstatic (outside itself), but only relatively so, indeed immanent in comparison with the non-synthesizable transcendence which initiates ethics: (a) the sensuous sensitivity or self-sensing of sensibility, which Levinas characterizes as enjoyment, contentment, satisfaction or a fragile happiness, and which is the deepest or innermost layer of the inwardness of selfhood; (b) the activity of labor or praxis which constructs and maintains a public and stable world; and (c) explicit representations of the world, including, among other discourses, the theoretical or scientific-philosophical objectification of the world in view of its universal truth.[24]

(2) Morality begins with absolute transcendence. Absolute transcendence is the asymmetrical exteriority—the moral "height and destitution" of the other person in his or her embodied singularity, *in relation* to the inwardness of the embodied subject in its first person singularity as responsibility. Moral subjectivity as responsibility occurs as a reconditioning of "for-itself" selfhood (immanence) into a for-the-other moral self of responsibility. As sentient beings morality begins therefore not in rational respect for law, but in and as a sensibility "suffering for the suffering of another," not through sheer sentiment, however, but by giving priority to materially aiding the other (feeding, housing, clothing, conversing, employing, comforting, financing, and so on).[25]

(3) Justice, equality, in contrast, arises at the level of society and the universal—of humanity and law. It arises as an extension and rectification of the infinite but first and second personhood (face to face) of the self as moral responsibility. To give all to one other (the one who faces) is to give nothing to all others (humanity), and hence to perpetrate an injustice. Justice, however, which requires law and institutions to rectify the inequality of moral responsibility, is at the same time judged by morality.[26]

(4) The final and highest end, therefore, is the combination of morality and justice such that in a fully just world all humans are morally responsible to and for one another without fault: a social world where giving all to one deprives no one else of anything. Therefore justice demands a world of plenty (goods, services, institutions, and the like) instead of scarcity. And therefore also, contra Heidegger,

for Levinas, "Science and the possibilities of technology are the first conditions for the factual implementation of the respect for the rights of man" (*OS* 119).

Such is Levinas's ethics of intersubjective responsibility and justice. The following citation, taken from his book *Difficult Freedom*, serves as our guide to understanding how this conception integrates religion and ethics: "The Justice rendered to the Other, my neighbor, gives me an unsurpassable proximity to God" (*DF* 18).

To explicate this proposition I turn to the five word epigram—it is only a sentence fragment—Levinas selected to place under the title *Difficult Freedom*: "Freedom on tablets of stone." The phrase is taken from section 2 of book 6 of the unique talmudic tractate *Pirke Avos*.[27] The Talmud is everywhere permeated with moral instruction, often indirectly expressed, but *Pirke Avos* is especially concentrated and particularly direct, almost entirely made up of moral maxims and favored moral proverbs enunciated by a wide variety of talmudic rabbis. The historical and continued importance of the Talmud, let me add, to all forms of contemporary Judaism, cannot be underestimated. One can say without exaggeration that all of Judaism is nothing more *and nothing less* than, as Levinas puts it, "reading the Bible through the Talmud" (*DF* 131).

First of all, "Freedom on tablets of stone," can be read as a reformulation of the very title of Levinas's book, substituting "tablets of stone" for "difficult." As such, it would be the first "talmudic reading" of the text of *Difficult Freedom*. The transposition indicates that freedom is not free-floating, abstract or pure, but is impressed onto and into the real world, onto stone specifically, but then too, quite logically, also onto a softer substance, human flesh. "Freedom on tablets of stone" would then suggest embodiment, efficacious action, transforming the world. Freedom is not immaculate: it is a real movement that always either becomes better and makes better or becomes worse and makes worse. So, too, freedom is itself affected by freedom. Freedom cannot be separated from what it frees, what it frees from, who it frees, and what it frees for, that is to say, it is inseparable from the concrete—historical, political, economic, ideological—social world wherein alone freedom makes sense.

The God-fearing Jewish person is often called a "living Torah." This is to say that the ideal person of Judaism—Jew or non-Jew!—is the *righteous person,* the *tzadik.* Piety is neither a precious sentiment, an exquisite sensitivity or mood, nor is it a privileged intellectual access to a hermetic knowledge. For Judaism piety is neither an anointment nor a revelation. Both are not enough. It is the person who is moral and just and hence the person learned and experienced in the ways of morality and justice, the one in whose very flesh, one can say, the Torah is written. "The pious man," Levinas writes, very simply and directly, "is the just man" (*DF* 131).

But there is more to the epigram. In keeping with the phenomenological insight that meaning depends on its horizon of meaning or context, and in keeping with long Jewish exegetical practice (which Levinas credits having learned from his Talmud teacher Mr. Shoshani), to understand the epigram of *Difficult Freedom* as Levinas no doubt wanted it to be understood, and to see just how very far it serves as an equivalent statement and further exegesis of the book's title and overall significance, it must be expanded to include all of section 2 of book 6 of *Pirke Avos* where this fragment appears. Here is that section:

> Rabbi Joshua, the son of Levi, said: "Every day a *Bat-kol* [a heavenly voice] goes forth from Mount Sinai, proclaiming these words, 'Woe to mankind for contempt of the Torah, for whoever does not labor in the Torah is said to be under the divine censure'; as it is said, 'As a ring of gold in a wine's snout, so is a fair woman who turns aside from discretion'; and it says, 'And the tablets were the work of God, and the writing was the writing of God, graven upon the tablets.' Read not *charut* (graven) but *cherut* (freedom), for no man is free but he who labors in the Torah. But whosoever labors in the Torah, behold he shall be exalted, as it is said, 'And from Mattanah to Nachaliel, and from Nachaliel to Bamot.' "[28]

Rabbi Joshua, the son of Levi, has given a very rich citation. In explicating it we gain access to Levinas's conception of the integral relation that inextricably binds ethics and religion, paying attention also to the contrast with Kant.

First, the "*Bat-kol,*" which is the "heavenly voice" or divine revelation. Elsewhere in the Talmud (*Baba Metzia* 59a), in an oft-cited story, it is made clear that the voice of God has no direct say in deciding Jewish law, for "the Torah has been given, it is not in heaven." After hard debate, Jewish law is decided by the majority opinion of the rabbis. But the heavenly voice in our citation is not interfering in legal argumentation; it is a voice of suffering. God suffers and his "divine censure" is aroused because the Torah He has given is neglected. To "labor in the Torah" is not simply a matter of study, burning the midnight oil, but is closer to the literal meaning of the term "Torah," which is "teaching," meaning to learn by following it, which is to say, to be morally uplifted and improved by it. This is what it means in Judaism to become holier, to become a "living Torah," to be imbued with more holiness (and always for the same "reason": because God is holy). "Learning," the broad Jewish term for serious engagement with the Torah, the teaching, is never an academic exercise alone, but always both intellectual and practical, two dimensions that Judaism refuses to separate. No doubt "learning" is a rigorous intellectual exercise, but that exercise and rigor as never divorced from practical consequences, the piety that is righteousness.

Second, let us notice that what turns a person away from the Torah are not worldly pleasures per se, because Jews are often enjoined to enjoy the world, and the Jewish Sabbath and Holy Days (with the exception of certain fast days), for instance, are celebrated with bread, with wine, and with festive meals. On Sabbath the Jew must be joyful; therefore there are no burials on Sabbath, or even mourning. On Passover Jews must drink a minimum of four glasses of wine. A Jewish man is obligated to have at least two children; hence he must marry. Furthermore, he is obligated to give his wife pleasure in their sexual intercourse, and that sexual intercourse is not restricted to procreation alone. He must also provide his wife clothing and housing to her liking. "The law for the Jew," Levinas writes, "is never a yoke. It carries its own joy, which nourishes a religious life" (*DF* 19). "Contempt of the Torah," then, comes not from the temptations of pleasure but from the temptations of pagan pleasure, from hedonism, from pleasures lacking the "discretion" of a moral modesty. The Hebrew Bible illustrates this distinction and admonition in its usual concrete terms: "As a ring of gold in a swine's snout, so is a fair woman who turns aside from discretion" (Prov. 11:22). It is not woman who is evil, but the immodest woman.

Freedom is written on stone, but it is the Ten Commandments that are written on stone. There is the first set of tablets, which entirely "were the work of God," and then the second set of tablets that Moses hewed after having smashed the first tablets, but in both cases "the writing was the writing of God." Letter and spirit cannot be separated without the spirit becoming ethereal, impractical, a fairy tale, an elsewhere in being rather than an otherwise than being, and the letter becoming opaque, inarticulate, pagan, and ultimately emptied of significance, nihilist, being persevering in its being.

Notice also in the citation the remarkable substitution of meaning from "graven" to "freedom." On its most superficial level this is derived from a different vocalization of the Hebrew consonants, which alone are given in the Torah and which are the same for both words. This play on words may at first sight seem like a purely arbitrary shift in meaning, akin to some of the later Heidegger's more inventive etymologies. But each Hebrew word has three core letters, its *shoresh* (root), from which plural meanings are indeed derived by different vocalization. In this way Hebrew words are already exegetical rather than literal. So, for instance, the Hebrew word for "peace" (*shalom*) has the very same three-letter root as the word for "wholeness" (*shalem*). Surely it is not merely an arbitrary vocalization that links the notions of peace and wholeness. Indeed, the same three letters, again with another vocalization, form the root of King Solomon's name, the king whom God allowed to build the Holy Temple in Jerusalem when his father was not allowed because as a warrior King David had shed so much blood. The interpretive bond joining "writing" and "freedom" is therefore not simply a case of the rabbis "running wild," as Spinoza said. There is a profound sense to it: spirit and letter are inseparable. For Levinas, "The human being is not only in the world, not only an *in-der-Welt-Sein* (being-in-the-world), but also *zum-Buch-Sein* (being-toward-the-book), namely, in relation to the inspired word" (*EN* 109). Here the specific teaching of the book is that divine command is *freedom*. Not pure freedom but spirit in letters, yes, in books, but also in flesh, in circumcision, for instance, which is at once a cut in the flesh and a cut in the heart, the "broken heart" (and one without the other, as the prophets taught, would be completely deficient and unacceptable to God). Or in the talmudic citation above, freedom is laboring in the Torah: mind and body joined in the moral responsibility for "the widow, the orphan, the stranger," which is a responsibility never responsible enough, never able to give enough, and which, furthermore, increases to the extent that it is fulfilled.

We must note also that in Levinas's epigram the talmudic interpretative substitute (*drash* in Hebrew) is employed and not the "plain" sense (*pshat* in Hebrew). The Hebrew Bible, which is acknowledged as sacred scripture for Christians and Muslims as well, is a *Jewish* text, a sacred scripture for Judaism, because it is read through the lens, as it were, or more accurately through the intonations, the vocalizations, the *voices* of Talmud discourse. In putting the exegetical meaning before the plain meaning, Levinas is not only reaffirming the unity of Oral Torah (Talmud) and Written Torah (Hebrew Bible), the unity of spirit and letter, oral and written, he is affirming and exhibiting the priority of *saying* over the *said*—the primacy of ethics as first philosophy. The significations of the said attain their significance not of themselves, but through the saying that is from the first a moral response to the other person.

To return again to our citation, its final sentence forces us to ask if Spinoza was perhaps right that the talmudic rabbis have indeed gone mad. What sense does Rabbi Joshua, the son of Levi, make when the exaltation of those who do labor in the Torah is explained by a biblical proof text that enigmatically does nothing more than present the names of three ancient biblical cities: "And from Mattanah to Nachaliel, and from Nachaliel to Bamot"? Again the answer lies in the Hebrew. Beyond their signification as place names, each of these proper nouns means something in Hebrew: Mattanah means "gift"; Nachaliel is made of two words and means "heritage of God"; and Bamot means "heights." Thus there emerges another homiletic interpretation (*drash*), a translation of this biblical sentence that otherwise appears almost mad and certainly is otherwise opaque in this context. Substituting the Hebrew meanings for the proper nouns, the sentence now can be read as follows: "From the gift of the Torah, man gains a Divine heritage, and that leads him to the heights of lofty ideals."[29] In this interpretive light one now sees clearly the nature of the exaltation that rewards laboring in the Torah, that is to say, which characterizes the difficult freedom of the Torah, the adherence to and heightening of moral responsibility for the other and for all others.

What Torah study, or Jewish religious life, or moral responsibility—which are equivalent expressions for Jews—produce is human entry into God's heritage on earth, where responsibility no longer depends on God but on man, as in the title of Levinas's article "Loving the Torah more than God" (*DF* 142–45). "Loving the Torah more than

God" means "loving the neighbor as thyself," which for Levinas means that "loving the neighbor," being "for-the-other" *is* the true self, the "humanity of the human." There is no other path to God than loving the neighbor. Or, as in the citation that began this section: "God rises to his supreme and ultimate presence as correlative to the justice rendered unto men." Religion is not, as Kant thought, a cloak which the moral agent puts on for his or her happiness. It is not a consoling fiction. Neither, then, is it a cloak that can be taken off in the rigor of a purely rational duty. It is the pedagogy—cut to the measure of flesh and blood human beings—which directs and guides individuals and all humanity to the highest height, the "holiness," toward which concrete moral behavior aims both in responsibility for the other and in the creation of a just world for all others. If this is Kantian, it is Kantianism with a human face. Levinas calls it, is "religion for adults." "It is a complete and austere humanism, linked to a difficult adoration! And conversely, it is an adoration that coincides with the exaltation of man!" (145). "[T]o deserve the help of God, it is necessary to want to do what must be done without his help. . . . The only absolute value is the human possibility of giving the other priority over oneself" (*EN* 109). Religion is not transcended and discarded in human striving for goodness and justice; it is accomplished and fulfilled.

Two

Being, Time, and the Ethical Body

INTRODUCTION

In the name of ethics, Levinas will challenge the apparently inescapable notion—dominant for millennia in the West—that the body must be understood in terms of *being*. The challenge seems untenable at first and second glance, fundamentally outrageous, irrational, and nonsensical. What can escape being? It is an all-embracing category, indeed, the most universal of all determinations. Whatever is has being, is being, *is*—being is, such is the tautology at the root of all Western thought. For Levinas, however, the deepest meaning of human embodiment is determined as *otherwise than being* (*autrement q'etre*). Not the human spirit alone, the "psyche" or "soul" independent of the body, but the embodied human, the human as embodied, would be the otherwise than being—not by being *beyond being*, however that might make sense, but by rising to a height, a moral height, *better than being*. Morality exceeds being. And the truly human body is the moral body inspired by the better than being. It is a radical thought, indeed, and opens a radical new direction for Western self-interpretation, for science, philosophy, culture and religion, but does it make any sense?

Levinas is sufficiently and rigorously phenomenological to acknowledge the *being* of the body. In its deepest origins, the body is a locus of enjoyments and needs, of strengths and weaknesses, a vulnerability, aging, suffering and mortal. The body requires nourishment, air, movement, and engages and is engaged by its natural environment across sensibility. Even if civilized beings dine, they must also eat, consume nutrients, and replenish their cells and organic systems. Even if civilized beings raise children, school them and establish various social, legal, political, and religious institutions for an unforeseeable future, nevertheless, like animal beings, these same humans age, suffer, ail, and perish. Civilization itself—the humanism of humanity—is moved by these two directions, between angels and beasts, ambiguous like the body, providing for self-preservation, but doing so above animal being, senses in the realm of the human. Humans, Claude Lévi-Strauss has taught, consume not the raw but the cooked; they do not eat, they dine. Humans are mortals, Heidegger has taught; they do not perish, they die. The body is not an alien vessel captained by the soul. Just as civilization is embodied in symbols, as Cassirer has taught,[1] the human lives across incarnation.

For Levinas, however, the "humanity of the human" lies elsewhere than under the categories of being, whether natural, cultural or both. The humanity of the human, the humane body, lies in the deeper imperatives of morality and justice. Ethics, the *otherwise than being* qua the *better than being,* nevertheless is not a fantastic region of beautiful spirits, angels, whispers or dreamy aspirations. For Levinas ethics is visceral, embodied, rooted in the significance of human suffering, in the priority that the suffering of the other can take over that of the self's own suffering. It occurs, Levinas writes, in "a shudder of incarnation though which *giving* takes on meaning, as the primordial dative of the *for another,* in which a subject becomes a heart, a sensibility, and hands that give" (*LR* 182). It is only as embodied beings, vulnerable and mortal, that ethical demands arise, and as embodied beings that ethical demands can be met. "The other's material needs," Levinas often cites the words of the great nineteenth century moralist Rabbi Israel Salanter, "are my spiritual needs" (*NT* 99).

To better understand these claims, one must first place them in the larger context of the history of Western thought regarding being. This means one must also place them in the context of the history of Western thought regarding the *time* of being. In the West, and no doubt elsewhere too, the two histories are one inseparable story. For it has always been within the framework of a conception of time—the time of being and the being of time—that the West has conceived of being, and hence also of the being of the body. The matter is not simple. In the following essay, two epochs are distinguished. First, there is the classical period, inaugurated by Parmenides, where being and time are conceived under the sign of *logic,* and where in the process the body is sacrificed to eternity. Second, there is the contemporary period, inaugurated by Bergson, where being and time are conceived under the sign of *existence,* and where for the first time the body is taken seriously.[2] Two contending avenues of thought are then distinguished in the latter period: the *aesthetic* body as interpreted by Bergson and Heidegger, on the one side, and the *ethical* body as interpreted by Levinas, on the other.

Time, in contradistinction to eternity, is clearly the central theme of contemporary thought. The body, whatever its ultimate significance, lives and dies in time, through time, across time. Because the body is such a temporal being, however one determines time so one determines the body. What, then, is time? Whatever time is, if it is anything at all, that is to say, if the proper category of time is even ontological—it has to do with the irreducible dimensions of "past," "present," and "future" and their irreversible sequence or unidirectional trajectory of "before" and "after." Time is inextricably bound to a transcendence of some sort because temporal dimensions, some irrecoverable sense of "before" and "after," remain separate or transcend one another. In our ordinary or common sense conception of time the *past* is that which occurs *before* the present and future; the *present* is that which occurs "now," that is to say, *after* the past and *before* the future; and the *future* is that which occurs *after* the past and present. The ordinary perception of time, then, grasps both its dimensionality and irreversibility.

When one tries to think more carefully about time, however, a variety of difficulties and perplexities emerge, severing more sophisticated explanations of time from the common sense experience of time. It is into this breach that philosophy and theology have stepped, and in doing so they have both classically gone quite wrong. Yet even without recourse to complicated or systematic philosophical or theological explanations, it is difficult to understand time. For instance, in the above simple sketch of the ordinary perception of time, there already appears a difference or confusion between time viewed from the *outside,* objectively, as it were, and time viewed from the *inside,* subjectively. That is to say, the natural privilege given to the present of time is subjective. It is "I" or "we" who view time from "my" or "our" present. Objectively, however, the present has no such privilege; it is simply one moment in the passage of time. The present occurs after the past and before the future in the same way in which any moment of time, whether past, present or future, occurs after a past and before a future. Thus even the most apparent understanding of the future, for instance, as what is "not yet present," already privileges the present experience of the present viewer. A purely objective view, on the other hand, would relativize time's dimensions without privileging any one of them. From this one can conclude that even the most straightforward or common sense *understanding* of time—one that naturally thinks of the future as what is not yet present, and the past as what has already happened—unwittingly mixes subjective and objective accounts of time.

This naive mixture of subjective and objective perspectives need not be considered, however, as the classical traditions of philosophy and theology have hitherto conceived it, namely, as a confusion, flaw or error to be overcome. Rather, more profoundly, as the contemporary understanding of time has grasped, it is an all-important clue to the nature of time. If understanding the genuine character of time is to have precedence over the niceties of systematic explanation or the consistencies of reason, then the ordinary mixture of subjective and objective perspectives must be accounted for rather than explained away. But it is precisely as something to be explained away, discounted, stigmatized, that the classical traditions of philosophy and theology have hitherto approached time's peculiar mix of the subjective and the objective. The consequences for any genuine understanding of the body and embodiment are, as indicated above, no less drastic.

ETERNITY: THE RULE OF PARMENIDES

Logical proofs are the eyes of the mind.—Spinoza, *Ethics,* V

The more sophisticated intellectual-spiritual traditions of the West (or of the East for that matter), have, until quite recently, been oriented not by time—by its irreducible dimensions and direction—but rather by the presupposition of their own logic or *ratio*. Time, and hence the body, very simply, have been made to conform to reason. So, instead of accounting for time, these intellectual constructions explain it away in the name of "eternity." In the same way the body, always a temporal body, is discounted in the name of the spirit, the eternity of the spirit. Time, in its apparent confusion of the subjective and the objective, is not understood but dismissed, and precisely this dismissal passes itself off for an understanding of time. Because nothing is wrong with reason, something must be wrong with time. In a word, it is an illusion of one sort or another. Time—the passage of time: past, present, future, before, after—is interpreted as an error (linguistic or real), ignorance (of the "many," who have no genuine understanding, in contrast to the "few" who do), degradation (a lower grade of reality) or evil (a tempting but wrong intellectual or spiritual path). So, too, then, the body: source of error, ignorance, degradation or evil. The allegedly higher mentality of the West (like the East in this regard) fundamentally misconstrued time as an *ontological illusion,* as the *corruption* of eternity. Time, exactly as error and evil, has to be explained away. Time and the body would then be a function of something else, something "truer" or "better," namely, eternity, true being, permanence, the divine. Time and the body would be anything but phenomena to be grasped in their own right.

For philosophers dedicated to truth, and theologians devoted to God, alike, this vast and consequential misconception of time occurs owing to a fundamental and relatively unquestioned allegiance to the categories of propositional or judgment logic. Philosophers and theologians strove to reduce time, along with the body and everything else, to the standards and intellectual parameters of affirmative ("S is p") and negative ("S is not p") judgments. These standards, at minimum, are two: the principle of noncontradiction ("No statement can be both true and false") and the principle of excluded middle ("Any statement is either true or false"). These two standards, in turn, both guide and constitute the possibility of any knowledge that claims to be systematic, that is to say, internally coherent. Within these strict confines, then, the passage, change, or transcendence of "before" and "after" become forms of nonbeing, absences whose sense is limited to the logical opposition of "is" and "is not." Time and being—the being of time, the time of being—are thus bound together by means of a copula limited to and ruled by the computational logic of affirmative and negative judgment.

Underlying the reduction of time and body to propositional logic, then, are two no less fundamental but perhaps even more hidden — or presupposed — reductions, both of which originate in ancient Greek thinking. First, the equation of being and *logos,* authorized by Parmenides' *Theogony.*[3] True being would be only that being certified by the order of the mind. Second, the equation of *logos* and logic, first articulated by Aristotle in his *Organon.*[4] The order of the mind would be only that order conforming to the principles of noncontradiction and excluded middle, and all the permutations (implications) linking propositions arising from and reflecting that conformity. The result of these two reductions — of being to *logos* and *logos* to logic — would be an understanding of time and the body subject to the paradoxes made famous by Zeno, Parmenides' student and fellow Elean. Subject to the philosopher's logic, all reality governed by time, from common sense to the five senses, would now be counterintuitive. The fleet-footed Achilles would be unable to defeat the slowest tortoise in a foot race. An arrow shot from a bow would never reach its target. These and other paradoxes, despite the obvious and profound challenge they immediately raised for classical thought, were — amazingly — recognized but never resolved by subsequent philosophy or theology. This Gordian knot was cut rather than untied. Provoked by these paradoxes, what came under question was not reason, however, but time and the body, which were dismissed as illusory in one sense or another. Time and all of temporally determined reality would have to conform to logic, however ludicrous the result. What Zeno's paradoxes show for a mind still free of philosophy, however, is that something is terribly wrong with the entire logic presupposed by the classical conception of time.

How does that logic work? According to the classical logic, the absence, difference or transcendence of past and future would be nonbeing. Time's passage — its dimensional interactions, its sequence, its one-way directionality — would be understood under the sign of propositional negation. They would not be being but mere becoming, and hence illusion. The dynamics of time, then, would be forced into the Procrustean bed of negative judgment. "S is not p," so past "is not" present (hence "past" has no meaning or being); future "is not" present (so "future" has no meaning or being). Being and all beings would thus be reduced to a *pure*—unreal, "ideal"—*present*, the present purified of nonbeing. But if past and future have no real being, then "before" and "after" make no real sense, and hence the movement of time, lacking meaning or being, has neither meaning nor being. Such were precisely Parmenides' conclusions. These are the same conclusions taken up by subsequent philosophy and theology, despite their obvious absurdity and their incongruity with common sense experience and the experience of the five senses. Philosophy and theology would henceforth require not only great intellect but also a great hardheadedness they would *laud*, each following its own star, as "intellectual courage" and "unshakeable faith." In this way, by subterfuge, *rhetoric*—Be courageous! Stick to thinking come what may! Believe because it is absurd!—would come to serve as the unmentionable underbelly and support of an allegedly rigorous rationality in philosophy and theology.

Nevertheless, taking this route, choosing eternity over time, being over nonbeing, philosophy and theology would both first be based on a faith in logic. Philosophy and theology would faithfully follow the propositional logic of the intellect into and despite its bizarre and obvious divergence from the evidence of the senses and of common sense, not to mention the unresolved logical conundrums articulated by Zeno. The interrelation and passage of past, present, future, the before and after, would be no more—and no less—than ontological illusion (opinion, falsehood, degradation, ignorance, evil, and so forth). To affirm the real *existence* of time, and hence the positive status of the body, contrary to the intellectual constructions following from the ironclad (and presupposed) rule of logic, would for the philosophers be an admission of ignorance, and for the theologians a fall into evil. Time and the body would henceforth be the enemies of knowledge and faith, the dark manifestations of one devil or another. The unyielding common sense of "the many," and the various intellectual perspectives that respected this common sense, would be denounced as ignorance and heresy. Seeing through the illusion of sense perception, philosophers and scientists—the "few"—would be the wise, theologians and the faithful—the "elect"—would be the saved—it is an old story.

EMBODIED TIME

To see a head, to see it alive, to maintain it so. — Giacometti

Bergson: The Creative Body of the Cosmos

A new story appears with the "vitalist" philosophy of Henri Bergson. Exposing and opposing the intellectual, spiritual, and ultimately rhetorical presuppositions that distorted classical philosophy and theology, the contemporary thought initiated by Bergson is at bottom the effort finally to take time and the body seriously. Instead of viewing time *sub specie aeternitatis,* from the point of view of logic, logic — and eternity — would be viewed from the point of view of time. Phenomenology, broadly conceived as an attention to the real independent of logicist presuppositions, would henceforth become the very mark and mode of philosophizing. For philosophy to retain its vocation as a true account of the real, it would have to ground itself in the real. The true would now depend not on its own inner logic, its *ratio,* but on the "logic" of the real. The real would no longer be made to conform to idea, but rather idea would conform to the real. Assiduously stripping itself of the prejudices of its Parmenidean heritage, henceforth phenomenological intuition would be the proper method and mode of a presuppositionless philosophy, "first philosophy," that is to say, philosophy made genuine for the first time.

Despite the appearance of a plethora of books on time (including Heidegger's *Being and Time*), contemporary thought has at bottom affirmed only two genuinely original and fundamentally distinctive theories of time: Bergson's notion of "duration," "creative evolution," on the one hand, and Levinas's notion of "dia-chrony," intersubjective time, on the other. Both thinkers inaugurated their own original philosophical careers with books centrally devoted to time: *Time and Free Will* (*Essai sur les données immédiates de la conscience*), published in 1889 by Bergson, and *Time and the Other* (*Les temps et l'autre*), published in 1947 by Levinas. Furthermore, for both thinkers, time and embodied subjectivity are intimately and inextricably linked. In taking seriously the transcendence of time — both its irreducible dimensionality (past, present, future) and its irreducible directionality (before, after) — both of these thinkers, each in his own way, reconceives the whole of philosophy and theology.

Bergson is of course the breakthrough philosopher, the one who first grasped the true significance and far reaching consequences of a phenomenology of time. While he was doubtlessly influenced by the modern appreciation for the biological opened up by the widespread popularization of Darwin's earlier theory of evolution, Bergson's theory of time, unlike that of Herbert Spencer, is far from being a philosophical appropriation of Darwinism. It is more like a transfiguration. His theory is well known: time is duration, the interpenetration of past, present and future through a continuous cumulative one-way movement of growth, accessible to philosophical understanding by means of a counterpractical suprarepresentational intuition.

What is perhaps not sufficiently appreciated is to what extent Bergson's notion of time—and his entire philosophy—is built on a single basic quasi-empirical insight: the real, like life, grows. Time and reality cannot be divorced without losing both to merely constructed representations. Imagine the flow of reality at Time 1, Time 2, and Time 3. Hold to the flow of the real, its one-way direction, rather than its stops. Only by not divorcing the succession from the real—the real as continuous cumulative growth—can one see that Time 3 is essentially different from Time 2 because Time 3, unlike Time 2, has Time 2 and Time 1 "behind" it. The cumulative growth of the real guarantees the reality of time. To grasp this insight, however, the philosopher must have a new phenomenological-existential courage. The philosopher must enter into the interior of the time of reality, into its movement or flow, its duration, rather than merely represent it at a distance in a representation which is always a retrospective reconstruction of time privileging a dead past rather than its living passage. Here time and the body are for the first time thought together, taking both seriously.

Both time and reality, taken in their integral unity, are creative. No two moments can ever be equal to one another. The present, while coming out of the past and linked to it, and to this extent delineating a future, is, insofar as it is unique and unlike anything in the past, in no way caused by the past. Freedom is thus assured. The uniqueness of each present, its novelty, whether consciously appropriated by an agent or not, is of the very essence of time and the real. The future, because it follows a unique present, unlike any other, is ultimately unforeseeable, unpredictable, unknowable in principle.

The more one enters into the uniqueness of the present, appropriating the uniqueness of the past, the greater is the openness of the future horizon. Time and reality would thus always be self-creation. Kandinsky's dictum of 1911 — "There is no *must* in art, because art is free."[5] — would speak not merely to the will of the artist (as thought Schopenhauer and Nietzsche), but rather to the unfolding of the real itself. The philosopher, like the artist, would simply have a fuller appreciation of the always novel unfolding of the real across time.

Heidegger: The Anxious Body of History

Heidegger's appropriation and revision of Bergsonian duration remains based in bodily being though with a different interpretative twist, and occurs in two steps, the first at the individual level, the second at the social or historical level. Let us remember, Bergson had said that one must look within, that one must enter into the inside of one's own duration as the starting point of thought. Heidegger — schooled in Husserl's more rigorously methodological "epoche" and "reduction" — did precisely that. Escaping the allure of casual everyday self-interpretations, what Heidegger calls the "they" (*das Man*), in both its theoretical and practical modes, the "existence" or "being-there" (Dasein) of the human subject would first have to appropriate its "ownmost" (*eigenst*) or "authentic" (*eigenlich*) being. Here, attentive to embodied existence, it is not a matter of self-reflection but of "mood" or "attunement" (*Stimmung*). No doubt under the influence of both Kierkegaard's brilliant and refined self-analyses of the temporality of subjectivity and his own Christian theological upbringing and training, Heidegger emphasizes the finitude of human being. Rather than seeing in the human self merely a self-conscious or self-reflective instance of Bergson's unique cumulative past and present and the unknowable but creatively ongoing future, Heidegger discovers in the prereflective *anxiety (Angst) of the body* the priority of the future as a projection limited and given meaning by *death*. Dasein senses in the recesses of its bodily being — in the mood of anxiety — its own finitude. "Being-toward-death is essentially anxiety" (*BT* 310). Death, and not an infinitely open horizon, would be the specific transcendence determinative of individual temporality. The "when" of death would remain unknowable, as in Bergson, but the "that" of death, its essential inevitability for an embodied existence, would nevertheless be most certain.

Whereas Bergson entertained the possibility, given the open creative horizon of the future, that even death, despite its overwhelming empirical probability, might one day be overcome,[6] for Heidegger, in contrast, death becomes the very significance of the future as such. Thus the transcendence of the future, "grasped" in bodily anxiety, takes on the existential significance of "being-toward-death" (*Sein zum Tode*). Individual time—the temporality of Dasein—is hence determined by anxiety and death-bound finitude. Facing such a finite future, the uniqueness of the present becomes the "moment of insight" (*Augenblick*), insight, that is to say, into one's own mortality, the merely "possible" character of all projections. The past, for its part, remains what it was for Bergson: that from out of which the present has come to be and that which the now authentic individual strives to appropriate but can only do so incompletely, inadequately (*Verschuldung*). The past is both the concrete history that produces Dasein and the same history that Dasein must but can only inadequately reappropriate.

Before moving to Heidegger's second revision of Bergsonian time, it should be noted that for both thinkers genuine time—duration or temporality—in contrast to represented time, is only grasped sporadically. The awakening of the individual, his or her appropriation of the genuine temporal character of its own being, via "intuition" for Bergson and "resoluteness" (*Entschluss*) for Heidegger, is episodic. The individual can only rarely pull together or appropriate the real past that leads to the unique present giving onto the open (Bergson) or death-bound (Heidegger) future, rather than being swept away by the superficial though powerful countervailing pulls of everyday practical or scientific theoretical interests, the dull residues of a once genuine time.

The second step of Heidegger's twofold transformation of Bergsonian duration is again a limitation. Dasein, in entering into the interior of its own anxious and death-bound temporality, discovers that the being it engages is historically determined being, what Heidegger later calls "epochal being." "The specific movement," Heidegger writes in *Being and Time*, "in which *Dasein* is stretched along and stretches itself along, we call its *historicizing* (*Geschehen*)" (*BT* 427). For Bergson, entering into the interior of time means entering into the duration of the cosmos itself—its blend of physics and biology, its "creative evolution." For Heidegger, no doubt owing to his Christian theological and German philosophical background,[7] this engagement is first and foremost one that reveals the *historical* unfolding of being. For Heidegger, in contrast to Bergson's cosmic approach, philosophical engagement becomes *Denken*, thinking or bespeaking the historical temporality of being, "attunement" to its epochal historical manifestations from the bottom up.

Despite his existential and historical-ontological revisions, Heidegger nonetheless remains profoundly Bergsonian in his overall outlook. That is to say, for both Bergson and Heidegger, the true life is a life attuned to the real, an engagement with being; and the real or being is fundamentally creative. Indeed, the late Heidegger's well-known critique of "technology" as the "end of metaphysics" is precisely a defense of the ontological-historical creativity or generosity (*Es gibt*) of being. The problem with the technological epoch of being, which Heidegger calls "the greatest danger," is only peripherally a concern with ecological disaster, mass death, soil depletion, nuclear proliferation, overpopulation and the like, that is to say, a concern with the host of moral issues raised by new technologies. Rather, more grandly as it were, it has to do with the unique historical-ontological potential within the present technological epoch to permanently occlude any further or new revelations of being. When Heidegger insists that the "essence of technology is not technological," his critical hermeneutics of "essence" follows Bergson's idea that the essence of the real is freedom, that is, a new as yet unknown unveiling of being. Based in bodily existence, whether cosmic or finite, both Bergson and Heidegger are wedded to an aesthetic interpretation of being and philosophy. Being is temporal, to be sure, but it is so as self-creation. The real or being is the ever deeper or further or new manifestation of manifestation, what Bergson, preferring biological-aesthetic terms over Heidegger's historical-aesthetic terms, calls the "creative evolution" of a protean "*elan vital*."

Levinas: The Ethical Body of Sociality

Levinas offers a radical alternative account of time. As a contemporary thinker, he agrees with Bergson and Heidegger that time and the body are unsurpassable structures, irreducible and to be interpreted in their own right. In sharp contrast to the Bergsonian and Heideggerian commitment to an aesthetic interpretation of being and time, however, Levinas's conception of genuine time is grounded in ethics, that is to say, in the embodied "face-to-face" encounter of intersubjectivity initiated in moral rather than ontological obligations and responsibilities. How is this so? How are time, the body, intersubjectivity and ethics intimately and irreducibly linked?

Like Bergson, Levinas takes seriously the transcendence of time's dimensions relative to one another as well as the irreversible directionality of time. The futurity of the future opens up an unforeseeable novelty; the passage of the past engages an "immemorial" heritage; and the present, as interpenetrated and traced by the irrecoverable excesses of future and past, is the bodily fissure — "denucleation" — of a time whose broken unity Levinas names "dia-chrony." To understand the transcendence of time, however, Levinas is not satisfied with the ontological ground upon which both Bergson and Heidegger construct their thought. Levinas argues that being is not capable of disrupting being. Does not being, he suggests, however "stretched" across history or creative evolution, always recuperate, reintegrate and reassemble itself into a whole? Is not something else, something even more radically transcendent, as it were, required to rupture being's identity with itself, its synthesizing and integrating powers? From whence comes the true source of an *alterity* capable of breaking the grip of being and opening up the dimension of time? We have seen that for Bergson it is the inner and essential creativity of being that outstrips being's integrating functions. Every present is the novel edge of an accumulating reality. Thus Bergson promotes "intuition," entering into the interior of creative duration. But such a conception, while acknowledging the novelty of the present and the unforeseeable character of the future, nonetheless remains formal, empty of content.[8] One is left to wonder how *meaning* accrues to being's ever-unfolding accumulation and building upon itself. How can being have a signification other than its own blind unfolding? It is not merely space and time that philosophy must grasp if it is to avoid the abstract reductions of classical thought, but also and *inextricably* bound up with space and time, it must grasp their essential *meaning*. This is also Heidegger's advance over Bergson: the meaning of individual temporality is embodied finitude, death-bound anxiety; the meaning of being is its epochal manifestation, the revelatory unveiling of historical determinations.

But neither is Levinas satisfied with Heidegger's ontological revision of Bergson. Regarding Heidegger's concrete determination of time as, first, Dasein's temporality, Dasein as anxious being-toward-death, though it is certainly not an empty formalism, Levinas nevertheless will challenge the phenomenological accuracy of this determination of futurity. Levinas will ask if one's ownmost death—unpredictable as to its "when" but inexorable regarding its "that"—is indeed the utmost and hence the paradigmatic sense of futurity. For Levinas, more compelling than the anxiety of one's own mortality lies the bodily suffering and mortality of the other. Not my own aging, sickness and mortality but the other's suffering has priority—moral priority. We will return to this key point shortly. Levinas challenges not only the priority of one's own mortality, but also the alleged individuation Heidegger attributes to death, its "ownmost" character. Even in the anxiety of death and dying, for Levinas the still living person remains bound to others, to the physician, family members (absent or present), neighbors, and so on. For Levinas, contra Heidegger, death takes its significance not from the solitude of individuation, but always from a social context, as an event that stands in relation to others.

As for Heidegger's second claim regarding the epochal historical unfolding of being, Levinas will again challenge the phenomenological accuracy of this interpretation. Is the deepest human relation to history really to be as the thankful thinker of being, its mouthpiece and herald, as Heidegger suggests, or are not humans called to a higher nobler vocation in relation to the historical unfolding of being? Would not that higher vocation lie precisely in moral judgment, in taking history itself to task for its immoralities and it injustices, rather than simply sensitively anticipating and opening up its as yet hidden ontological horizons? Is the history of being, as the final refuge of meaning, even in its epochal unfolding as narrated by the privileged thinker, capable of moral judgment? Is not history, taken as the final arbiter of meaning, always rather only the verdict of winners, the history of triumph, *realpolitik,* and therefore are not its judgments merely redundant self-congratulations? For Levinas, contra Heidegger, there is a indeed a deeper time to history, the time of "sacred history," an invisible history of moral agency and the struggle for justice, a "glory" that remains invisible to the self-congratulatory illuminations of visible history's survivalist triumphalism. Against Heidegger's notion of the epochal-historical revelations of being as the ground of temporality and the meaning of embodied existence, Levinas will argue that history by itself is incapable of the moral judgment that ultimately gives sense to all historical development. The veritable time of history is found in moral agency and the struggle for justice, both structures deeper than the time of epochal being.

In both cases, then, with regard to mortality and history, contra Heidegger, Levinas follows an ethical reading, finding a deeper sense of alterity emerging from the moral significance of embodied mortality and concrete history. Yes, humans, in their very embodiment, are mortal. Humans are vulnerable, open to aging, sickness, and death. Nevertheless, it is not my death but the death and suffering of the other that concerns me most—that should concern me most. One cannot only care for the other, but one can—*in extremis*—die for the other. To save the other, to sacrifice the self, to struggle for justice, have a *greater urgency*—are more significant—than the call to resolutely become oneself and care for being's epochal manifestation. To serve others takes precedence, is a higher calling, than to serve oneself. The deepest stratum of philosophy, then, contra Bergson and Heidegger, is not the issue of being, "to be or not to be," but rather the more pressing moral question of one's "right to be." Such is Levinas critique of the ontological conception of the body.

How are these considerations, Levinas's ethical critique of Bergsonian and Heideggerian ontology, the priority of moral responsibility and the call to justice, specified in terms of time and the body? Let us first of all remember that the matter of taking time and the body seriously hinges on the meaning of transcendence. For Bergson, the irreducible transcendence of time and the real hinges on the structure of creative evolution, the cumulative growth of being. For Heidegger, the irreducible transcendence of creative evolution takes on concrete significance as a resolute mortality caring for—"think-ing"—the epochal historicity of being. What Levinas proposes, to the contrary, is that duration, creative evolution, mortality and his-tory, far from being the sources of meaning, receive their ultimate significance—maintain their transcendence—from the absolute tran-scendence pressing in the higher claims of morality and justice. Time and the body, then, would not only be a matter of being, whether duration or epochal, but the impress or impingement of an alterity with a "face," the alterity, the humanity, of the other. In this way, via the alterity of the other person, the priority of the other person, we begin to see how time and the body emerge from and as morality and justice. Let us examine this novel claim more closely.

For Levinas, the past transcends the present not because it is the historical narrative within which the self finds its ultimate meaning across the inadequate work of recuperation for which the self is always too late (Heidegger uses the term "guilty" (*schuldig*) but in a non-moral sense). The self is not a snake racing to catch its tail, or if it is, it has no genuine past but only a past incompletely made present. Rather, more poignantly, the genuine past must be a past so past that it was never present and never can be present! Levinas will call it the "immemorial past." But such a past is found precisely and exclusively in the felt moral obligation that the other person imposes on the self prior to that self's circuits of self-sameness. One is obligated to the other before oneself—such is the very structure of moral obli-gation, beyond self-interest, and at the same time it is the trace of an absolute past, a past having passed before it was present. Or, we can equally say, the self-interested self discovers itself under greater obligation—is transfigured into its "true self," into its human-ity—insofar as its own self-interest gives way when faced with the moral imperative of the other's suffering. One's own way—always some form of self-presence—gives way to a *suffering for the other's suffering*, self-sacrifice. It is morality, then, obligation to and for the other, that has the kick—the transcendence—of a priority that is felt prior to the self's very identity, rupturing all self-presence with an "immemorial past."

What has passed irrecoverably before, earlier or prior to any self-presence "is" moral obligation impinging on the embodied feeling self, coming from the other. Here, then, in moral obligation, the subject morally *subject* to the other, *serving* the other, Levinas finds the source of the ultimate or paradigmatic sense of pastness: a past that never was or can be present. The other's needs taking priority over my own—such is a moral rather than an ontological structure. Only the other person as moral imperative, in an excessive proximity whose excess can only be moral, disturbing the subject deeper than its ownmost self, breaks self-presence across the passage of an absolute past. To be sure, it is not the empirical other, or an empirical necessity that breaks the self of its selfishness. One can always remain selfish or, as Levinas says, "one can always refuse the other." Being cannot break out of being. Being cannot be broken by itself. The other person, however, the one before whom one is already obligated, the one for whose suffering and mortality one is already one's brother's keeper, this alterity—as moral imperative—pierces through being from on high.

The past of time is transcendence, excess, rupture, the before that remains before. Only morality has the force of such an inordinate transcendence. It is only the absolute priority of the other person encountered as moral imperative that has the alterity to short-circuit all the syntheses of self-presence, whether Kant's "transcendental ego," Hegel's "negation of negation," Nietzsche's "will to power," Husserl's "intentionality," or Heidegger's "resoluteness" and "epochal being."[9] Time and the responsive humane body arise from a challenge coming from above. The past of the other cannot be recollected by the self. Such a piercing of the present, overwhelming self-presence, is in no way an ontological event. Time does not "appear," is not a "phenomenon," does not "make itself present," but rather "disturbs" as the priority of moral responsibility for the other, an obsession with the other that bears upon the self prior to the self's own natural or ontological perseverance. The embodied subject of morality is, to use Levinas's formulation, "more passive than receptivity." Precisely the other's moral command is already imposed, already obligates me, has always already passed—is forever "immemorial"—without ever having been present. In a word, the moral self is chosen before choosing. The past, then, emerges through and as compassion.

So, too, the future is also an event of intersubjectivity. The other person who has passed—who has surpassed me—as moral obligation is also the other who is always still yet to come. Not another mind, or another being who like the self is a manifestation of being, but another as suffering and mortal, encountered from the first as moral imperative, retains the otherness of the radically unknowable, unpredictable, nongraspable. The other whom the subject faces, toward whom the subject is obligated, escapes the prospective forestructures of futurity—whether Husserl's "protention" or Heidegger's "anticipation"—that are projected by the self. The other is neither transparent nor a function of some third and common term. The other is always still yet-to-come, always not yet fully arrived into the present. Nevertheless, to avoid an empty formalism, we must still ask what is the concrete sense of this "yet-to-come." For Levinas the "you" one faces has already passed, to be sure, but the third person singular, the "he" (or "she," if one prefers) is the one who has not yet arrived. What does it mean that in facing the other person one at once faces a "you" that is also a "he"? For Levinas "the third person singular," which he names "illeity," and the future, must be conceived from the first in terms of *justice*.

Yes, the other obligates the self, and hence has already passed prior to the subject's self-presence, but the one who faces, "you," is not the only other person in the world. We are not—or no longer—in the garden of Eden. One is born and lives in society; there are others. Responding to the other morally, the self is also required to take into consideration all the others who are other to the one who faces. That is to say, recognizing that "you" are also a "he," the subject takes upon itself not only moral responsibilities toward this particular obligating other, but also responsibilities toward all of humanity, all others. The future, then, is in no way an extrapolation of the present. As the impact of the other person and of other persons it remains not only forever unknowable, breaking into self-presence with a "not yet" always "to come," but does so specifically as the cry of all others, of humanity—the call to *justice*. The future that remains future even in the face of the present is the future of justice, a just humanity, where satisfying my moral obligations to "you" the self does not create injustice to the third person. The disjunction or disparity between what the self owes to "you" and what it owes to all others is precisely the future—the future as a call to justice. Thus the future is nothing abstract or disembodied. Rather it comes as the concrete demands to provide for the material and spiritual needs of humanity: to feed the poor, to house the exposed, to cure the ill, to regulate the ownership of property, to protect the weak, to guarantee accurate weights and measures, and the like.

What, finally, of the present? It too is moral noncomplacency. Broken by the priority of moral obligations, called to justice for all humankind, the present is the work of establishing a just society, a moral society regulated by just institutions. It is therefore the everyday effort to establish and maintain laws, courts, schools, democratic institutions, fair weights and measures, functioning economies of exchange, communications systems, equal rights, distribution systems for food, shelter and health care, good manners, entertainment, and the like. Obviously, such work requires all the resources of knowledge, both science and wisdom. It is interesting to note in this regard the parallel between Levinas's distinction between morality and justice, and the difference in the Jewish tradition between the Hebrew Bible and the Talmud. The Bible bursts with the broad demands of morality and the prophetic call to justice; the Talmud, in contrast, supplements and develops these imperatives via quantification, measurement, refinement, specification, in sum, concretizing of the demands of morality and justice. Guided and inspired by the Bible, the Talmud, like all wisdom, is the work—the "difficult freedom," to borrow Levinas's term—of the concrete and unredeemed present. In this way, for Levinas, the "secular" is not divorced from the "sacred," but rather becomes the very labor of sanctification, creatively bringing the high demands of morality and justice down into the everyday kingdom of God on earth.

Veritable time and the humane body, then, are structured as "diachrony," a moral responsibility torn and uplifted by a past that is not that of the self but the other's, and the same moral responsibility torn and uplifted toward a future not of its own but humanity's. In this way the inordinate overwhelming imperatives of morality and justice converge, without ever forming an identity, indeed, uprooting all identities, to "constitute" the deepest meaning of time and the body, of embodied subjectivity living in the demanding vectors of concrete sociality. Veritable time—the unsettled convergence of a transcending past, present, future, before and after—and the humane body—suffering for the suffering of others—occur as each person serving as a moral atlas, each responsible for each, and each responsible for all, and I (if this can be said without hubris, for it must be said in the first person singular, for it "is" the very singularity of the first person, the very firstness of the self, to be for-the-other before itself) responsible before all.[10] The body rises to its proper height, to its responsibilities, to its humanity. Thus time and the body are taken seriously together. In this way respiration rises to inspiration, the other-before-the-self. Here emerges the deepest sense of the past as moral compassion for the one who faces, of the future as the call to justice for all humanity, and of the present as sanctification, the "mundane" legal, organizational, economic, social and political labors serving the community of nations and seeking *shalom*.

THREE

Levinas
Thinking Least about Death — Contra Heidegger

INTRODUCTION

In fact Levinas thinks a great deal about death. The death he thinks least about (but not least of), however, is death as Heidegger understood it in *Being and Time*. Indeed, no thinker has analyzed human mortality with greater intensity, made it more central to human existence, given it more prominence for thought, especially the thought of being, or broken more radically with philosophy's millennial long flight from death, than Heidegger.

The flight from death is well known to us Westerners, and certainly not only from a religious point of view. We are familiar with Cicero's dictum "that to study philosophy is nothing but to prepare one's self to die." Socrates, the paradigmatic philosopher, had long before publicly declared after his condemnation to death by an Athenian jury, according to Plato's *Symposium*, that death is nothing, either literally as dreamless sleep or as a gateway to yet another world. From thereafter the denial of death is an intellectual drama with many acts. It reaches its systematic and rational peak, it seems to me, more than two thousand years after Socrates in the *Ethics* of Spinoza, according to which, in the now famous Proposition 67 of Part IV, "a free man thinks of death least of all."[1]

Prior to Heidegger, with a few notable exceptions (e.g., Montaigne, Vico, and Kierkegaard), philosophers would confine the love of wisdom to the virtual "life" of the mind, to the pure activity of thought thinking thoughts, preferring to cognize a deathless truth than to face the truth of death. All this changed with Heidegger, who brought human mortality to the center stage of philosophy. In an interview of 1982, published under the title "The Philosopher and Death," Levinas remarks: "Spinoza will say, as you know, that philosophers should think of nothing less than of death. Heidegger, by contrast, is the one who pursued philosophical thought's reference to death the farthest" (*AT* 155). Of course, let us add, when Spinoza says that philosophers should think of nothing less than of death, it not because he thinks of life and its vicissitudes, but because he has eliminated both life and death from the eternal and necessary truths which alone are meant to preoccupy the philosopher.

The task of this chapter is to explain Levinas's conception of mortality and in doing so to show how mortality and morality are inextricably linked. By showing this it will also show, by contrast, why and how Levinas rejects the Heideggerian account of death and its intimate link to ontology. Finally, in exposing Levinas's conception of death, I hope to leave the reader persuaded that what Levinas said of Heidegger's thought actually applies to his own—that it "pursued philosophical thought's reference to death the farthest." Thus, while thinking least about death as conceived by Heidegger, I want to show that it is Levinas, nevertheless, who thinks the most or farthest about death. And, if this is true, it means that Levinas has thought the farthest about human mortality not, as one might imagine, by standing on Heidegger's shoulders, but rather, more originally, by proposing a radically different but philosophically superior account of the nature and significance of human mortality.

Heidegger

I will begin, then, with a few words about Heidegger's conception of human mortality. I will assume this conception is not only better known than Levinas's, but, given its prominence, that it is reasonably well known. Accordingly, and also for the sake of brevity and because the real topic of this paper is Levinas's conception of death, I will provide only a summary review of Heidegger's conception instead of a full-blown exposition of it.

First of all it is important to note that it was not from some personal eccentricity or morbidity that Heidegger brought death to the center stage of philosophy. No doubt Kierkegaard and Rosenzweig had earlier given death a prominence it had never had before in philosophy. But Heidegger, in contrast to these and other prior thinkers of death, was trained in Edmund Husserl's phenomenology, which is, it seems to me, the first modern philosophical method fully equipped to grasp and present for scientific verification the meaning and significance of such phenomena as death, that is, significations whose sense lies outside of the confines of a conception of modern science hitherto restricted to mathematic or quantitative measurability. Heidegger, in other words, took full advantage of the expanded notion of science and the method for such a science that he learned from Edmund Husserl.[2] And so, too, as we shall see, did Levinas, Husserl's other most distinguished and original student.

One of Heidegger's central phenomenological discoveries in *Being and Time* is that a human being's relation to death is, first of all, of the utmost importance for that human being to discover his or her own basic, genuine or authentic being and, second, that such an "understanding of being," revealed in relation to death, is essential for being itself—the being of all beings—to be revealed for what it is genuinely or authentically. Thus, a human being's authentic relation to death, which Heidegger calls "being-toward-death" (*Sein zum Tode*), functions as the central revelatory moment which both defines authentic human subjectivity and opens up the root philosophical question of the meaning of being. Mortality, then, far from being the sort of thing the philosopher must flee or dismiss for the sake of purified intellection and eternal truth, is to the contrary the most philosophical of all moments. It is only in being-toward-death that the temporality of one's own being, and the historical-ontological context within which one's own being finds its ultimate sense, are disclosed.

How, then, does Heidegger understand authentic human mortality, what he calls "being-toward-death"? "Death," he says, "is the possibility of the absolute impossibility of Dasein. Thus death reveals itself as that *possibility which is one's ownmost, which is non-relational, and which is not to be outstripped (Tod als die eigenste, unbezugliche, unüberholbare Möglichkeit)*" (*BT* 294).

(1) Death is "ownmost"—nothing is more one's own than one's own death. For Heidegger the human subject is "individuated," becomes its "authentic" or "genuine" self, properly occupies it *Da*, the "there" of its of *Da-sein*, in being-for-death.

(2) Death is "non-relational"—in being-toward-death the authentic subject has broken its relations with others: "all its relations to any other Dasein have been undone" (*BT* 294). "*The they,*" as Heidegger calls everyday social life, "*does not permit us the courage for anxiety in the face of death*" (298).

(3) Death is "not to be outstripped"—in being-for-death Dasein understands death as the inescapable, unavoidable, certain future, in a certainty that "demands Dasein itself in the full authenticity of its existence" (*BT* 310).

(4) Death reveals Dasein as "possibility"—facing the "*possibility of the impossibility of any existence at all*" (*BT* 307). Dasein sees itself as a projection into possible futures.

(5) The mood consistent with being-toward-death is anxiety (*Angst*). Indeed, Heidegger claims, "Being-toward-death is essentially anxiety" (*BT* 310).

(6) Being-toward-death is a disclosure, a revelation; it is understanding in the sense Heidegger indicates: "Dasein . . . is ontically distinguished by the fact that, in its very Being, that Being is an *issue* for it. Understanding *of Being is itself a definite characteristic of Dasein's Being*" (*BT* 32).[3] What being-toward-death reveals to Dasein about itself is that Dasein is a temporal being, an "ecstatic" temporalizing being.

(7) Finally, because being-toward-death is not a self-understanding Dasein can maintain at all times, when Dasein does realize itself this way it enters into the back and forth movement of "fallen" (*Verfallen*) or "inauthentic" Dasein and authentic Dasein. Heidegger will speak of Dasein as being "resolute" (*entschlossen*) when it maintains itself in its authentic understanding of being as being-toward-death.

The most important, deepest, and founding question of philosophy is for Heidegger the "question of being"—the question of the meaning of the historical character of the being of all beings. This is because for Heidegger, as Levinas is quick to point out, being is thought as a verb, an event, rather than as a noun or substantive, first as the projective-retentive ("anticipatory"—"thrown"/"repetitive") movement of Dasein's temporality, and then, more broadly, as the projective-retentive context within which Dasein finds its meaning as part of being's "historicality" (*Geschichtlichkeit*) or "historicizing" (*Geschehen*), to speak properly of the eventfulness of verbal be-ing. Being, then, is the free or unbound source that gives meaning to beings, and hence gives meaning to the configuration or dispensation of meaning that is for each of us our own being, and for all of us and for all beings historical being, while at the same times never fully exhausting its generosity, withdrawing into and holding itself in reserve. Dasein, the distinctive manner in which humans are "there" in being—as a being-in-the-world and a being-with-others—is awakened from the superficiality of its worldly and social distractions to the distinctive manner of being which is its own and as such to its role as the language-speaking-opening of being's disclosure-withdrawal of itself. All this follows from human subjectivity grasping itself as being-toward-death.

In appropriating its own being by grasping itself as mortal, a fully resolute Dasein at the same time grasps itself as the mouthpiece, the voice, the opening wherein being itself is disclosed. The being of Dasein revealed in facing itself as mortal is precisely the issue or issuing of being as the "understanding of being." Human mortality is not only the key to the individuation and self-awareness of human beings; it is nothing less also than the key to the authentic being of being itself.[4]

LEVINAS

Levinas, like Heidegger, will oppose philosophy's conceptual flight into deathless eternal truth. Like Heidegger he is a contemporary philosopher, one who takes time—and hence movement, change, contingency, growth, embodiment, language, textuality and history—seriously. Like Heidegger he is a phenomenologist, one who bases his analyses on relevant evidence (the perceived for perceiving, perceiving for the perceived, the imagined for imagining, imagining for the imagined, and so on) rather than on the remains of reductionist presuppositions, however rational or logical or practical. Yet at the same time Levinas radically and completely opposes Heidegger's account of death—opposing each and every component of Heidegger's analysis, and opposing the larger ontological framing within which Heidegger makes ultimate sense of mortality. Indeed, the death that Levinas thinks least about, as I have indicated, is precisely Heidegger's notion of being-toward-death and the understanding of being it is said to reveal.

To confirm or challenge a phenomenological result is a natural part and indeed a methodological requirement in the ongoing and progressive development of phenomenological sciences. As a science, phenomenology is self-correcting: all of its results are subject to and demand confirmation or disconfirmation. Superficial or incorrect analyses are replaced with deeper or more correct ones. Thus the fact that Levinas's phenomenological analyses of death challenge and supersede Heidegger's on every point means, if Levinas's analyses are indeed superior, an advance in scientific knowledge, a better understanding, and a clearer and more distinct knowledge of the meaning of death. No one faults Copernicus for not being Kepler, or Kepler for not being Newton. We are grateful for every advance in knowledge. Levinas will force us to rethink the meaning of death. This is because—and the proof is only in the pudding—Levinas, like Heidegger, Michel Henry and Merleau-Ponty, is one of the masters of phenomenology. But, having said all this, it is also true that Levinas is doing more than simply advancing the state of phenomenological knowledge. And because Heidegger was also doing more than simply advancing the state of phenomenological knowledge, Levinas is also not simply correcting and supplementing Heidegger. Heidegger reinterpreted phenomenology as hermeneutic ontology, and he did so based on his account of Dasein as being-toward-death, and being-toward-death as the self-understanding of being. In challenging this account, therefore, Levinas is not only deepening Heidegger's phenomenological analyses, he is contesting the entire hermeneutic-ontological edifice Heidegger claims to have built upon and within which he ultimately framed those analyses.

By proposing deeper more insightful phenomenological analyses of death, and by following the significance traced in mortality beyond the limitations of a pure phenomenology, and thereby by discovering that the proper frame—or nonframe—of mortality is not ontological but ethical, Levinas is radically contesting the entire Heideggerian edifice of ontology and offering in its stead an alternative vision of ethics as first philosophy. Let us then turn to Levinas's positive philosophical contributions, both in phenomenology and in ethics.

Thinking least about Heideggerian ownmost death, Levinas nevertheless thinks most about the death of the other person. Indeed, it is precisely when and only when thinking least about one's own death and most about the other's death, precisely when care for the other's death takes precedence over care for one's own—all the way to the extreme point of "dying for" the other—that the human subject achieves its true humanity, and hence the proper height of a morally and socially responsible selfhood. Morality is not for Levinas a gloss on (or of) being, a merely "ontic" region of signification. Rather, it is at once beyond-being and better-than-being: beyond-being precisely because and insofar as it is better-than-being. To be for-the-other before oneself, caring for the other's mortality and suffering before one's own, is for Levinas the very height of a person's own humanity, the highest form of selfhood in the sense of the morally best—the kindest, the most compassionate, and in this sense the most excellent and noblest. It is also the most "individuated," in the sense that moral agency, moral responsibility, is irrecusable and nonexchangeable: it is incumbent upon me—in the first person singular, me, myself—to respond responsibly to the suffering of the other, independent and regardless of whether others are or are not also responding responsibly. Thus in the same interview mentioned above, Levinas will also say: "I think that *the Human* consists precisely in opening oneself to the death of the other, in being preoccupied with his or her death.... But above all, it is no longer just a question of going toward the other when he is dying, but of answering with one's presence the mortality of the living. That is the whole of ethical conduct" (*AT* 157–58, 164).

Although these inspiring formulations regarding the moral priority of the other's mortality and suffering express the lynchpin and culmination of Levinas's conception of the meaning of death, his position—refined and developed over half a century, based in phenomenological investigations but not limited to phenomenology—is in fact far richer and multilayered than these highpoints. For this reason the following exposition, aiming to be faithful to the complexity as well as the core inspiration of Levinas's thought, presents its key elements or dimensions under what I have identified as nine headings, which are to some extent (but not entirely) presented in a progressive development of conditions and conditioned.[5]

First, however, a final preliminary remark to obviate a potential misunderstanding. Levinas's thought is both phenomenological and ethical. In its epistemology, where it upholds and is upheld by the rigorous and universal standards of scientific knowledge and truth, Levinas's approach is phenomenological, based, therefore, on the descriptive and verifiable evidence of disciplined investigations into various fields of signification, such as, as in this case, the meaning of human mortality. Nevertheless, because the central claim of Levinas's thought is not ultimately a knowledge claim, and therefore not a thesis or a theme that can be fully represented in propositions, but a moral imperative—the "idea of infinity" as the irreducible height and transcendence of the other person and self-sensing as the irreducible independence or separation of subjectivity—his philosophy pursues phenomenology as far as it is able, as far as the evidence goes, but reaches a point, indeed the most important point, the very point of importance, where it encounters the imposition of a noncognitive significance (a "saying of the said," to use Levinas's formulation) whereby the imperatives of morality are traced in and overwhelm the very intentional ("consciousness of...") and constitutional (transcendental consciousness) structures which define phenomenology as a science. It is in the excess, the "more," the surplus of these moral imperatives that impose themselves beyond what are the most rigorous and specific phenomenological inquiries that one discovers the wisdom—the "love of wisdom" in the service of the "wisdom of love": ethics—which is Levinas's special contribution to the justified truth which constitutes philosophy.

Thus, in the following list of the distinguishable dimensions of sense which together constitute the full meaning of mortality, the lower or conditioning layers, let us say from one to six, are primarily or for the most part phenomenologically driven analyses, while the higher or more conditioned layers of sense, from seven to nine, are ethical significations. However, precisely because the ethical is ethical because it takes precedence over the ontological, because it disabuses naive or spontaneous subjectivity of its naivete, the ethical is already operative even at the most primitive levels of sense, all the way "down" to the most primitive layers of the self-sensing of subjectivity. In this sense one must read this list twice, first as a phenomenology which happens to build up to its own unworthiness as an instrument of understanding, and a second time to see how the ethical, because it is first philosophy, is already operative at all layers of meaning.

Suffering

While the ultimate meaning of death comes to the self from the other's mortality and not its own, death nevertheless does not come unannounced, as it were, as a complete surprise. For Levinas, however, death does not announce itself in the immanence or worldliness of subjectivity through the mood of anxiety as it does for Heidegger. Rather, death is first intimated in the phenomenon of suffering, "in the suffering," as Levinas says in *Totality and Infinity,* "called physical" (*TI* 238) which in *Time and the Other* he had identified somewhat more dramatically as "the pain lightly called physical" (*TO* 69).

Let us note right away, to avoid picturing Levinas as a philosopher of suffering and pain, as a morbid thinker, that in his constitutional analyses of the origin of subjectivity as such, Levinas describes the separation and independence of an existent out of anonymous existence as a sensuous reflexivity, a "hypostasis," which is originally an "enjoyment" (*jouissance*), the carefree joy and oblivious contentment of a sensibility satisfied with sensing sensations. Of course, neither do Levinas's analyses end with this primitive condition of contentment. As a sensible being the nascent human subject is also dependent being, a being vulnerable in its sensibility, subject to pain and suffering, and hence concerned to protect itself through the world. But death, the sense of one's own mortality, this comes first in suffering.

Of suffering, wherein lies the birth of a consciousness of death, which is for the most part a fear of death, Levinas notes that its acuity, the acuity of suffering, comes from the enforced passivity of the sufferer. That is to say, pain occurs in a doubling up of pain: there is pain and like a shadow there is also its inescapability, which is part of and increases the painfulness of pain. It is on the horizon of bodily pain, whose wretchedness comes from its insurmountable enchainment to itself,[6] the self burdened with itself as something it would rather escape but cannot, that there appears a fear (and perhaps, in extreme cases, a welcome?) of a complete enclosure, suffocation or compression—*per impossible*—of this doubling over of sensing and sensation. What is announced, that is to say, in the extremity of the acuity of suffering, of the flesh suffering insufferably from itself, is death. Obviously, not all suffering—I am thinking of minor cuts and bruises—raises the fear of death (though who has not on occasion dreaded death even in a minor bruise or ailment?). Nevertheless, it is in suffering that there opens a horizon in which even greater suffering, a suffering unto closure, as it were, is what Levinas characterizes "as the call to…the proximity of death" (*TO* 69).

In *Totality and Infinity*, as in his earlier texts, suffering is again interpreted as a doubling of pain owing to its inescapability. "The whole acuity of suffering," Levinas reiterates, "lies in the impossibility of fleeing it, of being protected in oneself from oneself; it lies in being cut off from every living spring. And it is the impossibility of retreat" (*TO* 238). Indeed, the physical pain of suffering brings one closer to death than a psychological fear of or anxiety before death: "In suffering," Levinas continues, "the will is defeated by sickness. In fear death is yet future, at a distance from us; whereas suffering realizes in the will the extreme proximity of the being menacing the will" (*TI* 238).[7]

Indeed, as we shall see, because for Levinas death is never present, it is actually in suffering, and not in fear-of or being-toward death, that the will is menaced: "The supreme ordeal of the will [or "of freedom"] is not death," Levinas writes, "but suffering" (*TI* 238). For this reason, too, Levinas rejects the alleged purity, the immaculate freedom of Jean-Paul Sartre's "for-itself," and instead finds "ambiguity" in the embodied will. "Suffering remains ambiguous: it is already the present of the pain acting on the for itself of the will, but, as consciousness, the pain is always yet to come. In suffering the free being ceases to be free, but, while non-free, is yet free" (238). Such a formulation upsets the niceties of logic, but it accurately describes a will both independent and dependent. The will is not absolute: though independent and free, it is nevertheless threatened, backed up against itself, fearful in suffering. But what is it that is glimpsed at on the hither side of acute suffering?

Mystery

For ages, common sense has understood that death is unknowable. As we say, "No one comes back." If you "come back," then you were not dead in the first place (despite all the so-called "after death" experiences hyped in the media)! For Levinas, it is not enough to say that death is unknowable. Its inscrutability goes beyond the known and unknown. It is not known, to be sure, but it is also not simply unknown, as if it were somehow within the realm of knowledge but not yet known or even unknowable in principle. The point, very simply, is that knowledge is not its proper medium. Levinas therefore calls death a "mystery" (*TO* 75). Although it was Gabriel Marcel (whom Levinas greatly respected) who a few years prior to Levinas gave this term a certain philosophical legitimacy; unfortunately, because he never defined it or presented precise formulations of its specificity, the term "mystery" in Marcel's usage remained vague and, let us say it, rather mysterious.[8] For Levinas, in contrast, when speaking of death as mystery he means something quite precise: "It is not unknown but unknowable, refractory to all light" (*TI* 76). "I have characterized this event as mystery because it could not be anticipated—that is, grasped" (77). We will return to the futurity of death shortly. The point at hand is its recalcitrance to knowing, not only with regard to its "when" (which is perhaps only a provisional unknown based on our current limited scientific knowledge of human genetics, biology and physiology), but more fundamentally death is recalcitrant to knowledge regarding its nature. It is not enough to say that one knows nothing and can know nothing about what death is. Rather, the mystery of death—that which is ungraspable—is not an object of knowledge, of any knowledge. It is beyond reach, outside of all grasp.

In *Totality and Infinity* Levinas reaffirms the impenetrable mysteriousness of death. "Death is a menace that approaches me as a mystery; its secrecy determines it—it approaches without being able to be assumed, such that the time that separates me from my death dwindles and dwindles without end, involves a sort of last interval which my consciousness cannot traverse, and where a leap will somehow be produced from death to me" (*TI* 235). It follows, as Levinas had pointed out in a footnote to the aforementioned citation from *Time and the Other*, that death or human mortality cannot be understood, as Heidegger thought, as "the possibility of impossibility," in which case it remains within the grasp of comprehension, but rather "the impossibility of possibility" (an expression he attributes to Jean Wahl), something essentially outside of or beyond all human capabilities whatsoever. "This apparently Byzantine distinction," Levinas notes, "has a fundamental importance" (*TO* 70n43). It is fundamentally important, as shall become even clearer as we proceed, because by treating death as that which is beyond possibility, as a mystery beyond the realm of any sort of comprehension, death transcends rather than confirms the self-understanding of human subjectivity, and in this way heralds the transcending of human subjectivity as understanding.

Passivity

Before turning to what is perhaps the most distinctive structure of death that has already been hinted at, that is, death as that which comes to me and not I to it, we must first underline another level of meaning that has just been touched upon, namely, the "passivity of the subject" (*TO* 70). In the approach of death, in the dying person's sinking into the closure of suffering, "in the crying and sobbing," Levinas sees the end of the subject's liveliness and verve, "the end of the subject's virility and heroism" (72). In this regard, dying is a "supreme irresponsibility" and "infancy" (72). In "the approach of death . . . we are no longer *able to be able*" (74; cf. *TI* 234). The subject in approaching death through suffering and illness, in dying, is emasculated, debilitated, incapacitated—rendered passive.

Levinas is clearly posing such passivity in direct contrast to Heidegger's claim that authentic Dasein must be "resolute" (*entschliessen*) in its being-toward-death, that in contrast to the pusillanimous and anonymous crowd the individuated Dasein must "have the courage" of its "anxiety before death." Furthermore, Dasein in being-toward-death is not only resolute; it is an understanding, a comprehension, a revelation of being—and it is this understanding that under girds its resolution: Dasein is resolute because it resolves to understand being. "Being toward death," Levinas writes of this, "in Heidegger's authentic existence, is a supreme lucidity and hence a supreme virility. . . . Death in Heidegger is an event of freedom, whereas for me the subject seems to reach the limit of the possible in suffering. It finds itself enchained, overwhelmed, and in some way passive. Death is in this sense the limit of idealism" (*TO* 70–71). Death, for Levinas, is not facing up to and grasping a possible future; it is rather, to face the impossibility of a future. It is therefore debilitating rather than strengthening. Marlow in Conrad's *Heart of Darkness* describes his own wrestling with death as "the most unexciting contest you can imagine. It takes place in an impalpable grayness, with nothing underfoot...without glory, without the great desire for victory, without the great fear of defeat, in a sickly atmosphere of tepid skepticism."[9] "There is only one thing that I dread," said Dostoyevsky, "not to be worthy of suffering."[10]

Here we must make a very important observation about the contrast between Levinas and Heidegger on death. Heidegger in speaking of being-toward-death is in no way necessarily talking about the dying subject, the subject critically ill or on a deathbed, the subject that Levinas seems to be invoking in his analysis of death. Being-toward-death in Heidegger is a basic ontological structure (an "existential") of Dasein's authentic being and not a specific reaction to a specific occasion, to a sickness or an injury, say. So are Levinas and Heidegger simply talking at cross-purposes, simply talking about two different meanings? Let us answer in the following way, linking these two approaches: insofar as being-toward-death is an essential structure of Dasein's authentic being, if and when Dasein does happen to suffer the pains of sickness or injury, if Dasein is authentic then it will remain resolute, self-possessed, a care for being, and in this sense courageous, active and virile. Looked at this way, we can see that Levinas's reading of the suffering and pain of dying is indeed an alternative directly critical of the Heideggerian account. For Levinas the meaning of death lies in suffering as incapacitation and passivity, not in a being-toward-death lucid and virile as an openness to being's free meaning-bestowal.

Futurity

While the passivity, incapacitation, irresponsibility, and intimation of death felt in the suffering of illness and injury, all establish that the subject maintains an intimate relationship with death, for Levinas, nevertheless, death itself remains forever future, and hence exterior to the self-presence that constitutes the separated subject. In *Time and the Other*, citing the adage of Epicurus that "If you are, it is not; if it is, you are not," Levinas approves of its recognition of the "eternal futurity of death" (*TO* 71). "Death," he writes, "is never now. When death is here, I am no longer here, not just because I am nothingness, but because I am unable to grasp" (72). It is true that for Heidegger also the primary temporal dimension of death is its futurity, but this does not derive from its aspect of "not yet," its being "something still outstanding" (an interpretation he explicitly considers an inauthentic construal of the futurity of death),[11] but rather from Dasein's comportment, from Dasein's being-toward itself as being-toward possibilities. For Levinas, in contrast, death is never now, is always to come, always remains future, not because the human subject somehow projectively integrates what is coming, which is impossible, but quite the reverse because the human subject cannot catch up to, cannot embrace, cannot be-toward death which is always and ever future. In *Totality and Infinity*, Levinas also affirms the absolute futurity of death, but, as we have seen and as we shall see, that futurity will be associated with the as yet unmet demands of justice.

Postponement[12]

Because death is always future, and when I am it is not, on the rebound, as it were, it is always in the "meantime" — not toward death but before death, prior to death — that human life is lived. This meantime is quite evident in the reaction of many people when faced with the immanent threat of death. "Prior to death," Levinas writes in *Time and the Other*, "there is always a last chance" (*TO* 73).[13] On this point Levinas invokes Shakespeare. "Like Hamlet," Levinas comments, "we prefer this known existence to unknown existence" (78). He cites Macbeth's final defiant words, perhaps said as much to himself as to McDuff, when it seems that all hope is lost: "Though Birnam Wood be come to Dunsinane, and thou oppos'd, being of no woman born, yet I swill try the last" (73). Macbeth refuses to accept death; death is precisely what cannot be accepted, precisely because it is always still outstanding, no matter how close or how inevitable it may seem. Levinas could equally well have cited verses from Dylan Thomas's now famous poem for his dying father: "Rage! Rage! Rage against the night! Do not go gently into that good night." Or the following more gentle verses from Edna St. Vincent Millay: "Down, down, down into the darkness of the grave,/ Gently they go, the beautiful, the tender, the kind;/ Quietly they go, the intelligent, the witty, the brave./ I know. But I do not approve. And I am not resigned."

In *Totality and Infinity* Levinas will speak of the time of this last chance, this interval between death and myself, the time that ever remains before a future that never arrives, as a "postponement" constitutive of time and of meaning (and, though I am putting this off, of sociality). "The postponement of death," he writes, "in a mortal will—time—is the mode of existence and reality of a separated being that has entered into relation with the Other. . . . In it is enacted a meaningful life which one must not measure against an ideal of eternity, taking its duration and its interests to be absurd or illusory" (*TI* 232). Or: "The will, already betrayal and alienation of itself but postponing this betrayal, on the way to death but a death ever future, exposed to death but not *immediately*, has time to be for the Other, and thus to recover meaning despite death" (236). Putting aside for the moment the announcement of the other person, it is within this meantime, in this last chance that lasts forever, in this time of postponement, that the entire dimension of human meaning is opened. Death is one of life's inevitabilities, so it seems—but it is not now. In this "being against death" (236), in the meaningful life that makes it possible, the mortal subject lives in a time where there is time to postpone violence and to establish the institutions that guarantee, as much as anything can be guaranteed across time and history, the postponement of violence.

The Grim Reaper

It is at this point that our attention must be drawn to something quite astonishing that Levinas saw, namely, the idea that time itself is neither objective nor subjective but is intersubjective (*TO* 79), something we have just heard in the citations above taken from *Totality and Infinity*. Death is not only a future that always comes but never arrives; its transcendence is like nothing so much as, is tantamount to, is as if it were the approach of another human being. The following passage by Levinas makes this same point even more pointedly:

> In the being for death of fear I am not faced with nothingness, but faced with what is *against me*, as though murder, rather than being one of the occasions of dying, were inseparable from the essence of death, as though the approach of death remained one of the modalities of the relation with the Other. The violence of death threatens as a tyranny, as though proceeding from a foreign will. The order of necessity that is carried out in death is not like an implacable law of determinism governing a totality, but is rather like the alienation of my will by the Other. (*TI* 234)

Before explicating this description of death as like another human being approaching, and hence death as if coming like murder, let me first focus more narrowly on Levinas's use of the expression "as though." It does not at all simply indicate a simile or metaphor. It has rather to do with Levinas's manner of doing phenomenology, and occurs in many places in his work. To understand the meaning of a term, any term, Levinas seeks out its most extreme sense. For instance, to understand the feeling of entrapment or enclosure, which we mentioned earlier with regard to the meaning of suffering, it is not enough to invoke the phenomena of claustrophobia, say, which leaves open the possible misinterpretation that one is merely psychologizing. One must rather seek out where or how this feeling originally gains the full force of its signification; one must search for more extreme forms of entrapment. Such a deeper sense derives from the way the body is encumbered with itself. And here, too, one can go farther. In his early article, "On Escape," Levinas will say that the body's nausea with itself derives its ultimate significance as an encounter with being, as that beyond which one feels it is impossible to go, an existence without escape, without exit. Being is encountered as that which has no exits, the ultimate trap, the ultimate enclosure, and it is from this meaning of being, being as entrapment or enclosure, that all "lesser" senses of enclosure, for instance "claustrophobia," gain their sense by near or far derivation. So, as a general rule of phenomenological investigation, it is from the most extreme meaning of a signification, the one without any presuppositions, that the lesser meanings in that same family of signification derive their meaning. And this is why Levinas sees in the futurity of death — murder.

It is an important transition, so let us review it carefully. We have seen that death is first intimated in pain, as a fear, as an intimation of an extremity of the doubling over of pain. It is experienced as that which lies over the border of an extreme passivity as an ever more extreme passivity to the point of a never-experienced but feared massive inertness. A living being, however much it may suffer, is never dead. Its passivity has limits. A body is not a corpse. Death never arrives. It always remains future. It transcends the present, opens up ·a meantime wherein everything meaningful occurs. But, the phenomenologist must ask a further question, hence Levinas must ask, what does it mean really to say that something never arrives into the

self-presence of the self, that it remains always future? Is this signification ultimate, irreducible, presuppositionless? And if it is not, from
whence does the futurity of the future derive its sense? It is because
he approaches meaning in this way that we can understand the justification for his answer: the transcendence of death as futurity makes
sense, or takes its sense from the even more transcendent futurity of
the other person. Death is thus *like,* or *as though,* or *tantamount to,*
the transcendence of the oncoming futurity of another person. Thus
death comes like murder. And with this signification we shift from
phenomenology to ethics, because for Levinas intersubjectivity, the
relation to the other person, *my relation to you,* is first significant as
an ethical relation. Nothing could be farther from the ontological
analysis of Heidegger which left ethics and other persons behind as
merely ontic or inauthentic.

The Doctor

Thus, too, even my mortality (before we consider the other's mortality) is not, as Heidegger thought, a matter of solitude. My own
death, my "ownmost" death, is not "non-relational." Being-with-
others is not merely inauthentic. For Levinas, a mortal being, most
especially when wounded, suffering, or dying, remains in relation to
that which is transcendent, remains in relation to the other, and hence
remains within an ethical relation:

> The solitude of death does not make the Other vanish, but remains in
> a consciousness of hostility, and consequently still renders possible an
> appeal to the Other, to his friendship and his medication. The doctor is
> an a priori principle of human mortality. Death approaches in the fear
> of someone, and hopes in someone....A social conjunction is main-
> tained in this menace. (*TI* 234)

My death, however much it remains mine in the compression of
my suffering, always retains its social and hence its ethical character: I
can be saved, and in the meantime of dying, in the ever future futurity
of death, hope remains for a cure or recovery. This is why some termi-
nally ill persons pay to have their dead bodies frozen—perhaps a cure
will be found in the future. This is why euthanasia is a risk—a cure
might be found. It is interesting, too, and too little considered, that
it is not inorganic matter than is infinite but rather the organic, life,

which through reproduction literally—though at the species level and not the individual level—has no end, goes on to infinity. A rock, however hard, eventually wears away, disintegrates and vanishes. But life, or at least species life, has absolutely no internal end and under the right conditions can go on forever. This interesting fact confirms Levinas's idea that death comes to the self from the outside, and comes to the self from the outside not, as Spinoza thought, "like an implacable law of determinism governing a totality" (*TI* 234), but *as though it were murder*. One can, in principle, even as an individual, live forever.

Every death, even the most natural death, comes as though it were murder. Under different conditions, in a different time, say, one might have gone on living. According to certain biblical interpretations, Adam was meant to live forever had he not eaten of the tree of the knowledge of good and evil. And the early biblical figures (so the Bible says) certainly lived very long lives. Death comes from the outside, hence it comes like murder. "The doctor is an a priori principle of human morality," because in principle life can be extended forever, and thus all deaths come as murders.

Morality: Dying for the Other

But there is another side to death: if all death comes as murder, it is not only my death that comes as murder, but so too does the other's death come as murder. And this consideration brings us to the ultimate sense of death, which lies not in my suffering or even in my dying, but rather derives from the primacy of the other person that we have already detected in the futurity of death, and the manner in which dying remains a social event. For Levinas, it is not my mortality and suffering that come first, but rather and precisely the mortality and suffering of the other.

Death remains a social event, and sociality is initiated in the primacy of the ethical, initiated, that is to say, in the primacy of the other person. So, considering the meaning of death, the death that remains social and hence ethical, the primary directive, the overriding moral imperative is to alleviate the suffering of the other, the one whose mortality comes first. The imperative of the face of the other, Levinas writes, "commands me to not remain indifferent to this death, to not let the Other die alone, that is, to answer for the life of the other person, at the risk of becoming an accomplice in that person's death" (*TO* 108). If the face of the other, as Levinas has taught, first appears in the imperative "Thou shall not murder" (*TI* 199), then to not murder the other I must tend to the other's suffering, to the other's mortality, and do everything in my means to avert the violence which produces the death of the other. "Thou shall not murder" means the "face" of the other person, but it means this not as an abstract and remote command, but as the concrete requirement, the command, to support the life, to alleviate the pain and suffering, and to forestall the dying of the other.

And the most extreme meaning, indeed, the paradigmatic meaning of "Thou shall not murder," in the sense of caring for the mortal other's suffering, is captured in the extreme formula that Levinas invokes in his later writings: "dying for the other." One can not only sacrifice one's own money, and time, and needs to alleviate the other's suffering, but one can be called to make the ultimate sacrifice for the other, the ultimate self-sacrifice, to give (as we say) one's life for the life of the other. This extreme notion, which of course is not simply an idea, is no idle fancy either, for it is precisely what many war heroes have actually done.

It is in the moral extremity of this notion, "dying for the other," that Levinas finds the ultimate sense of mortality, and perhaps also the ultimate sense of morality, living for and caring for others — "to not let the other die alone." Levinas will invoke this sense to understand the very humanity of the human. As he writes in his article, "Dying for...": "[T]he human, in which worry over the death of the other comes before care for self. The humanness of dying of the other would be the very meaning of love in its responsibility for one's fellowman and, perhaps, the primordial inflection of the affective as such" (*EN* 216). He goes on:

> The priority of the other over the I, by which the human *being-there* is chosen and unique, is precisely the latter's response to the nakedness of the face and its mortality. It is there that the concern for the other's death is realized, and that "dying for him," "dying his death" takes priority over "authentic" death. Not a *post-mortem* life, but the excessiveness of sacrifice, holiness in charity and mercy. This future of death in the present of love is probably one of the original secrets of temporality itself and beyond all metaphor. (*EN* 217)

Justice beyond Death

I have said that "dying for" the other is the ultimate meaning of mortality and morality, but it is nonetheless not the last word to be said about death. The last word must be given to justice, because justice supplements morality and as such provides another dimension to the meaning of "dying for." The moral person dies for the other, for the well-being of the other. The just person dies for all others, for the freedom and equality that in society at large make possible a moral life.

To die for another, to make the most extreme and ultimate sacrifice, is *not enough* because the world goes on after my death. Of course, to die for the other is indeed the ultimate sacrifice, and assuming that such dying is the morally right thing to do, a genuine requirement of an exceptional compassion, then nothing else is or can be required of he or she who gives his or her life. But morality, whatever the sacrifices it requires, is for Levinas not sufficient by itself, for morality must be supplemented by justice. To give all to one person does not (without further consideration) take account of what is needed by others, by those who do not face me but who face the other, say, or who face others who are not facing me. Society is made up of more than two persons. I am speaking, of course, of what Levinas calls "the third," he who is other to the other, of society at large. It is here that my compassion for the one who faces is insufficient. It is here that justice is demanded, where each person who is unique, singular, unequal to another, must be treated, under law, as an equal to others (*OB* 157–61). It is here that institutions—courts, legislatures, police, and so forth—are required to ensure justice and morality. But what has death to do with justice?

It has everything to do with justice! Indeed, just as justice is required by morality for the sake of morality, so justice is the final and ultimate meaning of mortality, even beyond the extreme sacrifice of "dying for the other." The meaningful world, we have seen, occurs in the meantime, in the time of postponement before death. But the meaning of the meaningful world derives from morality, from care for the other's mortality before my own. And, as we have just noted, morality must be supplemented by justice, by a care for all others, a care that cannot be accomplished solely in the love and compassion one person can have for another, but requires institutions and law also, to postpone violence and to secure a world in which the imperatives of morality can be fulfilled without fear or harm. All this is another way of saying that not only must the self place the mortality of the other before its own mortality, but the self must live for a time beyond its own time, beyond, that is to say, its own death.

"Signification," Levinas writes, "comes from an authority that is significant *after and despite my death*, signifying to the finite ego, to the ego doomed to death, a meaningful order significant beyond this death. This is not, to be sure, some promise of resurrection, but an obligation that death does not absolve" (*TO* 114).[14] To serve an authority—the authority of justice—beyond one's own life, "*after and despite my death*," is not as strange as it may first sound, and is indeed almost an everyday consideration. It is at work when one buys life insurance. It is at work when one votes for a bond issue for school financing, or for parks or bridges. It is at work when one plants a tree for one's children or grandchildren. The futurity of justice lies beyond the futurity of the one who faces.

The world, as I have said, does not disappear with one's own death. The world will need to be just beyond our own deaths, and our care to ensure and secure the institutions of justice is a requirement coming from the depth of our commitment to morality...all the way to the requirement of justice, of a world where everyone can be moral without violence. "In any case," Camus writes at the conclusion of *The Rebel*, "if he is not always able not to kill, either directly or indirectly, he can put his convictions and passion to work at diminishing the chances of murder around him."[15] The "stranger" toward whom Levinas directs our moral compassion is not simply or not only the other person who faces, or those who are far away, but also those who are not yet born. The ultimate sense of the future, the ultimate sense of morality, thus lies beyond morality in justice, for those as yet unborn, for all the generations to come:

> There is in the Other a meaning and an obligation that oblige me beyond my death! The futuration of the future does not reach me as a to-come, as the horizon of my anticipations or pro-tensions. Must one not, in this *imperative* signification of the future that concerns me as a non-in-difference to the other person, as my responsibility for the stranger—must one not, in this rupture of the natural order of being, understand what is—improperly—called super-natural? (*TO* 115)

Levinas invokes the much abused religious term "supernatural" not only because morality and justice move counter to our natural selfishness and clannishness, but also because the concrete meaning of the divine, of the God of Abraham, Isaac, and Jacob, the God of monotheism, makes sense to humans precisely in and as the work of justice. Whether we call it "justice" or call it "God," the ultimate "authority"—transcendent, better, "supernatural"—in whose imperative force death and mortality make sense, lies here. "The futuration of the future is not a 'proof of God's existence,' but 'the fall of God into meaning" (*TO* 115). The meaning of death as morality and justice is precisely and nothing less than the sense that God makes for the difficult freedom of an unachieved humanism. Not "God or Nature," as Spinoza thought, sacrificing morality and religion to an eternal and impersonal nature, or "temporality and historicity," as Heidegger thought, sacrificing a mortal humanity to the historicizing of being, but "God or justice," as Levinas claims, respecting transcendence and authority in the nobility of the quest for justice, the unfinished personal and communal adventure of social redemption.

Conclusion

Levinas's phenomenological-ethical account of death thus has a deeper "bottom" and a higher "top," as it were, than Heidegger's phenomenological-ontological account. It begins more deeply, in subjectivity conceived in the self-sensing of sensibility, thus in suffering, rather than in a subject first defined by the worldly (instrumentality) and social ("the they") distractions that are overturned in anxiety and the resolute self-understanding of one's ownmost nonrelational being-toward-death. And Levinas's account of death faces a more radical or greater transcendence in the priority and exigency of an infinite moral responsibility for-the-other's mortal being, ultimately a "dying for" the other person, and in the transcendence of an as yet unachieved justice of a for-all-others. All this contests Heidegger's account of Dasein's mortal and hence temporalizing understanding finding its authentic being in a bespeaking of being's never fully actualized historicizing. Transcendence for Heidegger requires that mortal beings be responsible not for other persons but for being, to be as the caretakers, the shepherds, the mouthpieces of the historicizing being of all beings. In critical contrast, Levinas saw that beyond the being of all beings, a responsibility was incumbent on beings as beings, specifically on mortal and suffering human beings, though separate from one another, to rise to a higher, nobler, responsibility, to care for one another, the I for-the-other, the other who as a mortal being suffers and should not face death alone, who requires help, who imposes the moral demand to be saved from the violence of death, imposing thereby—from the transcendence of the other's mortal separation from me—the infinite demands of morality and justice.

FOUR

Buber and Levinas — and Heidegger

The Levinas-Buber relation is a deep and instructive relationship.[1] Martin Buber is senior and far better known. His book, *I and Thou*, first published in 1923, was immediately and widely recognized as an important spiritual work and quickly translated into many languages. Buber is himself a recognizable figure, the bearded Jewish sage said to resemble a biblical prophet (even though, as Levinas once remarked, we have no photographs of the biblical prophets). Emmanuel Levinas, on the other hand, while a philosopher of the first rank, is never likely to be popular or well known. Although his many books and collections of articles have been translated into English, his name still often draws a blank — and this is almost as true within the academic community and the Jewish community as it is for the public at large.

What makes grasping the differences dividing Levinas and Buber of special importance, beyond the intrinsic value of gaining a sharp understanding of their thought separately and in conjunction, is the fundamental role that the ontological thought of Martin Heidegger plays for both of them. Both Buber and Levinas are critics of Heidegger. In an interesting twist of thought, however, their respective critiques of Heidegger serve, at the same time, as their critiques of one another. Buber accuses Levinas of being Heideggerian, and Levinas accuses Buber of the very same allegiance. Because for both thinkers these accusations are damning, their critiques of one another hinge in an important sense on the validity and depth of their respective critiques of Heidegger. The central thesis of the present essay is that it is Levinas—and not Buber—who fully critiques Heidegger. Levinas's critique of Heidegger is thus also a critique of Buber for unwittingly remaining within the orbit of Heidegger's thought.

BUBER ON LEVINAS AND ON HEIDEGGER

1957 Afterword to I and Thou

Although Buber wrote hardly anything directly about Levinas's thought, at a conceptual level, beyond explicit texts with proper names, he did respond rather directly to at least one of Levinas's central criticisms. He did this in the short Afterword of 1957 that he appended to the second edition of *I and Thou*. There Buber defended and focused on the topic—the reciprocity of the I-Thou relation—that is perhaps the central bone of contention in Levinas's 1958 article, "Martin Buber and the Theory of Knowledge."

Several Shorter Works

In this 1957 Afterword, Buber also indicates that "several shorter works" published after *I and Thou* function "to clarify the crucial vision by means of examples, to elaborate it by refuting objections, and to criticize views to which I owed something important but which had missed the central significance of the close association of the relation to God with the relation to one's fellow-men, which is my most essential concern."[2] These shorter writings are found in *Between Man and Man*. Here, as we shall see, the role of Heidegger becomes central. The "several shorter writings" of Buber are important, because they further develop and defend the central theses of *I and Thou* and because Levinas refers to them in his criticisms of Buber. But they are important also because in them Buber invokes and criticizes certain Heideggerian conceptions that play a key role not only in his own philosophy but also in his debate with Levinas. Opposition to Heidegger is important to Levinas's 1958 article on Buber and to all of Levinas's philosophy, and it is important as well, from Buber's perspective, in understanding Buber's short 1963 and 1967 responses to Levinas.

"What Is Man?"

One of Buber's most important criticisms of Heidegger, one to which Levinas often refers in his 1958 article on Buber, is contained in Buber's 1938 inaugural course of lectures as Professor of Social Philosophy at the Hebrew University of Jerusalem. These lectures were delivered shortly after Buber fled a hostile Nazi Germany. Among his many distinctions as a thinker, Buber has the honor of being one of the earliest and most trenchant critics of Heidegger. Buber's 1938 lecture on Heidegger appeared in English translation in 1965, in a monograph entitled "What Is Man?"[3]

"Religion and Modern Thinking"

The second and briefer of Buber's criticisms of Heidegger came shortly after the war, that is to say, shortly after the Holocaust. They were also delivered as lectures, but this time presented at several American universities (Yale, Princeton, Columbia, Chicago, and others) in November and December of 1951. This series of lectures was critical of what for Buber were the inadequacies of the philosophical stances of a variety of thinkers—Kant, Kierkegaard, Nietzsche, Sartre and Karl Jung—in relation to religion. One of these lectures, entitled "Religion and Modern Thinking,"[4] presents an extended criticism of Heidegger. For the most part, however, these 1951 lectures reproduce Buber's earlier criticisms of 1938.

HEIDEGGER

It is unfortunate that Heidegger wrote no response to either Buber or Levinas, though he certainly had ample opportunity—and legitimate reasons—to do so. Nevertheless, this void does not hamper our aims. The concern of the present essay lies not in texts and proper names but rather with thought, in this case with Heidegger's original and central contribution to philosophy, namely, the "ontological difference," the *Seinsfrage*, the question of being. It is important to grasp the unity of Heidegger's central question and position in order to see how and to what extent it influenced, positively or negatively, both Buber and Levinas. While we cannot assume that the reader is intimately familiar with Heidegger's work, neither can we divert a great deal of attention to elaborate introductions. Like Buber and Levinas, this essay will draw from Heidegger's magnum opus, the "funda-mental ontology" of *Being and Time*. It will also follow the "turn" (*Kehre*) of his ontology from its early orientation, found in *Being and Time*, which moved from beings—more particularly Dasein—to being, to its later and more original orientation, found in Heidegger's writings on language, poetry and thought, from being to beings.

BUBER AND HEIDEGGER, AND LEVINAS

As just noted, Buber gave two lectures critical of Heidegger, one before the war in 1938 and one after the war in 1951. In the ear-lier lecture, Buber considers Heidegger in relation to philosophical anthropology. Heidegger's philosophy is reviewed as part of a series of lectures published under the title "What is Man?" This publication is one of the "shorter works," as Buber says in his 1957 afterword to *I and Thou*, produced to "clarify the crucial vision" of *I and Thou*. It is an instance of Buber's desire "to criticize views to which I owed some-thing important but which had missed the central significance of the close association of the relation to God with the relation to one's fellow-men, which is my most essential concern."[5] It contains three criticisms of Heidegger; we will focus especially on the third that concerns Heidegger's notion of "solicitude," a notion that was critical in the exchange between Buber and Levinas in 1963 (*PN 33*). The later lecture of 1951 is also critical of Heidegger. It locates his thought as one of three inadequate ways of approaching religion in modern thinking, the other two being Sartre's existentialism and Karl Jung's psychology. Because the later lecture is less developed and less relevant to our concerns, I will turn to it first, but briefly.

Buber's 1951 Lecture

A second reason for considering Buber's postwar criticism of Heidegger first is that, with the exception of the adulatory cult of Heideggerians emanating from Jean Beaufret in Paris, certain histori-cal reasons for criticizing Heidegger and his thought were glaringly obvious in the postwar, post-Holocaust context. Heidegger was a member of the Nazi party from 1933 to 1945. After the war and until the end of his days, he never apologized or rendered a convincing moral justification for his behavior. The obvious criticism, then, is that Heidegger's thought—like Heidegger himself—was somehow too deeply embedded in history to have been able to recognize and to judge from a responsible critical distance the horrors of the Nazi terror. In his 1951 lecture, Buber states: "Heidegger creates a concept of a rebirth of God out of the thought of truth which falls into the enticing nets of historical time."[6] Such is Buber's basic criticism, namely, that Heideggerian thought—*Denken*—lacks an adequate notion of transcendence or the divine to be able to properly judge history. The notion of "resolution," which engages Dasein authentically in its temporality and history according to *Being and Time,* leads no further than to an embrace of personal "fate" (*Schicksal*) within the overriding context of a social-historical "destiny" (*Geschick*) (*BT* 435, 436)—even if that social-historical destiny and that fate are Nazi! The historical or "epochal" ontological difference, the source and provider of whole worlds of meaning, is all too apparently incapable of differentiating between right and wrong.

When Buber uses the expression "a rebirth of God out of the thought of truth," he is referring to Heidegger's reading of Hölderlin's claim that ours is a time of "indigence." According to Heidegger's reading, this claim means that ours is "the time of the gods who have fled and of the God who is coming."[7] Because his particular interest is in the most basic "I-Thou," the "I-Thou" with God, Buber interrogates Heidegger's thought to discover what this phrase, "the God who is coming," can mean. For Buber, speech faithful to the divine must be "a testimony to that which I call the dialogical principle."[8] This is not what Buber hears in Heidegger. Instead—and Buber invokes Heidegger's infamous "Rectoral address of May, 1933, along with a manifesto delivered to students dated November 3rd of the same year"—"here history no longer stands, as in all believing times, under divine judgment, but it itself, the unappealable, assigns to the Coming One his way."[9] Heidegger is guilty of having "allied his thought, the thought of being,...to the hour as no other philosopher has done," and in doing so he must, as he did, "succumb to the fate of the hour."[10] The dark syllogism is clear: Heidegger has so bound his thought to the truth of being, and the truth of being to history, that when the critical hour came to judge history rather than to embrace it, Heidegger embraced it along with the "sinister leading personality of the then current history,"[11] i.e., Hitler, whose name, by this circumlocution, Buber refuses to enunciate. This is what Buber meant when he said, "Heidegger creates a concept of a rebirth of God out of the thought of truth that falls into the enticing nets of historical time." No doubt Levinas would agree fully with Buber on this critical point.

Beyond the basic argument, that Heidegger's ontology falls into an uncritical historicism and the polemics that follow from it, the earlier lecture of 1938 explores why Heidegger embraces truth as a function of being rather than of dialogue so that he loses the capacity to judge history rather than to be swept along by it, and hence falls prey to the dark path of evil.

1938 Lecture

In this lecture, as I have indicated, Buber presents three criticisms of Heidegger, examined briefly below. The third, Buber's criticism of solicitude in Heidegger, will return in the Levinas-Buber confrontation.

Dialogical Relation More Real than Heideggerian Self-Relation

Buber's first—and primary—criticism of Heidegger is that "fundamental ontology" is neither fundamental nor in contact with the fullness of the real. Contrary to Heidegger's intention, his fundamental ontology is both narrow and abstract, representing only a limited or simple part, a fragment or aspect of being rather than the complex whole of what is genuinely real and meaningful. According to Buber's critical explication:

> Fundamental ontology does not have to do with man in his actual manifold complexity but solely with existence in itself, which manifests itself through man.... Heidegger abstracts from the reality of human life the categories which originate and are valid in the relation of the individual to what is not himself [death], and applies them to "existence" in the narrower sense, that is, to the relation of the individual to his own being.... Heidegger's modified categories disclose a curious partial sphere of life, not a piece of the whole real life as it is actually lived.[12]

Levinas criticizes Buber's fundamental philosophical commitment to ontology rather than to ethics. Quite clearly, Buber's critique of Heidegger is not based on a critique of ontology as such, but rather on a different version of ontology. For Buber, what is wrong with

Heidegger's ontology has nothing to do with the fundamental status of ontological notions such as "reality," "actuality," and "being," but rather with the narrowness, and hence the abstractness, of Heidegger's characterizations of these ontological notions. Buber's primary point is not directed against ontology as such, but rather lies in the positive and ontological claim that dialogue serves as a better basis for ontology than what Heidegger takes for its foundation, namely, Dasein's care for existence and resolute engagement in historical-epochal being. Buber has no argument, therefore, over the fundamental status of ontology as the final arbiter of all things. Rather, his challenge to Heidegger is an argument over which ontology is best suited for that status.

Buber rejects Heidegger's attempt to restrict Dasein to existence. For Buber "original guilt" derives precisely—and in direct contrast to Heidegger—not from a lack of resoluteness, not in an essential failure to be able to recover one's own ground in being, but rather "in remaining with oneself."[13] That is, for Buber true being lies in the being of dialogue rather than in Heidegger's self-referential being, even when the latter includes not only the effort at self-recovery but takes that effort into its social and historical context. Thus for Buber the "call of conscience" that in Heidegger is a call from being to Dasein's being, is in reality a call from the other as encountered in Thou-saying. Buber writes: "'Where were you?' *That* is the cry of conscience. It is not my existence which calls to me, but the being which is not I."[14]

But this persisting commitment to ontology, characterizing the alterity of the Thou as "the being which is not I," and the self's Thou-saying as an accomplishment of the self's "whole being," is also the ground of Levinas's critique of Buber. Levinas found Buber's recognition of the primacy of a nonepistemological relation to otherness praiseworthy. What he finds most praiseworthy is when Buber speaks of this relation as person-to-person encounter. But for Buber person-to-person encounter is but one instance, and not the privileged instance (despite what we have seen above), of nonepistemological relation. Levinas takes issue with Buber's failure to recognize both the proper structure and the radical consequences of giving primacy to a nonepistemological relation. Buber fails to appreciate that the only relation capable of escaping epistemology, including the hermeneutic epistemology of Heidegger's "fundamental ontology," is ethical intersubjectivity. Buber does not recognize the radical consequences of a grounding of thought in intersubjectivity, because Buber's interpretation of intersubjectivity in terms of the reciprocity of the "I-Thou" is a continuation of, rather than a break with, ontological thought. Dialogical thought, then, would be a "full" rather than a "partial" ontology, to cite Buber's own words. Levinas argues that Buber does not realize that intersubjectivity cannot be properly interpreted within the confines and according to the standards of ontology.

Transcendence of Dialogue versus Solitude of Dasein

Buber's second criticism hinges on the question of solitude and transcendence. Buber contrasts the self-enclosure of Heidegger's "monological" thinking with the transcendence or "absolute" of his own "dialogical" thinking. The problem with Heidegger's thought, based on its narrowness and abstractness, is that it improperly grasps the transcendence that appears only within the "I-Thou" of dialogue. Thus Heidegger's Dasein, despite its attachment to the whole of historical being, remains "solitary."

> Heidegger's "existence" is monological. And monologue may certainly disguise itself ingeniously for a while as dialogue, one unknown layer after the other of the human self may certainly answer the inner address, so that man makes ever fresh discoveries and can suppose that he is really experiencing a "calling" and a "hearing"; but the hour of stark, final solitude comes when the dumbness of being becomes insuperable and the ontological categories no longer want to be applied to reality.... Heidegger's man stands before himself and nothing else, and—since in the last resort one cannot stand before oneself—he stands in his anxiety and dread before nothing.[15]

Levinas, too, criticizes Heidegger's philosophy of being for its inability—even in the essential being-in-the-world of Dasein, as well as in its appreciation for the "ontological difference"—to surpass the category of *Jemeinigkeit* or "ownness." Levinas contends, however, that Buber's alternative, what he calls "dialogue," is itself unable to escape the solitude, monologue, *Jemeinigkeit*, or "closed system,"[16] that plagues Heideggerian thought. Dialogue, too, according to Buber's own account, becomes a relationship of being with itself.

Essence versus Solicitude

Buber's third criticism of Heidegger has to do with the latter's notion of care or solicitude.

> For the relation of solicitude which is all he [Heidegger] considers cannot *as such* be an essential relation with the life of another, but only one man's solicitous help in relation with another man's lack and need of it. Such a relation can share in essential life only when it derives its significance from being the effect of a relation which is essential in itself. . . . In its essence solicitude does not come from mere co-existence with others, as Heidegger thinks, but from essential, direct, whole relations between man and man. . . . It is from these direct relations, I say, which have an essential part in building up the substance of life, that the element of solicitude incidentally arises, extending after that, beyond the essential relations, into the merely social and institutional. In man's existence with man it is not solicitude, but the essential relation, which is primal.[17]

Here Buber rejects solicitude as merely a secondary gloss on the more "primal" or "essential" encounter.

Ironically, Levinas's later criticism of solicitude is really an echo of Buber's original criticism of Heidegger found here. I say "ironically" because Levinas in "Martin Buber and the Theory of Knowledge" appears to defend Heidegger's notion of solicitude against Buber's critique. In fact, Levinas's point is not so much to defend Heidegger, as Buber seems to have thought, as to attack Buber.

> Buber rises in violent opposition to Heidegger's notion of *Fürsorge*—or care given to others—which would be, for the German philosopher, the true access to others. It is not, surely, to Heidegger that one should turn for instruction in the love of man or social justice. But *Fürsorge*, as response to essential destitution, is a mode of access to the otherness of the Other. It does justice to that dimension of height and of human distress, by which (far more than by *Umfassung*) the Relation is characterized. . . . Is dialogue possible without *Fürsorge*? If I criticize Buber for extending the I-Thou to things, it is not because he seems to be animistic in relation to nature; it is rather that he seems too much the *artiste* in his relation to people. (*PN* 33)

Levinas is not defending Heidegger's notion of *Fürsorge* as such. Levinas is even more aware than Buber that its ultimate context is ontological rather than ethical. Rather, contra Buber, Levinas is saying that in the notion of Dasein's solicitude one can at least see a break with theoretical and practical reason instigated by an ethical intersubjectivity (even if Heidegger does not ultimately understand it this way) rather than via the allegedly deeper embrace (*Umfassung*) of Buber's "essential" relation, which by Buber's own account is not bound to intersubjectivity and hence is not bound to ethics. In other words, Levinas *uses* Heidegger's notion of Dasein's solicitude to the extent that it is an ethical notion (notwithstanding the use to which Heidegger puts it) to oppose Buber's notion of "essential" relation, which is ultimately not an ethical relation. Thus Levinas *also* rejects both Buber's "essential" relation and Heidegger's "ontological difference" by insisting that the transcendence proper to the origin of signification is ethical and not ontological.

It is interesting to note, because it confirms Levinas's criticism of Buber, that in this same discussion of solicitude in Heidegger, Buber links his notion of "essential" relation to reciprocity or mutuality. Against Heideggerian solicitude Buber writes, "In mere solicitude man remains essentially with himself, even if he is moved with extreme pity; in action and help he inclines toward the other, but the barriers of his own being are not thereby breached; he makes his assistance, not his self, accessible to the other; nor does he expect any real mutuality, in fact he probably shuns it; he 'is concerned with the other,' but he is not anxious for the other to be concerned with him."[18] Levinas would be the first to agree with Buber that the flaw in Heidegger's notion of solicitude lies in the irrefragable immanence of Dasein, in fact that "the barriers of his own being are not thereby breached." Nonetheless, while for Buber the issue and the alternative lies in the grace of reciprocal encounter, "for the other to be concerned with him," for Levinas the alternative lies rather in a more radical one-way "toward the other" without any consideration of return, mutuality, or reward. The ethical subject for Levinas is ethical precisely because its deepest self occurs as responsibility for-the-other before it is in any way for-itself, and certainly, therefore, also before any concern or anxiety regarding the other's concern for the self. Therefore Levinas criticizes Buber for precisely what Buber criticizes in Heidegger: "Heidegger's self is a *closed system*."[19] Heidegger's closed system includes all of being-in-the-world, and Buber's includes the holistic embrace of essential relation, but both remain closed off to the genuine transcendence deriving from the moral priority of the "height and destitution" of the other.

Society: Communion versus Justice

In his 1938 essay "What is Man?" Buber writes:

> But is there on this level something corresponding to the essential *Thou* in relation to the multitude of men, or is Heidegger here finally right? What corresponds to the essential Thou on the level of self-being, in relation to a host of men, I call the essential *We*.
>
> The person who is the object of my mere solicitude is not a *Thou* but a *He* or a *She* [i.e, objectified being, "It" world]. The nameless, faceless crowd in which I am entangled is not a *We* but the "one" [Heidegger's *das Man*]. But as there is a *Thou* so there is a *We*.[20]

The special character of the *We* is shown in the essential relation existing or arising temporarily between its members; that is, in an ontic directness holding sway within the We which is the decisive presupposition of the I-Thou relation.[21]

A full treatment of the topic of sociality and justice in Buber and Levinas goes far beyond the limitations of the present chapter. Even a discussion of Buber's position vis-à-vis law, a central and complicated topic much discussed in the secondary literature, is not possible here. What is clear, however, is the parallel which exists for Buber between the primal relation of I-Thou in contrast to the I-It, and the I-We relation which is built on the I-Thou and which is for Buber the primal social relation. The I-We relation is an *extension* of the I-Thou relation, perhaps even a *projection* of it: "But as there is a *Thou* so there is a *We*."

Because Buber elaborated his idea of the "We" in terms of "utopia," we turn to his book of 1949, *Paths in Utopia*. To extend or project the I-Thou onto society seems peculiar because an essential feature of the "I-Thou" is precisely its intimacy, that is to say, its inwardness, an experience of the "between" reserved exclusively for the two partners of the primal relation. Here lies Levinas's basic criticism: the "I-Thou" relation, by its very nature, cannot be projected socially. So how does Buber do it or claim to do it? "Community," Buber writes, "is the inner disposition or constitution of a life in common."[22] In

"What is Man?," written 11 years earlier, he had already said along the same lines: "The special character of the *We* is shown in the essential relation existing, or arising temporarily, between its members; that is, in the holding sway within the *We* of an ontic directness which is the decisive presupposition of the *I-Thou* relation.... Only men who are capable of truly saying *Thou* to one another can truly say *We* with one another."[23] In *Paths in Utopia* he writes, "A real community need not consist of people who are perpetually together, but it must consist of people who, precisely because they are comrades, have mutual access to one another and are ready for one another."[24]

So, like the intimate dyad of primal encounter, the community of the "We" is not only immediate and fundamental (socially), it is characterized as a relation of immanence, wholeness, mutuality and grace. It is "utopian" insofar as it represents only for some the "real community," the future for all, and as such is the social version of the primal relation existing sporadically between two in the I-Thou, against the backdrop of a world dominated by I-It relations.

It might seem overly clever to say of Buber's notion of utopia that it is utopian in precisely the sense that he faults Marx, that is to say, unreal, impossible, romantic fantasy, but there would be a kernel of truth to it. Just as the embrace of encounter happens by chance, by "grace," so too does the We of genuine social relations. Moreover, there is an additional problem: Buber shows no way to get from encounter to community. Each is self-contained and acciden-tal. "Community," he writes, "should not be made into a principle; it too, should always satisfy a situation rather than an abstraction. The realization of community, like the realization of any idea, cannot occur once and for all time; always it must be the moment's answer to the moment's question, and nothing more."[25] Just as anything that disrupts the moment of the "I-Thou" is an "I-It," anything that interferes with the "moment" of the "We" is no less extraneous and no less a loss of the between of the community. Thus, when Buber attempts to describe positively the community of the We, he resorts to the same poetic language that he had earlier used to point to the primal encounter of *I and Thou*. Both are based in experiences which Buber admits are "rare" and for which he can claim little more than that they have the seal of "wholeness" or "being."[26] In both cases, Arno Munster detects the residues of Buber's early partiality for

Hasidic enthusiasm and oriental mysticisms.[27] Another scholar credits Buber's "enthusiasm" to the influence of his reading of Nietzsche, while Levinas sees its genuine forebear in Bergson's notion of duration.[28] One might also think of Charles Peguy's notion of "mystique" in this regard. Regardless of its source, it is clear that Buber's "We" is intended as a community of *Gemeinschaft* in contrast to what he takes to be abstract sociality of *Gesellschaft*.[29] Nonetheless, his specific analysis, qua social theory, ends in a vagueness equivalent to abstractness of the latter, suggesting little more than a romantic, even mythological account of social being.

Levinas also speaks of "utopia" with regard to social being, but his is an account of justice, justice based in and derived from the morality of the face-to-face. Here "utopia," literally "no place," refers to the incomplete status—the ongoing task—of the justice demanded by morality. Insofar as a just world has not yet been established, and our world is thus an "unredeemed" world, a *u-topos*, no more important program is demanded by morality itself, and justice remains humanity's deepest and most pressing ideal. Its "place" is the future, the yet to come (*a-venir*: "to-come," and *avenir*, "future"). It is not a reality but an ideality. Still, it is neither an idea nor a fantasy, but the concrete day to day project of establishing exact measures and weights, fair courts, democratic polities, secure rights (speech, assembly, religion, press, and so on), equitable and universal distribution of food, clothing, shelter, health care, and the like. Of utopia and justice, Levinas writes: "Utopia, transcendence. Inspired by love of one's fellowman, reasonable justice is bound by legal strictures and cannot equal the kindness that solicits and inspires it" (*EN* 230).

While justice does not presently "equal the kindness that solicits and inspires it," its aim is to set up a world in which such an equivalence can occur, a world in which justice and charity, justice and kindness, that is to say, social justice and the morality of the face-to-face, are in harmony with one another. Justice, then, has a source and a guide: the moral transcendence of the other. Its aim to create a world where morality is everywhere and at all times actual. Such, is the "utopian" or "messianic" structure of justice and history from Levinas's fundamental ethics.

The difference that divides Levinas and Buber, then, is the same difference, ultimately, that divides Levinas and Heidegger, and unites,

paradoxically, Buber and Heidegger. For Levinas goodness is fundamental; the good grounds the real. For Buber and Heidegger, in
contrast—each in his own way, to be sure—being is fundamental.
What Buber upholds in both the I-Thou and the We is the fleeting
presence of a wholeness of *being*. In contrast to the I-It, whether the
objectification of the other who faces or the social objectification of
Gesellschaft, both of which produce mere "fragmentation," the experience or "embrace" of the "between" of "essential" relation presents being in its wholeness. The ground for Buber, as for Heidegger,
remains ontological: a relation to being, a relation of being. What
Buber calls the "problem of ethics" is in truth the problem of being,
the problem of attaining wholeness of being. For Levinas, in contrast,
in both the morality of the face-to-face and in the social call to justice,
what is most important lies in a transcendence "otherwise than being
and beyond essence"—an ethical metaphysics.

FIVE

Levinas, Plato, and Ethical Exegesis

Rabbi Huna said: "He who occupies himself only
with studying Torah acts as if he had no God."
— *Babylonian Talmud, tractate Avodah Zerah 17b*

The notion of "ethical exegesis" is not only inspired by Levinas's
thought, but expresses the essential character of it, its "method," as
it were, the "saying" of its "said." Accordingly, here I will begin by
reviewing some of what I have said elsewhere about ethical exegesis,
and then I will develop this notion further in relation to Plato and to
the question of moralizing.

Levinas reads the great texts of Western Civilization, the varied literature of both Athens and Jerusalem, by discovering in them truths
that depend on ethical conditions—whether these conditions are
explicitly acknowledged, as is often the case with Greco-Roman literature and, even more so, with the sacred writings of Jerusalem, or
whether they remain implicit yet operative, or, in the farthest extreme,
are explicitly denied, as occurred in early modern scientific thought.
Exegesis is the route, for Levinas, of and to "a difficult wisdom concerned with truths that correlate to virtues" (*DF* 275). The latter is a
phrase I emphasized in my book, where I took it, as I still do, to be
the root formula of Levinas's entire philosophical enterprise.[1]

To elaborate this notion, I have articulated "four interrelated
characteristics or dimensions" of ethical exegesis, namely, the:
"(1) concrete and productive integrity of spirit and letter; (2) pluralism
of persons and readings; (3) virtue, or existential self-transformative
wisdom; and (4) authority, or the renewal of a living ethico-religious

tradition."[2] I have contrasted these four aspects of ethical exegesis with their diametrical opposition by Spinoza's purely rationalist philosophy, and with the somewhat more muted, though ultimately no less radical, opposition to them in Nietzsche's and Heidegger's aesthetic manner of philosophizing.

I also contrasted ethical exegesis with *criticism*—biblical criticism. Ethical exegesis has an essential dimension of what I called "relevant hermeneutics," a sympathetic entering into texts, an inner understanding that applies to the life and not merely the intellect of the reader, which criticism not only lacks, but from which it deliberately withdraws in the name of an allegiance to a standard of objectivity borrowed from the natural sciences. Criticism withdraws primarily from the third and fourth aspects of ethical exegesis: the possibility of being transformed by a text and, related to this, the text's authority in the ongoing ethico-religious traditions within which readers live. "[E]xegesis," Levinas writes, "made the text speak; while critical philology speaks *of* the text. The one takes the text to be a source of teaching, the other treats it as a thing" (*LR* 263). Without neglecting the findings of the critical approach, ethical exegesis nevertheless emphasizes the teachings contained in texts.

What I want to further elaborate here is a related but somewhat different reason that ethical exegesis is too often and too easily dismissed by academics and intellectuals: its alleged moralizing. To do this I want to consider Plato. Socrates, the central protagonist of the Platonic dialogues, gave up his youthful pursuit of the natural sciences in order to discover the meaning of values more existentially relevant to him and his society, values such as goodness, love, piety, and justice. Whether or not he approached these values with the same epistemological standards he had found in the natural sciences remains an open question for Plato scholars to decide. That he shifted his focus to the fundamental human and social values is not. Nothing was more important to the Socrates depicted by Plato than the search for knowledge of the good.

Criticism, I have shown, can be criticized for its naivete. Levinas asserts: "[F]or these critical readers equally, transcendence continues to signify an exchange of data with God or an experience of the supernatural. Having descended to the underground of verbal signs, criticism has lost, under an artificial but apparently sufficient illumination, the philosophical certainties, right up to the desire to leave the Cave" (*NTR* 75). What is this loss of certainty, this fear of leaving the Cave? Ethical exegesis, for its part, does not fear leaving the Cave. Indeed, it requires such a departure. But what does this mean? I believe that critical philosophy's fear of leaving the Cave has to do, today, with the fear of moralizing.

Philosophy today defines moralizing as preaching. It sees moralizing as an unjustified edification, a didactic imposition, an insistent telling others what they should or should not do or think based on one's own groundless (or at least unexamined) and hence authoritarian moral certainties. The philosopher will simply not be told. He or she will decide for him or herself—or, is it not rather the case that the philosopher, as Levinas suggests, refuses to decide at all? Can one really know the good before doing it? Does this not insert a delay between theory and practice that is never bridged? Has the philosopher abdicated responsibility?

No doubt there are those who do preach in a way that no self-reflective person finds acceptable. There is certainly an important difference between slavishness before orders and obeying moral imperatives. No doubt for an adult, in many cases there is something very right about avoiding, deflecting, criticizing and otherwise tempering what becomes the immorality and totalitarianism of self-righteous excess. But Levinas's thought is not moralistic in this sense. Furthermore, in criticizing moralizing, philosophy is often doing far more—or far less—than deriding preaching. Unfortunately, it is rather succumbing to a fear of leaving the Cave. It seems to me there is in all learning—and what is philosophy if not teaching and learning?—a dimension of moral teaching, moral pedagogy. What is this dimension? When is moral edification right? And, even more important, when it is right, does it not follow that acknowledgment, intellectual assent, is insufficient, and that instead a certain obedience—call it *maturation*—is the only right response?

In one way or another, Plato raises all these questions of philosophy as a way of living the life worth living throughout all of his dialogues. But he does so especially in the three dialogues that are peculiar for being the least dialogic of all his dialogues: *Phaedrus, Symposium*, and *Apology*. These dialogues, in contrast to the rest, are primarily given over to speeches, and, even more oddly still, they are all given over to the topic of love, the desire for the desirable. *Phaedrus* presents three speeches on love; *Symposium* is a series of seven encomia on eros, of which only the two final speeches, those of Socrates/Diotima and Alcibiades, will interest us here; and *Apology* presents one speech, Socrates' unsuccessful self-defense before an Athenian jury against the charges of "corrupting young people" and "not believing in the gods," which is also a speech in defense of love, the "love of wisdom" that is the philosophic life.

Of the three dialogues, *Phaedrus* most directly raises the issue of moralizing and philosophy I am addressing. The first speech, Lysias's written speech read by Phaedrus, defends the starkly immoral idea—immoral for those, that is to say, who have retained their "certainties"—that one should give oneself over sensuously to a lover whom they do not love. In other words, physical gratification (or deliberately calculated benefit) is to be preferred to the passionate "madness" of loving a lover.

By arguing for what conventional morality knows to be an immoral position, this speech perhaps functions more as rhetorical proof that the Sophist can defend both sides of an argument than as a genuine argument for immoral love. This, at any rate, is how Socrates takes it. By itself, taken at its word, it is a moralistic, indeed a seductive speech promoting immorality in love: preaching calculation and a taking advantage of the lover's madness, advocating a nonloving, calculative but still sensuously gratifying response to love. It is, in short, a defense of prostitution—of oneself.

Socrates simply does not take it seriously. Obviously his certainties lie elsewhere. Boasting, rather, that he can give an even "better" speech while defending the same thesis, Socrates is cajoled by Phaedrus into also giving, though quite reluctantly, a no less immoral speech. In fact, despite his reticence, and covering his face in order to avoid "feeling ashamed" before Phaedrus, Socrates gives a speech arguing only that it is indeed wrong to give in sensuously to the passionate lover. He does not argue, however, that one should give in sensuously to the nonlover instead. In this way Socrates converts the immoral speech of Lysias into a moral speech. Nevertheless, Socrates—or the censorious "sign" or "voice" that sometimes comes to him—remains dissatisfied with his own "silly" or "blasphemous" speech, as he calls it, as well as with Lysias's original speech. Half-truths with their moral omissions are apparently an inadequate and unacceptable "improvement" over no truth.

To correct both speeches, then, Socrates recants his first speech and delivers a second speech on love, a speech he expounds without covering his head, hence without shame, silliness or blasphemy. Socrates develops the positive side of a distinction he made in his first speech, the distinction between higher love, of which he approves, and lower love, of which he disapproves and about which Lysias wrote exclusively. Lower love is bodily, sensual, passionate, while higher love is spiritual, intellectual, disciplined. In *Symposium* this distinction already appears as early as the second of the seven speeches, that of Pausanias. Lower love is a desire aiming for pleasure, an irrational and insatiable bodily desire that the true lover must avoid (as Socrates argued in his first speech), while higher love is a desire aiming at true excellence, which for Socrates means a rational desire for ideal or absolute truth. It is this the true lover must nurture, and this for which Socrates now argues.

Socrates' second speech is far more complicated than his first or than Lysias's speech. He begins by distinguishing four types of madness—mantic: the art of divining the future; psychological: an affliction requiring cure; poetic: possession by the Muses; and erotic: passion for another's beauty. He will later add a fifth—philosophical: the uplifting of the immortal soul to the perfection of knowing. He then proceeds, as Plato often does at crucial junctures of his thought, by introducing a myth or allegory, that is to say, an image. It is an image designed to persuade—*per impossible*—Phaedrus of the immateriality, immortality and perfection of the knowing soul and its object. The soul is somehow "winged," like a bird's feathery wings, and at the same time it is also like a charioteer riding a chariot drawn by unruly horses, the latter representing a person's body. If the body is properly disciplined, the "winged" soul "flies" upward toward the truth; if not, it falls downward under the sway of its bodily passions. "True knowledge," which is the aim of the true lover, i.e., of the philosopher, "is a reality without color or shape, intangible but utterly real, apprehensible only by intellect which is the pilot of the soul."[3] Thus in his second speech Socrates argues not only that one must prefer a higher nonsensuous love (nonlove in Lysias's lower sense) to passionate love, but, more importantly, that only by avoiding bodily passion can the true lover embrace what is the only genuine object of true love, that which is most desirable in itself, namely, true knowledge, immaterial, immortal and perfect in itself.

After finishing Socrates' second speech, the *Phaedus* turns to a discussion of language written and spoken, to which we will return shortly, and upon which Levinas has commented.[4] For the moment, however, we turn naturally to Plato's *Symposium*, because Socrates there, through the mouth of Diotima, presents the very same position regarding love that we find in his second speech of *Phaedrus*. The central idea is the same that true love is love of true knowledge, and the truest love is the love of absolute knowledge, "unalloyed" with any material elements. In *Symposium*, however, unlike *Phaedrus*, there is a counterspeech. Socrates' (Diotima's) speech about love is sharply challenged by an alternative and competing image of love, that declaimed and exemplified by the intoxicated—the mad—Dionysian-like Alcibiades.

In her penetrating commentary on the *Symposium*, Martha Nussbaum reminds us of Gregory Vlastos's criticism that Socratic love strangely seems to require a complete indifference to the love of any particular person, whether in loving or in being loved.[5] Alcibiades' subsequent description—and only the speeches of Socrates and Alcibiades explicitly claim to be true rather than flattery[6]—of his failed attempts to love or be loved by Socrates, is certainly one strong testimony to the truth of this criticism. In *Symposium*, Diotima is quite clear that the true lover only begins by loving the one beautiful beloved, but if on the correct path the true lover then discovers that beauty itself, something found in all beauties, becomes the purer, higher or truer object of love. But the path of love continues, leaving all particulars behind, stripping itself of all bodily manifestations. Diotima states:

> This is what it is to go aright, or be led by another, into the mystery of Love: one goes always upwards for the sake of this Beauty, starting out from beautiful things and using them like rising stairs: from one body to two and from two to all beautiful bodies, then from beautiful bodies to beautiful customs, and from customs to learning beautiful things, and from these lessons he arrives in the end at this lesson, which is learning of this very Beauty, so that in the end he comes to know just what it is to be beautiful...to see the Beautiful itself, absolute, pure,

unmixed, not polluted by human flesh or colors or any other great nonsense of mortality.[7]

The true Socratic lover, in other words, loves not only ideas, but the very idea of ideas.

One understands after reading this text the truth of what Schopenhauer and Nietzsche meant when they said that Christianity is Platonism for the masses. Platonism is for the few, the intellectuals: pure intellectual love of perfect knowledge. Christianity is for the many, driven by will rather than intellect: pure faithful love (submission of the human will to the divine will) of the Perfect God. Both require more than a rigorous taming of the body (*askesis*). They require a surpassing of the body altogether, an absolute transcendence, not toward the other person who is loved, but above all lovers to the pure Idea. Hence, from a rhetorical point of view, surpassing the plodding logic of what can be reasoned from premise to conclusion, or from cause to effect, the speech of Socratic love requires the "myths" of winged souls and horsedrawn chariots, the "mystery"[8] of Diotima's speech or, in another context, the "Mystery" of the Church (of all churches).

But then the drunken Alcibiades arrives with noise, flute girl, and drunken crowd, "all of a sudden"! As Nussbaum points out, if Socrates represents the surpassing of flesh and blood, the surpassing of images (despite his therefore paradoxical because necessary use of myth, already more than a hint of a problem), Alcibiades represents flesh and blood in flesh and blood in all its drunken passion. His speech of love—by which, again *in* sharp contrast to Socrates, he means his particular passionate love for the flesh and blood individual man Socrates—begins and ends with the image of Socrates as a Silenus (Dionysian-like) statue. If Socrates' speech represents, as I think Nussbaum is correct to discern, intellect without body, an absolute love of absolute knowledge, Alcibiades' boisterous shameless speech represents body without intellect, a wildly passionate fully incarnate love. Or, since these two possibilities surpass the possibilities of mortal life: Socrates advocates a body as fully as possibly ruled by the mind, while Alcibiades represents a mind as fully as possibly ruled by the body. Notice, too, that Plato has both and only Socrates and Alcibiades claim to speak the truth—but obviously their words and actions present two conflicting incompatible "truths."

Therefore, again as Nussbaum points out, this leaves *Symposium* with an unresolved antagonism, an *agon* of eros: mind versus body and body versus mind. Each, driven to its extreme, produces an inherent failure: Socrates can love no one in particular, the lover of wisdom can neither love nor be loved as a person; Alcibiades can only lose his identity, shattering into momentary passions, and hence can offer no stability in love, no long-term enduring love. As Nussbaum writes:

> I can follow Socrates only if, like Socrates, I am *persuaded* of the truth of Diotima's account; and Alcibiades robs me of this conviction. He makes me feel that in embarking on the ascent I am sacrificing a beauty; so I can no longer view the ascent as embracing the whole of beauty.... I can, on the other hand, follow Alcibiades, making my soul a body. I can live in *eros*, devoted to its violence and its sudden light. But once I have listened to Diotima, I see the loss of light that this course, too, entails—the loss of rational planning, the loss, we might say, of the chance to make a world.... *Those* two—philosophy and literature—cannot live together or know each other's truths, that's for sure.[9]

This point regarding the divorce between mind and body is further confirmed in *Apology,* where Socrates, who claims in *Symposium* to only know about love,[10] cannot—while keeping to the integrity of his life, the life of the philosopher, loving only wisdom—he cannot save his own mortal life. Blame it on the imperfection of an unjust society? Blame it on the ignorance of Socrates' fellow Athenians? But why not blame it on Socrates? With what tenderness can a gadfly (of the Absolute, no less) be a lover or beloved?

Nevertheless, it seems to me that Plato, as author of the Platonic dialogues, provides an alternative to both Socrates and Alcibiades. Does not the dialogue itself represent the form of philosophy that remains embodied, remains a literature, while loving wisdom, loving knowledge? Is not dialogue itself the place, the interaction, the encounter, the proximity of flesh and blood individuals as well as of their winged ideas, the extraordinary u-topia of saying and said? Let us return to the second half of *Phaedrus,* to Socrates' discussion with Phaedrus of the difference between speech and writing, and to Levinas's comments on it, to see what it is that happens in dialogue that neither Socrates nor Alcibiades are able to represent by themselves, or at least that they unable to represent in *Symposium.*

In the second half of *Phaedrus*, Plato has Socrates once again resort to a myth to explain the origin and significance of writing. The Egyptian god, Theuth (or Thoth), so Socrates tells Phaedrus, is said to have invented writing. He presented his gift to the Egyptian king Thamus (called by the Greeks Ammon), praising it by declaring that it will "improve both the wisdom and the memory of the Egyptians."[11] Despite its divine origin, King Thamus, exercising his sovereign judgment, is not equally impressed and disagrees. It will harm memory, he insists, because instead of exercising their memories, possessors of written texts "will rely on writing to bring things to their remembrance by external signs instead of on their own internal resources."[12] It will harm wisdom, he continues, because readers of texts "will receive a quantity of information without proper instruction, and in consequence be thought very knowledgeable when they are for the most part quite ignorant. And because they are filled with the conceit of wisdom instead of real wisdom they will be a burden to society". To these two criticisms, Socrates adds two of his own, contrasting written texts unfavorably, as a "kind of shadow," to "the living and animate speech of a man with knowledge": "a writing cannot distinguish between suitable and unsuitable readers. And"—this is Socrates' second criticism—"if it is ill-treated or unfairly abused it always needs its parent to come to its rescue; it is quite incapable of defending or helping itself."[13] Levinas takes these last criticisms to heart. He writes:

> Plato maintains the difference between the objective order of truth, that which doubtlessly is established in writings, impersonally, and reason *in* a living being, "a living and animated discourse," a discourse thus "capable of defending itself... and which knows those to whom it should be addressed and before whom it should be silent" [*Phaedrus*, 276a]. This discourse is therefore not the unfolding of a prefabricated internal logic, but the constitution of truth in a struggle between thinkers, with all the risks of freedom. The relationship of language implies the transcendence, the radical separation, the strangeness of interlocutors, the revelation of the other to me. In other words, language is spoken where a community between the terms of the relationship is wanting, where a common plane is wanting or is yet to be constituted. It takes place in this transcendence. (*TI* 73)[14]

Precisely the absolute transcendence of dialogue, the proximity of two speakers who remain separate yet conjoined, who, retaining their individuality, "ab-solve" themselves, to use Levinas's term, from the relation within which they meet, is the transcendence proper to the discourse from out of which the relative transcendence of true knowledge is discovered. Accordingly, dialogue is not extraneous to truth, it is its very condition. This is what Plato understood. This is why Plato himself is absolved from his own dialogues, except in the one instance where he appears in the *Symposium* attempting to rescue Socrates from the hubris that will (and in fact does) lead to his condemnation to death—in such cases, of life and death, one can no longer distance oneself, no matter what knowledge is at stake.

"A universal thought," Levinas writes, "dispenses with communication. A reason cannot be other for a reason. How can a reason be an I or an other, since its very being consists in renouncing singularity?" (*TI* 72). This is the problem with Socratic love: it loves only the universal at the expense of the singular. And it is equally the problem with Alcibiades' love, which is the mirror image of Socratic love, for it loves only the singular at the expense of the universal. "But love as analyzed by Plato," Levinas writes, "does not coincide with what we have called Desire. Immortality is not the objective of the first movement of Desire, but the other, the Stranger" (63). The first desire is the desire for-the-other, the speaking that begins in a moral responsibility responding to the vulnerable and obligating face of the other. Moral responsibility is the condition of truth, and is not itself first conditioned by the truths that will later—but too late, and too early—in the time of history and historiography (in a temporal structure Levinas describes as the "posteriority of the anterior" [54])[15] have built up the courage to provide explanations for everything. Nevertheless, despite all its stratagems, whether sophistical or sincere, "Truth arises where a being separated from the other is not engulfed in him, but speaks to him" (62). The dialogic form of philosophy, the brilliant invention of Plato, preserves this unity in difference, this nonindifference of one person to another person, which is the condition and the manner in which truth arises from speakers speaking to one another because they are first and each uniquely responsible one for the other.

Perhaps, someone may object, it is precisely because we cannot say what Plato thinks that he is guilty of intellectual irresponsibility. On the contrary, Plato inaugurates a discourse that remains alive to this day precisely because we cannot say finally what Plato thinks. In other words, the world of Plato—for it is a world—demands commentary. It demands exegesis—ethical exegesis. Not to discover the "moral of the story" as in Aesop's fables, say, as if morality could be contained in a neat concluding postscript,[16] but rather to discover the moral *in* the story: the persons, places, times and issues that have troubled all of us and continue to trouble us without losing their anchor in concrete situations. In this way, through dialogue, Plato preserves the saying of the said, the ethical condition of truth without which truths—reduced to the said, to writing—become monstrous, like Socrates and Alcibiades in *Symposium,* or totalitarian, in their political formulation. Indifferent to flesh-and-blood persons, persons in need of guidance, such "truths" become inhumane, whether because they are more than human or less than human it does not matter.

Another world that is, as Levinas modestly characterizes it, "at least as large as that of Plato"[17] is the world of the Talmud. Here, coming from Jerusalem (and, in fact, also from Babylonia) rather than Athens, the language is consciously charged with moral seriousness. Conscientiousness guides consciousness. The Talmud is both intense and rigorous, but sometimes lighthearted too, as are humans; all its discussions and often long and complex arguments contain truth so long as they are expounded, to use the Talmud's own expression, "for the sake of Heaven." Everything in the Talmud, as in Plato's dialogues, is said in the name of someone, some flesh-and-blood person. No subject matter is too large or too small, too near or too far, and no interlocutor too important to be challenged or too insignificant to be ignored, because it is a text driven by a moral desire, or more precisely, by a holy compassion for others, to alleviate the suffering of others, and to in this way come close to God, to bring God's will to earth and to raise human will to God. Nothing is more serious than the search for truth in such a context. And no discourse takes the individuality of its interlocutors more seriously, even when the sages are engaged in discovering the strict parameters of the "right path" (*halachah,* often translated as "law") applicable to all Jews for all time. "Language is universal," Levinas writes, "because it is the very passage from the individual to the general, because it offers things which are mine to the Other [*Autrui*]. To speak is to make the world common, to create commonplaces" (*TI* 76; cf. *EE* 99).

Commonplaces congeal, however, losing their life and their truth, without the saying that animates and inspires them. The Talmud lives because all the moral seriousness, all the compassion of its interrogatory discourse continues to this day in the life of the Jewish community guided by it. Plato lives not only because of the dialogical *form* of his writings—a written discourse that enables a maximum obviation of "all the betrayals against which Plato himself struggled" (*BV* 28), as Levinas says—but also because we today continue to comment upon his dialogues. And this commentary itself only lives when and because we take it seriously, take it to heart, are disabused of the distancing conventions of academic jargon, and not because we are alien scholars, Martians observing the human condition. It lives because and when we are part of a philosophical dialogue that has and continues to stimulate our own dialogical lives. "But," Levinas writes in the concluding sentences of his preface to *Totality and Infinity*, "it belongs to the very essence of language, which consists in continually undoing its phrase by the foreword or the exegesis, in unsaying the said, in attempting to restate without ceremonies what has already been ill understood in the inevitable ceremonial in which the said delights" (*TI* 30).

There is no final word because the infinite obligations and responsibilities of morality and justice remain incomplete, unfulfilled, however well formulated their expressions and institutions have become. If we are to retain our humanity, our human dignity, if in the process we are to search and to find truth, as justice itself requires, we must continue speaking to and hence caring for one another. Why are we always looking for ways to get off the hook, to justify our selfishness, to limit our responsibilities? These lower demands somehow find by themselves, as it were, all too much satisfaction; they surely do not need additional support. And if our worse "crime" is to sometimes fall into moralizing, to sometimes care too much—as if this were even possible for a responsible person in a world such as ours—would it not be far worse to be always too afraid to make this oh-so-grave error? Perhaps it would do us all a great deal of good to be sometimes guilty of saying and doing too much, and correcting ourselves on this score, rather than being guilty, as we almost always are, of saying and doing too little.

Levinas does not flinch from pointing to the infinity of the responsible self's moral obligation to another person when he writes: "It is impossible to fix limits or measure the extreme urgency of this responsibility. Upon reflection it is something completely astonishing, a responsibility that even extends to the obligation to answer for another's freedom, to be responsible for his responsibility" (*LR* 180). Surely, the biblical prophets demand no less; surely Plato's Socrates demands no less, either. I am not here advocating a gratuitous meddling into the private affairs of others, or a moral imperialism that makes mockery of the first-person initiative of moral responsibility. Rather, I am supporting an intelligent, difficult and humble moral path that would seek to have each one of us declare in an irreducible singularity—along with Levinas when he advocates "attempting to restate without ceremonies what has already been ill understood" (*TI* 30), and means his own book!—the words of Plato's Socrates in *Phaedrus:* "Grant me forgiveness for my former words and let these that I have now uttered find favor in thy sight."[18]

SIX

Some Notes on the Title of Levinas's *Totality and Infinity* and Its First Sentence

Being and Time, Being and Nothingness, Totality and Infinity — these short titles, made up of two ponderous words connected by an "and," modest in its indeterminacy, spanning the twentieth century, announce big books, important books about the most important things. There are, of course, other big books in twentieth century philosophy. One knows the authors, the contentions, the struggles, as well as the abyss that divides continental and the Anglo-American debates.

Twentieth century continental philosophy commenced at the dawn of the century with Husserl's call for a renewal and extension of science through a rigorously descriptive and transcendental phenomenology. As he veered into idealism — the natural tendency of all philosophical science — his two greatest students, Martin Heidegger and Emmanuel Levinas, staked out alternative paths. In this regard, perhaps no two books are more important or stand in more fateful or closer quarters — with one another and with their teacher — than Heidegger's *Being and Time,* which challenged Husserlian science through the disclosure (*Entdecken, Erschliessen, Geben,* etc.) of an ontological-aesthetic path for phenomenology, and Levinas's *Totality and Infinity,* which challenged the nature and status of both Husserlian science and Heideggerian ontology by calling attention to the primacy of the ethical-social condition (or, properly speaking, "noncondition," transcendence) of both scientific knowledge and ontological disclosure.[1]

The aim of the present all too brief notes is to approach these issues and others as well by examining the title and the first sentence of *Totality and Infinity*.

Regarding the term *Totality*, for instance, we might consider that it would have been more natural for Levinas to juxtapose it to the term *Part* or *Individual* rather than *Infinity*, for parts or individuals stand in opposition to totality, the whole, as the many, the multiple, the plural stand in opposition to the one. In this way *Totality and Individuality* would have made a striking title that would recall an ancient opposition with a fine pedigree, found at the very origins of philosophy and continuing throughout its history. How does the one become many? How are the many one? Are not these two questions—so prominent in the pre-Socratics, in Plato, in Plotinus and, much later in German Idealism, not to mention in monotheism—the alpha and omega of metaphysics, ontology, cosmology as well as theology?

Or, moving east of Greece proper and past Persia, where these questions first arose in the West, surely the opposition between individuals—"dualities"—and the totality is the issue at stake in India's two great monisms, Hinduism and Buddhism. They strive to show how beings, more particularly how human individuals who are self-conscious and free, can and should unite themselves to the whole, to realize their identity, to annihilate their differences, in order to achieve liberation or deliverance (*Moksha*) from all the dualities of individualism and thus to return to the oneness of the all, the absolute One (whether World Soul, Reality, *Brahman*, or World Not-Soul, Emptiness, *Shunyata*, it does not matter). In this way, they can attain complete being (or nonbeing), complete enlightenment and complete freedom.

While Levinas's title does not go back to the Greeks alone, or out toward Persia or India, it does draw—especially in its invocation of the term *Infinity*—from the deep wells of Beersheba, that is to say, from the heritage of Abraham, of "Jerusalem," which in its own way goes even farther than Greece or India, indeed to the farthest reaches and beyond, forging a path at once without exit and without return. That is to say, for Jerusalem—for Levinas—humanity is created and responsible at once, irreducibly multiple and yet each existence bound to the infinite through and not despite that very multiplicity. It is also a path that opens out across a history moving from bondage to freedom, from injustice to justice, in a great exodus and redemption. To give such an absolute priority to the good without diminishing the integrity of the multiple—this will demand an extenuated existence and an exceptional thinking, developments perhaps too troublesome, too disquieting, too risky, apparently, for the longed for composure and tranquility of a Greek or Persian or Indian cosmos.

As for the crucial term *Infinity,* one could also make similar suggestions regarding alternative conjunctions. *Finite* or *Finitude* would seem to be the more natural or logical complements than *Totality*. *Finitude and Infinity* or, alternatively, *Infinity and Finitude*—these would also have made striking book titles. Here, in addition, Levinas would have been in the good company of his teachers and contemporaries, with Heidegger and Sartre, for example, with their phenomenological-ontological analyses of human being as temporal being, as mortality, as condemned to choices or to having been thrown into history, and the like. The finitude of human being, its "historicity" especially, was all the rage in post-war Paris. In 1957, just a few years before the publication of *Totality and Infinity,* Alexandre Koyré published his scholarly work entitled *From the Closed World to the Infinite Universe,* in which he placed all of modernity under the sign of a disconcerting "infinity," a loss of moorings, a failure of absolutes, literally a "dis-aster," that he contrasted to the immanent or closed "finitude" of the entire medieval, ancient, and prephilosophical conceptions of the universe that girded humankind prior to the rise of modern science. Furthermore, in addition to its subtle and penetrating descriptions of a variety of finite structures (enjoyment, nourishment, dwelling, work, and so on), on the very pages of *Totality and Infinity* Levinas defends the notion of an embodied or "finite freedom," On this basis, like Merleau-Ponty, he argues against the more extreme but also more rarified, indeed the merely abstract or "angelic" freedom of the self-consciousness upon which Sartre tried to base his existentialism in *Being and Nothingness.*[2]

Yet both of these imaginary alternatives — *Totality and Individuality* or *Finitude and Infinity,* however logical or tempting, would have diminished Levinas's project. For they would refer only to internal oppositions and accordingly would only have elaborated, explicated, analyzed the terms "totality" or "infinity," and not set into motion the greater opposition triggered by Levinas's actual title. Totality, Levinas argues in *Totality and Infinity*, is totality precisely because it does organize, integrate, synthesize, subsume and ultimately eradicate the independence of the multiple into modes, parts, roles or ventriloquists of a "higher" identity, such as Spinoza's substance, Hegel's concept ("identity of identity and difference"), Husserl's infinite horizon (or its shadow, Derrida's *différance*), or the billowing historical world withdrawal-disclosure of Heidegger's "thinking." The idea of "part" or "individual," then, is contained analytically in the very notion of totality, which would be the goal and fulfillment (the "sublimation") of parts, and hence in no way sets up or maintains the transcendence of a genuine or irreducible opposition. Precisely to the extent that separate beings are absorbed and find their meaning solely within a larger whole are they "totalized," reduced, denied and stripped of their independence. Totality is, as Levinas says immediately in the preface, the *war* of the whole against the independence of the individual, the war against the singularity of the singular. Levinas's opposition to this totalitarianism in all its dimensions, from the alleged serenity of contemplation (purchased at what cost!) to the outright violence, the concentration camps, the gulags, the thought-control of all real-politics,[3] is perhaps the central philosophical and political teaching of *Totality and Infinity*, which is able to make good on this lesson precisely because it opposes *Infinity* to *Totality*, an *Infinity* that cannot—or rather that *ought* not—be totalized. It is odd, let us add, to see how many academic commentators of Levinas have not yet seen to what extent and how thoroughly Levinas's thought is political—a radical politics—and not merely moralist (or, hard as it is to believe, "amoralist," i.e., postmodern). It is a dimension of his thought that did not escape the insight of political activists such as Václav Havel or certain prominent South American liberation theologians. In any event, the title of *Totality and Infinity* is already a call to arms, the provocation of a continuous revolution, and an absolute resistance to totalitarianism—but as peace, not war. A peace, let us say it immediately, that does not exclude the use of violence, and that all too often in our world, sad to say, requires it.[4]

In a like manner, *Infinity*, as the word itself seems to suggest, is the in-finite, literally the not-finite, a negation of the finite, as if the pair "infinite" and "finite" were necessarily already coupled across negation to make the least sense of either. To oppose *Finitude* to *Infinity*, then, would in this way be an analytic distinction but not a radical opposition. By *Infinity,* however, Levinas means something more and something different in kind than the internal opposition produced by this negative conception. "Transcendence Is Not Negativity," he cleverly entitles an early subsection of *Totality and Infinity* (*TI* 40–42).[5] The transcendence or irreducible alterity of Infinity refers to a surplus rather than a deficit: the height of the other person. On the side of the subject it refers to a noble desire rather than a need: a "metaphysical Desire," as Levinas calls it in *Totality and Infinity.*[6] It is a desire for transcendence that increases rather than decreases to the measure that it approaches that which it desires. Levinas admits his agreement with Descartes' "astonishment" in his third meditation, that in some way he, the cogito, "has the infinite in himself prior to the finite," and not, as his philosophical critics argued, the other way around (see *TI* 210–12). The infinite is not the finite negated. Rather, the finite is elevated by the infinite or is a refusal of it—in either case, the infinite has priority. *Infinity* bursts, breaks, ruptures, disturbs, troubles, traumatizes, awakens, inspires, ruins, obsesses, and otherwise exerts the pacific force of a "more" ("greater," "nobler," "better") on the "less." *Infinity*—a dimension of height—is not contained or containable in the congealing economies of totality; exceeding them, its very surplus makes them possible and returns them to the contentiousness or humaneness of the intersubjective dimension from which they arise. Such is the always exceptional structure of Levinas's thought, a thought that exceeds thought, a "saying" that exceeds and makes possible what is "said," an inspired or "prophetic" thought nevertheless speaking the universal language of philosophy, higher than all complacency.

It is precisely because Levinas sees that it is properly *Totality* that is opposed to *Infinity* that his thought exceeds and escapes the internal and conditioned opposition of finitude and infinite, just as by opposing *Infinity* to *Totality* it surpasses the most philosophical of all oppositions, indeed the opposition that originally gave rise to philosophy and defined its parameters of thinking and being, namely, the opposition between being and nonbeing. "To be or not to be," is not for Levinas the ultimate question or alternative (*OB* 3). With the title of Levinas's second great work, *Otherwise than Being, or Beyond Essence,* the exceeding of philosophy—philosophy as the thinking of being and nonbeing, philosophy as launched by the ancient Greeks—could not be made clearer. In the title *Totality and Infinity*, this surplus, which awakens the very self-consciousness of philosophy, occurs more succinctly in the single term *Infinity*. Infinity is neither a thought nor a being, neither is it the thought of being or the being of thought—not because it is less than thought or being, a "stammering" thought or a nascent being, but rather because in exceeding them otherwise than as being or essence it first makes them possible. Infinity in any register, from mathematics to the humanities (the "face of the other"), exceeds the thought that attempts to think it. To think infinity is to think beyond thought. Thus thought and being are broken by infinity. Its proper or most radical register, however, the one from which the others ultimately derive their sense, is found in ethics, in the responsibility of one for another, an infinite responsibility. What impels thinking and being is not wonder or disclosure but closer to the bone, as it were, it is human vulnerability and the moral responsibility it elicits.

Accordingly, at the heart of his thinking, reflected in the title of his *magnum opus,* Levinas has, *per impossible* (in the eyes of philosophy), hit upon a far more radical opposition. He has stirred up what is perhaps the most radical opposition of all: totality (including its synthesized parts, indeed as the very synthesizing, identifying, integrating of its parts) opposed to and by infinity, that which transcends the finite and the not-finite. Not being and nonbeing, not the thinking of being and nonbeing, not philosophy's perennial but internal debate therefore, but Athens *and* Jerusalem, reason and revelation, evidence and excess, being and the "otherwise than being," the true and the good beyond-being—such are the far reaching issues, beyond all horizons that can be converted into origins, that guide and elevate Levinas's "ethical metaphysics."[7]

In the title of *Totality and Infinity*, as in the titles *Being and Time* and *Being and Nothingness*, the connecting term "and" has, as this seemingly innocent connective often has, a certain provisional neutrality. Of course, by contrast, we can say that it is already not exclusionary like "or," or prioritizing like "in," or determinative in the various ways that other possible conjunctions or prepositions might have specified this title. The initial indetermination of the "and" makes all these titles tantalizing—we read these books to see how the "and" is specified. We know for Heidegger the genuine meaning of *Being* is *Time*, and time is not "clock time" but an existential-ontological temporality and historicity. We know for Sartre *Being,* which is the massive impenetrable opacity of the "in-itself," is inescapably and solely made meaningful by the transparency of pure consciousness, the *Nothingness* of the "for-itself," a thoroughly free human subjectivity. The entire issue of *Totality and Infinity* will be to articulate the character of the "and," the nature or manner of interaction that in bringing infinity to bear prevents the totalizing—the totalitarianism—of totality. We know Levinas's answer: ethics as moral responsibility and the call to justice. It is morality, the imperatively demanding and transcendent face (*visage*) of the other person, eliciting the response of responsibility for that other person, that bursts the totality with infinity and charges, invests, elects what would otherwise congeal into a totality with the higher and "denucleating" exigencies of kindness and justice. Determining the meaning of this "and," saying it without reducing it to a theme that can be known and grasped and catalogued by the mind, proffering it without limiting it to the logic (or illogic) of propositions, therefore, is the very task of the "argument" and sweet rhetoric of *Totality and Infinity*—often achieved by what Levinas calls "an abuse of logic" or what Ricoeur identifies as "hyperbole."[8] Unlike traditional philosophy *Totality and Infinity* heralds neither an opposition nor the dialectical overcoming of an opposition. Rather it announces—in a speech as close to prophecy as to philosophy, but even farther from mythology—obligations and responsibilities going to infinity, going, that is to say, to the other person as other, in a "love thy neighbor" that does not follow from love of the self, but that "is" the self, the true self, the self invested with and by a greater exigency than its own being. It is to put the mortality and suffering of the other before one's own—such is the imperative that drives ethics, such is the nontotalizable infinity of *Totality and Infinity*. In an always-renewed reversal of the priority that had hitherto determined philosophy, it is "love of wisdom" in the higher service of the "wisdom of love."[9]

While the "and" in the title of *Totality and Infinity* seems neutral at first sight, in fact and profoundly there are no neutral grounds between totality and infinity. From the side of totality, "neutral grounds" can only be a mask, an "ideology" serving ulterior and hidden constellations of forces (instinctual drives, infantile desires, economic classes, semiotic structures, and so on); while from the side of infinity, the "disinterestedness" of scientific justification (verifiability, evidence, repeatability, and the like) already reflects the project of justice which itself stems from the exigencies of moral imperatives. Totality and infinity are never neutral toward one another, nor can their relationship be symmetrical. That which infinity transcends, that which confines infinity, is itself opposed to infinity precisely insofar as it forms itself, or tends to form itself into a totality, a whole which treats its members not as independent individuals but as parts, components, constituents. A totality, however characterized, is that which remaining self-contained, self-sufficient, without exterior, ultimately complacent, is an imperial refusal of the otherness, the transcendence, the "beyond" — which is ultimately a moral dimension — of infinity. Totality, seeing only itself, thinking only its own thoughts, self-absorbed, inevitably promulgates a vicious circle of amoral cynicism. The state is right, why? — For reasons of state! Who can forget Orwell's *1984* or Koestler's *Darkness at Noon* or the twentieth century totalitarian realities they warn against?

There is no doubt that Levinas is on the "side" of *Infinity*, of justifying and increasing rather than rationalizing and decreasing responsibilities. "Ethics," he has written, "is first philosophy." Infinity gives totality no rest, no excuses, unravels the knots of its identifying syntheses to turn what would otherwise ossify into an identity into the "non-identity" above identity of life lived with others, a movement that goes out to the other without recuperation. Our true identities are not the identities identified on identity cards. Abraham does not return home. His voyage, like the movement of one-for-another, and the historical project of justice, is one-way. Ulysses, in contrast, ventures outward only to invariably, inexorably return home (*TI* 271). His going out is for the sake of his coming home. It is this same homecoming, as a return to self replenished with experiences, an "identity of identity and difference," a haughty colonization, a Crusade or Jihad to eliminate the Infidel, that in the name of a total comprehension, an absolute intelligibility (present or deferred, perfect or imperfect, it is the same) — that has hitherto served as motive and aim of philosophy, and fueled its self-applauding rhetoric of greatness. The whole point of Levinas's philosophy, in contrast, is to recognize infinity not as a problem or failure, a stubbornness or satanic rebellion, but as a surplus, a "more," something greater than, beyond, above, better than the totality which always claims to be the be all and end all of all things. Such an "escape" from the totalizing grip of a comforting and self-congratulatory homecoming is only possible, so Levinas argues, if we appreciate the surplus of infinity not in epistemological, ontological or aesthetic terms, not in terms of disclosure at all, but in ethical terms, as the "better" than being, the nobler, higher, more important, the glory or *holiness* of moral responsibility for the other person, as kindness toward the "the stranger, the widow, and the orphan" (*TI* 78, 215), and as a responsibility which extends to all others, starting with the human community, in the sacrifices of a social activism that aims to institute and maintain the laws and institutions of a just society for all.

These words are inspiring, to be sure, but are they duplicitous and hollow, filled with air rather than spirit? So much in our technological "age of publicity"—with its staged media events, superficial news bites, instant celebrity, "reality" television shows, and the like, when theatre and politics are often indistinguishable—has led not merely to a general suspicion regarding motives, but to an outright cynicism regarding all lofty sentiments. In China innumerable posters promise "friendship and harmony," but what does China really want? The presidents of the United States speak endlessly of "freedom and democracy," but what does America really want? Continually bombarded, saturated with an unending stream of ever more stimulating commercial sales pitches, "human interest" stories, political and financial scandals, scenes of catastrophic floods, hurricanes, mass starvations, all accompanied by the "spin" of praise and blame, we of the "first world" are increasingly jaded, inclined to agree that "talk is cheap," and to retreat into our private gardens, our "home entertainment systems," our "McMansions," and video game obsessions. But Levinas is not proposing a quick fix or a pie-in-the-sky idealism. His words are not consoling. The level of his philosophical discourse is not in the least condescending. Nothing in his philosophical project enables yet another intellectualist escape route of self-righteous self-indulgence, of utopian or dystopian nostalgia. In fact, nothing is more serious than the demands to which Levinas's philosophy recalls us. No tasks are more pressing or more concrete than the alleviation of the suffering of others—for each other and for all others, near or far, associate or stranger, for each of us, our loved ones, our friends, our social institutions, our economic relations, our political structures, our environmental and our global future, indeed, for our very humanity if we are to remain truly human, i.e., humane, and perhaps most of all (and perhaps simply to restate these same obligations in

another register) for the nobility and glory of our religious aspirations and communities as well. Religion is nothing, or is infantile, for
Levinas, if it is not responsible and just.

Totality and Infinity is an unremitting attack on mythological thinking and all naturalist and anthropocentric rationalizations (scientism,
logicism, psychologism, sociologism, historicism, and the like), an
attack accomplished based on close and careful phenomenological
analyses supplemented by an ethical sensitivity accepted with the priority proper to it, and with nothing vague, superficial, arbitrary or sentimental about it. I have elsewhere outlined the inner "logic" — both
phenomenological and ethical — of its overall structure.[10] Like the
sobering dialogues of Plato and the provocative inquiries initiated
by Socrates, *Totality and Infinity* moves in an upward "curvature"
toward and with other human beings. The title, we have said, brings
to mind Sartre's *Being and Nothingness* and Heidegger's *Being and
Time*, to be sure, but this title, or the idea driving this title, the infinity that ruptures *Totality*, the *Infinity* that cannot be "contained" in
a *Totality*, also brings to mind certain Kantian themes, for instance,
the opposition first articulated by Kant in his *Critique of Pure Reason*
between reason (*Vernunft*) and understanding (*Verstand*), both of
which in their own way harbor infinities: the absent cause, the absent
whole. Based on these infinities and their irresolvable conflict, Kant,
like Levinas, also gives priority to morality over knowledge. It far
exceeds the capacity of these brief notes to explicate Kant on reason,
understanding, infinity, and morality, let alone to make careful comparisons with Levinas, important as the latter are, so the following
few words must be taken (but cannot suffice) as hints or pointers.

The necessity of and the irresolvable conflict between the different
interests of reason and understanding led Kant to the philosophical
necessity of his most fundamental distinction, that between appearances, subject to scientific objectification and causal explanation, and
the unknowable "x," the "thing-in-itself," forever beyond objective
knowledge but serving as its source and goal. Precisely the irreducibility and the absolute unknowability of the "thing-in-itself," in turn,
make room for the irrefutable possibility of free will and hence for the
legitimacy (as well as the priority) of moral judgment. The interest of
reason is to gather or synthesize all true representations into absolute
unity. The interest of understanding is to seek all the conditions of
representations, hence to reach their absolute ground. Given their

divergent aims, however, neither faculty can satisfy or overcome the interests of the other. Reason fails to achieve the completed totality it requires precisely because understanding continues to seek, in a quest essentially infinite, the totality of conditions it requires (see the "Antinomies" in the "Dialectic" of the *Critique of Pure Reason*). To believe or insist that either reason or understanding has accomplished its aims and is therefore already self-sufficient, as if the infinite could be totalized, leads to unjustifiable and hence merely "speculative" claims on the side of reason (e.g., "All is will to power"; or "Being is *Ereignis*"), or to a close-minded dogmatism on the side of understanding (e.g., "Only measurable reality is real"; or ".099999...n really = 1").

Kant's "solution" to this inevitable yet irresolvable "conflict of the faculties" is the "transcendental idealism" for which he is justly famous: the separation of the fields of science and ethics (and ultimately the separation of science, ethics, and religion), based on the irreducibility of the distinction between knowable appearances and the unknowable "x."[11] For our purposes, let us note two things about Kant's solution. First, it is interesting that Kant, like Levinas, recognizes the inherent limitations of both understanding (scientific inquiry) and reason (philosophical comprehension). Of course, for Kant they are limited by one another, which is to say, one form of rationality limits the other, while for Levinas both forms of rationality seek totality, and hence, are disrupted by infinity from the start conceived in ethical rather than epistemological terms. For Levinas, the absolute limit of rationality is found not within but outside of rationality, in ethics, and it is found there not merely as a boundary and possibility (that cannot be refuted but which also cannot be proven) but as what is most concrete and immediate, as a surplus rather than a lack or negative, as the "better," the moral imperative that elicits the responsibility for other persons which at the same time requires and conditions science even while exceeding it. It is true that Kant also recognizes the priority of morality over science, because the unknowable "x" is somehow (inexplicably) prior to phenomena, but given Kant's basically epistemological orientation his conception of morality remains for him bound to the domain and standards of logical possibility.

Second, then, and related to this first observation, Kant's transcendental idealism respects modern science (as Heidegger's ontology, for instance, does not), and it does so without undermining the possibility of an alternative or extra-scientific *ethical* "kingdom." In short, Kant and Levinas defend science while criticizing scientism, the overestimation to the point of exclusivity of the range of science. Yet Levinas has seen more clearly than Kant the proper relation separating and at the same time joining science and ethics, and he therefore gives to ethics the proper priority they both recognize it as having. This is because Kant, almost despite himself, continues to determine the nature of ethics according to standards borrowed from science, i.e., as rational and hence autonomous obedience, as acquiescence to self-generated because rational (noncontradictory, universalizable) maxims. For Levinas, in contrast, it is not only a matter—in the face of the hegemonic tendency of modern nonteleological science—of "making room" for ethics and religion. What Levinas does that Kant intended but failed to accomplish is to present a fully ethical account of the primacy of morality and justice. No longer does rationality determine ethics, since by that path the priority that is the essential moment of the ethical—the moral "better"—inevitably succumbs to the nonmoral totality of knowledge. And by taking this approach, what Levinas is also able to accomplish is the *justification* of modern science via a nonscientific but nonarbitrary ethics. In this way, altering but fulfilling the Kantian project, determining the limits of a purely scientific perspective (often taken to be equivalent to philosophy itself, philosophy as science) is accomplished not by a ratcheting up of science (*a la* Spinoza, Hegel, or Husserl), but by means of an even greater ethical-metaphysical philosophy. Husserl's philosophy expanded science from "object" to "evidence," but kept philosophy within the exclusive orbit of science; Kant expanded philosophy from science to include ethics, but conceived ethics under the ruling standard of science. Levinas expands philosophy from science to ethics, but does so by grounding science in ethics and conceiving ethics ethically.

Regarding the relation of science to infinity, furthermore, there can be little doubt that with the term *Infinity* Levinas has in mind (among other things) Husserl's last philosophical writings, especially his article "Philosophy and the Crisis of European Man" and his book, *The Crisis of the European Sciences*. Written in the 1930s, one hears in this defense of phenomenology an impassioned call to overcome the crisis of a "Europe" which had chosen fascism in Italy and Spain, anti-Semitic fascism in Germany, and Stalinism in Russia, though Husserl never mentions these social-political developments by name. What is the true or essential ground of the crisis? Husserl's answer is direct: naivete regarding the meaning of science. What is the solution? Again a direct answer: return to the true meaning of science as an "*infinite task.*" "The spiritual *telos* of European Man, in which is included the particular *telos* of separate nations and of individual human beings," Husserl wrote, "lies in infinity; it is an infinite idea, toward which in secret the collective spiritual becoming, so to speak, strives."[12] He continues:

> [S]cience designates the idea of an infinity of tasks...the idea of truth in the scientific sense is set apart...from the truth proper to pre-scientific life. Scientific truth claims to be unconditioned truth, which involves infinity, giving to each factually guaranteed truth a merely relative character, making it only an approach oriented, in fact, toward the infinite horizon, wherein the truth in itself is, so to speak, looked on as an infinitely distant point.[13]

For Husserl only science—more and better science, i.e., transcendental phenomenology—driven by the infinite idea of truth, could save the West. Alas, it did not, and one thinks of Husserl's reliance on science as itself yet another naivete in the West's crisis. Levinas understood, as Husserl did not sufficiently, that the quest for truth is not self-justifying or, obviously, self-evident, and that it requires justification and protection outside itself in the social imperatives of morality and the institutions and sanctions of justice. Levinas understood this because he understood that the deepest meaning of infinity is not to be found in the infinite tasks of science according to the self-understanding of science, for which the value of truth is self-evident, but beyond and buttressing the legitimate tasks of science, giving them their proper support and nobility, the deepest meaning of infinity is traced in the moral transcendence imposed by the face of the other person.

So, the famous opening sentence of *Totality and Infinity:* "Everyone will readily agree that it is of the highest importance to know if one is not duped by morality" (*TI* 21).[14] How does this question—which is also, let us note right away, Nietzsche's question!—begin to illuminate, to introduce the meaning of the title and, as one expects from a first sentence, the inner sense of *Totality and Infinity?*

Immediately, in the highest tradition of philosophy's argumentative and critical style, in the full integrity of philosophy's commitment to reason, it turns directly, radically, bravely against Levinas's own thinking. It asks if morality is not perhaps something else than itself, a mere epiphenomenon, the disguise, mask, ideology, symptom, or superstructure of what (or who) is not moral. Perhaps there is no morality at all! Instances of morality-denying perspectives are legion in our day: morality, or rather the evaluative, prescriptive, imperative language of moral judgment, the language of "good" and "evil," "right" and "wrong," "better" and "worse," would be the dissimulative front for class relations, physiological drives, oedipal-familial repressions, sociological impositions, personal or social immaturity, slave mentality, anthropology, naturalism, world historical spirit, being, cosmos, God, ideology, ignorance, and so forth. The list is long. Morality would be the public tool by which these deeper and more powerful configurations of signification mask themselves to better seduce and rule. The snake sweetly reasons with Eve. Machiavelli taught the Prince, he who wants to rule, to be sovereign, *not to be good but rather to appear to be good.* Here lies all the difference between morality and machination, and we moderns, we "masters of suspicion," know, as Machiavelli did not, that this difference need not be consciously known or willed, indeed, that the true Prince (class relations, chemical imbalances, and the like) may rule entirely unbeknownst to ruler and ruled.

Kant—again Kant—in the *Foundations of the Metaphysics of Morals,* had already established as a matter of *principle,* hence not by some oversight, failing or accident, that regarding both perception and introspection: "It is in fact absolutely impossible by experience to discern with complete certainty a single case in which the maxim of an action, however much it may conform to duty, rested solely on moral grounds and on the conception of one's duty."[15] He continues: "One need not be an enemy of virtue, but only a cool observer who does not confuse even the liveliest aspiration of the good with its reality, to be doubtful sometimes whether true virtue can really be found anywhere in the world."[16] Again, perhaps there is no morality at all—and from the mouth of a moralist! Accordingly, Kant's "argument" for morality is a "deduction," meaning a transcendental argument, which never proves the existence of morality, but having already taken it for granted only explains the conditions necessary for its possibility. In our age of suspicion, in the face of a century of mass murder (with no end in sight: witness Sudan or the continuing AIDS epidemic), we are perhaps no longer so willing to take morality for granted. Is it possible that along with astrology, phrenology, and augury, morality too is a hoax, and more than a hoax, a deception, the mask of something else? Such is the power of the upheaval implied in the question with which Levinas begins *Totality and Infinity.*

As a "strong man" question, Levinas's doubt would be analogous to the hyperbolic doubt of Descartes, so admired by Husserl. That doubt, of course, was raised to discover if knowledge had a sure foundation, to see if and how knowledge was truth, an account derived from the real, or merely a construct, a fanciful, convenient or powerful imposition upon the real. In Levinas's case, however, doubt or questioning is not simply an epistemological device. Here it is raised to discover whether morality is mere rhetoric, merely a language of imperatives and judgment in the service of nonethical ends, or no ends at all, or whether it is genuine, sincere, the expression of an irreducible dimension of significance worthwhile and valuable in its own right. Unlike Descartes and Husserl, whose doubts were launched in order to establish truth, for Levinas, his opening question aims to undermine truth, or more precisely it aims to undermine those points of view which claim to establish that morality is merely an epiphenomenon, a derivative and dependent discourse based more deeply on truths, on knowing, on a hidden science, or rather on a science known only to the few, always a vanguard intelligentsia, rather than on goodness, about which "everybody" already knows (but in whose obedience they, the ignorant many, are really only duped!). Levinas's question—questioning morality, but really questioning the doubt about morality—is therefore anti-Spinozist to the extreme. This is because we know Levinas's answer, we know the teaching of *Totality and Infinity:* morality is an unconditional independent register of meaning. Furthermore, truth, far from grounding morality, is itself dependent on and conditioned by morality!

Why is the question of the integrity of morality of the highest importance? Certainly making this question the very first question, indeed, the very first sentence of *Totality and Infinity* highlights its importance. But the answer is deeper. It is of the highest importance because it is precisely morality that determines the meaning of "importance." Without morality there are only differences in quantity (only differences in "ratios of rest and motion" says Spinoza), differences in force, differences in taste, indeed, in our age of subjectivity, in our Nietzschean times, there are only differences in will power—in will to power—to determine the better and the worse, the more and the less important. What could the meaning of hierarchy, rank, orientation, direction, up and down, be without morality?

Accordingly, let us also not fail to notice that Levinas has begun his book with a fallacy! "It is of the utmost importance…" well, in what is meant to be the radical questioning of morality, morality is already at work! (It is the same "informal" fallacy, known as "complex question," used with such bravado by Nietzsche in each of the titles of the four chapters of *Ecce Homo*. Is it possible to discuss ethics without invoking Nietzsche?!) Reason is tweaked. A touch of humor, a certain human personality, is already at work from the very start of *Totality and Infinity*, like the skepticism that in *Otherwise than Being* Levinas praises not for its validity—its argument is not valid, or there would be no truth—but for the humanity and the personality to which it gives voice. Let us not confuse this light touch with mockery, with the bite of Nietzschean wit, for Levinas is no mocker of reason. He is a critic of reason, and *Totality and Infinity* is a critique of pure reason, insofar as we understand that criticism is itself an essential moment of reason, ultimately a moral surplus, that keeps reason reasonable.

To seek for that which is important, to acknowledge without preparation the importance of importance, the exigency of what is important, is already to be engaged in ethics. The real beginning of *Totality and Infinity* thus precedes the first sentence of *Totality and Infinity* neither as the naivete of opinion nor as the authority of tradition, which precede philosophy provisionally only to eventually succumb to its recuperation of their origins in what Levinas calls the "posteriority of the anterior" (*TI* 54), but as moral responsibility precedes philosophy and in its immemorial precedence gives to philosophy (and to opinion and tradition) its ultimate significance. The prephilosophical is not less than philosophy but is rather the ethical, unless philosophy, rising to its true height, were to accept "ethics as first philosophy," as is precisely Levinas's entire point.

The allusion to Nietzsche via the fallacy of double question, whether intended or not, is not merely whimsical. Certainly the question of the importance of importance, what he calls the "value of values," is the very center of all of Nietzsche's philosophizing. This is especially the case when Nietzsche argues, in the concluding sections of the Third Essay of *On the Genealogy of Morals*, that science, for all its vaunted objectivity, is not the opponent of religion (as the now standard Enlightenment critiques of religion argue), but rather the most refined form of religion, "natural" rather than "unnatural" religion. For Nietzsche, science, even more than the Judeo-Christian religion from which it first obtained its marching orders (Thou shall not lie; thou shall not bear false witness, and so on) is based "on the same belief that truth is inestimable and cannot be criticized."[17] But what interests us, beyond his vitriolic denunciation of the nihilist asceticism of both religion and science, is that Nietzsche too, like Levinas, recognizes a human dimension as the irreducible ground and meaning of scientific objectivity. Truth, no less than lie, is first of all the expression of a will, an all too human will. But because, far from Levinas, he denounces religion and morality as well as science, when Nietzsche turns to artistic creativity—in the radical form of art for art's sake, art as life, life as art, but always art as absolute giving, solar will—his is but an empty gesture, the dark side, as it were, but still but the other side of the scientific illumination he aims so desperately to extinguish. There can be no "revaluation of all values," in contrast to outright nihilism, without a prior acceptance of the value of values, the importance of importance—something Nietzsche did not understand, or refused to acknowledge.

In this light we can understand the informal fallacy that introduces *Totality and Infinity* not, as with Nietzsche, to affirm an aggrandizing will to power, but rather in peace, *shalom*, to remind readers from the start that *Totality and Infinity* is a book with a human face, a book by a human being and for human beings. *Totality and Infinity*, unlike *Thus Spoke Zarathustra*, is not a book "for everyone and no one," by which Nietzsche meant that he wrote his book for "no one" else except himself, "the greatest solitude," and "for everyone" only in the sense that it is for all others who, essentially alone, monads, atoms in a void, "ships passing in the night," must also bravely live their own essentially solitary lives. Nor, on the other hand, is *Totality and Infinity* a book by or for an anonymous "transcendental ego," a pure objectivity, or by a transpersonal "world historical spirit," an absolute objectivity. Nor, finally, is it a book that must be published pseudononymously, like those of Kierkegaard, because it usurps a position that essentially defies communication, knowing too much about God. Rather, it is a book for each and every reader, a book by someone who retains his humanity, by Emmanuel Levinas, who writes for and for the sake of the humanity of other human beings, in a discourse of the universal—philosophy—which nevertheless speaks for each and everyone in his or her particularity. Precisely the *singularity* of author and readers retains its force in the ethical discourse of Levinas's philosophy.

From it very first sentence, then, without trumpets, with a touch a humor, but in the greatest possible seriousness also, *Totality and Infinity* is a *human* discourse of truth, a philosophical discourse aware of its moral momentum, a book aware of its communicative context, in an accusative voice, driven not only by the "infinite tasks" of science announced by Husserl, but by a relation to the infinitely other, the other human being. It is this *importance*—this emphasis, this exigency—that is already at work prior to and in *Totality and Infinity*. Just as an unacknowledged will to total truth, a will to the complete articulation of the determinate totality, is already at work in the first sentences and before the start of Hegel's *Phenomenology of Spirit*, so, too, *mutatis mutandi*, is there a moral imperative already at work in Levinas's *Totality and Infinity* and, if Levinas is correct, in the prior importance that Hegel must always already give to truth in his *Phenomenology of Spirit* as well. Against the reductions of scientism and its obverse, skepticism and nihilism, Levinas's discourse is designed neither to ignore nor to overestimate—and certainly not to underestimate—the ethical signification of its own humanity.

Here the "circularity" of what is prior in relation to what is posterior, the ethical in relation to the discourse of philosophy, of knowledge, of science, is not the familiar hermeneutic circle, which moves from what is only somewhat familiar to what is truly known, from the merely implicitly known to the more fully, or more explicitly, or completely explicitly known. Rather, ethics involves a different sort of circularity altogether, that of a responsibility that increases in the measure that it is taken up, where an inescapable imperative that precedes discourse—a "saying" of the "said"—nonetheless gives to discourse its seriousness, its direction, its importance (*OB* 5–7). This, too, is hinted at in the human face intimated in Levinas's use of a fallacy, and perhaps, too, it is hinted at in the self-depreciating humor that like the slightest glimmer of a smile also accompanies and in no way belies the infinite seriousness of that same first sentence.

To begin by saying that it is of the *highest importance* to know if we are not duped by morality is in any event to have already sided with morality, for only morality introduces the hierarchy of the more and less important into human affairs. The precise nature, or rather the precise sociality and time of this "already"—one must already be moral to be moral—will be the central issue, the central concern, that which is of the highest importance, to be clarified, elucidated, illuminated, explicated throughout *Totality and Infinity.* Its task is to show the trace of an anteriority not fully submerged in the posteriority, the representations, of thought. But it will not be shown or illuminated at all! It may be "of the highest importance *to know* whether we are not duped by morality," but to know the priority and sincerity of morality demands a different sort of "knowing" than what is found in and by objective theory, phenomenological representation or ontological disclosure. The priority and primacy of moral responsibility will be born, traced, achieved, and emphasized across a new form of philosophical discourse appropriate to ethics: an ethical account of ethics. I say "new," but ethical discourse, ethical exegesis, also "appears" (it never *appears*) in the conversational character of Plato's dialogues where it is not merely ideas that clash but persons who speak and seek the truth from one another, where Socrates is but one voice among several. Aristotle, too, despite a certain ambivalence, suggests in his *Nicomachean Ethics* that friendship may be essential to truth. The ethical circle is a circle of people, each independent yet linked across language—out of relation and in relation and not even "at the same time." More precisely it is not a circle at all, but a one-way movement of transcendence from one person to another. It occurs in the asymmetry of the face-to-face: in the infinity of the other's mortality, the other's vulnerability which in its suffering obligates and calls out for a response; and no less, then, does it occur in the infinity of a responsibility for-the-other which awakens from and rises above the selfishness of its own needs. Morality occurs in obligations and responsibilities which also require justice and thus spread across and link all humanity today and from generation to generation past and future. The *Infinity* of ethics, of moral sociality, of justice for all, is better—higher, more important—than the *Totality,* with the inevitable violence of its suppression of the independence of inalienably independent beings, and its homogenizing epistemology and aesthetics or rather, to expose what these are in truth without morality, of its oppressive politics and its cults of personality each of which demand total loyalty and permit no dissent.

Levinas makes the close link between the title of *Totality and Infinity* and its first sentence explicit several pages later in the preface. It turns out that the first sentence is indeed an elaboration of the title; or, conversely, it turns out that the title is a succinct summation of the first sentence. Levinas writes: "Do particular beings yield their truth in a Whole in which their exteriority vanishes? Or, on the contrary, is the ultimate event of being enacted in the outburst [*tout éclat:* splintering, shattering, bursting] of this exteriority? Our initial question now assumes this form" (*TI* 26).

In other words, we are duped by morality—there is no morality and "morality" expresses a "false consciousness," as Marxist ideologues would say—if particular beings gain their sense from their placement within a whole, as parts of a totality. On the other hand, morality is serious, and we are not duped by it, if infinity has priority over totality—if the orders of totality are the false consciousness, a greater or lesser violation of an infinity that forever precedes and exceeds totality and is the source of significance.

We are duped by morality if *Totality* has priority over *Infinity*, and not duped if *Infinity* has priority over *Totality*. *Infinity* does have priority over *Totality*, and it does so precisely in the moral responsibility one person has for another. Such responsibility can be shirked, to be sure. Evil is always possible and brute force is quite real. Let us not, by some angelic flight of utopian fancy, underestimate the power of their regime. They are all too real. Nevertheless, it is to give a full account of the infinite *exigency* of moral responsibility—including its conditions, its emergence and its consequences in all registers of human signification—all the while attentive to its irreducible *elevation*, which is the nonthematizable theme—the "relation without relation" (*rapport sans rapport*) (*TI* 295; my translation)—that is the exceptional ethical subject-matter of Levinas's *Totality and Infinity*. At the conclusion of this book, and mirroring ideas already articulated in the concluding paragraph of its preface, Levinas writes: "The description of the face to face which we have attempted here is told to the other, to the reader who appears anew behind my discourse and my wisdom. Philosophy is never a wisdom because the interlocutor whom it has just encompassed has already escaped it" (*TI* 295).

The "wisdom of love," so Levinas expresses this point elsewhere, precedes and gives meaning to the "love of wisdom."

SEVEN

Choosing and the Chosen
Levinas and Sartre

INTRODUCTION

Let us straightaway acknowledge that the vision and intentions of Sartre the man seem at times to exceed the confines of Sartre the philosopher, whose philosophy is articulated most precisely in *Being and Nothingness* and in several books and articles preceding and following this magnum opus. Nonetheless, we are with good conscience bound to the philosophy of Sartre. It is this philosophy, after all, for which Sartre is famous. And it is to this philosophy, it seems to me, that he remained essentially faithful throughout his intellectual career, even if sometimes seemingly despite himself, as one senses in the intellectual convolutions of his (unfinished) *Critique of Dialectical Reason*.[1] Although the subtitle of *Being and Nothingness* calls the book an "Essay of Phenomenological Ontology,"[2] the name by which its philosophy became famous—and in some quarters infamous—was "existentialism," a label Sartre more than any other so-called "existentialist" accepted and used. It is a philosophy centered on and determined throughout by the Archimedean opposition between "being for itself," (*l'être pour soi*), by which Sartre means human freedom as an objectifying negativity, and "being in itself" (*l'être en soi*), massive inert impenetrable being, the *Nothingness* and *Being* of the book's title.[3]

One should not mistake Levinas's professed admiration for Sartre "at a personal level,"[4] and also at a certain philosophical level, as no more than the good manners of fellow philosophers or, later, with

Sartre's death, an obligatory eulogizing kindness. Levinas genuinely admired Sartre, and repeatedly said so, and said why. It is certainly not simply a matter of the gratitude he felt because it was Sartre—world famous in the 1940s, 50s, and 60s, when Levinas was relatively unknown[5]—"who," as Levinas says, "guaranteed my place in eternity," because Sartre's introduction to phenomenology came through reading Levinas's prize winning book, *The Theory of Intuition in Husserl's Phenomenology*.[6] No, the affinities that bring these two thinkers together are not merely sentimental or personal—contemporaries, known to one another, living in the same city, writing in the same language, engaged by the same intellectual milieu, reading one another's writings, and experiencing the same historical events.[7] There are philosophical affinities.

And these similarities occur not merely at a level of generality that make them seem forced or charitable rather than genuine and illuminating. It is true, however, the similarities that bring their respective philosophies close to one another do occur at a higher level of generality, and are expressed in broader strokes, than the differences, to which Levinas devotes precise analyses. Levinas, as we shall see, is a severe critic, indeed a fundamental and profound critic of Sartre. But for all that, there is nothing ingenuous when in 1947, for instance, responding to Sartre's book *Anti-Semite and Jew*, Levinas writes: "The overall philosophy of Sartre is simply an attempt to think man, encompassing his social, economic, and historical situation within his spirituality, without making him a simple object of thought. It recognizes commitments for the mind that are not knowledge. Commitments that are not thoughts—that's existentialism!" He continues: "[T]he existence of an existentialist humanism—that is, where all scholastic dogma, even a modern one, is set aside—a humanism that integrates the fundamental experiments of the modern world...this is Sartre's essential contribution to our cause, the cause of humanity" (*UH* 74–75).[8]

Or, even more glowingly, in an article on Sartre written in 1980, Levinas's first sentence reads:

> The idea that human freedom could be retrieved in the midst of everything that is imposed on man came from Sartre like a message of hope for a whole generation that grew up under fatalities through all the expectation of our century and for which the humanism of eloquence,

however much it glorified human rights, was totally unconvincing. (*UH* 91)

There can be no doubt that Levinas respected Sartre. But there can be no doubt, either, that Levinas opposed Sartre's philosophy of freedom, and that he opposed it frequently and fundamentally (In this, of course, in its own way, there is also respect: Sartre is worthy of criticism.). Perhaps the most trenchant, detailed and sustained criticisms appear in *Totality and Infinity,* but Sartre is also criticized in *Otherwise than Being* and in many of Levinas's shorter philosophical writings written before, between, and after these two great works.

For all his criticism, Levinas remains far closer to Sartre than to Heidegger, his primary target of criticism. The contrast is instructive. Regarding Levinas's opposition to Heidegger: it is not only because Levinas has phenomenologically contested and surpassed every single phenomenological analysis that Heidegger ever made—such disagreement is certainly possible (and ultimately healthy!) between philosophers who are joined by a shared phenomenological method (in the scientific communal sense as Husserl interpreted it). Far more profoundly, Levinas stands on fundamentally different "grounds" than Heidegger. What separates Levinas and Heidegger is a chasm: the difference between ethics as first philosophy and ontology as first philosophy. In his adoration for ontology, Heidegger explicitly rejects the ethics of human responsibility as willful, subjectivist, constructivist, mere "world-picture" (*Weltbild*) and nihilist. With Sartre, in contrast, both thinkers stand—or want to stand—in solidarity on the side of ethics. Levinas endorses Sartre's claim that the human subject is a radical responsibility. He must criticize Sartre, nonetheless, for articulating a philosophy incapable of justifying this claim, and for sinking instead into an ontological quicksand of his own devising. To say this of Sartre is no "excuse," certainly, but it indicates in a rough way his proximity with Levinas. In sum: against Heidegger, Levinas is fighting a grand war without quarter, a *gigantomachia* of the excluded middle: either ontology or ethics comes first. With Sartre, in contrast, theirs is an argument between allies both on the side of human freedom and responsibility, but only one of whom, Levinas, is able to escape totality and justify freedom in moral responsibility.

AFFINITIES: SARTRE AND LEVINAS

Let us turn first, then, to the links that bring Levinas and Sartre close. I do not want to say Sartre "influenced" Levinas because the issue of influence is difficult to determine at best, and is especially difficult in the case of Sartre and Levinas whose philosophical worlds overlap to such a great extent. For instance, in the following I show that Sartre and Levinas, despite their enormous differences regarding religion, are quite close in that both defend a necessary dimension of "atheism." But one would be closer to the truth regarding Levinas's position on atheism to say it was Franz Rosenzweig's *Star of Redemption,* with its assertion of the absolute independence of the world from God, which was the greater philosophical *influence* on Levinas rather than Sartre's atheism, which is ultimately quite far from Levinas. The term "affinity," then, serves better than the term "influence" to capture their philosophical proximities.

In fact there are too many affinities to review all of them in a chapter of this size. Accordingly, in the following I am going to focus primarily on three interrelated philosophical positions of central importance to Sartre which are also of central importance to Levinas: (1) the independence, freedom, or atheism of the human subject; (2) responsibility as the very selfhood of the subject; and (3) the asymmetry of social relations. (If there were room to add a fourth focus, it would be the notion of the "third," which for both Sartre and Levinas—in differing ways and with differing success, to be sure—opens up a dimension beyond moral responsibility: the realm of social justice.)[9]

A proviso: in elaborating these three affinities, do keep in mind that Levinas's criticisms of Sartre—which are fundamental—will not appear until the third section of this chapter, where these affinities will be reexamined under a sharper and more critical light. This is another way of restating that Levinas's agreements with Sartre occur at a higher level of generality than his disagreements.

Independence, Freedom or Atheism of the Human Subject

It is to state the obvious to say that Sartre in *Being and Nothingness* articulates a radical philosophy of freedom. It is perhaps the most radical philosophy of freedom possible. Sartre completely eliminates any reification of human selfhood by interpreting human subjectivity as the pure activity of negating. Consciousness, being for-itself, is precisely this activity, in contrast to the inert, massive, or opaque character of being in-itself.

What Sartre means when he interprets human subjectivity as the pure activity of negating is that human consciousness freely bestows meaning on the world, indeed, creates a world of meaning, precisely because it is *not* a thing or object and cannot be determined as a thing or object. Wilfrid Desan, in his perceptive study of *Being and Nothingness*,[10] correctly distinguishes the three types or levels of the for-itself's pure activity of negating: (a) prereflective consciousness of the world, where one sees, tastes, hears, touches, and smells the world but is *not* the world seen, tasted, heard, touched, or smelled; (b) reflective consciousness, where there is a second order or representational awareness that one is conscious of (negating) the world, but one is also, as with prereflective consciousness, *not* the consciousness of which one is aware; and (c) consciousness that one's own self is also *not* the thing, object or role—the reification—that it would be according to another person's meaning-bestowal. In each case, whether it is not the world, not self-consciousness, or not the other's signifying, the for-itself is nothing more and nothing less than the sheer activity of *negating,* which is at the same time the pure activity of giving meaning.

Human subjectivity, therefore, where consciousness, freedom, and negating are equivalent expressions, is a radical inescapable choosing of meaning. Nothing—not the world, not a reflection, not the other's meaning—can possibly determine the pure freedom of the for-itself. Entirely unmotivated, it is entirely free. When Sartre famously declares that "existence precedes essence," he is referring precisely to this freedom from any determination whatsoever. The human subject chooses meaning based on nothing. Such is what Sartre calls the "anguish" of the self: it is free, completely free, without recourse, without exit, without excuses. It is on its own, independent. True, the for-itself has been born, has a past, is located in a place, has a surrounding world, looks forward to a future, and the like, but such "facticity" takes all its meaning from the meaning given to it by the for-itself. The only thing, as it were, the for-itself is not free to negate is its own freedom! As such, it is "condemned" to its freedom, condemned to invent itself at each moment—wholly on its own.

Absolute freedom also provides the reason for Sartre's atheism. The unlimited freedom that Descartes attributed to God is for Sartre the freedom of the for-itself. The meaning of God, then, depends on the freedom of the for-itself, and not the other way around, *per impossible*. But if that is so, if the meaning of "God" results from and cannot exceed human creation, then God is not God, not a transcendent absolute; hence Sartre's atheism. A second reason for Sartre's atheism derives from the contradictory character of the notion of God. To put the matter in philosophical terms: God is imagined to be "being-in-and-for-itself." But for Sartre this is as impossible as a round square because a for-itself, being wholly free, cannot therefore also be unfree, an in-itself.

While Sartre thus rejects the notion of God as doubly impossible, let us nevertheless not overlook the fact that the inner tendency of the for-itself is—like the impossible God—precisely to try to be an in-itself. True, the for-itself is *not* the meanings it invents, but it does invent them, project them, and it "is" them by not being them. The for-itself is thus always in "bad faith," whether it pretends to be its projections or acknowledges the nothingness that separates itself from its projections. In this way, in the independence, freedom or atheism of negating everything outside itself, Sartre joins a long philosophical tradition of philosophers who, having killed God, wish to be God in his stead.

One of the pillars of Levinas's philosophy is also the independence and the consequent atheism (or, more precisely, the possibility of the atheism) of the self. The essential structure revealed by the phenomenological analyses found in their most detailed form in the first three subsections of *Totality and Infinity*, is precisely the independence, "separation," or "hypostasis" of the self. To be sure, this independence is accomplished not, as with Sartre, in the activity of negating, but rather in the felt sensuousness of sentient being, which Levinas calls "enjoyment" (*jouissance*) or "living from..." (*TI* 109–51). "*Living from*...is the dependency that turns into sovereignty, into happiness—essentially egoist" (114). "Enjoyment accomplishes the atheist separation...existence at home with itself of an autochthonous I" (115).

We shall see that for Levinas the atheism of the I, its separation and independence from anonymous existence (the "there is"), its freedom, because it is originally produced as sensibility rather than consciousness, is a self-relation at once closed *and open,* secure *and vulnerable,* or what Levinas characterizes as "an independence higher than substantiality" (*TI* 113). Egoist subjectivity in its independence, in its refusal of otherness, in its atheism, *can* be maintained against the moral authority of the other person (even if, under duress of violence, of torture, for example, its "freedom" can be broken). It is indeed for this reason, in its egoist resistance, that Levinas calls it "atheist," in an atheism that is neither illusory nor ignorant, that is, which is not merely nugatory or an epiphenomenon. Such an independence is necessary, Sartre and Levinas agree, for the subject to be truly free and hence truly engaged in actions for which it can be held morally responsible—subject to ethical rather than merely ontological determination. It is to this topic that we now turn.

Responsibility as the Very Selfhood of the Subject

Another way Sartre understands the independence, atheism, and freedom of the for-itself, is as responsibility for all and everything. That the for-itself is absolutely free means that nothing else, no condition or motivation, can be held responsible or blamed for the world of meaning it creates.

We have seen that the for-itself is responsible for its situation, its place, its surroundings, its death, its future, its past, its birth... for all and everything. That it is responsible for all and everything means that the *meaning* of all and everything, from birth to death, from past to future, from here to there, is produced, created, invented by the for-itself and by the for-itself alone. Near the conclusion of *Being and Nothingness,* Sartre writes:

> [M]an being condemned to be free carries the weight of the whole world on his shoulders; he is responsible for the world and for himself as a way of being. We are taking the word "responsibility" in its ordinary sense as "consciousness (of) being the incontestable author of an event or of an object." In this sense the responsibility of the for-itself is overwhelming since he is the one by whom it happens that *there is* a world.... I must be without remorse or regrets as I am without excuse;

for from the instant of my upsurge into being, I carry the weight of the world by myself alone without anything or any person being able to lighten it.[11]

In an essay written three years later, in 1946, entitled "Existentialism Is a Humanism," Sartre reaffirms this absolute responsibility: "Our responsibility is thus much greater than we might have supposed, because it involves all mankind.... I am responsible for myself and for all men, and I am creating a certain image of man of my own choosing. In choosing myself, I choose man."[12]

In the face of this Himalayan responsibility, one thinks immediately of the equally enormous responsibility borne by the moral self of Levinas's philosophy. One of the most striking and disturbing features of Levinas's thought is precisely that it does not let the self off the moral hook, as it were: the responsibility of the self to and for the other is infinite. There are no excuses. Further, responsibility, beginning with the other person who faces, extends in a demand for justice to all others, to all of humankind, to all sentient life, and in the final account to all of creation[13]—a truly biblical responsibility. Levinas repeatedly and approvingly quotes from Dostoyevsky's *The Brothers Karamazov*: "We are all responsible for all for all men before all, and I more than all the others."[14]

The moral self for Levinas as for Sartre, is not only infinitely responsible, but is absolutely irreplaceable in its responsibility; and as such, as the one and only one who is responsible, the human is thereby individuated by it, or, to use Levinas's preferred term, "*élu*"—"elected" or "chosen." "Obligation," Levinas has written, "calls for a unique response not inscribed in universal thought, the unforeseeable response of the chosen one" (*OB* 145).

Furthermore, again for both thinkers, on a social plane extending beyond the face-to-face the subject's unconditional responsibility is responsible to the point that it judges history itself. It is precisely this unparalleled responsibility which upholds the very "humanity of the human" that creates what Levinas calls "holy history" (*BV* 63), the history of moral responsibilities undertaken and changing history even if morality is invisible to the historiographer who deals exclusively with the husks of history, its documents, artifacts, and monuments. Kant saw that responsibility cannot be proven empirically; Levinas, along with Sartre, adds that neither can it be delegated to history.

In a word, for both Sartre and Levinas the human subject is the moral atlas[15] of the universe, responsible for all and everything without excuse and without exception, not merely resolute,[16] but in its freedom and independence "ab-solute," to use Levinas's precise term.

The Asymmetry of Social Relations

For both Sartre and Levinas, being-for-the-other is not: (a) a reciprocal or transitive relation, whose terms are interchangeable, as one finds, by contrast, with the account of "appresentative" or "associative" "pairing" in Husserl's Fifth *Cartesian Meditation,*[17] or the "mutuality" of Buber's I-Thou;[18] (b) a dialectical relation, whose terms, self and other, are surpassed and gain their sense from a higher level organization of meaning, as one finds, by contrast, with Hegel's "world historical spirit" or Marx's "communism"; (c) a prior structure inherent in and common to all subjects, as one finds, by contrast, with Heidegger's "being-with" (*Mitsein*). Rather, to speak affirmatively, intersubjectivity for both Levinas and Sartre is a relation that remains irreducibly dyadic and asymmetrical.

For Sartre the asymmetry of being-for-the-other is a function of the irresolvable clash of two consciousnesses each of which projects the objectification of its other, on the one hand, and, on the other, of the inescapably first-person singularity of the for-itself as the absolute zero, as it were, of all meaning bestowal. It is as impossible for two consciousnesses to objectify one another and remain consciousnesses, as it is for one consciousness to objectify itself and remain a consciousness. In fact, because there is no outside perspective from which to speak of what occurs to two consciousnesses in relation to one another, it is simpler and closer to Sartre's claim to say that the for-itself, as pure freedom, cannot be objectified—even in its relation to another for-itself. Whatever Sartre may have gleaned from Kojève's lectures on the Master-Slave dialectic in Hegel's *Phenomenology of Spirit,* he in nowise accepts the Hegelian "resolution," of slaves overcoming their masters through the work of history.[19] Rather, the for-itself remains irreducibly opposed to the other, negating the other. It can neither be objectified by the other nor can it objectify the other.

What Sartre calls the "masochist" for-itself tries to become an object for-the-other, but fails, since a for-itself cannot become an in-itself. What he calls the "sadist" for-itself tries to objectify the other, but fails, since no for-itself—myself or another—can become an in-itself. And there is no alternative other than that of a masochist or a sadist for-itself. This is yet another way of saying that the for-itself, no matter what its intentions, is always in "bad faith." Sartre sums up the character of intersubjective relations with a famous line from his play *No Exit:* "Hell is—other people."[20]

For Levinas, too, while intersubjectivity is not Sartre's hell, the "face to face" relation is from the first and always an asymmetrical relation. It is "diagonal": the other stands above the self with moral priority, a "height" that obligates the self prior to the self's self-interests. This diagonal asymmetry is the very meaning, for Levinas, of the morality of the moral self: obligated to the other before itself, responsible for the other before itself. When asked by an interviewer about this: "But is not the Other also responsible in my regard?", Levinas answered: "[T]he inter-subjective relation is a non-symmetrical relation.... I am responsible for the Other without waiting for reciprocity" (*EI* 98).

Of course, this asymmetry is not in every way the same as that found in Sartre. In *Totality and Infinity,* Levinas indicates that in being called to a moral service by and to the other, the imposition of the other is in no way that of an enemy or opponent:

> The being that presents himself in the face comes from a dimension of height, a dimension of transcendence whereby he can present himself as a stranger without opposing me as obstacle or enemy.... The Other who dominates me in his transcendence is thus the stranger, the widow, and the orphan, to whom I am obligated. (*TI* 215)

In contrast to Sartre, the self in Levinas is truly "for oneself" only insofar as it is "for the other." Nevertheless, in agreement with Sartre, for Levinas the interpersonal relation establishes the very first person singularity of the human subject, "elects" the subject, who is "chosen" across a nontransitive, nondialectical, nonshared relation to the other's nontotalizable transcendence. In short, there is no exterior point of view that can determine, coordinate or comprehend the first personal singularity of the responsible subject in Levinas or Sartre. Thus both philosophers begin their philosophies in an unsurpassable asymmetry that characterizes and begins in the responsibility of the human subject.

DIFFERENCES: LEVINAS'S CRITIQUE OF SARTRE

Despite their many points of general agreement, Levinas remains in fundamental opposition to Sartre's philosophy. The titles alone of several of the subsections of Levinas's two major works are already objections to Sartre: "Transcendence is not Negativity," "Freedom Called into Question," "The Investiture of Freedom, or Critique," "Freedom Invested," in *Totality and Infinity;* and "Finite Freedom" and "The-One-for-the-Other is not Commitment," in *Otherwise than Being or Beyond Essence,* come to mind.[21] Just as I have presented only three of the many affinities that bring Levinas and Sartre close to one another, in the following I will focus on only three of Levinas's major criticisms of Sartre. For Levinas, contra Sartre: (a) The human subject does not ultimately aim for being but for the beyond-being; (b) Freedom is not pure, transparent, impregnable, a matter of consciousness alone, but embodied, vulnerable, or as Levinas expresses it, "created" and "difficult"; (c) the other person has priority—being "for-the-other" is higher, better, more excellent, and hence more genuinely oneself than being "for-oneself" (A fourth major point of disagreement would have to do with the notion of the "third").

No doubt Sartre's existentialism has had many critics. This is due in large measure to the artificial and abstract, indeed the Cartesian and procrustean character of his central opposition between being for-itself and being in-itself. Let us say, then, that this does not diminish the depth of Levinas's criticisms, nor their importance, and all the more so because Levinas is not merely a critic. His own positive philosophy, an ethical and social metaphysics, is able to articulate and accomplish what Sartre's existentialism cannot: an ethics of responsibility.

Metaphysical Desire versus Being for Being

The thesis of what is perhaps Levinas's first original philosophical publication, his 1935 article entitled "On Escape," is that the movements of the self which return to itself—whether praxis or theory—are not enough and cannot be enough to satisfy the deepest desire of subjectivity. According to the nuanced phenomenological studies presented in this article, the deepest desire of subjectivity is to get out, to be disburdened of itself, to escape the weight of being, of "ownness" itself, to experience a transcendence that does not and cannot return, to venture out on a one-way trip. The meticulous phenomenological investigations Levinas began in this article are refined and broadened from his first two books, *Time and the Other* and *Existence and Existents,* to his two major works, *Totality and Infinity* (especially Section II) and *Otherwise than Being or Beyond Essence.* These investigations show that the inaugural "hypostasis" of "separation" which establishes the existent in existence originates in a circuit of self-sameness, the sensuousness of the sensing of sensations ("enjoyment"), and remains within such circuits through several higher levels of self-constitution such as labor and possession, and representation and knowledge. But the inner desire of the existent is nevertheless not exhausted by these circuits of sensations, possessions and objects, however wide they may become, all the way to the higher levels of constitution that include scientific knowledge and world history. The inner desire of subjectivity, through all these constitutions of sense, altogether exceeds needs that can be satisfied.

Such a desire—a desire for what exceeds self-satisfaction—is what Levinas calls "metaphysical desire." In contrast to the self-interest inherent in the circuits of self-sameness, such a desire would be "disinterested." Yet its disinterest would not be that of knowledge and objectivity. The "objectifying" consciousness of knowledge, like he who wears Gyges's ring, operates as a pure spectator, the unseen and undisturbed onlooker of a world of pure objectivity. Such, in any event, is the ideal of objectivity, and such is also, as we have seen, the very structure of the Sartrean for-itself, which bestows meaning on the world but remains untouched by that world. Metaphysical desire, in contrast, seeks to break out of its own consciousness, to go beyond the known world by—however paradoxically—maintaining a relation with that which exceeds all relation, namely, transcendence. It is well known that for Levinas such a peculiar relation—a "relation without relation" (*rapport sans rapport*)[22]—is found not in representation and knowledge, but in the "face" of the other to whom the self is morally obligated. For Levinas, human subjectivity, while *originating* in structures of being for-itself (which are not, however, limited to "negation"), and rising via praxis and knowledge to higher cultural and spiritual levels of being for-itself, is neither ultimately nor exclusively limited to structures of return.

Obviously, then, both from the point of view of its *sensuous* origin, and even more importantly, from the point of view of its ultimate desire for *transcendence,* Levinas rejects Sartre's claim that human subjectivity is fully grasped as a negating, objectifying consciousness for-itself—a nonbeing or nothingness that aims for nothing other than being. It makes no difference, in this regard, that for Sartre the for-itself cannot be the being it aims to be. What matters, and where Levinas takes sharp exception, is Sartre's claim that the for-itself aims exclusively to be, to be in-and-for-itself, whether or not it can fulfill its aim. There can be no doubt, either, that this is Sartre's position. As Hazel Barnes has correctly emphasized in his introduction to his English translation of *Being and Nothingness:* "[T]he For-itself is a revelation of Being, an internal nihilation of Being, a relation to Being, a desire of Being, and a choice of Being."[23]

Even more succinctly, we note Sartre's title to his own introduction to *Being and Nothingness:* "The Pursuit of Being." "[B]eing," Sartre writes, "is the ever present foundation of the existent."[24] Indeed, Sartre dubs "the ontological proof" his claim that "consciousness is born *supported by* a being which is not itself."[25]

For Levinas, in striking contrast, at the heart of subjectivity lies not the desire to be (or not to be), but a desire for the beyond-being: "The metaphysical desire tends toward *something else entirely,* toward the *absolutely other*" (*TI* 33)." "To be or not to be," he writes, "is not the question where transcendence is concerned" (*OB* 3; cf. *EN* 132; *AT* 159–60). It is not that the self is devoid of for-itself structures, which Levinas calls "egoist," but rather that such structures do not plumb its true depths.

> Metaphysics therefore does not consist in bending over the "for-itself" of the I to seek in it the solid ground for an absolute approach to being. It is not in the "know thyself" that its ultimate movement is pursued—not that the "for itself" be limited or be of bad faith, but because by itself it is only freedom, that is, arbitrary and unjustified, and in this sense detestable; it is I, egoism. (*TI* 88)

With such terms as "only," "arbitrary," "unjustified," and "detestable," it is clear that Levinas has departed from the plane of ontology determined, as it always is, by the dyad of being and nonbeing. It is not being that the subject seeks; the subject is all too caught up in being. Rather it is the beyond being.

Difficult Freedom versus Absolute Freedom

What the previous citation shows is that for Levinas pure freedom, whatever its value for a self-reflective consciousness—for the "freedom of thought," that is to say—is not ultimate. To take the structure of such freedom as the very definition of subjectivity is to be neither objective nor neutral but, in its egoism, "detestable." It is detestable because, as Levinas has written, it is "arbitrary and unjustified." To understand this claim, we must turn to an important discussion, in *Totality and Infinity* of the significance of the *limitation* of freedom. It is here Levinas both criticizes Sartre and defends "created freedom" (*TI* 83). The argument hinges on a central distinction Levinas makes between two basic ways of interpreting the lack of justification and hence the arbitrary nature of freedom: either this limitation is understood as "failure" or it is undergone as "unworthiness."

"European thought," Levinas will say, has preferred to interpret the limitation of freedom as "failure." By doing so, however, "The spontaneity of freedom is not called into question; its limitation alone is held to be tragic and to constitute a scandal. Freedom is called into question only inasmuch as it somehow finds itself imposed upon itself: if I could have freely chosen my own existence everything would be justified" (*TI* 83).

The failure of freedom, in other words, is that it is not free enough! No doubt Heidegger's notion of *Geworfenheit*—"thrownness"—is meant here, for Dasein is said to be "guilty" not in any ordinary moral sense but rather because its authentic or resolute self-appropriation comes "too late." Always already determined by its historical situation, Dasein can never fully reappropriate itself from the bottom up. But Sartre also interprets the limitation of freedom as tragic failure, a "condemnation" to freedom. "I am condemned to be free," Sartre writes and explains: "This means that no limits to my freedom can be found except freedom itself or, if you prefer, that we are not free to cease being free."[26]

Elsewhere Sartre writes that the free human subject is "forlorn" because "he is without excuse."[27] The for-itself cannot become an object, cannot be a being for-itself-in-itself, cannot escape its freedom. To be sure, its failure is also its very freedom, but that is Levinas's point: Sartre interprets the limitation of freedom as failure—as "bad faith"—not unworthiness.

Despite the enormous differences which separate Sartre and Heidegger (because for Heidegger it is not the human subject who is free but rather being itself[28]), both thinkers conceive of freedom and its limitations in ontological terms. Levinas is all too aware of the inner relation between ontology and self-determining freedom: "Ontology," he writes, "which reduces the other to the same, promotes freedom—the freedom that is the identification of the same, not allowing itself to be alienated by the other" (*TI* 42). Sartre's being for-itself remains unperturbed, untroubled, one can even say complacent in its freedom, even in the face of the freedom of others. Whether it tries to submit to the other's objectifying gaze (the masochist for-itself) or tries to objectify and reduce away the freedom of the other (the sadist for-itself), the freedom of the for-itself remains completely uncompromised. The freedom of the for-itself is exclusively negative or, as Erich Fromm might express it, it is a "freedom from" being but not a "freedom to" become.[29] It is trapped ("condemned") in the purity of its always and forever unmotivated—"arbitrary and unjustified"—freedom.

For Levinas the problem with freedom is not that it fails to be freer. Can one even conceive of a human freedom freer than Sartrean freedom? Rather, the problem with freedom is precisely its spontaneous and unjustified character. The problem with freedom, in other words, is not ontological, not tragic, but moral. What is truly disturbing about the spontaneity of freedom is its capacity to do violence, to harm or even to kill others. Freedom unjustified is also the freedom to *murder*. The problem with freedom by itself, then, is not at all its failure to be freer, but rather its potential harm, its unworthiness.

Levinas's critique of freedom derives not from the isolated subject, or from being in relation to itself, but rather from the self in relation to the other person. Taken on their own, individual subjects or the whole of being are indeed free, or one might say they are never free enough. But when one begins with the other person, with a self in relation to the other, then the spontaneous freedom of the individual self becomes egoist, detestable, unworthy—put into question by the other. The other person is not simply an obstacle to my freedom, thinking which is once again to approach the limitation of freedom through ontology as if it were no more than a failure, an ontological shortcoming but not a moral issue. Instead, as Levinas writes:

> The first consciousness of my immorality is not my subordination to facts, but to the Other, to the Infinite. . . . The Other is not initially a *fact,* is not an *obstacle,* does not threaten me with death; he is desired in my shame. To discover the unjustified facticity of power and freedom one must not consider it as an object, not consider the Other as an object; one must measure oneself against infinity, that is, desire him. . . . [I]t is accomplished as shame, where freedom discovers itself murderous in its very exercise. (*TI* 83–84)

Freedom, in other words, is not its own justification, is not based solely on its own freedom. Rather, freedom is justified, to the extent that it is justified, only in relation to the other person before whom my freedom is secondary, subordinated to a moral service, the "wisdom of love": "Morality begins," Levinas writes, "when freedom, instead of being justified by itself, feels itself to be arbitrary and violent" (*TI* 84). Freedom unjustified is not failure; it is shameful.

To feel oneself ashamed of the spontaneity of one's own freedom in the face of the other is to appreciate the primacy not of the other's freedom, as if the other were reducible to consciousness, but of the other's suffering, the other's mortality, the other's needs. In this appreciation, ashamed of its capacity to hurt, the self is at the same time elected to its obligations to help the other person. In other words, the other and the self are not dueling negations, not battling pure activities of freedom, but vulnerabilities, flesh and blood beings with weaknesses and susceptibilities, in a relation which is from the first not a matter of being but of what is *otherwise than being or beyond essence,* the ethical. The other is not pure freedom but someone in need of shelter, clothing, food; someone requiring an education, a job, medical care; someone enjoying books, music, dance; someone with dignity worthy of respect; someone who along with all others should be accorded justice, the rule of law, recourse to courts, police protections, and so forth. These are not simply meanings invented by an aloof for-itself, but meanings and institutions whose sense ultimately derives from moral imperatives obligating the self—me—with responsibilities for the other and for all others, obligations and responsibilities of greater worth and impinging closer to myself than my freedom. Levinas writes:

> Existence is not in reality condemned to freedom, but is *invested* as freedom. Freedom is not bare. To philosophize is to trace freedom

back to what lies before it, to disclose the investiture that liberates freedom from the arbitrary. Knowledge as a critique, as a tracing back to what precedes freedom, can arise only in a being that has an origin prior to its origin—that is created. (*TI* 84–85)

The basic problem with Sartre's philosophy of freedom, then, is that despite its cleverness, "[f]reedom is not justified by freedom" (*TI* 303). Freedom is not an immaculate conception. It is justified, and requires to be justified by responsibility. Responsible freedom is more difficult than a freedom that can never be challenged; it is more demanding than a freedom that is forever choosing but is never chosen.

Being-for-the-Other versus the Evil Genius

Obviously, then, a sharp difference dividing Levinas and Sartre and the basis for Levinas's critique of Sartre, is that for Levinas it is the other person who has priority over the self, the other person who comes first. This priority has nothing to do with being or levels of understanding of being, with qualities or attributes, say, found in or achieved by the other person. From the first it is a moral priority, a moral imperative, a matter of ethics: the other person *obligates* the self; the self is *responsible* for the other—such is the asymmetrical relation whose priority lies at the root of all of Levinas's originality as a philosopher.

In a penetrating interview conducted by Richard Kearney, Levinas criticizes Sartre's adherence to ontology and his consequent inability to put into question the immanence or "sameness" of being, his inability, that is to say, to appreciate the *alterity* of the other person. Levinas says:

> I was extremely interested in Sartre's phenomenological analysis of the "other," though I always regretted that he interpreted it as a threat and degradation, an interpretation that also found expression in his fear of the God question.... In Sartre the phenomenon of the other was still considered, as in all Western ontology, to be a modality of unity and fusion, that is, a reduction of the other to the categories of the same. This is described by Sartre as a teleological project to unite and totalize the for-itself and the in-itself, the self and the other-than-self. It is here that my fundamental disagreement with Sartre lay.[30]

What Sartre could not see, blinded by his categories of being and nonbeing, was how to articulate and establish the primacy of ethics, the primacy, that is to say, of the other person.

For Levinas the human subject is not at bottom a being or a nothingness trapped in its "bad faith" (*mauvaise foi*), but rather the singular one—me, I, myself—who is elected in the face of the other, "invested." The human subject is a "creature" with vulnerabilities and susceptibilities, who rises above its animal vitality because exposed to the other, shamed, rises to its obligations, to "bad conscience" (*mauvaise conscience*), its insufficiency to the exigency of an infinite responsibility for the other, to be for-the-other before being for-oneself up to the point of being able to die for the other. As Adriaan Peperzak has well noted:

> Levinas opposes the idea that humanity can be defined by autonomy, because the term *autonomy* suggests easily the idea of a *causa sui*—a suggestion made into a thesis by Sartre's exaggeration of an existence choosing its own essence. The other reveals to me that the "essence" of the self is to be a subject in the accusative: not *I think, I see, I will, I want, I can*, but "*me voici*" (*Here I am*).... In the ethical "experience," the ego of *I think* discovers itself as an *I am obliged*.[31]

The priority of "I am obliged" over "I think" is not something that in its turn can be thought; it is rather responsibility taken on, enacted, performed, in and as the priority of the other person—"proximity and not truth about proximity" (*OB* 120). "No freedom, no commitment undertaken in a present, a present among others, recuperable, is the obverse of which this responsibility would be the reverse, but no slavery is included in the alienation of the same who is 'for the other'" (135). The primacy of the other signifies neither the other's mastery or sadism nor the self's slavery or masochism; it is rather my responsibility, my investiture as a moral self.

To make the structure of subjectivity "negation," as Sartre does, is simply to absolutize the dominant tradition of Western philosophy, namely, the primacy of cognition, thought, knowledge, intellect—"Western philosophy, which perhaps is reification itself" (*OB* 110).[32] Although, as we have seen in his article "Existentialism Is a Humanism," Sartre *claims* that the for-itself, in it absolute nonmotivated freedom, is responsible for all humanity, in fact the for-itself is responsible only for the *meaning* that it alone—each one alone, and each one is necessarily alone — gives to what after all is only and can only be its own projected sense of "humanity." Commenting on this failure, which is at the same time nothing less than an absolute imperialism, the totalitarianism of the ego, Theodore de Boer has noted:

> Exteriority can only appear within the circle of this sense-giving center. This is the reason why Levinas can also characterize existential phenomenology as a philosophy of the same. It is at the same time a philosophy of totality, because existence is the perspective point from which the world of experience is "totalized" (Sartre).[33]

For all its vaunted freedom, the being for-itself lives within an airtight bubble of its own meaning-bestowing, solipsist like a windowless monad. It has no contact and cannot have any contact with anything or anyone genuinely outside the reach of its own objectifying consciousness. But its solitude — one begins to think of it in psychological terms of delusion — is not benign because in fact we do live in a social world. Of this Levinas writes:

> [I]mperialism of the same is the whole essence of freedom. The "for itself" as a mode of existence designates an attachment to oneself as radical as a naïve will to live. But if freedom situates me effrontedly before the non-me in myself and outside of myself, if it consists in negating or possessing the non-me, before the Other it retreats.... [T]he Other imposes himself as an exigency that dominates this freedom, and hence as more primordial than everything that takes place in me. (*TI* 87)

Sartre's for-itself can choose, indeed it must choose, but because it never is and never can be chosen it is never responsible for what is not its own, much less for what is better — the other human being.

Sartre's being for-itself is an artificial and false intellectual abstraction, the absolute reification of the freedom of thought. At the same time Sartre's being in-itself, the obverse of being for-itself, is equally an artificial and false intellectual abstraction. While being-for-itself remains enclosed within an arbitrary prison of meaning of its own making, being-in-itself, in revenge, as it were, sinks into an abyss of equivocation. In a thesis that seems astonishing to a culture nurtured by philosophy and science, Levinas argues that the distinction — perhaps the most fundamental distinction of philosophy and science — between appearance and reality, or truth and falsehood, is itself a function of a deeper distinction between truth and lie, or sincerity and mendacity—a function of ethical significa- tion. Propositions about being and nonbeing, he argues, depend on being said, on a speaking or "saying" (*dire*), and hence on an inter- locutory relationship irreducibly characterized by an ethical asymme- try—"the veracity that is prior to the true" (*OB* 143). The argument, a transcendental one, runs as follows:

> [A] world absolutely silent that would not come to us from the word, be it mendacious, would be an-archic, without principle, without a beginning. Thought would strike nothing substantial. On first con- tact the *phenomenon* would degrade into *appearance* and in this sense would remain in equivocation, under suspicion of an evil genius. (*TI* 90)

This is precisely *what Sartre himself understood* as early as 1938, or at least it is what Antoine Roquentin discovers in that famous scene in *Nausea* where, transfixed by the root of a chestnut tree, he sees a "profusion of beings without origin," where "all these existents which bustled about this tree came from nowhere and were going nowhere," because "this veneer had melted, leaving soft, monstrous masses, all in disorder—naked, in a frightful, obscene nakedness," leaving a root that "*looked* like a color, but also . . . like a bruise or a secretion, like an oozing—and something else, an odor, for example."[34]

Because being in-itself is nothing more than what being for-itself projects, the projections of the for-itself, without anchor, collapse upon themselves, have no exigency or finality. "The 'for itself,'" Levinas writes, "closes in upon itself and, satisfied, loses all significa- tion; to him who approaches it, it appears as enigmatic as any other apparition" (*TI* 97). He continues: "In the *cogito* the thinking sub- ject which denies its evidences ends up at the evidence of this work of negation. . . . [I]t is a movement of descent toward an ever more profound abyss which we elsewhere have called *there is,* beyond affir- mation and negation" (93).

The for-itself and in-itself, linked only by negation, both end by sinking into an amorphous existence without existents. It is not negation that breaks this mystification, this enchantment and endless equivocation, but speech, speech between interlocutors, the other who speaks to me and to whom I respond. "Speech introduces a principle into this anarchy. Speech disenchants," Levinas continues, recalling one of Socrates' arguments in the *Phaedrus,* "for the speaking being guarantees his own apparition and comes to the assistance of himself, attends his own manifestation" (*TI* 98). The anchor of the very reality of the world, then, its being in contrast to its mere appearance, is not found in consciousness, and certainly not in a consciousness whose only relation to being is to project meanings upon its surface like a kaleidoscope. Rather, the difference between reality and appearance depends on a prior and more fundamental *orientation*—the asymmetry of the one-for-the-other, which Levinas appreciates in its ethical rather than ontological significance. "The world is *said* and hence can be a theme, can be proposed" (98).

The significance of being itself thus depends not on the freedom of the for-itself, which is finally lost in its own world of meaning independent of the others who in becoming objects are not even objects but masks, veneers, always "oozing—and something else." Rather the significance of being depends on the incarnate or created freedom—"the pneuma of the psyche" (*OB* 69)—that in its exposure to the other becomes inverted into a for-the-other "despite itself" (*malgré soi*) (51–53, 141). Only such a being—obsessed by the other before itself—can be "responsible for the freedom of others" (109), and in that responsibility become responsible for a world serving justice. Levinas writes:

> In opposition to the vision...of a freedom without responsibility, a freedom of play, we discern in obsession a responsibility that rests on no free commitment, a responsibility whose entry into being could be effected only without any choice.... It is the setting up of a being that is not for itself, but is for all, is both being and disinterestedness. The for itself signifies self-consciousness; the for all signifies responsibility for the others, support of the universe. (*OB* 116)

"Finite freedom" is thus not inconceivable, a misunderstanding of freedom, but an ethical proximity, an election to responsibility for the other first of all, and for the world in which all others live, a world which in the demand for justice attains its truth and its being. "Justice, society, the State and its institutions, exchanges and work are comprehensible out of proximity" (*OB* 159).

CONCLUSION

Sartre's notion of freedom—an unmotivated choosing based in consciousness, a freedom of thought interpreted in ontological terms, with ontology reduced to the purely abstract opposition of being and nonbeing—is guilty of what Levinas in one of his "talmudic readings" calls "the temptation of temptation,"

> the condition of Western man.... What tempts the one tempted by temptation is not pleasure but the ambiguity of a situation in which pleasure is still possible but in respect to which the Ego keeps its freedom, has not yet given up its security, has kept its distance. What is tempting here is the situation in which the ego remains independent.... What is tempting is to be simultaneously outside everything and participating in everything. The temptation of temptation is thus the temptation of knowledge.... Its starting point is an ego which, in the midst of engagement, assures itself a continual disengagement. (*NT* 34–35)

In critical contrast to such detached freedom, despite all its compensatory talk of "commitment" and "engagement," and to philosophy conceived as the free "love of wisdom," with its inherent and imperial but disavowed egoism, Levinas poses the priority of ethics, the "de-posing" of the egoist self in the "wisdom of love," a self exposed to the other before itself, responsible for-the-other prior to its own choices or choosing, in a "created" or "difficult freedom," a "mode of consent that cannot be reduced to the alternative freedom-violence" (*NT* 37), already chosen by the other—scandalous for philosophy, but better. "To be a self," Levinas continues, "is to be responsible beyond what one has oneself done" (49). The true self, always already responsible, chosen before choosing, is thus "hostage" to the other. "This condition (or uncondition) of hostage is an essential modality of freedom—its primary modality—and not an empirical accident of a freedom always remaining above it all" (50).

EIGHT

Some Reflections on Levinas on Shakespeare

A MEDITATION OF SHAKESPEARE

To link Emmanuel Levinas, twentieth century Jewish French philosopher of ethics, and William Shakespeare, sixteenth century Elizabethan dramatist and poet, is neither an idle fancy nor an arbitrary academic exercise. Even beyond a natural curiosity that wants to understand the links that bring together all spirits who are of the first rank, regardless of whatever differences in epoch, culture, station, language, and genre may separate them, there is in this case a special reason for making this conjunction. It is the unforgettable claim made by Levinas at the start of his own career in 1947, in *Time and the Other:* "[I]t sometimes seems to me," he declared, "that the whole of philosophy is but a meditation of Shakespeare" (*TO* 72).[1] Then, too, there is the no less memorable but more general claim made by Shakespeare, or rather, Shakespeare's Hamlet, (after being told by his "father's spirit" that his father did not die a natural death but was murdered) to his friend Horatio: "There are more things in heaven and earth, than are dreamt of in your philosophy." While Hamlet's claim is congruent with Levinas's, since both deny the usual self-proclaimed comprehensiveness and finality of philosophy, the claims are nevertheless asymmetrical. Hamlet's claim declares that philosophy is limited, a view oft expressed, especially in Western religious thought, while Levinas's claim, in contrast, determines the limit of philosophy as one that Shakespeare surpasses. Let us add that we have no doubt that for Levinas, Shakespeare is but one instance, and not the exclusive instance, of the surpassing of philosophy.

What is striking about Levinas's assertion is the combination of its universal quantification of philosophy, its grand reference to "the whole of philosophy," and its use of the possessive "of" to link philosophy to Shakespeare. What this means is not that all of philosophy is a meditation about Shakespeare, which by itself would already be a remarkable and thoughtworthy possibility, but rather that the whole of philosophy is a meditation *by* Shakespeare, Shakespeare's meditation. What Levinas is suggesting, then, is that Shakeseare — whatever is meant by "Shakespeare," and this is what we will have to investigate — subsumes philosophy, and not, as one might ordinarily suppose, that philosophy, which has always held itself out to be an account of the whole, and ideally as the whole account of the whole — subsumes Shakespeare. If by Shakespeare, he means, minimally, "great literature," and I think this is so, then what follows is that instead of philosophy being the truth of the art of literature, the art of literature would be the [. . .] the what? — this is our question — of philosophy. In any event, we must ask what is the meaning of this reversal of the personal and the impersonal? Not philosophy meditating on Shakespeare, but Shakespeare meditating on philosophy.

What can it mean for philosophy to be conceived as a Shakespearean meditation? Shakespeare lived and died before the birth of Kant, Hegel, Feuerbach, Marx, Bergson, Nietzsche, Husserl, and Heidegger. Does Levinas's statement mean, then, that philosophy ended before these thinkers? Levinas, who in the 1930s and 1940s introduced Husserl and Heidegger to twentieth century French thought, can hardly mean this. Does it not mean, more broadly and more decisively, that discursive or conceptual thought, contrary to the self-proclamations of philosophy, is subsumed by a more concrete dimension or element beyond discursive or conceptual thought, a dimension or element manifest in the world of Shakespearean drama and poetry? I think here lies the key to Levinas's statement. Philosophy lives in thought, in concepts, in knowledge, in "making the unequal equal," in the "life of the mind," while Shakespeare presents a world, an artistic rendition of the life-world in its unfinished, temporal, and dialogical character. It is a matter of closeness to the unique. A literary world, in contrast to a philosophical concept, does not simply refer but replicates — highlights — such characterizations as the one way directionality of time and history, or, more importantly, the exigencies of morality and justice. Truth lies in neither mute particularity nor abstract universality but in singularity, where particular and universal meet. In a word, Shakespeare's dramatic world is more *concrete* than philosophy's discursive universe. Merleau-Ponty correctly taught that philosophy does not surpass the world when it abstracts its truth, rather it reduces and eviscerates "the flesh of the world," the ambiguities of an always unfinished and always already ongoing discovery and construction of meaning.

Let us remember, too, that in its French context Levinas's use of the term "meditation" in a personal possessive construction has a specific resonance. To anyone versed in French culture, it directly calls to mind the famous *Meditations on First Philosophy* of René Descartes. And as a matter of historical fact, Shakespeare and Descartes were contemporaries. Descartes was twenty years old when Shakespeare died in 1616. Had he wanted, he could have attended the openings of *The Tempest* or *Henry VIII* in England. And yet, beyond an accident of chronology and geography, to link Shakespeare and Descartes is to juxtapose nearly opposite sensibilities: the rich humanist morality, the divine comedy of the dramatist and poet; the clear and distinct analytical epistemology, the geometrical method of the philosopher of science. In the estimation of French thought, and in numerous histories of European philosophy, Descartes is considered the greatest of French philosophers, the first modern philosopher, and sometimes even the greatest of all philosophers *tout court*. Whatever the appraisal of his reputation and status, Descartes is acknowledged to be the first modern philosopher, the first philosopher, that is to say, committed fundamentally to the calculus of a thoroughly mathematical science. In its intention, Descartes's meditation and method are "first philosophy" in the most profound modern sense. Descartes's philosophy would be a self-contained cogitation, truth thought from the ground up without any dependence external to intellect, autonomy, and absolute freedom in the strictest most rational sense (even if in certain respects Spinoza, Kant, and Hegel would more consistently carry out elements of Descartes's own intention). This digression from Shakespeare to Descartes is intended to indicate that Levinas's use of the phrase "meditation of Shakespeare" carries enormous philosophical weight, even more than might be imagined at first glance. Thus Levinas's claim that "the whole of philosophy is but a meditation of Shakespeare" gives incalculable philosophical prestige to Shakespeare and literature, and perhaps more broadly still to *poesis*.

Would philosophy then be a subset of art? Would truth, then, be a special case of lie, as Plato warns in the *Republic* and Nietzsche celebrates? Is Levinas's praise for Shakespeare the sign of his adherence to a long Western tradition of aesthetics, whether Bergsonian, Nietzschean, Heideggerian, or Deleuzean, to name only recent avatars of this tradition? No one can in good faith think that this is so. All of Levinas's thought stands against it. Which is to say all of Levinas's thought is a prolonged and profound defense of ethics as first philosophy. Indeed, *Time and the Other*, wherein Levinas articulates his extravagant claim regarding Shakespeare and philosophy, is already a work of ethical metaphysics. It is already a work that grounds labor, mortality, meaning, and time in social relations, and hence in morality, and ultimately in justice. Throughout his long philosophical career Levinas, with great subtlety and penetration, criticizes the irresponsibility of philosophies and worldviews devoted to the manifestation of being, in all its semantic and semiotic sophistication. Nevertheless, in the pursuit of this ethical task he will freely invoke literary works such as Dostoyevsky's *The Brothers Karamazov*, Vasily Grossman's *Life and Fate*, and Paul Celan's poems, not to mention an entire book—*On Maurice Blanchot* (cf. *PN* 127–70, 183–87)—on the novels of Maurice Blanchot. Philosophy, for Levinas, is certainly not a subset of art. And yet Levinas will find in literature, even more than in epistemological (including theology) or aesthetic theories and philosophies, the expression of the transcendence he insists must be approached under the sign of an ethics.

Levinas's recognition of the dangers of aestheticism occured early and decisively in his intellectual career. In 1948, shortly after the publication of his first two original philosophical works, *Time and the Other* and *Existence and Existents*, where Levinas refers to Shakespeare more often than any other time in his career, Levinas published his most sustained reflection on the meaning of art, an essay entitled "Reality and Its Shadow" (*LR* 129–43).[2] In that essay Levinas attacks the artwork as the mere shadow of reality, as a temporally frozen and semantically closed world unto itself. In a certain sense, then, art would be guilty of the same abstraction for which one might fault philosophy—abstraction from life, from ethical life. As if utilizing Bergson's philosophy *au rebours*, Levinas finds in art not an open, dynamic, fluid world but a closed, static, frozen one instead. Detached from the morality and justice that for Levinas make life and history serious, and hence irresponsible to its core, the telos of the artwork requires—for its own redemption—the supplement of recontextualization, the work of criticism. And every reader is a critic, a commentator, and an exegete, in a word, an interpreter. Rather than becoming lost in the warp and woof of its internal relations, the critic reweaves the isolated artwork into what Levinas will later call "sacred history," the world historical work—whether seen or unseen, known or unknown, recorded or unrecorded—of morality and justice. To read is to translate. But to translate is not to betray but to redeem. The reader must outwit the essential betrayal of the work of art, the silence and impersonality about which Socrates warned in the *Phaedrus*.

True, in this early essay Levinas may have reduced all art to a mythic dimension, and hence to that morally regressive manner of being—participation in being—which he will later criticize, and see in Judaism, in particular, a religion against myth and mythic consciousness. In this case one might think contra Levinas that myth is not co-extensive with the whole of art. But then again, maybe it is. Maybe there is a way of approaching or understanding art whereby art takes the role, the place otherwise occupied by myth. Perhaps, that is to say, without the work of criticism, without a critical reinsertion of the artwork within the exegesis of morality, art becomes myth, idolatry, return to animality. A critic as sensitive as Nietzsche, in any event, was explicit on this point, writing about the irrepressible theories of "art for art's sake," he declares (in his usual clever manner): "The struggle against purpose in art is always a struggle against the moralizing tendency in art, against the subordination of art to morality. *L'art pour l'art* means: 'the devil take morality!'"[3] Lionel Trilling makes this point more positively: "Literature doesn't easily submit to the category of aesthetic contemplative disinterestedness—so much of it insists '*De TE fabula*—this means you,' and often goes on to say, 'And you'd better do something about it quick.'"[4]

In the expansion of the artwork beyond itself effected by criticism, Levinas—already in his early essay of 1948—is pointing to a process whereby art and philosophy are joined together and uplifted through what I have elsewhere called "ethical exegesis."[5] The idea of a self-contained artwork, like the apparently opposite idea of a literal meaning, are illusory, mythic. The literary work and the work of commentary are inseparable. Of course, one can distinguish literature from criticism, just as one can distinguish both from scientific treatises, but all signification relies ultimately on the larger context of an interhumanity whose significance is not merely a matter of signs referring to things or to other signs. The literary-interpretive enterprise, in other words, is inseparable from the human. Inseparable from the human, it is inseparable from the humanity—humaneness, humanism—of the human. Like all significations, then, literature is inseparable from an ethical context.

This suggests the answer to our question: In what sense is "the whole of philosophy" a "meditation of Shakespeare." Or to rephrase the question in light of our reflection above: In what sense is the truth philosophy claims to love—wisdom—found in Shakespeare, Dostoyevsky, Grossman, Celan, and others? Answer: literature is closer to the humanity of the human, to the transcendence constitutive of the ethical category of the human, than are the abstract reflections of philosophy. What is the difference? Not that every novel is moral and every philosophy is immoral. Not at all. Levinas's ethical metaphysics is not reducible to a moralism. It is not at all driven by an omniscient and hence pretentious self-righteousness as was, for example, the officially approved "socialist realism" of the Soviet Union in the twentieth century under and after Stalin. Rather, it is the texture of literature, its "life"—excepting those instances when art slavishly apes the theoretical perspective of a philosophy, such as the "new French novel" of the 1960s[6]—that is thicker, closer, "truer," to the ethical exigencies, to the obligations and responsibilities, the imperatives of social life, than is philosophy. What Levinas says of the world of talmudic disputation is no less true of the world of Shakespearean drama: "faithful to the Real, refractory to the System" (*OS* 130).

I want to emphasize the moral dimension in Shakespeare. Shakespeare is not a moralist, in the sense that like Aesop each tale must have its lesson, or that crime is always punished and virtue always rewarded (*Hamlet* belies any such notions). Rather, because in his literature one finds at play the tension, the drama of good and evil, their contention, the play of conscience, dastardly betrayal, noble self-sacrifice, moral ambivalence, and the like. It is important to emphasize this point, because the thickness, the vividness, the reality of Shakespeare's world has long been remarked. "*The Complete Works of William Shakespeare* could as soon be called *The Book of Reality*,"[7] is how Harold Bloom has recently put this point. What I want to emphasize in contrast to the admiration expressed by Bloom and many other Shakespeare scholars before him for the concretude or reality of Shakespeare's world,[8] is the even deeper link that binds the true to the good. What makes for the much-admired concretude or reality or "understanding" of Shakespeare's world, what brings his characters to life beyond caricature, is, Levinas would say, the moral dynamic that drives intersubjectivity, the worldliness of the world, and any account, scientific or otherwise, of these. Here, then, the Shakespearean scholar Alfred Harbage was right to link the vividness of Shakespeare's characters not only to the detail or accuracy of their descriptive portraits or contexts, but more specifically to the concretude of their ideality. It is not an abstract moral sentimentality Harbage and Levinas find and honor in Shakespeare, but the drama of men and women with concrete moral (or immoral) aspirations, achievements, and failings.[9] And it is precisely this that Levinas values in all the great literatures of the world, and what permits him to speak of such literature in terms of the "religious" category of prophecy: "Can one not read Plato as a Bible, or other great texts where humanity has acknowledged a testimony to the Infinite? . . . There is a participation in Holy Scripture in the national literatures, in Homer and Plato, in Racine and Victor Hugo, as in Pushkin, Dostoyevsky or Goethe, as of course in Tolstoy or in Agnon" (*EI* 116–17).[10] And as of course, "there is participation in Holy Scripture"—"testimony to the Infinite"—in Shakespeare too.

Though appreciative of certain insights based in creativity as understood by Bergson and Heidegger, Levinas is not suggesting that philosophy, the search for truth, or reality, its "object," is in a fundamental sense a form of art, a creative production. He is not proposing, therefore, that the basic task of philosophy, whether symbolic or conceptual, is epistemological or ontological, to expose or uncover [Heidegger's *entdecken, aufdecken, unverdect*] what is hidden in the manifestation of manifestation. Nor is Levinas endorsing the slightly more modest claim of Hegel, that philosophy and art, though distinct in kind, each in its own way says the same thing, the absolute, which art expresses in images and philosophy in concepts. Levinas's objection to aesthetics derives not simply from an opposition to the frozen shadow world of representational art, but more profoundly from his appreciation for what the frozen world of art leaves out. To be swept away in an enthusiasm for the aesthetic, for the manifestation of the manifest, for the show of what is, is at the same time to evade the exigencies of moral obligations and responsibilities. Levinas opposes what he understands to be the downward movement of an aesthetic worldview because it is irresponsible or is conducive to irresponsibility. Thus Levinas opposes what he sees to be the necessarily sentimental and escapist dimension of the aesthetic, its artful illusions. For art can just as easily serve evil as good. And if it serves only itself—"art for art's sake"—it sooner or later serves evil. The beautiful—like nature, like being—is indifferent to the good.[11] The great verisimilitude of Shakespeare, as of all the great literatures, making them all prophecy and revelation, "biblical" in this sense, is not that they present philosophies, quests for the truth of being, but rather, and more broadly, because they present human worlds, that they depict and animate "characters" with character—the humanity of the human—driven by the higher and more pressing imperatives of morality and justice.

We must take seriously, still, Levinas's opposition to the fascist inclination—whether avowed or, as is more usual and ordinary, hidden—of all aestheticism. There is a certain "devil may care" attitude of indifference built into the self-circuits of all art. It is precisely the imitative—or referential—connection of art's artificial world to the real world, fortified by the critic that is severed by the telos or work of the artwork itself. Picasso's "Guernica" is perhaps intended to remind us of the horrors of war, but it is also a painting with its own internal values, its own color scales, its own formal relationships. From an alleged reference to horror one easily shifts into a purely aesthetic mode of appreciation for the artwork itself. Good and evil are defused by purely formal qualities of art appreciation. It is certainly something like this that in 1934 Levinas included and denounced in "the philosophy of Hitlerism," about which he warned: "More than a contagion or a madness, Hitlerism is an awakening of elementary sentiments."[12] Levinas's opposition to the moral vagaries and temptations of a purely sentimental sociality, permits us to better appreciate what is at stake in his own thought: its ethical height. The "more than philosophy" found in Shakespeare is a dimension of the human irreducible to any theory of "art for art's sake," to aestheticism, to an "attunement" (again we think of Heidegger: *Befindlichkeit, Gestimmheit,*

Gellasenheit) to the manifestation of manifestation. What Levinas is saying is that in Shakespeare, in the world of Shakespeare, as in the work of other great writers, in other great literatures—the world of Plato, the "ocean" of the Talmud—one finds depicted that fundamental moral exigency that constitutes the very humanity of the human.

Beneath the artificial identities, the constructed identities of reason and aesthetics, lies the fundamentally moral "non-identity" of morality: the one-for-the-other before being for-itself. If we name "wisdom" that worldview that is greater than knowledge—whether scientific or sentimental—then it is wisdom to recognize that what is most significant in the concrete significations of the real, the very "signification of signification," is in the first instance an ethical rather than an ontological imperative. What is most real "is" paradoxically what exceeds the real, what "is" more pressing than the real.[13] But this excess is not ontological but ethical, and as such "otherwise than being or beyond essence." It is no "is" at all, but an "ought." It is the surplus of moral exigency above and beyond all the masks of being, whether the latter be conceived in terms of an essentially conservative *conatus essendi* or alternatively in terms of an expanding *wille zur macht*. "'To be or not to be,'" Levinas once wrote, "is that the question?" No, he answers: the genuine question is not contained in the alternative of being and nonbeing, but in the deeper, more profound, more troubling question of one's right to be—rectitude, righteousness, justice. What Levinas seeks, then, and finds in great literature—as the very greatness of a literature—is a world whose veritable concretude comes neither from epistemological nor ontological considerations alone, but from the greater exigencies of moral responsibility, of one's obligations to another and to all others. These are the exigencies and this is the world—what Coleridge, in his 1818 *Essays and Lectures on Shakespeare,* called "Keeping at all times in the high road of life"[14]—that drive Shakespeare's drama, making his characters lifelike and large at the same time, and enabling his world to challenge our own to this very day.

While the whole of philosophy may be Shakespeare's meditation, to the extent that what Shakespeare animates are the moral pressures of a life world, meditating on Shakespeare is nevertheless not the whole of Levinas's philosophy. It is not even a large or sustained part of it. Very little of Levinas's philosophical reflections concern Shakespeare, or, for that matter, any other literary figure. This contrasts sharply with the focus of many of his contemporaries, for instance Albert Camus and Jean-Paul Sartre. Sartre, though recognized as the author of many abstract conceptual works, was certainly no less well known as the author of numerous novels, stories, and plays, lengthy critical volumes on such literary figures as Genet and Flaubert, and not to mention his own extensive autobiography. The same can hardly be said of Levinas's oeuvre: no novels, plays, or poems, and only a five page intellectual autobiography. While in his philosophical works Levinas never entirely neglects literary figures, he refers or alludes to them far less than to other philosophers—and almost every sentence Levinas writes contains a reference or an allusion to one or more figures from Western spiritual history. Fragments taken from Shakespeare's plays appear and are analyzed only in Levinas's earliest philosophical writings. Levinas uses these exegetical opportunities, as we have seen, to bring to life certain "phenomenological" insights.[15] Shakespeare is hardly visible, however, in *Totality and Infinity* and *Otherwise than Being*. This does not, however, prevent Levinas in 1981 from summing up his critique of ontology in relation to his defense of justice in the following way: "To be or not to be—this is probably not the question *par excellence*."[16]

True to his precise word, then, it is only "sometimes" (*parfois*) that Levinas chooses to explicate his own thought by means of lessons derived from the dramatic universe of Shakespeare. But the limited number of references made specifically to Shakespeare does not undermine the broader and deeper point of Levinas's claim. An artwork—like the face of the other which signifies as a "signification without context" (*EI* 86)—stands by itself, and hence is "exotic, without a world" (*OB* 41). But it must be awakened from its own slumber, awakened by criticism, interpretation, exegesis. Indeed, the artwork, for Levinas, is at its best nothing less than a "call for exegesis" (41). The "success" of its call—the "greatness" of a great literature—comes both from the integrity and insight of the exegete, to be sure, but no less from the "thickness," the amplitude, the "life," of the artwork's artificial world. One can comment on a comic book or a can of Campbell's soup, but the weight of such commentary lies nearly transparently on the shoulders of the exegete, and hence the "accusation" of subjectivism. To comment on Shakespeare, Dostoyevsky, or the Bible, in contrast, requires that the exegete listen as much as speak—it is like breathing on hot embers (Levinas invokes this talmudic image of rabbinical hermeneutics) to bring out their potential heat and light (not just light, but heat also—it can burn!). Shakespeare's world—like the world of Dostoyevsky, Plato, or the Bible—is a very rich world indeed.

The concrete "literary" *world* to which Levinas's ethical exegesis is primarily dedicated, however, is not that of Shakespeare, Dostoyevsky, or even the Bible. Rather it is the Talmud, the "Oral" Torah (*Torah she-b'al peh*), given, according to Jewish tradition, to Moses and the Jewish people at Mount Sinai, the Jewish "new testament" which to this day continually renews the Jewish people. The world of talmudic Judaism, began in the conversations, discussions, arguments, explanations, tales and anecdotes of the rabbis of the *Mishna* and *Gemara* (the "classic" Talmud, circa 200 B.C.E. to 500 C.E.), but also and no less in the long and unbroken tradition of learned commentary that followed from these early texts and continues to this day.[17] It is in this "world," a world of relentless but committed interrogation, "not an obedience but a hermeneutic" (*EI* 116), where for Levinas "God is real and concrete" (*DF* 145). For Levinas—"for me" he would say—it is in the drama and dialogue of the Talmud, its narrative or *aggadic* dimension (rather than its legal or *halachic* dimension), far more than in the works of Shakespeare or Dostoyevsky, that he finds and enters into an engaged reflection on the nuances of moral life. The world of the Talmud, the discourse—the "oral Torah"—of Judaism, is a world not because it reveals the being of beings, the truth of being, but more profoundly, and with greater urgency, because it is permeated and elevated by a extremely subtle reflection on the innermost workings of ethical imperatives as humans understand and live them—and not merely cogitate them—in order to rise to their proper humanity. The Talmud is a world because its element is not simply knowledge, the world as object, but wisdom, and its correlate, an inspired world. Levinas's thought is also such a wisdom and like the Talmud itself it engages critically with the discourse of its times, including the long history of philosophical discourse.

Levinas's thought is not simply imbued with a vague "rabbinical" or "talmudic" flavor, the sort of thing that secondary scholarship often thoughtlessly attributes to thinkers who happen to be born Jewish, especially when such thinkers happen to treat Jewish themes.[18] There is nothing, after all, exclusively Jewish about ethics.

No doubt it is true that Levinas's thought is true to Jewish tradition and Jewish sources, and this says a great deal. But what is incontestably true is that Levinas has commented profoundly, and commented sympathetically and not merely "critically," on talmudic texts. In close commentaries on specific passages taken from the various tractates of the Talmud, Levinas renews an ancient but perennial wisdom by bringing it to bear upon the profound questions—of technology, education, youth, urbanization, secularization, and so on—of our day. These textual treatments now appear in several volumes in English translation.[19]

Elsewhere in his "Jewish" or "confessional" writings Levinas freely cites and comments on other biblical and talmudic passages. He will not hesitate to reach into the depths of Jewish "sacred" writings—into the *yeshiva,* into Jewish learning—to comment on certain statements and texts by such "authoritative" figures in Jewish religious tradition as Rabbi Moses ben Maimon ("Maimonides") or Rabbi Hayyim of Volozhin. But unlike Paul Ricoeur, for instance, who explicitly divorces his confessional Christian writings from his universal philosophical writings, for Levinas no such divorce can be true either to religion or to philosophy as a love of wisdom. There is a strict coherence and continuity between the exegetical writings of Levinas primarily focused on Jewish sources and the philosophical writings of Levinas primarily oriented by the language of philosophy and Western culture. This does not, however, and this is the important point, *diminish the universal import of Levinas's thought.* It neither compromises the conceptual rigor of knowledge for the sake of a partisan and parochial particularity, nor does it compromise the concrete traditions of religion for the sake of an abstract and detached universality. To the contrary, Levinas's philosophy—ethical metaphysics—forces us to rethink the nature of universality. It forces us to rethink the nature of universality by reminding us of the inextricable link joining the universal to the particular in the singularizing imperatives of the ethical. To grasp this point is to understand why and how philosophy, for Levinas, can be no less a meditation of (and on) Shakespeare, or a meditation of (and on) the talmudic rabbis, than a meditation of (and on) Plato. Here, perhaps, lies the greatest originality of Levinas's new conception of philosophy.

As I have indicated, Levinas's talmudic readings do not present theses at variance with those found elaborated in his philosophical books proper. Levinas's thought, though it has developed in its elaboration over time, is a seamless unity. Not the artificial and forced unity of a System, to be sure, but the unity of the priority of the appeal of the good over the true and the beautiful. Even Levinas's method—phenomenological to the point of ethical rupture[20]—remains basically the same in his talmudic readings in relation to his philosophical works, though perhaps their emphasis is more directly ethical. He certainly nowhere relies on "proof texts" or "religious experience" to establish the validity of his thought. His work neither begins nor ends in blind faith or dogmatic adherence. Rather, it operates by breaking through the origin of thinking to the more radical beginning of moral obligation and responsibility. It ends through and above the morality of the face-to-face in the "utopian" social call of justice, a call that is no less, for Levinas, than the witness to God's "presence" on earth, "and does not rest on any positive theology" (*OB* 147). Indeed, all of Levinas's writings—from his philosophy books, philosophy articles, to essays on Judaism, and talmudic readings—express an "ethical metaphysics," an ethical exegesis, that is to say, "a difficult wisdom concerned with truths that correlate to virtues" (*DF* 275). It is this difficult wisdom—this call of the Infinite—that Levinas finds in all the great literatures of the world.

SHAKESPEAREAN READINGS

Before concluding with a few schematized observations regarding the broad issue of the relation of universality to particularity from an ethical point of view, let us first (all too) briefly review the specific insights Levinas finds in his early philosophical writings—*Time and the Other* and *Existence and Existents*—in Shakespeare.

In *Time and the Other* scenes from Shakespeare's plays are introduced three times. In the first of its four parts (*TO* 50), and first in order of appearance, Levinas invokes specific scenes and lines from *Macbeth, Hamlet,* and *Romeo and Juliet,* to support two of his positions regarding the meaning of death. Contesting the opinion Albert Camus expressed in *The Myth of Sisyphus* in 1942,[21] and then again, later and more fully in 1951 in *The Rebel,*[22] which celebrates the power given to the individual by virtue of the possibility of suicide, Levinas will argue that the oblivion and hence the power allegedly promised by suicide are in fact uncertain. The second point of Levinas's account of death, this time contesting Heidegger's well known notion of "being-toward-death" [*Sein zum Tode*], as found in *Being and Time,* is the claim—reminiscent of the Stoics and Epicureans—that the approach of death is, until its final arrival, forever only an approach. Thus, far from being the principle of individuation it is for Heidegger, the living, in relation to a death that never arrives, live in a time of "postponement," always leaving room, however desperate, for more life. Death, as one old American blues song has it, is always "too quick."[23]

The second appearance of Shakespeare, at the beginning of the second part of *Time and the Other,* is more general. Levinas invokes "[t]he buffoon, the fool of Shakespearean tragedy" (*TO* 59), to distinguish madness, as one limited response to life's existential anxieties, from the more common and more practical responses to the same existential anxieties. Again, as with his earlier interpretation of the meaning of suicide and death, Levinas invokes Shakespeare as part of his challenge to certain well known, but rather extreme positions regarding the significance of anxiety that were trumpeted in Parisian intellectual circles in the 1940s.

Third and finally, Levinas returns to an analysis of *Macbeth,* to the scene of Macbeth's immanent death at the hands of Macduff, to again find support for his earlier thesis—contra Heidegger—regarding the ever impending yet never arriving character of death for the living (*TO* 72–73).

In all three instances, let us note straightaway, Shakespeare is not invoked as a "proof text." The authority of Shakespeare does not prove or cinch an argument. Rather, it lends credibility—owing to the depth and verisimilitude of Shakespeare's world—to Levinas's account of the meaning of such "things" as suicide, death, and anxiety. Nor, then, do these invocations of Shakespeare simply illustrate or serve as examples of an argument whose force could otherwise be completely independent of the sort of existential situations—the drama—found in a writer such as Shakespeare. Other "literary" works could have been invoked. By now we should be clear on this point: for Levinas the prophetic dimension of speech is not confined to the Bible or to any favored literature, national or otherwise (gender, class, etc.). Shakespeare's dramatic situations serve Levinas as both existential illustrations and confirmations of the theses for which Levinas "argues" in his phenomenological-ethical philosophy. In his prize-winning book, *The Theory of Intuition in Husserl's Phenomenology*, Levinas recalls a "paradoxical" thought Husserl enunciated in paragraph seventy of the first book of *Ideas*. "'Fiction is the vital element of phenomenology as well as all other eidetic sciences'" (*TTI* 141). Levinas's truth claims are at no point detachable from the context of their validation, the human situation and conditions that are part and parcel of their meaning. Meaning is ideal in this sense, that it must remain open to reconfirmation or disconfirmation by continual referral to the intuitive context that originally confirmed its meaning. And thus, too, philosophical truths—essences—are found exhibited in writings that also capture—depict, represent, show—the central and revealing conditions and situations of our humanity, as do the dramas of Shakespeare. This in no way reduces phenomenology-ethics ("ethical metaphysics," according to Edith Wyschogrod's felicitous title)[24]—and therefore philosophy—to a literary enterprise. Neither does it suggest that truth is fiction, hence merely relative. These extreme formulations are merely the irrepressible claims of a sophism forever seduced by intellectual abstraction. Rather, Levinas here underlines the fact that the concretude and creativity involved in imagination—the domain of literature—is also and inextricably linked to philosophy's task of achieving truth and conceptual clarity.[25] In other words, concepts, ideas, truth, essences, are all made clearer when they stand in relation to the context of concrete significations that do not obscure but are part of and give rise to their very significance. "Here," says Levinas, continuing the above citation, "is one of the most laborious tasks of phenomenology" (141).

Turning to Levinas's second early philosophical work, *Existence and Existents*, Shakespeare appears in a two-page discussion of death and nothingness (*EE* 61–62). Levinas invokes, first, the "spectors, ghosts, sorceresses," the darkness of night, and death, in both *Hamlet* and *Macbeth* (62). From the latter tragedy he recalls, more specifically, the famous scene with the three witches wherein Banquo's ghost appears to Macbeth (Act IV, Scene 1), to speak about what Levinas calls "the fatality of irremissible being" (61). This latter is a crucial dimension of signification (or nonsignification) that Levinas labels the "there is" (*il y a*), a fundamental stratum and manner of prepredicative being that Levinas finds defended by Bergson, but not recognized by Hegel· or Sartre (61–63). Characterizing the "there is" as "a decisive experience of the 'no exit' from existence" (62),

Levinas is clearly alluding to the wartime play of the same name by Sartre, whose philosophy of absolute freedom (*néant*) and absolute being (*l'être*) Levinas always criticized for its abstraction. Levinas cites several lines of Macbeth including one that specifically includes the word "shadow"—"Hence horrible Shadow, unreal mockery hence"—a term central to Levinas's 1948 article on art, "Reality and its Shadow." At the conclusion of his two-page commentary on Shakespeare, in a footnote Levinas writes: "*Thomas l'Obscure*, by Maurice Blanchot, opens with the description of the *there is*" (63). Levinas's use of literature and his references to literary works could hardly be more in evidence. Even the Greek tragedians appear, again with regard to the "there is": "This return of presence in negation, this impossibility of escaping from an anonymous and incorruptible existence, constitutes the final depths of Shakespearean tragedy. The fatality of the tragedy of antiquity becomes the fatality of irremissible being" (61). It is clear that literature, for Levinas, is capable of far more than the presentation of a parallel but slightly deficient version of an absolute truth that can only be found in its purity and glory in the "pure" Concept, as it is for Hegel. Rather literature—in its concretude, its verisimilitude, its moral drama—provides the always necessary "shadow" or preface of truth, the impact of the transcendence of an exigency—the humanity of the human—that wisdom keeps continually on the alert, in a wakefulness, a vigilance, whose very animation comes by way of philosophical commentary. In these two pages devoted to Shakespeare in *Existence and Existents*, in any event, we find Levinas discovering the "there is" already in Shakespeare. Thus Shakespeare has already grasped and presented in his own way what Levinas grasps and presents philosophically as the foundation—or the nonfoundation—of signification.

Levinas invokes Shakespeare with marked less frequency subsequent to these first two books published shortly after WWII. He occasionally refers to Shakespeare, to figures in his plays, even to certain well known Shakespearean lines, but the references are for the most part made in passing or repeat ideas already elaborated in relation to Shakespeare in *Time and the Other* and *Existence and Existents*. For instance, to take a relatively late reference, in *Totality and Infinity*, Levinas invokes *Macbeth*, but as in *Time and the Other*, it is in order to understand the meaning of the limitations of suicide and the exteriority of death (*TI* 231). In 1972, the apothem Levinas selects to precede the preface to his collection entitled *Humanism of the Other* is taken from Shakespeare's *King Lear* (IV, 7): "I should e'en die with pity to see another thus" (*HO* 3). This citation recalls a central theme of Levinas's ethics, namely, "substitution," the exigency of moral agency whereby one's suffering becomes suffering for the suffering of others. But beyond this apothem, there is no mention or discussion of Shakespeare in the text of this collection. To take an early reference, indeed perhaps the earliest: Shakespeare's name appears as one possible existentialist (along with Kierkegaard, Pascal, and Socrates), in passing, in 1937, in a published letter on Jean Wahl's *Short History of Existentialism*.[26] In the introduction to his first collection of talmudic readings, published in 1968, Levinas distinguishes his own sympathetic or committed exegetical approach from the objectifying and externalizing discourse of critical science as follows:

> Our first task is therefore to read it [the talmudic text] in a way that respects its givens and its conventions, without mixing in the questions arising for a philologist or historian to the meaning that derives from its juxtapositions. Did audiences in Shakespeare's theatre spend their time showing off their critical sense by pointing out that there were only wooden boards where the stage sign indicated a palace or a forest? (*NT* 5)

But most of Levinas's other references to Shakespeare occur in the same general time period as *Time and the Other* and *Existence and Existents*. Shakespeare is mentioned once in an article of 1947 on the writings of Marcel Proust, entitled "The Other in Proust." There, Levinas characterizes Proust as

> the analyst of a world of preciosity and artificiality, a world frozen in history, caught up in conventions more concrete than reality itself; a world that (remarkably) offers its inhabitants, by its very abstractions, those dramatic and profound situations that, in a Shakespeare or a Dostoyevsky, probed the humanity of man. (*PN* 99–100)

More important, Shakespeare is twice mentioned in Levinas's most extended discussion of art, "Reality and Its Shadow."[27]

Finally, and perhaps only to round out this account, Levinas mentions Shakespeare in one of his very few autobiographical remarks, in this case made on French radio in early 1981. When asked about the "the first great books encountered, Bible or the philosophers?" Levinas concluded his response by going between the horns of this question:

> But between the Bible [encountered as a child] and the philosophers [encountered at university], the Russian classics—Pushkin, Lermontov, Gogol, Turgenev, Dostoyevsky and Tolstoy, and also the great writers of Western Europe, notably Shakespeare, much admired in Hamlet, Macbeth and King Lear. (*EI* 22)

What are we to conclude fmm these various invocations found throughout Levinas's writings—from Levinas's remarkable statement regarding philosophy as a meditation of Shakespeare, from the several general and specific references to Shakespeare in *Time and the Other* and *Existence and Existents*, as well as from the various shorter references and allusions to Shakespeare in other of Levinas's writings, including his autobiographical testimony? At the very least it is clear that in the mid to late 1940s, when he was first formulating his own original philosophy of ethical metaphysics, Levinas recognized and was impressed by the profundity—at once philosophical and ethical—of Shakespeare's "literary" world, most especially *Hamlet* and *Macbeth*. More broadly, however, Levinas's comments and his short commentaries manifest the truth of his claim that the ethical elevation of humanity and hence of discourse itself—its prophetic or revelatory dimension, the height of the good that is the ultimate significance of signification—are not exclusively limited to a canonized "sacred text" such as the Bible (whether Christian, Jewish, or the Koran). This means, too, that the ethical height which defines the human—which Levinas will in the end call the "holy"—is not limited exclusively to the Talmud or to philosophy, which are clearly the two sorts of endeavor which together constitute Levinas's preferred world of discourse. But, and this is the conclusion we draw, even more broadly, the elevating exigencies of an ethical metaphysics find their full expression in a Shakespeare as they can find their proper articulation in all the world's great literatures.

Only slightly less formally, we can also conclude that what permits Levinas's appreciation for Shakespeare, as for Don Quixote, Plato, the Talmud, etc., is his conception of a universality based not in epistemology or ontology but in the singularizing exigencies of morality and justice. The "unique" is not the particular that escapes the grasp of the universal, but the singular called to respond to the suffering of the other and out of this appeal and response to rise to the call of justice and hence to engage in redemptive history. Such universality rooted in the unique singularity of each moral agent at the same time cannot be reduced to its historical situation. The morally singularized individual—me, I, "here I am" (*me voici, hineni*)—is both engaged in the concrete exigencies of the moment, the suffering of the other, and, driven by these same moral obligations by a justice that demands that even history must be judged.

Careful to avoid the abstract and hence depersonalizing universality of modern Rationalist or Enlightenment thought, neither is Levinas's conception of a universality bound to singularity, growing out of singularity, the "concrete universality" of Hegel, whose notion of "historic" individuality remains in the final analysis that of being a node or locus of abstract universals heedless of the particular. Nor, finally, is the singular universality of Levinas's ethical metaphysics—the face-to-face, the call of justice—another version of all those pretended universalisms—those One Churches and Final States—that at bottom are but militant particularisms heedless of the rights of all other particularities. Singular universality—one responding to the other—stands in opposition to the pretended universality achieved at the high price of an exclusivity, of a parochialism masking its own finitude through a more or less ruthless totalitarian magnification and obliteration of difference.

Rather, the manner in which philosophy is a meditation of Shakespeare, is precisely philosophy beholden to the higher exigencies of an ethical "way" that finds its concrete expression in the non-substitutable responsibilities and obligations of the one-for-the-other, in the infinite responsibility of each for each and for all. Or, as Levinas often expresses this point, invoking the words of Dostoyevsky in *The Brothers Karamozov:* "We are all guilty of all and for all men before all, and I more than the others" (cf. *EI* 98, 101).

NINE

Defending Levinas

Interview with Chung-Hsiung (Raymond) Lai

NOVEMBER 9, 2007

Lai: I still remember when we met at the international conference on Levinas at Purdue University last year. You gave a plenary address on "The Reception of Levinas in the States," so perhaps you could first briefly tell us about what is the reception of Levinas in general in the States?

Cohen: The first step in Levinas's reception depended on the translation by Alphonso Lingis of Levinas's major work, *Totality and Infinity*. This appeared in 1969, just eight years after the original French edition. Duquesne University Press put out a beautiful paperback edition with large margins on every page; I still have my copy. Then Levinas's *The Theory of Intuition in Husserl's Phenomenology* appeared in 1973, translated by André Orianne. *Existence and Existence* and *Otherwise than Being or Beyond Essence,* both also translated by Lingis, appeared in 1978 and 1981, respectively. The latter, *Otherwise than Being,* is of course Levinas's second masterpiece. My translation of Levinas's important article, "God and Philosophy," appeared in the journal *Philosophy Today* in the summer of 1978. And my translation of *Time and the Other,* published by Duquesne University Press, appeared a few years later in 1987. My collection of secondary writings on Levinas, *Face to Face with Levinas,* including such thinkers as Maurice Blanchot, Theodore de Boer, Jean-François Lyotard, Jan de Greef, Adriaan Peperzak and Luce Irigaray, had appeared the year before in 1986. At that time, in the 1980s, there were relatively few

American scholars who had even heard of Levinas, and those of us who realized his enormous importance, as you can imagine, were an even smaller number. The benefit, however, of this obscurity was that for the most part we all knew one another personally or knew of one another through publications.

Professor Edith Wyschogrod has the eternal honor of having written the first dissertation in English devoted exclusively to Levinas (which also appeared as the first book in English on Levinas, and remains in print), *Emmanuel Levinas: The Problem of Ethical Metaphysics* (1970). The second was by Phillip Lawton, *Emmanuel Levinas's Theory of Language* (1973), and the third was my own, *Time in the Philosophy of Emmanuel Levinas* (1980). Let me also mention two early dissertations on Levinas that were comparative studies: Leonard Grob's *The Renewal of Philosophy: A Study of the Thought of Sartre and Levinas* (1975), and Steven G. Smith's *Totaliter Aliter: The Argument to the Other in the Thought of Karl Barth and Emmanuel Levinas* (1980).

Regarding the reception of Levinas in America you must remember that American philosophy in the mid-century was dominated by Anglo-American or analytic philosophy, and in fact remains dominated by philosophers trained in that tradition. Although the Society for Phenomenology and Existential Philosophy, where Continental Philosophy was discussed, was the second largest philosophical association in America, its membership was miniscule compared to the American Philosophical Association which was—and to a large extent remains—controlled and dominated by analytic philosophers. So to say that Levinas was not well known in the 1980s and even in the 1990s, must be put into a context where continental philosophy as a whole was little known, and where such important continental thinkers as Merleau-Ponty or Habermas were also little known. Though it spans its own continent from the Atlantic to the Pacific oceans, America is in general insular in this way.

In the last five years or so, within the limited academic world of continental philosophers, Levinas's reputation has certainly blossomed. Indeed, he is now recognized as the major philosopher that he truly is. Now there are dozens of dissertations, and every year several books on Levinas are published. One can hardly keep track. As you have said in your question, there is now in America a Levinas Society. Now he is known, or his name is known, throughout the entire American philosophical community, and his stature has risen to the uppermost tier owing to a general recognition of his great originality and importance.

Let me make one final point about Levinas's reception in America. As you know, Jacques Derrida—who was famous years before Levinas, even though in a profound way Derrida was Levinas's student and not the reverse—wrote two long articles on Levinas: "Violence and Metaphysics: An Essay on the Thought of Emmanuel Levinas" (1964) and "Here I Am at This Very Moment in This Work" (1980). The former has exerted great influence in Levinas studies, and appeared in English in 1978 in Derrida's collection, *Writing and Difference,* translated by Alan Bass. Given the popularity of Derrida at that time and through the 1980s and even into the 1990s (and even, especially in Comparative Literature and English departments to this day) in America, one can to some extent distinguish two "schools" of Levinas studies in the United States. There are those, like myself, Richard Sugarman and Edith Wyschogrod, for instance, who came to Levinas through Levinas. And there are those, like Robert Bernasconi and Hent de Vries, who came to Levinas through Derrida, or like Leonard Lawyor who in 2003 had the temerity to write in a book on contemporary French philosophy that "it is difficult to differentiate between Derrida and Levinas."[1] The result, not surprisingly, is two quite different Levinas readings. I would be misleading you and be falsely modest if I did not say that I prefer the former to the latter.

Lai: Besides being an early pioneer to explore the thought of Levinas in the States and to introduce it to the English world, you later became one of Levinas's students in France. So you know Levinas not only in terms of philosophy but also through personal acquaintance. Could you tell us (1) why you decided to go to France to study philosophy under Levinas, (2) who he is as a "person," and (3) what is your special memory of him?

Cohen: I had been introduced to Levinas's thought while I was an undergraduate majoring in philosophy at Penn State University, where Lingis was then teaching. In fact it was at Penn State that I not only first read Levinas, but where I first saw and heard him! He came in 1971, during the time when he was in America as a Visiting Professor at Johns Hopkins University. I cannot remember the precise date. He gave a lecture, read in English translation, which was published in a later version as "Ideology and Idealism." In any event, when I finished my undergraduate studies, Lingis suggested that I apply to the University of Stony Brook (SUNY) for graduate studies in philosophy.

The graduate program in philosophy at Stony Brook was new then and under the chairmanship of Don Ihde, who taught Ricoeur and Heidegger, and was then beginning to develop the philosophy of technology for which he is known. So, I was in the second class of graduate students. Though it was new, Stony Brook already had an outstanding faculty in contemporary continental philosophy. However, despite its commitment to contemporary continental philosophy, no one at Stony Brook really knew Levinas's work, and no one was teaching him. Despite my many philosophical interests and curiosities, for me Levinas was already *the* philosopher, the one whose philosophy was *truth*. It occurred to me one day that Levinas was not simply a set of books but a real person, indeed someone alive and teaching in Paris at that very moment. So I told my teachers at Stony Brook that I was leaving to study in Paris—no grants, no scholarships, nothing: a "leave of absence." As it turned out it was a very timely decision since 1974–1975 was Levinas's penultimate year teaching full-time at the University of Paris-Sorbonne.

I definitely wanted to meet Levinas as well as attend his classes. So I fabricated an excuse: I called him by phone and said I wanted to know what books he wanted us to be reading for his classes. Of course I knew that in the French university system it is up to the students to read whatever is necessary, and not up to the professors to assign books as in the American system. Levinas immediately made this clear, but he invited me to visit him at his apartment anyway, perhaps on the strength of the fact that I was a student of Lingis, his primary American translator.

At his apartment he welcomed me warmly. His wife brought us coffee and small pastries. In my inadequate French, I tried my best to discuss his philosophy, but when I look back at it I do not think I made the best impression. In fact I was in awe of Levinas and immediately felt I was "wasting" his precious time. Levinas, for his part, made me feel completely at home and discussed some of his current ideas.

I attended Levinas's two classes at the Sorbonne. One was on Heidegger's *Being and Time*, and the other was on what became

Otherwise than Being. In the Heidegger class I would bring my English translation of *Being and Time.* Now remember that in French university classes (or at least then) the students never speak, never ask questions. In the course of his lectures Levinas was often referring to specific passages in Heidegger. So one day, I raised my hand and asked Levinas if he would give the references to the page numbers. All the other students laughed at this, no doubt surprised I had spoken up and had requested something so prosaic from a professor. For his part Levinas quieted the class, and with great respect, said he would certainly henceforth provide the page numbers (which lasted only a week!). I felt as if he had not only responded positively to my question, but that in his manner he had defended me in front of the class. It is a very small story, but I remember it.

What to say about Levinas the person? Joelle Hansel, the wife of his grandson David, summed it up with one word: affable. Brilliant and creative though he was, certainly aware of his position within contemporary philosophy and all philosophy, and hence aware of the respect which was due him, never compromising his proper thought, whether in exposing it or defending it, Levinas in conversation was nevertheless always personable, courteous, warm, very open. And he had a fine sense of humor. A philosopher of world class stature, with great obligations, he would take the time to personally send me signed copies of his books.

Lai: In an earlier conversation, you mentioned to me that there are three kinds of Jewish people in respect of their relation to Judaism nowadays—reformist, conservative, and orthodox. Each group of Jews not only has a different attitude toward Judaism but also leads a different way of life since they interpret Jewish holy discourse differently. Is Levinas also a pious Jew? Which category does he belong to in France? In his writing, Levinas is always very cautious and tries to avoid mixing up philosophy with his Jewish belief. If this is so, should we read his philosophy from the perspective of Judaism? Why?

Cohen: Levinas was indeed a pious Jew, an "orthodox" Jew, but this did not mean what "ultra-orthodoxy" in Judaism has often come to mean today: a fundamentalism, what Heidegger called "onto-theology." In France and elsewhere, Judaism can be divided into orthodox and liberal strands (the American Reform and Conservative movements would in this division both be liberal). The liberal strand evaluates the validity of Jewish tradition from an Enlightenment perspective, the perspective of reason and universality. It focuses therefore on the universality of morality and justice in Judaism, especially as enunciated by the biblical prophets. The orthodox strand, in contrast, adheres to Jewish tradition, which means primarily the rabbinic or talmudic elaborations of postbiblical Judaism. There are many subsets of both strands, but Levinas can, with qualifications, be located in what is now called "modern orthodoxy," an adherence to traditions (rituals, prayer services, holidays, rabbinic interpretations, talmudic study) but one engaged in the modern world, the world of science and culture, the world of reason. He combines a commitment to the Jewish prophetic tradition, within which ethics is central, with adherence to the practices and sacred texts of Jewish religious tradition; the latter interpreted in terms of the former. So unlike much of liberal Judaism which jettisons a great deal of tradition in favor of a universal morality and justice, Levinas retains but *interprets* tradition in favor of universal morality and justice. It may not seem so, but it is a big difference. In *Totality and Infinity* Levinas has written: "Everything that cannot be restored [*ramener*] to an interhuman relation represents not the superior form but the forever primitive form of religion" (*TI* 79; my translation). And this is the position he takes within Judaism.

Let me say here that I do not subscribe to the view that Levinas's "philosophical" and "confessional" writings are essentially different. In fact they both teach precisely the same message, the same ethics. Levinas rejects Leo Strauss's sharp opposition between Reason and Revelation, Athens and Jerusalem. The difference in Levinas's writings, therefore, does not depend on a different point of view or a different ground, but rather on their different audiences. The philosophical writings, like all philosophical writings, are directed to intelligent readers, especially those familiar with the history of Western philosophy and civilization. His so-called "confessional" writings, in contrast, are directed to and take up topics of especial relevance to Jewish readers, readers familiar with the texts and traditions of Judaism. But the teaching is precisely the same. Remember, despite its small number of adherents, Judaism too sees itself as a "universal" religion, a religion with teachings for all humanity.

Lai: As we know, Levinas went to Freiburg University to study phenomenology under Husserl in 1928. And he often sees himself as a phenomenologist, not to mention that his dissertation is still regarded as one of the best books on Husserl. However, while Husserl introduces the method of phenomenological reduction to pursue the pure transcendental ego, as opposed to the concrete empirical ego, Levinas argues that ethics is first philosophy which emphasizes our "sensibility" with the absolute Other, as opposed to the pure ego. Also, in Levinas's early work, *Existence and Existents,* he rightly points out that the problem of Husserl's phenomenology (and also of Heidegger's existential philosophy) is that it is structured by the ontological passage from the existent to existence and focuses on the intentionality (or thinking) of the existent. Therefore, he moves in the opposite direction—from existence to the existent, and concentrates on the priority of the Other. Do you see Levinas's philosophy as a continuation of Husserl's phenomenology or a confrontation (or even a decisive break) with it?

Cohen: It is an excellent question and in its formulation you have highlighted an important dimension of Levinas's thought. Levinas's work both continues and breaks with phenomenology. That is to say, it is because Levinas is such a fine phenomenologist, which is to say, a scientist in the realm of thought, doing "rigorous science" in Husserl's expanded sense of science (expanded beyond "objects" to "phenomena" and hence to description instead of only quantification), that his phenomenological studies are so penetrating, insightful, revealing. It is because Levinas is such a fine phenomenologist that when he discovers the limitations of phenomenology, the point where moral encounter precedes and under girds intentionality itself, that he breaks with phenomenology in a way that establishes the decisive priority of ethics over phenomenology. Levinas is able to establish the primacy of ethics not by fiat but precisely because he takes science all the way to its limits, to the point where an imposition—an ethical responsibility—bursts through the interests of epistemology and ontology and gives them—against their will, as it were—their highest significance and indeed their *raison d'etre.* In this way, committed to the truth all the way to its limits, Levinas remains a philosopher and not only a moralist. In this way ethics becomes first philosophy.

Lai: Unlike science, philosophy presupposes radical resistance and conflict. And yet no great philosopher, even Plato, Kant, or Hegel, can think creatively without thinking his/her previous thinkers first.

What are the major influences on Levinas's thought besides Husserl and Heidegger?

Cohen: Well, beyond Husserl and Heidegger, I would suggest Henri Bergson. Levinas famously includes Bergson's *Time and Free Will* as one of "four or five" "of the finest books in the history of philosophy" (*EI* 37–38). Levinas understood that Bergson's theory of duration was a breakthrough in the development of philosophy from its modern, medieval, and ancient adherence to eternity and representation to a genuine appreciation of time and existence. Time is of central importance to Levinas's thought, where time is no longer conceived in terms of self projection but rather as intersubjective disruption, what Levinas in his later works calls "diachrony."[2]

Also one cannot leave out Immanuel Kant. Levinas wrote an early short article on Kant's *Critique of Practical Reason,* but otherwise published nothing exclusively devoted to Kant, yet Levinas's differences from Kant are perhaps the most instructive differences to see what is new in his thought. For instance, Kant speaks of ethical respect for the other person as respect for the law in the other person, as in the first and third formulations of the categorical imperative.[3] Levinas would be closer to the second formulation: "Act so that you treat humanity, whether in your own person or in that of the another, always as an end and never as a means." But even this formulation is not quite Levinasian. It is still too subject oriented. For Levinas, as you know, morality arises not in respect for law, in oneself or the other (the law for Levinas has to do with justice, which is built upon morality but not equivalent to it), but in "respect" for the other as other. I put the term "respect" in scare quotes because for Levinas morality does not begin with the self but with the other, with being-for-the-other before being for-oneself. The other ruptures the equilibrium of the self, disrupts all its synthesizing abilities; indeed, the other disrupts the very *ability* of the self, in a movement that starts with the other person and as the other-in-me reverberates in the self as moral responsibility. The other *affects* the self in its *sensibility,* and not merely as an intellectual or rational encounter. These sorts of considerations are what I meant by saying that the contrasts with Kant are instructive, and I think Levinas was always aware of them. No doubt, too, Levinas has a great and nuanced appreciation for the writings of Plato, though little sympathy with Platonism.

Lai: Can you describe the "major ideas" in Levinas's earlier work, *Totality and Infinity,* and his later work, *Otherwise Than Being?* Which one is more important than the other to you?

Cohen: Gigantic question! These are Levinas's two most important works, the heart and soul of his philosophy. Regarding importance, for me *Totality and Infinity* is more important because it is first, that is, the work in which we find all the major themes of Levinas's philosophy, including those which reach an even more refined articulation and development in *Otherwise than Being.* There are too many major ideas to elaborate here, but to scratch the surface I would say that the central idea of *Totality and Infinity* is the emergence of morality from out of the encounter with the other as transcendence. Hitherto philosophy refused even the possibility of a "relation" with transcendence, with that which exceeded the transcendental. At best it was the "unknown," for example Kant's thing-in-itself. What Levinas saw was that there is a relation to transcendence but it is not epistemological or ontological: it is ethical. It is the relation of the self and other, not seen from the outside, however, but coming from the other and impinging on the self in its most first person singularity, if I can speak this way, the singularizing of the self as responsibility, responsibility for the other. This is the great moment of part 3 of Totality and Infinity, prepared by careful phenomenological analyses of the genetic constitution of immanent selfhood found in part 2.

Otherwise than Being, while assuming all that was accomplished in *Totality and Infinity,* turns back from the transcendence of the other person to the moral impact of that transcendence on the very sensibility of the responsible self, the self as "vulnerability," as "hostage" to the other, a "suffering for the suffering of the other." It is also more refined in its analyses of language than *Totality and Infinity,* not disagreeing with the earlier analyses but elaborating and deepening them. Here Levinas raises the important distinction between "saying" (*dire*) and the "said" (*dit*), and shows how the latter, on its own, occludes the former, even though the former—saying as moral encounter—is the deepest (or highest!) significance of the significations and matrixes of significations of the latter.

Lai: Goodness always comes first for Levinas. Indeed, the priority of the good over the true is surely one of the most debatable and central themes of Levinas's philosophy. And you once gave an example to support this ethical assumption: "knowing that the drowning child must be saved, even when coupled with knowing how to save the child, is not the same as saving the child, unless knowing and doing are synonymous, which in our world they are not."[4] Could you further elucidate this argument?

Cohen: The true has a tendency of its own. It wants to see itself to its own completion, to its own wholeness, its own end, even when, admitting the failure of the notion of "system," it allows that truth is an "infinite task" as in Husserl (or Peirce), or a giving and simultaneous withdrawal of being according to Heidegger, or an infinite deferral of sense as with Derrida's notion of "différance." In this context, however, the immediacy—but it is better to say the "greater importance"—of moral responsibility is derailed and lost, is absorbed in the allegedly larger and unfinished project of truth, a project, however, that because it never ends also never gets back, as it were, to the immediate exigency at hand, in this case saving the life of the drowning child. This is perhaps a too complicated way of putting the matter, but the same point is evident in the painful fact that Heidegger ignored the Holocaust, not simply while it was being prepared, and not simply while it was happening, but also for decades afterwards when he was completely dedicated to "the question of being." It is precisely his complete devotion to the question of being that blinded him to the cries of victims unjustly murdered. But which is more important? For Levinas the answer is obvious and without question. Paradoxically, for philosophers only the search for truth—the alleged purity of the "freedom" of truth—could confuse us or anyone on this point.

But let me also state clearly that Levinas is not against truth. He is a philosopher. But as an ethical philosopher he is against giving over to truth the priority that truth always claims for itself. Rather, ethical obligations have first priority. Not only do they have first priority, the very notion of priority, or "importance," comes to us from ethics. Truth is important precisely because ethics precedes epistemology. And let there be no mistake: truth is very important. Without truth morality itself would suffer, for it could not be supplemented, as it must be, by justice, by a concern not simply for the other person in his or her singular transcendence, but for all others, for those who are not present, and hence a concern for the law, for courts, for the efficient production of food, housing, clothing, and all the material goods that sustain us, and no less for their fair distribution. It is only when truth listens only to itself, is absorbed in itself, that one loses sight of these obligations, first of moral obligation, and no less the quest for justice, which can only be accomplished with truth, with science, with knowledge.

Lai: In Chinese culture, there are three pillars which hold our ways of thinking and life together: Buddhism, which deals with the relation between the gods and people; Daoism, which deals the relation between nature and people; and Confucianism, which deals with the relation between people and people. Personally, you like Confucianism. You believe that Levinas is much closer to Confucianism than to Buddhism and Daoism. Could you elaborate this idea to us?

Cohen: Well first let me say that I do not presume to know Confucianism, Buddhism, or Daoism as well as I expect these great spiritual movements—and the complex and varied historical developments flowing from them—are known in Taiwan. Nor, with regard to Confucianism specifically, which you are right to say I admire greatly, do I know much more than the writings of Confucius and to a lesser extent those of Mencius, and in English translation, hence I am ignorant of the long development of Confucianism and neo-Confucianism. Nor, if I may be allowed a final disclaimer, am I sufficiently aware of the contemporary political significance of Confucianism in the context of modern China. However, for more than 40 years I have continued to read the primary texts and to reflect on all these traditions.

So what brings Levinas close to Confucianism? It is, as you say, that Confucianism deals with the relation between people and people, and it does so in from a base of morality and virtue, propriety and respect, rites and deference. As for Levinas, the interpersonal relation is asymmetrical, as one finds concretely in Confucius's four relationships. Furthermore, moral responsibility is always greatest upon oneself, as, for example, in Confucius's great "principle of the measuring-square." Basing the justice of the state on morality, both leaders and led, who are also members of families, ideally must always think of others before themselves—this is Levinasian. In addition, Confucius's avoidance of useless metaphysical questions, his avoidance of theology, his adherence to rituals, these too are all congenial to Levinas's biblical-humanistic approach. These are some, and there are many other areas of congruence, but each one really requires a more careful and nuanced explication of comparisons and contrasts.

This topic is one that requires much further study, and which will prove, in my estimation, to be a very fruitful research area.

I have recently read William de Bary's book, *Asian Values and Human Rights: A Confucian Communitarian Perspective* (1998), and have been very favorably impressed by its scholarship and certainly by its overall thesis: that Confucianism provides no excuse to evade the defense of human rights in political community, and indeed provides compelling positive reasons for such a defense. I do not know if it has been translated into Chinese, but I recommend it.

As for Buddhism, if I may say a word here, while I have not been drawn into its popular devotional forms, as a philosophy, which I believe was the Buddha's original intent—of a fearless commitment to truth aligned to the greatest compassion to alleviate suffering: the Bodhisattva ideal—I have always felt an enormous kinship, and feel that it speaks to a core truth and the core imperative of all the world's great religions. Daoism, again as a "philosophy," is elusive, perhaps too complaisant, even erotic, but certainly it speaks to a yearning humans have for nonalienation, acceptance and homecoming. For myself, "exile"—a notion important to the Jewish tradition—is closer to my experience of worldly life, and not to be understood negatively solely in terms of "alienation." It rather speaks to the open future, the human adventure, our prospects.

Lai: Since you also teach Levinas, can you tell us in what ways we may open the necessary space for continuing collaboration between the generations of Levinas thinkers and to draw together those working on seemingly disparate projects into a more robustly pedagogical community?

Cohen: As you know, in America we have just created, two years ago, a Levinas Society. There is a Levinas journal coming out of Israel, and another in America. But I am ambivalent about such structures. Yes, they bring together Levinas scholars and provide a forum for high-level scholarly work, for detailed analyses, for examination of the lacunae of Levinas's thought. On the other hand, I think Levinas's thought is relevant to all human endeavor, to all the humanities, say, within the global academic community, but not only there, also to the social sciences and more broadly to social, religious, and political thought and action. His central idea, that ethical considerations are the very "humanity of the human" and hence that they *should* govern all that we do, this idea is one not limited to any specific discipline or group, though it also has ramifications for all specific disciplines and groups. I do see the influence of Levinas increasing throughout many disciplines, and I think this is a very good development.

Lai: Now we should move to a serious business. Levinas is not a thinker without criticism. Actually, his idea of ethics as the first philosophy has attracted "slings and arrows" from different quarters. Since you are a "Levinasian" scholar it is, in a Levinasian sense, your "responsibility" to seriously respond to these criticisms and accusations. So my following questions will focus on the major problems raised by six of Levinas's critics; namely, Derrida, Lyotard, Ricoeur, Irigaray, Žižek, and Badiou.

Although you published your first paper on Derrida, I know you are not really "Derridean." In fact, you don't like Derridean readings of Levinas. So, let us start with Derrida. In his cogent interpretation and famous critique of Levinas's ethics in "Violence and Metaphysics," Derrida questions Levinas's nonviolence oriented ethics, which privileges peace over war. He believes that were there a nonviolent language, it would have to be one that goes without verb, without predication, without *to be*. "But since finite silence is also the medium of violence, language can only indefinitely tend toward justice by acknowledging and practicing the violence within it."[5] Levinasian absolute peace, for Derrida, only exists in the domain of the pure nonviolence and of the absolute *silence,* or, in an unreachable Promised Land, a homeland *thither* without language. Accordingly, in contrast to Levinas, Derrida calls for an "economy of violence:" "an economy irreducible to what Levinas envisions in the word. If light is the element of violence, one must combat light with a certain other light, in order to avoid the worst violence, the violence of the night which precedes or represses discourse."[6] For Derrida, discourse can only do itself violence and negate itself in order to *affirm* itself. In other words, how can Levinas build up his critique of the violence of ontology without using the ontological language? Is Derrida's criticism justified to you? In what sense, do Derrida's deconstructive interpretations of Levinas in general not do Levinas justice?

Cohen: All that you have said in the name of Derrida in your question is already present in Levinas's work. Levinas is perfectly aware of the relative violence that is necessary in order to move toward peace.

You are quite right that I am no follower of Derrida, though I did attend his classes in Paris in 1994–1995 and have written often—critically, to be sure—about his thought. To characterize his thought in the way your citations from Derrida suggest would be to turn Levinas into a naive utopian, an absolute pacifist, which he is not. In *Otherwise than Being*, for instance, Levinas writes: "The true problem for us Westerners is not so much to refuse violence as to question ourselves about a struggle against violence which without blanching in non-resistance to evil, could avoid the institution of violence out of this very struggle" (*OB* 177). I think this is a very important insight.

But the philosophical issue between Derrida and Levinas lies elsewhere, in a theory of signification, which has important political consequences. Derrida sides with Hegel, as it were, in rejecting the notion of absolute transcendence. The argument is not so obscure, as it was Hegel's argument against Kant: if you say it then what you say occurs within the said and all talk of a transcendent "saying" is just that, talk, a signification *within* the said. This was Derrida's original argument in "Violence and Metaphysics": signification occurs within a system or context of signs referring to signs, a differential matrix ("language"), even if unlike Hegel, Derrida rejects the idea that there can be a "system" of such signs and proposes instead that there is a continual "differánce" or "deferral" of meaning without closure. But Levinas is perfectly aware that at the level of the "said" signs refer to other signs in a continual deferral of sense within the context of historical languages and indeed of an unfolding history. His point, however, is that this entire edifice, the matrix of signs, depends on an upsurge of signs in what in *Totality and Infinity* he called "expression" and in *Otherwise than Being* "saying." This is not an ontological upsurge, as in Heidegger's "ontological difference," nor is it the "play" of signs that Derrida—following Heidegger by taking seriously Heidegger's later shift from being to language—discovers in language itself, as if language were somehow speaking without speakers speaking. No, speakers speak. And the speech of speaking comes from the proximity—a moral proximity, based in responsibility: the responsibility to respond to the other person—Levinas calls the "face to face" or the "inter-human." Here is a context, as it were, that cannot be objectified or "closed" not because signs continually slip in meaning, but because it begins in the first person singular, in a singularity in closer contact with another singularity—I and you—than the slippage of meanings enunciated in what is said. It is precisely the absolute alterity of the other person, and not only the relative alterity of signs, that makes discourse, speech, and conversation an obligation. And that obligation is from the first a moral obligation: to listen, to respond to the other person and not merely to what the other person has said.

It seems to me that after Levinas's death in 1995, perhaps beginning with his lecture on "Friendship" in Aristotle, Derrida himself tried to appropriate Levinas's moral perspective. He certainly appropriates Levinas's language of the alterity of the other person and of morality. But he can only do so legitimately, consistently, hence philosophically, if he repudiates his earlier philosophy of "différánce," which I do not see he has done. Either he becomes Levinas, which is a strong tendency in the language of his later writings, which are so "Levinasian," or he remains Derrida, in which case he cannot, in principle, be Levinasian. Nor can this alternative remain yet another "undecidability," though it seems to me that this is precisely what the later Derrida tries to maintain, like a tightrope walker, but which also made him remain himself and not Levinas. I think Derrida's response to the famous "Paul de Man Affair," to take one concrete instance, his defence of the ruses of Paul de Man in hiding his pre-WWII anti-Semitic writings, and his attack on the critics of those ruses when they were finally discovered, is sufficient evidence that his thought and Levinas's are irreconcilable. Insofar as Derrida was, as I have called him, "the most faithful disciple of Heidegger," his thought is also and quite obviously in radical conflict with Levinas's ethics.

Lai: In "Levinas's Logic," Lyotard aims to scrutinize the situation of Levinas's thought, especially "in the face of Hegelian persecution." In so doing, he also explains his main question of commentary and the confrontation with Kant's second *Critique*. He believes that "Levinas's riposte against ontology is refutable and that the project of emancipating ethical discourse in relation with the same fails in view of the enunciative clause."[7] What do you think about his criticism?

Cohen: In the end I was not convinced that Levinas's notion of moral imperative had been "refuted" or, for that matter, actually engaged. I am not so sure Lyotard's appropriation of the language of analytic philosophy proves very helpful. It seems to me that in this article and elsewhere when he writes on Levinas (e.g., in *The*

Different), Lyotard ends more with questions about Levinas than a critique, as if he is unsure of his own position vis-à-vis Levinas. For my part, I think Lyotard is stronger in his analyses of the dangers of the ambiguous and fluid character of the "said" (a point about which Levinas would agree) in our contemporary world of commercial and political propaganda and transnational corporations. But it would be Nietzschean or Machiavellian, and hence narrow and brutish, indeed sophistic, it seems to me, to affirm, as he does in *The Postmodern Condition* that "to speak is to fight."[8]

Lai: Ricoeur's idea of "the self is just another self" in his late work *Oneself as Another* is regarded as a mature representation of themes in philosophy of ethics, language, narrative, and action theory discussed in his early works. His ethics is obviously different from Levinas's. He questions some arguments in Levinas's ethics, especially moral selfhood and the premise of asymmetry relation between the self and the other, although his criticism is comparatively friendly. Confronting his criticism directly, you did write a strong paper to defend Levinas—"Moral Selfhood: A Levinasian Response to Ricoeur on Levinas."[9] I know it is long and complicated paper. Can you briefly tell us your main arguments in this paper?

Cohen: It is indeed a lengthy and concentrated paper, one which tracks down and responds to every instance and nuance of Ricoeur's reading of Levinas in *Oneself as Another*, both positive and negative, a testimony to the power and sophistication (in a positive sense) of Ricoeur's thought and his long engagement with Levinas's ethics. It is also, as you say, a defense of Levinas against Ricoeur. Levinas had a very high regard for Ricoeur, and Ricoeur helped Levinas personally in his professional career, and their philosophical training was quite similar (both wrote very early books in France on Husserl's phenomenology). Nevertheless, at bottom, Levinas remained at odds with Ricoeur. What is this "at bottom"? While Ricoeur admirably does reorient the notion of "the voice of conscience" from Heidegger's "listening to being" to a listening to the other person, he nevertheless cannot fully escape from the orbit of Heidegger's thinking. What this means in *Oneself as Another* and in relation to Levinas, is that for Ricoeur—who also wants to retain Aristotle's insights regarding "virtue"—is that morality, while inescapably concerned for the other, ultimately derives from the self's own sense of "self-esteem." In the final account, then, "at bottom," moral conscience remains an affair of the self with itself, despite having acknowledged the great impact of the other person, which Ricoeur freely admits and credits to Levinas. All of Ricoeur's criticisms of Levinas derive from this, then, the notion that Levinas has gone too far, has credited too much to the impact of the other person. This is to say, from Levinas's point of view, that Ricoeur retreats from the disturbing transcendence of the other, from the other's "face," from Levinas's defense of the "infinite obligation" that raises the moral self to its proper height, one that elevates and disturbs even if—indeed, especially because—it cannot be accomplished or completed.

I have heard this critique, though expressed in less subtle form and without philosophical scholarship, from my students: Levinas demands too much. Levinas lets no one off the hook, as it were, or, rather, ethics lets no one off the hook of responsibility, even if all of our responsibilities (even most of them) cannot be met. However, ethics would not be ethics otherwise, but psychology, anthropology, or sociology, a reduction to something else. I ask in response: Is the human problem really that we are all too ethical, that we are all sacrificing too much of our happiness in order to be good, in order to serve others, to serve justice? Is it not rather the reverse: that we are hardly ethical enough, that we do indeed satisfy our need for happiness all too often and all too sadly at the expense of others who suffer? Each must answer for himself or herself. Levinas, for his part, had no illusions about how much morality and justice occur in the world today.

Lai: Levinas's idea of woman as "the absolute Other" is still an ongoing debate. The first female thinker who raises the feminist criticism of Levinas is perhaps Simone de Beauvoir. In *The Second Sex,* she argues: when Levinas "writes that women is mystery. He implies that she is mystery for man. Thus his description, which intended to be objective, is in fact an assertion of masculine privilege."[10] Irigaray, in "The Fecundity of the Caress," also makes some harsh criticisms of Levinas's idea of "feminine," "love" and gender relationships. She contends that the female is, for Levinas, "brought into a world that is not her own so that the male lover may enjoy himself and gain strength for his voyage toward an autistic transcendence."[11] That is, for her, Levinas's woman may be a wonderful, brilliant, mysterious other, yet she is bound to lack a face, home and transcendence of her own. Believing "lovers' faces live not only in face but in the whole body,"[12] so she also argues that Levinas "knows nothing of communion in pleasure," in which there is "immediate ecstasy" between lovers, but only solitary love between distant selves.[13] Do you think Levinas's idea of "feminine" is purely transcendental? Is Levinas's ethics patriarchal as Irigaray criticizes?

Cohen: The issues raised by contemporary feminism are indeed important and challenging. Simone de Beauvoir initial "critique" of Levinas, however, arose, it seems to me from a fundamental misunderstanding. For Levinas the alterity of the other person is neither male nor female but the interiority or "secrecy" of the other's person's irreducible transcendence in the face of my subjectivity. Of course the other is always a concrete other, a male or female, a family member or not, a policeman, banker, or doctor, and so forth. Nevertheless, otherness for Levinas has priority—it is that toward which the subject is obligated, beholden, responsible—and does not mean, as Beauvoir seems to suggest, a secondary status. On the other hand, perhaps Levinas was mistaken in Part Two of *Totality and Infinity* to characterize the notion of "dwelling" as "feminine mystery" (*TI* 156). As I argued in "The Metaphysics of Gender" in my book *Elevations,* Levinas appropriates the ordinary language of "feminine" and "masculine" not as biological categories but as regions of signification, the former referring to the protective environment of the home (whether set up and inhabited by biological males or females) and the latter to the public sphere of work and objectivity (again, whether performed by biological males or females).[14] One can debate the wisdom of this terminology, to be sure, and its political ramifications, but I think it is a mistake to misunderstand or simplify that to which Levinas refers when he invokes it.

As for Irigaray's criticism of the analyses of eros in part 4 of *Totaliy and Infinity,* again, it is a matter for phenomenological inquiry. Is Levinas right that two lovers remain separate in their erotic embrace or is Irigaray right to suggest that there is a "communion in pleasure"? I am inclined to think that Irigaray has a point, but so too does Levinas. And this is Levinas's point: in eros one strives for communion, but that communion, even if it occurs, is transitory, ephemeral. One could also challenge Levinas's account of erotic embrace as tending to paternity-maternity, that is, as aiming beyond itself to the birth of a child. Could it not also be pleasure for its own sake, shared pleasure? Perhaps eros has these two dimensions, one wrapped up in itself in pleasure, in dual pleasure, two bodies enjoying one sensation, and the other tending beyond itself, infused with transcendence, in paternity-maternity? Must one decide which is primary? Furthermore, there is the larger question of the relation of the responsible body to the erotic body. It seems to me that eros should occur within the bounds of morality (one would not approve of nonconsensual violence, of abuse), but within the rule of that context, does morality provide any special further guidance for erotic behavior? I would think not.

I think in his later writings, Levinas backs away from his earlier terminology, especially what he called the "feminine presence" of the dwelling in *Totality and Infinity* (*TI* 156–58). I think the idea remains, the idea of dwelling. In his later writing, however, Levinas comes to call the responsible self, the self for-the-other before being for-itself, "maternal" (*OB* 67), inviting us to think of the moral self as so deeply introjected with the other, penetrated by the other, as if it were carrying the other inside itself, pregnant with the other, the other-in-the-same. Here "maternity" is no longer an erotic concept but a moral one, the very "definition" of selfhood as responsibility. Is this "sexist"? I think not, but there are feminists for whom any use of gendered terms is a patriarchal violence toward women. For my part, I agree with Nietzsche—though I put an entirely different value on his claim—that religion, discourse still in contact with a higher or elevating transcendence, in Levinas's case ethical transcendence—effeminizes, "makes tame," or as I would rather say, sensitizes the self to the suffering of the other. Of course, when I use the term "effeminizes," or I could equally say "emasculates," I run the risk of sexism. Certainly one must be careful and attentive to current usage, denotations, and connotations as well. But there is no pure language, no immaculate conception: we must use the significations that are our heritage. The main thing is to steer them toward what is good and just, adjust them, criticize them, in some cases eliminate certain terms if possible, raise them if possible, or as Buber said, "sanctify the world," and not simply overthrow them all (which was Nietzsche's apocalyptic flaw) which is never possible in any event if we are to continue to converse with one another.

Lai: Other critics believe Levinas seems to dismiss animals as too stupid to have a "face." In *Zoontologies: The Question of the Animal*, for instance, Cary Wolfe contends that Levinas in *Difficult Freedom*

directly addresses animals in general and a dog named Bobby in par-
ticular, and then implies that a dog has no "face" simply because
Bobby has no brain to universalize (*DF* 151–53).[15] Do you think
Levinas's ethic has a problem of speciesism as Wolfe argues?

Cohen: Well I could only agree if I thought "speciesism" were a
problem! I do not know Wolfe's book, but John Llewelyn and others have also raised this objection. At the first meeting of the Levinas
Society in America, Diane Perpich give a paper that to my mind was
a careful, balanced, and quite convincing Levinasian response to this
objection.[16]

The deeper issue is the question of hierarchy and humanism. Is the
human an irreducible and privileged dimension, as Levinas argues,
or must it be assimilated and reduced to a larger context, such as the
cosmic mechanism of the seventeenth and eighteenth century rationalists. Or, in our day, a time in which environmentalism is a serious
global concern, must the human be assimilated to naturalism? The
answer depends on whether there is something distinctively and irreducibly human, and whether that dimension gives to the human its
special privilege in the face of all else. And on this point there have
been several answers. The classical or Greek answer is indeed that it is
rationality that is distinctively human, so that a dog, lacking human
rationality, would be lower on a scale of value than the human. From
what you have said it is to this that Wolfe objects, as did Spinoza ages
before, and Diogenes before him.

What makes Levinas's thought able to respond to this objection
is that Levinas does not define the human in terms of rationality but
rather in terms of morality. There are many things, no doubt, of which
one could argue that humans alone are capable: a certain abstract
rationality, symbol use (language), creativity, play, and so on. But for
Levinas, the "humanity of the human" lies in morality, in being-for-
the-other before oneself, self-sacrifice, responsibility, giving, and in the
justice built upon this morality. I think this is what is at issue in
the arguments made about Levinas not caring sufficiently for animals,
or for sentient nature more broadly. But I think these arguments are
misguided, indeed mistaken. For how can we *value* animals and the
environment, how can we be *morally concerned* for them if we humans
did not, as humans, already "know" what morality is? Do we derive
our morality from nature? From animals? Hardly. I think the Marquis

de Sade put a rest to this argument forever: all things can be derived from nature, from loving one's children to eating them, from caring for others to torturing them, from protecting forests to burning them down, and so forth. It is only the naive prejudice of a romantic sentimentality that sees in nature beauty rather than ugliness, the awe-inspiring sunrise or sunset rather than hurricanes, earthquakes, and tsunamis, or the vigor of health rather than disease, plague, and deformity. Nature, of itself, provides no values whatsoever. Spinoza summed up nature in a phrase: big fish eat little fish. It is "perseverance in being," or in Nietzsche's biological perspective: will to power, aggrandizement. But even these characterizations say too much. It is we humans who interpret nature, see nature through our eyes.

Because Levinas defines the human in terms of morality, rather than rationality, his philosophy is in a better position to care for nature starting from the human, that is to say, starting from morality. Because the responsible self is a suffering for the suffering of other persons it also, by extension, suffers for the suffering of animals. And not only from a utilitarian point of view, because their suffering will hurt us, deprive us of pets and food. No, insofar as the human is in essence (or "non-essence," since it is no fixity) a suffering for the suffering of other persons—is responsible—the human is a response to all suffering, even if that responsiveness starts with and has its primary concern for other persons. Ethics means not only moral responsibility but justice, and hence hierarchy of values, prioritization of concerns. The other human being comes first, but that does not leave dogs or sentient life out in the cold; in fact, it makes possible care for them also.

Let me add that these critics of Levinas regarding animals are often unaware of the great Jewish biblical and talmudic tradition of concern for animals. When the biblical Eliezer, the servant of Abraham, selects a wife for Abraham's son Isaac, he chooses Rebecca, a shepherdess, because she not only gives him water but gives water to his many camels (Gen. 24:18–21). In the Talmud it is a law for Jewish farmers—actually for all Jews—that they must feed their domesticated animals before they feed themselves, because the animals are in their care and are unable to get food for themselves. The Jewish dietary laws require that kosher animals be killed in the least painful manner possible. The Jewish dietary laws greatly restrict what animals (and birds and fish) can be killed at all. Indeed, of the seven "laws of Noah"—the laws of righteousness for all nations (and not just for Jews)—besides the expected prohibitions against murder, stealing, adultery, and so forth, one of the seven laws prohibits cruelty to animals! So we can say that the "humanism" of Levinas, at least as it manifests itself in his own Jewish tradition, is deeply involved in and concerned in great detail, in real practice over long tradition, for the welfare of sentient life, and indeed for all creation, beyond its inaugural emergence in the face-to-face between human beings.

Lai: Your example of kosher food is convincing to me to show the Jewish tradition of caring and loving animals. Yet, allow me to be direct, so you are saying that animals have a "face" in Levinas's ethics? As far as my knowledge is concerned, Levinas himself seems reluctant to recognize the "face" of animals directly.

Cohen: Yes, I can understand that reluctance. It speaks to the priority of the human other, the other person. It is really starting from the "face" of the other person that humans are also obligated toward animals, all sentient life, plants, and all of creation. It is because it is there that humans become human, become moral. It does not happen in the world of animals by themselves. That a lion eats a lamb is not a moral issue, neither for the lion nor for the lamb. That an earthquake occurs or a volcano erupts, these are "natural" events, indifferent—if considered in themselves—to morality and justice. So, to answer your question, it is indeed only "indirectly" that animals have a face, a face—a moral imperative—deriving from the interhuman. But this does not at all say that we therefore have no obligations to animals. Quite the reverse, it is because the human arises in the face-to-face, in morality, that we absolutely have moral obligations and responsibilities toward animals, sentient life and, as I have said, all creation. Such is our contribution, as it were, the significance of the human, to sanctify the world. It is not "dominion" in the sense of tyrannical or self-serving rule, but caretaking, the extension of what is most human, most noble, the alleviation of suffering, to all of creation.

This is why the environmentalists are right to value the saving of endangered species above profit making. But such decisions do not come in a mindless reflex; rather they reflect a careful and thoughtful weighing, discretion, considerations of "better and worse," in a

justice that must never lose sight of consequences for human suffering. For instance, a person may personally choose to starve for
the sake of feeding his or her beloved pet, but that person does not
thereby gain the right to make others starve also. I remember when
I first visited Holland in the early 1970s I stayed with a couple in
Amsterdam whose home was also a hostel. Our hosts regaled us with
stories of their remarkable pet rabbit, which they had trained to go
to the bathroom on the toilet. When we asked what happened to the
rabbit, they said they ate him, because it was during the war and they
had no food. There was a silence, and we all felt the sadness, but we
all also understood.

Lai: Sometimes we just cannot help wondering how we continue
to hold beliefs in this postmodern age, where truth has lost its legitimacy. In *On Belief*, Žižek, as a prominent follower of Lacan, draws
on psychoanalysis, film, and philosophy to answer this question by
exploring some cynicism and fixation with the Other in multicultur-
alism and elsewhere, which includes Levinas's ethics. He tries to get
behind the contours of the way we normally think about belief, in
particular Judaism and Christianity. He argues that nothing could be
worse for believers than their beliefs turning out to be true. He contends that the self might simply appear to desire goodness and justice
for its own sake. That is, the so-called absolute Other is just a self-
projected imagination to justify the Self's interest and desire. Here is
one of his arguments: when Levinas says that one must respond, even
to the point that not to respond is still a response, he is mistaken.[17]
What would give an ethical value to indeclinable responsibility is no
less than the sort of genuine commitment to the destitute other that
is lacking in the self's interest. I think this core doubt rooted in Žižek
is the question: is the ethical relation between the self and other transcendental or immanent?

Cohen: I am not sufficiently conversant in Žižek's thought to
properly respond to his specific criticisms. But from what you have
said, it strikes me as something Kant already articulated: every moral
action can be recast as a selfish action. From a strictly empirical point
of view there is no morality whatsoever. I return someone's wallet;
it seems like a good deed, but who knows? Perhaps I only want the
reward or to be seen as a good person. Such is Machiavellian doubt,
cynicism. There is no stopping it. Here is not the place to enter into

the refutations of such skepticism, which in fact does refute itself even as it enunciates its doubts.

But perhaps I can give an answer that is related. Recently I have returned to Jean Baudrillard's notion of "hyper-reality" and "simulation": the unfathomable mediation and mystification of our contemporary world where truth and lie can longer be distinguished in the public square. So much of our public world is indeed mediated, through newspapers, radio, television, and now the internet. Public information indeed has come to resemble a "witch's brew," phantomlike, a set of masks of masks of masks without end. There is no "getting to the bottom" of anything, so it seems, and hence no way to assign culpability, to distinguish not only the true and the false, but good and evil, just and unjust. All efforts to make these distinctions, even in the best of faith, are appropriated by the very institutions that one wants to criticize, neutralizing all criticism. It is what Marcuse described earlier in *One Dimensional Man,* and what he equally hopelessly saw no alternative to except the futile gesture of a "great refusal." Or, as you put it, if transcendence is really immanence, then why pretend there is ethics? This of course recalls the famous opening sentence of *Totality and Infinity:* "Everyone will readily agree that it is of the highest importance to know whether we are not duped by morality" (*TI* 21).

What can I say here other than that Levinas's entire ethical philosophy is the effort to say that we are not duped by morality, and hence that we are not duped by the justice that is built upon and aims to institutionalize morality. Yes, global technology has made doublespeak, dissimulation, spin, lying, and the like far more powerful, but it does not ultimately undo the difference between the true and the false, good and evil, justice and injustice, even if it makes the effort to support goodness and justice, and to speak truth, that much more difficult. Nobody ever said morality or justice would be easy. Indeed, Levinas explicitly names our freedom and our humanity "difficult." But difficult is not impossible, and even cynicism is a moral posture. Here I am inspired by the writings and life of Václav Havel, who was himself inspired by Levinas. When Havel describes "the power of the powerless" as "living wihin the truth," all the sophistication, erasures, ambiguities, deceptions, repressions, and simulacra cannot efface or distort the moral power of his witness.[18]

Lai: Now comes the final, and most mordacious, critic—Alain Badiou. Badiou's criticism is so far ruthless, provocative, and relentless to Levinas's thought, I dare say. In *Ethics: an Essay on the Understanding of Evil,* he claims that philosophy is a militant pursuit of truth and that we should not succumb to the temptations of the post-Heideggerian tradition, which includes Levinas. Similar to Žižek's contention of immanence against transcendence, he argues that if selves are all different, as an ethics of difference insists obstinately, then difference is a property we all share, which entails that in the end there is nothing but the Same. He believes that Levinas's hyperbolic language fails to "guarantee" the primacy of the ethics of the Other over the truth of the Same and "the ethical primacy of the Other over the Same requires that experience of alterity be ontologically 'guaranteed' as the experience of a distance, or an essential nonidentity, traversal of which is the ethical experience itself. But nothing in the simple phenomenon of the Other contains such guarantee." Accordingly, he believes that Levinas's unintelligible and religious ethics should be abandoned.[19] Therefore, he concludes: If we take away Levinasian ethics's religious aspect, there is nothing left but a "dog's dinner," a "pious discourse without piety."[20] What do you think?

Cohen: I'm afraid I must agree with you that Badiou's writings are, as you say, ruthless and provocative. I think a slightly less provocative way of saying this is that he is an avant-gardist with a philosophical vocabulary. He sets up his militant position cleverly. First he would have us think that ethics has become fashionable. This is already an attack on ethics and on philosophy as well. No doubt after the "death of man" pronounced first by Heidegger, but then also by Althusser, Foucault, Lacan, and Deleuze, the work of Levinas has indeed forced the philosophical world to reconsider and once again take seriously the position of ethics. But even with this backdrop, ethics is certainly not a fashion and never can be. But it is this that bothers Badiou—he is tired of this fashion and wants next year's fashion. What disturbs him, apparently, is that morality and justice do not play to his avant-garde enthusiasms, to his craving for whatever is or seems new, the latest thing. At the same time he wants to don the persona of the intellectual master. Thus he is the one who sees through ethics, is not duped. But, I would say in response, the imperatives of morality and justice are not fads. Their demands are indeed ancient, but far from obsolete, and even farther from fulfillment. Indeed their central elements—responsibility, kindness, respect, horror of murder and violence, fairness, and so on—do not change at all. For all his sociological positioning and the high sounding language of truth seeking, Badiou's stance remains, if I may label it this way, adolescent.

Beyond the rhetoric of his revolutionary frustration, however, Badiou's actual argument is unconvincing. It hinges on a fallacy learnt by all beginning students of logic: equivocation or ambiguity. Unfortunately the term of Badiou's equivocations is an important one: "difference." You have referred to his criticisms of Levinas. I will respond. The central argument Badiou proposes is as follows: "the self-declared apostles of ethics and of the 'right to difference' are clearly *horrified by any vigorously sustained difference.* For them, African customs are barbaric, Muslims are dreadful, the Chinese are totalitarian, and so on."[21] Clearly these are two sorts of difference: one refers to the human condition, the intersubjective situation, while the other refers to cultural, sociological, historical, and political differences. The difference Levinas articulates, and upon which his thought is centered, the alterity of the other, must not be confused with the social, cultural, political, and historical differences it conditions. Badiou would conflate them.

But regarding the latter differences, there is no question that everyone, every society, every culture, indeed everything that can be identified, is "different" like fingerprints, each having its unique set of spatial-temporal characteristics. Philosophers have called these distinguishing differences "particularities," unique nodes of universalities (Hegel's "concrete universal") from the point of view of knowledge. What lies at the center of Levinas's thought, in contrast, is something else: singularity. There occurs—or can occur—an irreducible transcendence in the encounter of the singular other as other relative to the singular self as singular. Such a transcendence, so Levinas argues, does not appear, is not a phenomenon, is not fully grasped as a unique node in the economy of being or truth, but rather ruptures all continuities and identities because it is from the first a moral imperative, a "thou shalt not murder," an asymmetrical order. One can call this "religious," but I think Levinas prefers to call it ethical because it is as moral imperative that it arises. The demand or command coming from the other's singular "height and destitution" which escapes the powers and capacities of the self, including its search for truth, but nonetheless hollows the self out into a responsibility singularly beholden to that other is an ethical structure. The other in his or her particularity as a cultural, sociological, historical, and political being does not disappear however. Levinas in no way neglects or belittles the concrete differences which constitute the other's particularity — quite the reverse. It is because the other is first other, irreducibly different and beyond appropriation, that the I can take seriously and respond to another's social, cultural and historical differences in their specificity.

Badiou prefers particularities, to be sure, but this aesthetic taste does not provide him grounds for criticizing moral responsibility outside of a high-spirited but ultimately arbitrary celebratory attitude, one that remains quite subjective. But Badiou wants to claim more, he wants the mantle of the metaphysician, so like Nietzsche's speculative pronouncements about will to power, Badiou proclaims the universe to be modeled on his aesthetic taste: the "the multiple 'without one' — every multiple being in its turn nothing other than a multiple of multiples — is the law of being."[22] Why this exaltation of multiplicity over unity? Of course, it is fashionable, in French intellectual life in any event. But it is really a valuation of the body freed of values, what Deleuze calls "desiring machines." Despite his enthusiasm, however, it is not by means of this approach that even the particular differences Badiou claims to support are maintained let alone respected. The reverse holds true: in this vision all particular differences — cultural, political, historical, and so on — erode, dissipate into an unending series of masks of masks of masks. Nietzsche declared himself "all names in history" precisely at the moment when he was not even one name. One does not respect the specificity of the other, or of other cultures, by exalting historical differences over ethical difference.

Ironically, Badiou's position ends by supporting the globalization it claims to oppose, promoting leveling, homogenization, and the trivialization of whole societies, histories, and cultures. By wanting to undermine the irreducible nonidentity of ethics, its "for-the-other," where the other remains other, for the sake of the nonidentity of being and truth, which is really a defense of the body as delirious or "schizoid," Badiou perpetuates the colonialism he pretends to oppose. It is a permanent revolution antithetical to cultural integrity. Once again it is propelled by a claimed quest for truth. Everything must be shattered, all pasts must be unmasked in their naivete, all present "truths" must be surpassed for the truth that will come. Perhaps his enthusiasm for the future comes less from a genuine desire for truth than from the frustration of a romantic nihilism that devalues everything it touches beforehand. The Heideggerian "ontological difference" lies at the root of Badiou's rhetoric—a yearning for what will come to "save" our terrible unredeemable present. But morality and justice—both their accomplishments and the tasks they open up for our future, resist the avant-garde's constant need for new thrills. As Kierkegaard already understood, for the aesthete, ethics is simply boring. But being bored is no critique. And thrills are no real future and no hope for those who suffer today. Ethics is far more serious, and far more serious than Badiou would prefer.

You can see from my response that I am not impressed by Badiou's rhetoric. That the artist squirms under the imperatives of decency and regard for the other, this should come to us as no surprise. But it is not an argument. In fact it is a form of violence. I have not even mentioned that the quest for truth, which Badiou claims so fervently to renew, does not and cannot depend on the Nietzschean aesthetics he in fact renews, but rather on a "taking seriously" that is neither slavish nor colonialist but derives, as Levinas argues, from ethics.

PART TWO

Religion for Adults

Part Two

From a theological perspective, religion is a challenge to human freedom. Here I will speak of the monotheisms, but monists face problems of a similar order. If God is omnipotent, then how can humans be free? If humans are free, then how can God be omnipotent? Lacking freedom, humans would be no more than puppets, their morality and justice rendered risible, their salvation or damnation completely arbitrary. Despite the sound and fury of rhetorical subterfuge, or a retreat to "mystery," theology has no answers adequate to its own pretentions to *logos*. But what if the problem lies not with religion, not with the practices and beliefs of monotheists, but with theology? What if knowledge, rationality, comprehension, logic, disclosure, revelation, and all the various resources and approaches of intellect, with its logical and ontological alternatives of being and nonbeing, freedom and necessity, as well as their possible dialectical interplay, what if these are all simply inappropriate registers of the deepest or highest sense of religion? Unless religion is a form of self-deception, surely the answer must be yes.

Would the result then be affirmation of the irrational and foolishness, idiocy or madness of beatitudes? Would the monotheisms then be asylums? Certainly there have been preachers aplenty who have proclaimed such beliefs, perhaps in defensive reaction to the irresolvable conundrums of theology. Heedless of its own long hostility to paganism and hedonism, monotheism would then be indistinguishable from mythology, from the worship of miracles through a faith confirmed in and by its very blindness.

In the name of religion, of monotheism in particular, Levinas offers an emphatic no to both alternatives: the self-deception and mystery of theology and the self-stupefaction and mystification of mythology. The irrational, after all, is but the flip side of rationality, not its alternative. Irrationality is not only inferior to monotheism, the sort of thing monotheism abhors as "superstition," "sorcery" "witchcraft," and the like, it is inferior to rationality. For Levinas, emphatically, the proper significance of monotheism is found neither in the rational nor in the irrational. Monotheism is ethical religion. "Ethics," Levinas has written, "is not the corollary of the vision of God, It is that very vision....To know God is to know what must be done" (*DF* 17). And the ethical, as we have seen in part one of this volume, is both the condition for the possibility of rationality and that in whose service rationality finds it very purpose. For rationality, for science, the irrational is exactly that: irrational; in the context of monotheism, however, where science is made possible by morality and made necessary by its service to justice, the irrational has a deeper signification: it is the ground or the abyss of evil and injustice. It derives from a refusal of the other person and an indifference to the needs of a suffering humanity, the reduction of the needs of the other and of all others to the desires of the same.

One sees right away, then, that there is no essential division in Levinas's thought between his philosophical writings and his so-called "confessional" writings. One can distinguish Levinas's writings in this manner, to be sure, but the resulting differentiation depends on their intended audience and not their message. Levinas everywhere propounds the same primacy of ethics, the primacy of moral responsibility before the other, and the call to justice demanded by that same responsibility.

Levinas was a Jew and a philosopher. Furthermore, as a Jew he was a "Litvak," a Jew of *Lita*, Jewish Lithuania, a mentality—an extreme intellectualist sobriety—even more than a geography. When Levinas writes for his coreligionists, for his fellow Jews that is to say—and let us not forget that he was principal of a Jewish high school and teachers' college long before and then during his appointments as professor of philosophy—he can and does assume a shared familiarity with Jewish traditions, practices, rituals, holidays, commentaries, historical experiences, language, sacred texts, and the like. He cannot, of course, make these assumptions when he writes for a general audience. In his philosophical writings, then, Levinas elaborates his ethics for all intelligent and educated human beings, regardless of their historical particulars. To be sure, Levinas assumes a familiarity with Western cultural and intellectual history, but here, too, as I indicated in the introduction to part one, the idea of the "West" is not only a geographic notion.

This difference in rhetoric has been characterized as that between "Greek" and "Hebrew," or one might say between "Athens" and "Jerusalem." It is said that Levinas speaks in the language of Greek science—the universal science that originated historically in ancient Greece—an ethical wisdom that is found in the Hebrew Bible and the commentaries of the rabbis in the Talmud. In other words, Levinas forces the universal language of philosophy, where primacy is given to knowledge, to acknowledge the transcendence of the good, which is ethical: the teaching that ethics is first philosophy. No doubt there is some truth to this framing. However, one could equally say that Levinas speaks Hebrew in his philosophical texts and Yiddish in his Jewish writings. Or is the wisdom of Israel less universal somehow than the science of the Greeks? Levinas precisely challenges such a suggestion. Conceptual reductions to alleged oppositions between Athens and Jerusalem, reason and revelation, progress and return, and the like, are simplifications familiar to conceptualization, but as simplifications they are ultimately tendentious and misleading. The real point is that for Levinas there is no rupture between philosophy and religion. Instead, "there is communication between faith and philosophy and not the notorious conflict. Communication in both directions" (*ITN* 170).

There is continuity and communication between religion and philosophy insofar as one recognizes religion not as the defender of the irrational, but as sustaining and sustained by the irreducible surplus of the ethical. Just as kindness, compassion, mercy toward the other is holy, so also holiness occurs in the vocations of righteousness. "Justice, justice shall you pursue, so that you will live and possess the Land that the Lord your God gives you" (Deut. 16:20). And speaking of a Judaism whose concrete life is guided by its oral as well as its written "law," indeed invoking a Judaism wherein spirit and letter are inseparable, Levinas writes: "The ritual law of Judaism constitutes the austere discipline that strives to achieve this justice" (*DF* 18). As we have seen in part one, morality demands justice, and justice serves morality—a teaching that remains the same throughout all of Levinas's writings. This is, without contradiction or mystification, the teaching of Judaism in every aspect of its existence, from the most ordinary actions and courtesies of everyday life to the most exacting demands of its rituals. It is the thread that binds—as it uplifts—all its various components across a history as old as civilization itself.

To be sure, one does not have to be a member of a monotheist religion to acknowledge and enact the primacy of the ethical. All discourse, all communication, finds its possibility and purpose in the extraordinary moral proximity of the face-to-face which is the inspiration of Levinas's ethical philosophy. The transcendence proper to monotheism is precisely the surplus of the good over being, as it is the impatience and the patience of humanity—"the little humanity that adorns the world" (*OB* 185), Levinas mentions twice on the final page of *Otherwise than Being*—in its long hope for a better, more just, world. The universality of religion, then, is a responsibility to the neighbor as it is a responsibility to all human beings in the exigency of moral obligations. Levinas is a Jew, his Bible is the Hebrew Scriptures read through the lens of the Talmud and Jewish tradition, but he would not disagree with Spinoza when he wrote "that books that teach and tell of the highest things are equally sacred, in whatever language and by whatever nature they were written."[1] The elevated transcendence of morality and justice are not the exclusive privilege of one religion, or of religions alone, or of the nonreligious either.

Jewish monotheism, then, or Jewish ethics, is without exclusivism, open to all others, who are welcome to join or to not join, just as Judaism is open to the ongoing viability of other monotheisms in their independent integrity. "Their particularity," Levinas says in one of his "confessional" writings, and hence speaking of the monotheism of the Jews, "does not compromise, but rather promotes their universality" (*DF* 13). Or, in an exegesis alerting readers not to an undeserved Jewish arrogance but rather to the paradigmatic character of all things Jewish, to the inherent universality of its covenant, Levinas notes: "a Talmudic text, even when it does not try to prove it, always proves that Judaism and the Jews are necessary to the world" (*NTR* 72). Judaism and Jews are necessary to the world insofar as their teachings and life are imbued with the universality of what Levinas elsewhere calls "biblical humanism": compassion for one another, justice for all others. Judaism is nothing if it is not this difficult teaching.

No doubt Levinas is not the first and not alone in the Jewish tradition to teach the primacy of ethics. Judaism is permeated and sanctified by its long prophetic tradition. He is preeminent, however, in teaching the primacy of ethics to an audience of readers steeped in a contemporary thought often oblivious of or antithetical to the primacy of moral responsibility—from Marx, Bergson, Nietzsche, and Freud, to Husserl, Heidegger, Merleau-Ponty, Sartre, Foucault, Derrida, and Deleuze. The genius of Levinas is not to have invented a new morality or new religion, but rather to have pierced through and unmasked the pretentions of many of today's most sophisticated cultural and philosophical perspectives to have done precisely that. Regarding Levinas's predecessors in Judaism, in the following, I have singled out the great Italian rabbi and kabbalist Eli Benamozegh who, one hundred years before Levinas, articulated a brilliant and philosophically informed vision of Jewish universalism embedded within Jewish particularism or talmudic Judaism.

It seems undeniable that Levinas shares with many other Jewish thinkers a certain skepticism regarding Christianity. Perhaps he was influenced by the essays collected in Leo Baeck's *Judaism and Christianity*, where Judaism's concrete commitment to redemptive justice and its moral and holy adherence to law without legalism is contrasted favorably to what Baeck takes to be Christianity's merely personal and sentimental notion of salvation, which, coupled to its otherworldly faith, promotes a social and political quietism and fatalism and in that way justifies irresponsibility and escapism. No doubt, Levinas pays homage to that Christianity and those Christians, lay and ecclesiastical, that have made morality and justice central to religious life. Levinas is quite aware—along with thoughtful Christians such as Kant, Rauschenbusch and Bonhoeffer, to name only three—that Christianity is fully capable of rising to its ethical vocation. But he does not shy away from criticizing religiosity which fails to rise to the heights of an ethical mission, which subscribes to a primitive spiritualism or a magical ritualism and thereby avoids and sullies the higher and greater responsibilities of holiness.

Levinas opposes not only mythology, the refuge of paganism and its worship of the body, but also onto-theology, the notion that God must be represented as a preeminent being, a being somehow "above" and somehow—always inexplicably—"ruling" over all other beings. The transcendence of God for Levinas is not an absence, lack or negativity, not the product of epistemological failure or nothingness in being. Rather it is manifest as a superlative, an excess or surplus, a "more" in the less—"benevolence" as humanity's call to the *better*. God's transcendence is no manifestation at all, not a play of presence and absence, a hide and seek of revealing and withdrawing, but the very surplus of the good above being. Thus for Levinas: "The fact that the relationship with the Divine crosses the relationship with men and coincides with social justice is therefore what epitomizes the entire spirit of the Jewish Bible" (*DF* 19).

I have taken this and several previous citations from the short article from which the title of the present part is borrowed: "A Religion for Adults." Clearly, Levinas radically opposes irresponsibility sanctioned by religion. He opposes childishness, immaturity, and irresponsibility everywhere, but especially in religion—it demeans both God and humanity. For Levinas humans are not God's pets; they are his partners. Thus Levinas who opposes stupidity and ignorance, who opposes the oracular assertions of a blind faith, opposes all of these most especially in religion. God demands not abject submission but justice, self-sacrifice in a worthy cause. Here Levinas sides with Nachmanides in his disputation in Barcelona nearly a thousand years ago: God and religion demand that humans stand on their feet, not arrogantly, but with the pride and humility, and the courage—indeed the nobility—of the obligations and responsibilities to their fellows inspired by God's demand for compassion and justice.

It seems to me that religion for adults should not be on the defensive against the childishness, the stupidities, the foolishness, the escapism and fantasies of fundamentalist religion. Rather the relation should be reversed: it is the fundamentalists who should feel embarrassed, indeed, ashamed of how they have distorted and undermined religion. Stupefaction and mystification are not religious; they are tools of a political manipulation. It is high time that religion recognized and took up the real responsibilities of holiness: ethical responsibilities. Religion should be the greatest spur and not the most despicable obstacle to what are in fact the most difficult and yet the highest aspirations of a morality and justice which are still far above our present state. Religion is not an opium, not some pie in the sky. It is the work of bettering the world. Its true road, as Levinas understands and teaches, is the one initiated in that ancient and yet still paradigmatic exodus from slavery to freedom, the difficult march forward and upward, which Mahatma Gandhi and Martin Luther King Jr. knew so well and for which they gave their lives.

The other person suffers: I must help. "Fear of God" is neither a cowering or a private anxiety, but resistance to evil, acts of kindness, opposition to injustice, defense of justice. "The fear of God," Levinas writes, "which reveals itself concretely as the fear for the other man" (*BV* 96). "The justice rendered to the other person, my neighbor, gives me an unsurpassable proximity to God" (*DF* 18).

TEN

Levinas, Judaism, and the Primacy of the Ethical

God tells us to be holy, not meaning that we ought to imitate Him, but that we ought to strive to approximate to the unattainable ideal of holiness.

— Immanuel Kant, *Lectures on Ethics*

To every judge who judges truly, even for an hour, the Scripture reckons it as if he had been a partner with God in the work of creation.
— *B. Talmud, Tractate Shabbat,* 10a.

INTRODUCTION: FROM KOVNO TO PARIS

Emmanuel Levinas was born on January 12, 1906,[1] in the Lithuanian city of Kaunas, known as "Kovno" to both Poles and Jews. In 1923, at the age of sixteen, Levinas left Kovno to study philosophy at the University of Strasbourg in France. During the 1928–29 academic year, he studied in Freiburg under Edmund Husserl and Martin Heidegger. In 1930 he moved to Paris; married Raisa Levy, who as a child lived on the same block in Kovno as Levinas; became a French citizen; found employment at the *Ecole Normale Israelite Orientale;* published academic articles on Husserlian phenomenology, his Strasbourg thesis, the prize-winning book *The Theory of Intuition in Husserl's Phenomenology,* and short pieces in Jewish journals on Jewish topics; and otherwise entered into the vibrant intellectual life of Paris. Conscripted into the French army in 1939, Levinas spent the war years in a German prisoner-of-war camp. After the war, he became Director of the *Ecole Normale Israelite Orientale,* and in 1947 published his first two original philosophical books: *Time and the Other* and *Existence and Existents*. After the war Levinas also began his talmudic studies under the hidden talmudic master known only as "Monsieur Shoshani" or "Professor Shoshani," who was also at the same time teaching Elie Wiesel, amongst others.[2] In 1959 Levinas delivered the first of his many talmudic readings at the annual colloquia of French Jewish Intellectuals, a group that had been formed two years earlier in 1957.

In 1961, Levinas published his magnum opus, an ethics, *Totality and Infinity*, which served as his thesis for the French Doctorate in Letters. With the support of Jean Wahl, Levinas obtained his first academic post at the University of Poitiers in 1963. In 1967 he moved to the University of Paris-Nanterre, to join Paul Ricoeur there; and finally from 1973 to his retirement in 1976, Levinas finished his academic career at the University of Paris-Sorbonne where, as an Emeritus Professor of Philosophy, he taught courses until 1979.

In 1974 Levinas published his second magnum opus, *Otherwise than Being or Beyond Essence*. In addition to the four philosophical books named above, from the 1930s to the 1990s Levinas published many articles both in philosophy and Judaism, almost all of which have by now been collected into various volumes, most of them having been put together and prefaced by Levinas, but some also edited by others and published posthumously.

Levinas died at the age of 89 on December 25, 1995 (the eighth day of Chanukah), after a few debilitating years suffering from Alzheimer's disease.

The central message of Emmanuel Levinas's philosophy is in fact quite simple, well-known, and ancient, though at the same time notoriously difficult in execution: "Love your neighbor as yourself." Nevertheless, despite the straightforwardness and near-universal consent to this essential moral teaching, the language Levinas utilizes to set his philosophy in motion and the context to which his philosophy responds are rather complex and at least initially quite daunting. Many neophyte readers of Levinas complain of the density of his texts, and it is true that Levinas makes little concession to mass opinion or taste. He is writing on the basis of the entirety of Western civilization, from Athens to Jerusalem to Rome, and writing with all of its greatest contributors and interlocutors in mind.

Levinas's thought is not only engaged in philosophy and committed to modernity, fully open to the discoveries of the modern sciences and the phenomenological extensions of science; it is also faithful to a long tradition of Jewish monotheist spirituality and wisdom. Levinas is at once and without compromise both a philosopher and a Jewish thinker. "There is," he once said in an interview, "a communication between faith and philosophy and not the notorious conflict" (*ITN* 170). In the following we shall have to see more precisely how Levinas harmonizes, or rather begins in the continuity of, the thought of Judaism and philosophy, but we can say right away that because he avoids the tempting simplicity of certain all too obvious dichotomies, entrance into his thought is for this reason, too, made more difficult.

It is time to enter into Levinas's thought, which we will do by first grasping the meaning of *monotheism*. Judaism, whatever its specific character, is a monotheism. What then is the essence of monotheism? Furthermore, how does *modernity*, the shift from the ancient and medieval standards of intellection, permanence and eternity, to those of will, change and time, mark a difference for monotheism? How is the ethical metaphysics of Emmanuel Levinas to be thought in relation to monotheism in general, to the ethical monotheism of Judaism in particular, and, with regard to both, to the intellectual and spiritual shift from a classical to a modern sensibility? These are the questions that guide this chapter.

I have said that Levinas's thought is at once philosophical and Jewish, and that Judaism is a monotheist religion. "The God of Abraham, the God of Isaac, and the God of Jacob"—the God of the Jewish people, of Judaism—is a monotheistic God. Nevertheless, beyond Bible stories, rituals, dietary restrictions, holy places and times, beyond everything that constitutes the particularities of the particular monotheist religions (Judaism, Christianity, Islam), to *comprehend* monotheism is impossible because monotheism, by its very nature, *exceeds* human understanding. But how exactly does *monotheism* exceed human understanding? Let me explore this question by examining what I call the "paradox of monotheism."

THE PARADOX OF MONOTHEISM

The paradox unravels in three steps. All three are necessary, and all three together lie at the core of all monotheist religions. First, the monotheist God is *perfect*—by definition. This is not something one can argue over. It is the basic irrevocable premise of monotheism. If one worships an imperfect God, one is not worshipping the God of monotheism. Moreover, the perfection of God's perfection is absolute. No attributes, qualities, or adjectives can be applied to God's perfection insofar as all attributes, qualities and adjectives are taken from *our* finite world and can therefore only be applied to God by analogy or negation. God's absolute perfection, what Levinas, citing from Rabbi Hayyim of Volozhyn's *Nefesh HaChayim* (*The Soul of Life*), refers to as "God *on his own side*" (*BV* 162–63), is perfection without duality, multiplicity or contrast. Here the "oneness" (*echud*) of God is not numerical, one among other ones, but unique, incomparable. Levinas invokes a phrase from Deuteronomy 4:39: "there is nothing outside him" (164). Here is God prior to or without creation. It is what kabbalists have called *ayin*, literally "nothingness," or "pure spirituality" (if we leave the term "spirit" undefined and indeterminate), in contrast to *yesh*, "existence" or "palpable reality," literally "there is."

Second, the perfect God of monotheism *creates* an *imperfect* universe. The process of creation—which is one of the central topics of Kabbalah, or so, at least, are the opening verses of *Genesis*—is a mystery unto itself. What is important for the paradox, however, is the imperfection of creation (possible, so say the kabbalists, only through the "withdrawal" of God, whatever that means). It includes, in some sense, ignorance as well as knowledge, evil as well as good, ignoble feelings as well as noble feelings, the profane as well as the holy. Here, then, in "this world," instead of a unique and absolutely perfect One with no other, there is *hierarchy*, the above and the below, the better and the worse. In contrast to absolute perfection, here one has "God *on our side*," to again invoke the language Levinas takes from Rabbi Hayyim of Volozhyn's master work. In Judaism the term "holy" (*kadosh*), according to the classic interpretation given by Rabbi Solomon ben Isaac (Rashi), refers to "separation": of the holy from the profane, the pure from the impure, the noble from the vulgar. Separation refers, on the one hand, to the fundamental difference between Creator and creation, and on the other hand, to the differences within creation, between beings. "Before you could feast your eyes" directly on God, the rabbis have taught in the Midrash, "you fell to earth."[3]

Regarding the differences within and between the three great monotheistic religions, these occur by determining in what primary sense creation is a diminution, an imperfection of God's original perfection. Each must answer the question as to the meaning and nature of creation in relation to God. What follows from the answers to this basic question is the very legitimacy, the appropriateness and the hierarchy of the religiously sanctioned countermeasures—such as wisdom, faith, prayer, charity, repentance, good works, sacrament, sentiment, righteousness, asceticism, and so on—of which creatures are thought to be capable in order to rectify the imperfection of creation. That is to say, determining the meaning of creation's imperfection determines the meaning and function of the actual monotheist religions: Judaism, Christianity or Islam. So, step one: the perfection of God. Step two: the imperfection of creation.

Third, however, because God is perfect everything that follows from God is also perfect, completely perfect like its source—including creation! Only the perfect follows from perfection, otherwise perfection would not be perfection. Because all is perfect, nothing is required, no countermeasures are called for, and no legitimation or rectification is needed. From the point of view of this third element, even for a creature to be grateful for perfection is essentially an ungrateful attitude, since grateful or not, all remains perfect. Nothing is required. Perfection cannot require anything without diminishing itself. And perfection, because it is perfection, is undiminished. Here, then, latent in this third element, *taken by itself,* lies the seduction of *nihilism,* a *holy nihilism,* the temptation of *excess,* let us call it, in contrast to *surplus.* "The spiritualism beyond all difference that would come from the creature," Levinas has written of this excess originating in creation, "means, for man, the indifference of nihilism. All is equal in the omnipresence of God. All is divine. All is permitted" (*BV* 166). But so too nothing is permitted because nothing is forbidden...whatever is, is—without hierarchy, without orientation, without motivation. *Nihil obstat* (nothing stands in the way), but also *nil admirari* (to admire nothing). But no less, or, more accurately from the monotheist perspective, far more: this perfection is nothing less than the pure splendorous glory of God's perfect holiness, pure unadulterated plenitude without end or limit. All is God and God is all.

The paradox of monotheism derives from the simultaneous truth of all three elements: God is perfect, and creation is at once both imperfect and completely perfect.[4] It is precisely *the surplus of this paradox that lies at the root of all monotheism.* It is upon this paradox (metaphorically called a "foundation stone" or "rock") *and because of this paradox* that actual monotheist *religions*—not "religion in general" but Judaism, Christianity and Islam—are built, and which they reflect in all their concrete particularity from liturgy to daily activity to theology. It is precisely *this paradox* that cannot be grasped or known, for it exceeds human understanding. This is the specific incomprehension that lies at the root of monotheism.

THE PARADOX BENEATH OR ABOVE

Like any paradox, the paradox of monotheism is fundamentally *nonrational*. It oversteps the two constitutional principles of propositional logic, namely, the principles of noncontradiction and excluded middle. In the case of monotheism, however, these conditions of logic are not only unmet, they *must* be broken. Hence monotheism "is" *beyond* the logic of being and the "sense" it makes (if it makes sense at all), is *beyond* the logic of rationality. The very language of *being*, as understood by philosophers, is thus inadequate to the paradox of monotheism. Being adheres to itself, subsists in itself, develops from itself, while the God of monotheism is both being (God as the im-perfection of creation) and beyond being (God prior to or without creation) at once—"otherwise than being," to use Levinas's formula. One cannot "think," "feel," or "obey" the God of monotheism without invoking an absolute *transcendence*—God's perfection, with or without the world—whose "content" overflows its "container," whether the latter, the container, is conceived as thought, felt as emotion or enacted via action. It is not by accident, then, but by necessity that paradox lies at the core of monotheistic religion.

This otherwise-than-rationality, does not mean, however, that monotheism is *irrational*. Indeed, the key to the *sense* of monotheism—whether in thought, feeling or action, or somehow otherwise—depends on seeing as precisely as possible how the monotheist religions concretely *express* the extra-logical "relation" between God and creation. While a genuinely atheist nihilism might claim that "because there is no God, everything is permitted," it is nevertheless never the case that for monotheistic religion everything is permitted. And everything is not permitted precisely *because* there is God. The entire effort of the monotheistic religions—Judaism, Christianity and Islam—is to highlight the significance of, without utterly confining, what cannot be contained, to reveal without reducing that which ruptures manifestation. Revelation is thus never *only* a particular "content"—for instance the specific texts, rituals, declarations, services, saints and sages revered and exalted by the faithful of the three monotheisms. It is also and more profoundly and closer to the true essence of monotheist religion, a *more* in the *less*—the *surplus* of the paradox. It is often pointed out that a sacred text, in contrast to a profane text, is inexhaustible, indeed infinite. This does not mean that it has one "literal" meaning, allegedly God's meaning. Rather this implies that the sacred text has an infinite number of readings, equal only to the infinity, the perfection of the God whose will it is said to reveal. To determine and make concrete the explosive *sense* of the surplus of the paradox of monotheism, whether primarily it is love, compassion, intellection, command, grace, action, meditation, or something else—this is the task of religion, of the concrete religions, in contrast to philosophy.

There have been two broad and fundamentally opposed responses to the paradox of religion. For those persons like Spinoza and Western philosophers generally, those who adhere consistently to the logic of rationality, the paradox indicates that monotheistic religious mentality is *less* than rational, *subrational*. The real, as Parmenides first insisted and as Hegel later elaborated, conforms to the rational: "The real is rational and the rational is real." The actuality of Jewish, Christian and Muslim monotheistic beliefs and practices, based as they are in paradox, would thus be explained away as the psychological-sociological products of ignorance, primitivism, pathology, herd instinct, grand politics, mass delusion, class consciousness, and the like. For all forms of rationalism the nonrationality of monotheism is merely subrational, merely the symptom a deeper unacknowledged failure.

In contrast, for those persons who adhere to monotheism, the nonrationality of the paradox indicates that religious mentality is *more* than rational, *suprarational*. All that is not rational is not therefore illusory, superstitious, mere appearance. Unlike the "either/or" dualism of the rationalist, the monotheist makes a tripart distinction: irrationality, which one opposes; rationality, which one exceeds; and religion, to which one adheres. *Religion is the making sense of paradox.* The monotheistic religions account for their superior significance as the gift of divine revelation, Holy Spirit, prophetic inspiration, celestial grace, or other like elevated sources. The critical objections of the rationalists are met by characterizing rationality, contrary to its own self-serving claims, as narrow, blind to the transcendence of the divine. The basic effort of monotheist religions is to point toward and approach a "dimension" (what *is* the proper way to speak of this? — *that* is the question) of the *holy* unknown to and unattainable by rationality alone.

REFERENCE, INTENTIONALITY AND CONSCIENCE

It has often been said that between science and religion there can be no middle ground or term and hence only conflict without quarter, because they are mutually exclusive. One side exalts the paradox at the expense of rationality, while the other exalts rationality at the expense of the paradox.[5] Leo Strauss, who has done much to propagate this raw dichotomy, has also shown that when posed in such an opposition neither side can convince the other of its errors because each is based on different grounds entirely.[6] But we must take more seriously the notion that science and religion are not mirror images of one another: neither accepts the other's contextualization. In contrast to the distinction between the rational and the irrational recognized by rationality, religion would offer a third alternative, one based on a positive appreciation of the paradox of monotheism. "This human impossibility of conceiving the Infinite," Levinas writes, "is also a new possibility of signifying" (*BV* 165).

We know that and how rationality rejects religion as a species of the *subrational*. The intelligibility of religious persons would be rejected for being stubborn, infantile, deluded, and the like. But our question and Levinas's is neither how rationality rejects religion nor how religion rejects rationality. Rather, the question is how monotheism admits its fundamental paradox without producing the chaos of irrationality. The real may not be rational, but for all that it is not irrational. The answer of religion is that the *sense* of the paradox finds expression in the *symbol*, not the symbol as a corruption of thought, nor the symbol as a mystification of matter, but rather the symbol as the unstable unity—the "singularity," to use the current term—of the proximate and the distant, being and the otherwise than being. Oriented upward, diagonally, it functions as a pointing, a disruption, a challenge. The great originality of Levinas is to argue that the *symbol*—the *sense* of monotheism as a surplus—is at bottom neither an ontological-epistemological structure nor an aesthetic structure, but an ethical one. In *Totality and Infinity*, he had already written: "God rises to his supreme and ultimate presence as correlative to the justice rendered unto men" (*TI* 78) and: "Everything that cannot be brought back to [*se ramener à*] an [ethical] interhuman relation represents not the superior form but the forever primitive form of religion" (79; my translation).[7]

The problem, then, is one of establishing a level of sense independent of the rationalist dyadic worldview, and yet generative of rationality. It is a question, beyond the paradox of religion, that has troubled, and whose effort to answer it, has determined most of modern thought. In general, however, these various "middle term" alternatives to sense and nonsense have relied on what we can call an *aesthetic ontology*—an attentiveness to the manifestation of manifestation in its own right taken as a new form of epistemology. One sees this quite clearly in the poetry of Heidegger's "ontological difference," where the source of the significance of beings is not their rational or irrational interrelations, whether scientific or historical, but their upsurge from the opening of an openness, a "giving" (which is simultaneously a withdrawal) that is the very "be-ing" (verb) of their being. Such would be the prerational, but not irrational, structure of the revelation of being. Until Levinas, however, no one has thought this new sense of origination in terms of ethics, and even less has it been thought in terms of an ethics based in intersubjectivity. Furthermore, Levinas thinks ethics *ethically*. That is to say, Levinas thinks ethics as the "metaphysics" of the paradox of monotheism, such that its noncoincidence concretely "is" the self morally "put into question" by the other person, in contrast to all the philosophical accounts which remain based in one form or another self-positing, self-consciousness, or aesthetic upsurge.

The Significance of Signifying

One of the best avenues into Levinas's thought is to follow his understanding of the intimate link between the semantic and communicative functions of language. Levinas's own careful study of signification led him to discover a dimension of meaning whose true significance was overlooked by the "intentional" or "noetic-noematic" analyses of meaning laid out by his teacher Husserl as well as by the "revelatory" hermeneutics of Heidegger.

We must remember, first of all, that Husserl's great discovery was a turn to consciousness as the source of meaning for the true, that is to say, for *science,* the "hard" objective sciences. Hitherto, natural science, in contrast to philosophical idealism, had wrested truth out of meaning by correlating signs to their referents. This was its realism, based on a simple correspondence model of truth. Here is the model:

> *Correspondence Theory of Truth:*
> Sign/symbol → (refers to) — Signified/thing itself

What Husserl saw was that a complete understanding of meaning would also require an elucidation of the production of signs by consciousness, a turn to "meaning-bestowing" or constitutive acts. Thus Husserl supplemented the realist sign-referent structure with its "origin" in the signifying acts of consciousness. Here is the model:

> *Intentional (or "Transcendental") Analysis of Signification:*
> Signifier/consciousness ⇨ (Sign/symbol → (refers to) — Signified/thing itself)

Of course this "transcendental" approach opened the door not only to a clarification of the origin in consciousness of scientific or representational significations, but also to a clarification of the origin in consciousness, broadly interpreted as "intentional" meaning-bestowal, of many more regions of meaning besides those of representational consciousness, such as the significations opened up by perceptual, imaginative, practical and emotive signifying. Heidegger, for instance, early in *Being and Time,* analyzed the ground of theoretical significations in instrumental significations, in the "worldliness" of the subject's primordial "being-in-the-world" (*BT* 78–148).

What Levinas saw, however, was that in his legitimate concern to provide a broader ground for signification by turning to consciousness,

Husserl still favored a representational model of meaning, a model he had unwittingly borrowed from the objective sciences he aimed to supplement. What struck Levinas's attention, beyond Husserl's broader signifying-sign-signified structure ("intentional" consciousness), was the *communicative* dimension of meaning. Not only is realist meaning, the sign-signified correlation, intended or meant through an act of consciousness, meaning is also that which is said *by* someone *to* someone—it has an *accusative* dimension.[8] There is not only what is *said*, even adding that what is said is produced by consciousness and thus has an "intentional" structure, there is also the *saying* of the *said **to someone***. Here is the model, but in a moment we shall see why there can be no model, no outside perspective with which to thematize what it is that Levinas is pointing to in highlighting the accusative dimension of signification:

InterSubjective Event of Meaning:

Someone/Other

/

(Sign/symbol → (refers to)—signified/thing itself)—to

⇧

Signifier/Subject

What Levinas saw was not only that the *accusative* dimension of meaning could not be recuperated within the signifying-sign-signified structure of intentionality that Husserl had advanced. What he saw, and here lies one aspect of his originality, was that the recognition of the irreducible accusative dimension of signification meant that signification was a function ultimately neither of correspondence with things nor of an intentional origination in consciousness (which, thinking so, led Husserl back to idealism), but rather it is a function of the intersubjective relation. But this is not all. Second, and even more significant, is what comes into play with this recognition of the role of intersubjectivity. It is precisely because the intersubjective relation is fundamental to signification that it is an error to understand and interpret the intersubjective relation in terms of signifying structures that are themselves derivative and not constitutive of it. Rather, then, signification must be interpreted based on the structures of intersubjectivity. And intersubjectivity, to say it again, cannot be interpreted in terms of signifying-sign-signified, that is to say, in terms of language as a system of signs (coherent, revealed, deferred, or otherwise) or as a product of consciousness. The proper interpretation of intersubjectivity, the very essence, as it were, of intersubjectivity, its very upsurge—such is the second aspect of Levinas's claim and his most profound and original insight—is an *ethical* structure: the moral priority of the other person over the self, the self responsible for the other person. The asymmetrical priority of the other person, the other as infinite moral obligation, and the self as moral responsibility in the face of ("accused" by) the other's transcendence—this ethical orientation of the "I" and "You" is what cannot be contained within the signifier-sign-signified structure of language, what cannot be "viewed from the outside," cannot be represented, but nevertheless makes language significant, meaningful, important in the first place.

So, unlike the later structuralists, for instance, for whom this surplus indicated the impact of a larger web of historical-cultural signs, and unlike the later deconstructionists, for Levinas this surplus does not indicate the impact of a semiotic slippage, which would again occur at the level of signs deferring to signs. Rather, for Levinas the irrecoverable *accusative* dimension of signification must be "understood" beyond signs, beyond the *said* (*dit*). What it brings to bear is the impact of an intersubjective or interhuman dimension, a *saying* (*dire*) that is from the first an ethical exigency. The impact of the communicative situation of a self brought into proximity with another self across discourse cannot properly speaking be "understood" because as exterior, transcendent, other, it also cannot be captured in a theme or represented. Beyond the structure of signifier-sign-signified, discourse, speaking, expression—what in another context J. L. Austin conceived in terms of "performance"—do not indicate some failure of signifying to be sufficiently precise, or the intrusion of larger cultural or semiotic determinations (which would undermine the subject's freedom) relative to the sign. Rather the necessity of discourse, of communication, would not be neutral, but would point to an irreducible *priority* deriving from the intersubjective relation, a priority that would overcharge—give meaning to—the entire signifying-sign-signified structure without undermining its validity. This *priority* of the intersubjective dimension can only be accounted for in *ethical* rather than epistemological, ontological or aesthetic terms. The alterity of the other person to whom one speaks and, even more importantly, the alterity of the other person who speaks and to whom the I responds, even in listening, would have the *moral significance* of an *obligation*. *Responsibility*, then, the responsibility to respond to the other person as other, would be the nonintentional root of the intentional construction of signification. The entirety of Levinas's intellectual career is the effort to articulate as precisely as possible this *overriding social and moral surplus* of meaning and its consequences and ramifications for all the dimensions of human life.

INTERSUBJECTIVE ETHICS AND MONOTHEISM

Our guiding questions have to do with Levinas and Judaism. Perhaps the connection is now not so difficult to see. The paradox of monotheism can be construed as the irruption of transcendence within immanence, without that transcendence either absorbing immanence into itself or itself being absorbed by immanence. The paradox, in other words, mimics the structure of *saying-said* that for Levinas is the root structure of ethics. But does monotheism only mimic the structure of ethics, or is ethics rather its best articulation, its closest most faithful realization, monotheism's highest and most holy dispensation? Levinas will say yes. "Ethics is not the corollary of the vision of God, it is that very vision"—at least for a "religion of adults" such as Judaism (*DF* 17). Let us consider the parallels.

Monotheism characterizes transcendence as perfection and immanence as imperfection (and perfection), neither divorcing the two nor identifying them, but holding them in paradoxical relation. What Levinas understood was that the paradox of monotheism could be neither an ontological nor an aesthetic structure, for both of these dimensions of sense, which ultimately reduce away the independence or separation of selfhood, are essentially incapable of maintaining the extra-ordinary "relation without relation" (*relation sans relation*)—transcendence in immanence—characteristic of the monotheistic paradox (*TI* 80). Ethics, however, maintains the self in relation to absolute alterity across responsibilities and obligations. It is the very structure of transcendence in immanence. *Monotheism is an ethical structure.* "Religion," Levinas writes in *Totality and Infinity*, "where relationship subsists between the same and the other despite the impossibility of the Whole — the idea of Infinity — is the ultimate structure" (80). "To know God is to know what must be done" (*DF* 17).

Thus it is not the abstract philosophical omniscience of God, but his concrete personal *benevolence* that is the key to understanding creation. Creation in its relation to God, in the paradoxical conjunction of imperfection and perfection, is constituted by the work of *sanctification as the responsibility of morality* and *redemption as the striving for justice.*[9] The paradox of monotheism is ethics as *tikkun olam,* "repairing the world" through a justice tempered by mercy. One could cite many elucidating texts by Levinas to support this claim such as the entire subsection entitled "The Metaphysical and the Human," of *Totality and Infinity,* from which the following *philosophically* oriented citations are taken.

> The proximity of the Other, the proximity of the neighbor, is in being an ineluctable moment of the revelation of an absolute presence (that is, disengaged from every relation), which expresses itself. . . . God rises to his supreme and ultimate presence as correlative to the justice rendered unto men. . . . The work of justice — the uprightness of the face to face — is necessary in order that the breach that leads to God be produced. . . .
>
> The establishing of this primacy of the ethical, that is, of the relationship of man to man — signification, teaching and justice — a primacy of an irreducible structure upon which all the other structures rest (and in particular all those which, in an original way, seem to put us in contact with an impersonal sublime, aesthetic or ontological), is one of the objectives of the present work. (*TI* 78–79)[10]

Morality and justice are not only "like" religion; they are religion. The path to God is not beneath, around, or above morality and justice but through them. "The harmony between so much goodness and so much legalism constitutes the original note of Judaism" (*DF* 19).

I have cited from *Totality and Infinity* as much as from Levinas's so-called "confessional" writings (for my part the only difference between these two sorts of writings is not in what Levinas says, but in who he says it to). We cannot indulge in the misleading notion that Levinas interprets monotheism *ethically* in his philosophical works alone, as if this manner of speaking were merely the public and acceptable face of what otherwise and more authentically derives from a tribal field of significance from which non-Jews are forever excluded. This is incorrect. There is nothing exclusionary about Judaism (except that it struggles to exclude and eliminate evil and injustice), and nothing supraethical, no faith or blind faith (in the manner of Kierkegaard's Knight of Faith) undergirding Levinas's conception of Judaism. For Levinas the "highest moment" in Abraham's near sacrifice of Isaac, to take the apparently most difficult "religious" counterinstance, is not any rejection of morality on Abraham's part, but precisely Abraham's submission to the moral imperative, the "no" of the angel of God who will not allow murder (*PN* 74). Murder is not evil because the angel or because God forbids it; it is evil, and thus God forbids it. And we find this affirmed, so Levinas argues against Kierkegaard, shortly after the near sacrifice story when we learn that Abraham, who has obviously learned the lesson well, argued with God about saving the cities of Sodom and Gomorrah *in the name of the justice that both humans and God must obey.* Such is "covenant" religion, for covenant—"in the name of justice"—is the *political* expression of the paradox of monotheism. Already in 1937, in an article on "The Meaning of Religious Practice,"[11] Levinas understood Jewish ritual practices not by reducing them like Aesopian fable to moral lessons, or to a hygiene or symbolism, but by seeing in them an interruption, a pause, a check before the passions of the natural attitude and its absorption in the gathering of things (that so impressed Heidegger), hence a distance-taking from any purely natural or naturalist reality. In his mature thought, this hesitation—taught by religious ritual—will be understood in its deepest sense as shame before the evil of which our vital powers are capable, ultimately the recognition, in the face of the other person, that "Thou shall not kill."

In his philosophical writings Levinas focuses a great deal of attention, some of which I have tried to indicate, on the disruptive trace of morality as a nonintentional surplus giving meaning to the signifying functions of intentional consciousness.[12] In his Jewish writings, too—without in the least reverting to an abstract and reductive universalism, hence faithful to the concrete spiritual world of the normative rabbinic tradition—Levinas will no less articulate the "breach" of the absolute in the relative, the disruption of the *said* by *saying*, in terms of morality and justice. The primacy of ethics, to say it directly, is articulated and defended throughout Levinas's writings, both philosophical and Jewish.[13] Insofar as the aim of philosophy is *wisdom* rather than *knowledge*, there is no need and there can be no justification, from the point of view of philosophy itself, for separating philosophical from confessional writings. Not surprisingly, however, since the very topic of "monotheism" is a religious topic, the most explicitly monotheist readings of the primacy of ethics are found in Levinas's "Jewish" writings. There are several, but I refer now to the concluding pages of two essays published in 1977: "Revelation in the Jewish Tradition" and "*In the Image of God,* according to Rabbi Hayyim Volozhiner."

In "*In the Image of God,*" for instance, Levinas recognizes that when Rabbi Hayyim finds the paradox of monotheism in the very syntax of Jewish blessings, which begin addressing God in the second person and conclude referring to God in the third person, the coordination of "God *on our side,*" the immanent God who acts in history, and "God *on his own side,*" the transcendent God in his pure perfection, is *also and no less* a reference to the *moral* imperative placed upon the I facing a You, on the one hand, *and* to the demand for a "disinterested-ness" that, striving for perfection, aims at *justice* for all (*BV* 163), on the other hand. "In this radical contradiction [between *God on our side* and *God on his own side*], neither of the two notions could efface itself before the other....And yet this *modality* of the divine is also the perfection of the moral intention that animates religious life as it is lived from the world and its differences, from the top and the bottom, from the pure and the impure" (165). In the conjunction of proximity ("You") and distance ("He") enunciated in Jewish prayers, Levinas finds *in a certain sense* precisely what so many previous Jewish commentators had found before him — the conjunction of this world and another, the conjunction of the human and the divine, the conjunction of the God's deeds and his Essence. But in Levinas's hands, these conjunctions rest not on an impossible "knowledge" (or mystification) but on the commands, the exigencies, the imperatives of a morality obligated to infinity — a "glory" that "does not belong to the language of contemplation" — yet rectified by justice, a justice serving morality.[14]

The imperfection-hierarchy of creation is precisely a moral imperative, from and to perfection. When Levinas continues, writing of this as "[a] spiritualization that dismisses the forms whose elevation it perfects, but which it transcends as being incompatible with the Absolute," he means precisely religious life as ethical self-over-coming. Religion, in this holy-ethical sense, would no longer be a miraculous or predetermined escape from nothingness, a flight from the utter worthlessness of creation, from its "husks," but rather the perfecting of a creation whose highest sense would be precisely this movement—not necessary or impossible, but *best*—toward moral perfection. In the order of the face-to-face this would mean acts of kindness and compassion. At the social level this—what Levinas calls "political monotheism" (*BV* 186)—would mean the struggle for jus-tice, just laws, just courts, just institutions, not only enforcing but promoting and improving fairness in access and distribution of basic goods and services.[15] Ethics as the ground of the real, Levinas writes, is "a new possibility: the possibility of thinking of the Infinite and the Law together, the very possibility of their conjunction. Man would not simply be the admission of an antinomy of reason. Beyond the antinomy, he would signify a new image of the Absolute" (166–67).[16] Man in the "image and likeness of God" would be ethical man. "His compassion," says the Psalmist, "is upon all His creations" (Psalm 145:9).

The concluding pages of Levinas's article entitled "Revelation in the Jewish Tradition" are even more explicit regarding the height of ethics as the ultimate and irreducible *sense* of the paradox of mono-theistic Judaism:

> The path I would be inclined to take in order to solve the paradox of the Revelation is one which claims that this relation, at first glance a paradoxical one, may find a model in the non-indifference toward the other, in a responsibility toward him, and that it is precisely within this relation that man becomes his self: designated without any possibility of escape, chosen, unique, non-interchangeable and, in this sense, free. Ethics is the model worthy of transcendence, and it is as an ethical *kerygma* that the Bible is Revelation. (*BV* 148)

Elsewhere, in another article, Levinas has this to add: "the Bible...is a book that leads us not toward the mystery of God, but toward the human tasks of man. Monotheism is a humanism. Only simple-tons made it into a theological arithmetic" (*DF* 275). The paradox of monotheism cannot be thought, but it can be enacted as righteous-ness. Such, indeed, was the demand of the prophets and the refine-ment of the rabbis.

In this way, through ethical exegesis, the hollowing out of self-hood as *sacrifice*, as *circumcision of the heart*, as *prayer*, is "brought back" to its sense as infinite obligation to the other person, as "hostage" — "the opposite of repose — anxiety, questioning, seeking, Desire" (*BV* 149). Such is a selfhood "more awake than the psyche of intentionality and the knowledge adequate to its object" — "a relation with an Other which would be *better* than self-possession" — "where the ethical relation with the other is a modality of the relation with God" (149). Levinas continues in the same article: "Rather than being seen in terms of received knowledge, should not the Revelation be thought of as this awakening?" (150). Levinas is not merely serving up homiletics for what in truth are ontological or aesthetic structures: the real is itself determined by the "messianic" ideality of morality and justice. It is perhaps this more than anything else that monotheism "understands" better than philosophy.

Judaism is based in the paradox of monotheism; it is not a Manichaeism. God transcends the world but "is" also within it. God transcends the world without having separated Himself from it: he has given His Torah, His instructions. For many Jews, the most direct path to God is through Torah study. Levinas gives his assent to this emphasis, but with a twist. Torah study does not mean pure intellection, pure erudition, or knowledge for the sake of knowledge. Nor is it the province of the intellectual elite alone. Rather, for Levinas Torah study means learning to be ethical, and not just "learning" to be ethical. It is the teaching of ethics, a goad to moral behavior and a call to justice. Torah study is thus an ethical activism for Levinas.

Levinas's originality, his interpretation of the paradox in ethical rather than epistemological terms, opens up the possibility of a new way to resolve certain conflicts that continue to haunt Jews, Christians, Muslims, and the religious of the world more generally. What Levinas has to contribute is an escape from the hardened and hence inevitable and irresolvable clash of *theologies* for the sake of the shared values of interhuman kindness, the morality of putting the other first, and interhuman fairness, the call for justice for all.

This is not to say that a shift from epistemological grounds, from the clash of theologies and ideologies, to an ethical ground, to love of the neighbor and the call to justice, will automatically solve or resolve all human problems. Not at all. But by opening lines of communication between people, rather than simply between ideas, by placing *saying before the said,* Levinas's thought opens up opportunities for discourse, communication, exchange, and interhuman understanding that are lost from the start when one begins with the *said as said*. Levinas took the title of one of his articles from a phrase in a fictional newspaper feature on which he had been asked to comment: "Loving the Torah More than God." What he means, of course, is not that one loves the Torah *more* than God, but that "loving the Torah"—that is, loving your neighbor—is precisely the way and the only way one loves God. To love God before or above or without loving one's neighbor is to turn away from God. Such is the meaning contained in the Hebrew word *shalom,* "peace," which refers not to the peace of conquest, the peace which is really the victor's continual suppression of rebellion, an order Levinas calls "totality," but to the peace of harmony, the peace of respect for and learning from the otherness of the other.

The *sense* of Judaism, as of all genuine humanism (the two are in no way in conflict—Levinas writes of a "biblical humanism" and a "Jewish humanism"), would be to preserve the surplus of the more in the less, the perfect in the imperfect, via the demands of an imperative voice from beyond: the voice of the other person, commanding the self to "its unfulfillable obligation" to one and all (*BV* 150). The perfection of a personal God would be the perfecting of the world. And the perfecting of the world would be to care for the other before oneself, for "the orphan, the widow, the stranger," and from there to care for humanity, for animals, for all sentient life and finally for all of creation. Not sentimentality but morality, morality requiring justice. "And with justice, judge in your gates" (Zech. 8:16)—upon which Rabbi Simeon ben Gamaliel comments: "where justice is wrought, peace and truth are wrought also."[17]

ELEVEN

Emmanuel Levinas
Philosopher and Jew

Religion is the excellence proper to sociality with the Absolute, or, if you will, in the positive sense of the expression, Peace with the other.... This seems to me fundamental to the Judaic faith, in which the relation to God is inseparable from the Torah; that is, inseparable from the recognition of the other person. The relation to God is already ethics; or, as Isaiah 58 would have it, the proximity to God, devotion itself, is devotion to the other man.

— Emmanuel Levinas, *In the Time of the Nations*

For the philosopher and Jewish thinker, Emmanuel Levinas, there is no divorce between philosophy and religion. "There is a communication between faith and philosophy," he writes, "and not the notorious conflict. Communication in both directions" (*ITN* 170). No doubt the continuity between the two derives from the fact that Judaism is obligated to no "theology," to no *logos*, or dogma in conflict with philosophy. Judaism is rather a way of life in covenant with God, and such covenantal life includes knowledge, reflection and questioning—the mentalities traditionally associated with philosophy. But the relationship is deeper. Philosophy and religion are not simply united by life, two of the many activities—like sports, art, or humor—of a human life. For Levinas monotheism provides the ultimate *justification* for philosophy, satisfying philosophy's innermost demand for justification, but in a way that a philosophy detached from religion is unable. How is this possible?

Like many Jewish thinkers before him, Levinas's basic message is that religion (institutionally endorsed relationships with God) and ethics (morality at the interpersonal level and justice at the social level) are inextricably united. Indeed, before they are separate and reunited, they form an integral union. The elevation of genuine piety can neither discard religion for ethics (secular humanism) nor sacrifices ethics for religion (Kierkegaard's "knight of faith"). Rather, one is the expression and fulfillment of the other, and both require obedience to Law. "The justice rendered to the Other, my neighbor," Levinas writes, "gives me an unsurpassable proximity to God.... The pious person is the just person. Justice is the term Judaism prefers to terms more evocative of sentiment" (*DF* 18).

Speaking even more broadly of the social or covenantal character of the human in relation to the divine, Levinas writes in *Totality and Infinity:* "Everything that cannot be reduced to an interhuman relation represents not the superior form but the forever primitive form of religion" (*TI* 79). The origin of theory is not simply praxis, as Marx thought; nor is the origin of both theory and praxis a more primordial aesthetics of sensation or worldliness, as Locke and Heidegger respectively thought. Rather they begin and are permeated by the imperatives of social life as ethics. Prayer and ritual, moral care and juridical structures, as well as knowledge and scientific inquiry, are all ventures in a human sociality driven not by myths and fantasies but by respect for others.

The primacy of ethics—metaphysics as ethics—was also the position taken in mid-nineteenth century Germany by Rabbi Samson Raphael Hirsch, who wrote: "The Sanctuary of the Law in particular and the Law of God in general, strive solely for moral objectives."[1] The primacy of ethics, then, is not the invention of the Renaissance or the Enlightenment or of Reformed and Liberal branches of religion, nor is it merely a defensive or polemical position within faithful orthodoxy. To obey *mitzvot,* the divine commandments (all of which are also "good deeds"), like the compulsory annual reading of Torah and a lifelong Talmud study, requires a constant renewal in the present. Only in this way are the commandments "living," the word of a "living God," operative in the created world that God declares "good" right from the start. In this way eternity and time intersect, require and elicit one another.

One special and important characteristic of Levinas's thought is that it takes the dialectic of tradition—preservation through renewal—seriously in relation to the most important historical and intellectual events of the twentieth century. Such engagement does not date his thought, however, making it outdated in the twenty-first century. Rather it shows the path of genuine thinking, which becomes increasingly profound throughout its historical unfolding, without, for all that, losing its perennial bases and relevance. Levinas responded insightfully to such contemporary events as World War I, the Russian Revolution, World War II, the Holocaust, nuclear weaponry, the State of Israel, space exploration, and others. His philosophy responded critically to the various philosophical formulations and ideologies that underlay these events and that served and continue to serve (explicitly and implicitly) as the intellectual environment of our times. Vitalism, socialism, liberalism, democracy, fascism, phenomenology, existentialism, hermeneutics, structuralism, and deconstruction—these are the intellectual currents of the twentieth century. To be sure, these philosophies are often expressed in a language arcane and unknown to the general public, but serious thought is hardly a matter of journalism or editorializing. The special virtue of Levinas's philosophy is that it responds—and offers a positive alternative—at the highest level to the highest level of thought.

Levinas defends and renews a specifically Jewish vision, driven by Torah, Talmud, and rabbinic commentary, which is at once faithful to *halachic* Judaism (normative, orthodox, or rabbinic Judaism) and relevant to all humanity. To be Jewish and to be human are in no way contradictory postures. To speak the language of Judaism and to speak to all humanity are compatible projects—certainly in Levinas's hands they are. Indeed, the language of humanity, if it is not to become overly abstract and empty, is precisely the language of particular languages and particular communities of speakers. "Jewish universalism," he writes, "has always revealed itself in particularism" (*DF* 164). A fidelity to Judaism which is at once a fidelity to humanity is possible, however, not as a parochial "witnessing," which lacks any criteria of verifiability, but as an exemplary moral responsibility. "A truth is universal," Levinas affirms, "when it applies to every reasonable being. A religion is universal when it is open to all. In this sense, the Judaism that links the Divine to the moral has always aspired to be universal.... This election is made up not of privileges but of responsibilities" (164).

Levinas defends the morality and justice exalted by rabbinic Judaism not with grade school simplicities but rather, like Moses Maimonides in his classic *The Guide for the Perplexed*, by responding to and utilizing the very language of the most clever intellectual ruses and evasions of today's various "cultured despisers of religion." In thus presenting Judaism as a "religion for adults" (*DF* 11–23), a particular but nonparochial religion, Levinas defends it not against windmills and imaginary enemies, or against obsolete ghosts who haunted times past, but rather against the real intellectual and spiritual options that are in fact seducing the fine intelligence of contemporary Jewry and contemporary humanity. The devil of yesterday is not the devil of today, even if the direction he points us to remains the same. No doubt he or she now carries a credit card and can be found shopping with everyone else at malls. No doubt he speaks philosophy too, and can even be "religious."

The enemies of Judaism, and of religion more generally, whether "religious" fundamentalists, agnostics, atheists, or simply those who are indifferent, have taken on new guises, created new vocabularies, and speak the latest lingo. It is at the deepest levels of thought, then, that Levinas steers a course between assimilation and alienation, renewing the message of Judaism for Jews and of ethical monotheism for the whole world. In the present day world of ideas and ideologies, Levinas has urged Jews that "we must return to Jewish wisdom; this is why in our recitation of this wisdom we must reawaken the reason that has gone to sleep; this is why the Judaism of reason must take precedence over the Judaism of prayer; the Jew of the Talmud must take precedence over the Jew of the Psalms" (*DF* 271). Note well: for Levinas the "Judaism of reason" is the Judaism of the Talmud (287)! And the *reason* of the Talmud is for Levinas far closer to the classical wisdom of a Plato than it is to the modern rationalism of a Spinoza or the (mirror image) antirationalism of a Derrida.

Levinas does not invent a new ethics—how absurd! (How dangerous!). Rather, he traces the irreducible and unsurpassable priority of ethical transcendence in the imperatives of the "face" of the other person. What is new, first of all and as I have indicated, are the opponents of monotheism, who are no longer confined to the quaint but obsolete figures of pagan idolaters or superstitious simpletons, though these too, alas, find their contemporary avatars. In our world, the modern world, the "Western" global world, the most sophisticated and danger-ous opposition to religious-ethical life comes from two related fronts.

First, there is the rise of modern science, which in its legitimate search for verifiable evidence deepens an ancient Hellenic disdain for biblical wisdom with a new disdain for the notion of purpose and value altogether. Second, and in a seeming paradox, there is the rise of relativism, both subjective and social, psychologism and his-toricism. The two are related because a science that denies the value of values in the name of realist objectivism produces, as a necessary byproduct, a subjectivism of values. If values are not real or true, in other words, they must be merely subjective and arbitrary. If Locke celebrates "primary qualities," inevitably a Nietzsche will celebrate "secondary qualities." Leibniz, before Nietzsche, so Ernst Cassirer teaches us, had already glimpsed that to even make such a distinction is to reduce them both to anthropology.[2]

For Levinas, however, values are very real, or, rather, they are not real at all: they are *better,* higher, more pressing than the demands of reality or the curiosity of knowledge. "The impossibility of killing," Levinas writes succinctly, "is not real, but moral" (*DF* 10). The hard won and now pervasive success of modern science has falsely accus-tomed us to taking "the real"—especially what can be objectified via quantity and measure—as the standard of values. It is an old associa-tion, deriving from ancient Greece: what is best must be what is most real, and what is most real is what rationality (today's empirical objec-tive sciences) says is real. All of contemporary thought is an effort to come to terms with this reduction, this exile of values. But instead of exasperating it, or celebrating it, or retreating before it, only the thought of Levinas has overcome the hegemony of "value free" sci-ence all the way to its roots. It has done this neither in the name of a deeper notion of being, whether Bergson's *élan vital* or Heidegger's ontological difference; nor in the name of a more inclusive knowl-edge, whether Husserl's phenomenology or Foucault's archaeology; nor, finally, has it escaped in the allegedly playful name of less stable language, whether Nietzsche's nominalism or Derrida's *différance;* but rather "otherwise than being and beyond essence." It has done so in the name of a more fundamental understanding of ethics.

Let us not forget that this solution, the ethical, is far from obvious or self-evident. Several alternatives have offered themselves as competing "solutions" to the problem of value. I will briefly mention three, which I label scientism, aestheticism, and infantilism. Science presents the truth of reality. The true is real and the real is true. All the rest is illusion, error, ignorance—the "not yet" scientific. The problem with this view, however, is that science remains obstinately blind to its own inability to scientifically justify its original resolution, its own unscientific faith in science. Science denies values but still values itself!

Aestheticism, in contrast, claims that scientific knowledge is a limited form ("slavish" says Nietzsche) of the imagination, which is then installed in the hegomic place denied to science. Here the artist, the creator of values, whether a person or a projected person (Heidegger calls it "being" or "*Es gibt*"), reigns supreme. Unfortunately, a multiplicity of incompatible and conflicting viewpoints results from this substitution. Each ultimately seeks its "day in the sun" by means of a violence—overt or hidden—that, having rejected the objectivity of science, each lacks the wherewithal to criticize or morally resist.

The third "solution" is a stultifying and obstinate retreat into premodern ignorance. But unable to answer even the most common sense questions with regard to scientific truths, the adherents of this ostrich-like position end up silencing those who ask them.

None of these worldviews—popular or sophisticated though they can be—are able to satisfy the mature, sober, and worldly wisdom of normative Judaism. "Hebrew studies," Levinas has written, "do not bring man to an exotic wisdom, but reawaken one of the souls of his soul. They herald a man freed from myths and identify spirit with justice" (*DF* 276). Science without values cannot be total. Aestheticism without criteria cannot control violence. Infantilism without truth or reality is enslavement. The unacknowledged motor of all three is an ethics to which they refuse a voice.

The task Levinas sets for himself is to enter into the heart of the most sophisticated twentieth century philosophical "justifications" for the above three worldviews and to expose them—at close quarters, in intimate terms—for their inadequacies. He reveals their overt and latent egoism. And he does this not by citing the Bible or telling tales of pious rabbis or raising his voice, but by engaging and challenging the most advanced discourses of contemporary philosophy and Western civilization.

For Levinas the very "humanity of the human" is constituted as a moral relation—an intersubjective relation—requiring kindness to one's neighbors and justice for all. Instead of thinking of humans as real beings who take on moral behavior as a gloss, or as intellects surpassing common morality, Levinas conceives of humans as moral beings for whom the real—both as science and culture—takes on sense based upon personal responsibility, moral obligations, and justice. Not freedom and culture but responsibility and justice lie at the heart of human selfhood.

Such a perspective demands a radical reorientation in philosophy and the Western scientific outlook as a whole. Socrates, retaining his distance in the freedom of thought, said that "one must know the good to do the good." Levinas, faithful to the decisive declaration of the Jews at Mount Sinai: "*n'ase v'nishmah*" (Exod. 24:7)—"We will do and be obedient," and to all genuine religious "obedience"—says one must do the good to know the good. Obeying the order of goodness is to be neither ignorant nor duped, but to become one's unique human self. "I am irreplaceable in my assumption of responsibility. Being chosen involves a surplus of obligations for which the 'I' of moral consciousness speaks" (*DF* 177). Moral election is not an easy path. It requires effort to help others and effort to keep oneself morally ready to help others. Ethics and religion go hand in hand. "The law is effort." Levinas also writes, "The daily fidelity to the ritual gesture demands a courage that is calmer, nobler and greater than that of the warrior.... The Talmudist does not hesitate to link this royal awakening to the sovereign power of a people capable of the daily ritual.... The law for the Jew is never a yoke. It carries its own joy, which nourishes a religious life" (19). The joy is not the exuberance of animal vitality, and certainly not any pleasure in domination, but rather the heightened and grateful consciousness of contribution—service to others, and hence service to God.

The Hebrew Bible advocates that one "love your neighbor as yourself." Levinas comments that the true meaning of this expression is that loving one's neighbor is oneself. The human cannot be grasped on the basis of a reality as determined by science or a reality as determined by culture and its rhetoric. Rather, the human is called to be *better,* called to and as the task of redeeming the world through morality and justice. Such is the highest task of humanity, the "definition," or rather the election of humanity and the source of all meaning, including all scientific and cultural meanings. It is a joy in the humility of giving rather than receiving, or receiving through giving.

It is noteworthy that for Levinas even the infinite obligations of morality, the ever inadequate deeds of kindness one person performs for another, the obligations that no one can fulfill fully but that no one can rightly shirk — even these obligations are insufficient to the human task. There is a difference, that is to say, between morality and justice. If I give everything to my neighbor then I am neglecting others who are not present! Morality, with its infinite obligations, is not enough! The world is not a garden of Eden; there are more than two people in the world. There are many: family, friends, communities, countries and humanity as a whole, and each requires its fair share. Even if I give everything — even my life — to and for another, I still have no right to remain indifferent to the harm that another may suffer from a third party.

To give a fair share to others and to protect the other person from others, equal treatment under law is required. Furthermore, all the quantitative and rational resources of modern science are required to equitably distribute food, clothing, and so on; to transport goods; and to increase agricultural and manufacturing productivity. In other words, science, properly understood, is far from being an enemy of value. Rather, its true vocation is to be in the service of justice. This insight is important in our day of disenchantment with science. Yes, science is not the *alpha* and *omega* that its early enthusiasts thought it might be. But no, it is not therefore a sham. Morality, to be fair, requires justice; justice, to be possible, requires knowledge and science. Value is therefore not a supplement to modern science; it is its very *raison d'être.* Weapons, scientifically produced, can kill, but medical equipment and training, scientifically produced, can heal. And weapons, in our unredeemed world, can also protect innocent victims. At the bottom of science — the very justification of science — lies service to justice which is based on an irreducible moral obligation to love the neighbor as oneself.

I will conclude beginning with a citation by Levinas, taken from an article devoted to the biblical expression "in the image of God"

(Gen. 1:26) as found in Rabbi Hayyim of Volozhin's *Nefesh Ha'Hayyim,* and testifying to the unsurpassable import of human responsibility:

> Man occupies an exceptional place. Everything depends on him who is at the bottom, in contact with the matter on which his actions are carried out....The 'roots of his soul' reach the top of the hierarchy....There is here an ethical significance to religious commandments: they amount to letting those who are other than self either live or, in the case of transgression, die. Does not the being of man amount to being-for-the-other? Man exercises his mastery and responsibility as mediator between *Elokim* [God] and the worlds by ensuring the presence or absence of *Elokim*....This mastery is interpreted without hesitation as responsibility....Man's interiority derives from his responsibility for the universe. The power of God subordinated to responsibility becomes a moral force. Man does not sin against God when he disobeys commandments; he destroys worlds.[3]

Each human is a moral Atlas upon whose shoulders rests God's creation.

The prophet Micah expressed this same thought: "What does the Lord require of you but to do justice, and to love kindness, and to walk humbly with your God?" (Micah 6:8). We would comment: To walk humbly with God is to love kindness and therefore to do justice. Mercy without justice is mere sentiment, helpless against the onslaughts of violence. Justice without mercy is inhuman, abstract and rigid. Both without God become arrogance. Together mercy (morality in the face of the other person) and justice (law and equality) establish the Kingdom of God on earth, for such a "kingdom" is nothing other than "the brotherhood of man" found in the peace (*shalom*) that respects rather than reduces difference.

To put the other before the self is not to diminish but to elevate the self. In turning itself inside-out, as it were, for the other, the self rises to the responsibilities that constitute its very humanity. Such elevation is holy, for it rises above being which aims only to persevere in (*conatus essendi*) or aggrandize more ("will to power") being. It is a kind of miracle—without mystification—in being, an election higher than being, a demand for self-sacrifice evoked by and put into question by the other. Such a response-ability requires far more than lofty sentiments or beatific feelings, for it is the other's

material needs, the suffering of the other, Levinas insists, that constitute the spiritual needs of the human self. To care for the "widow,
the orphan, the stranger" before oneself is to feed, cloth, house, to
provide education, jobs, public safety, health care, old age security,
political enfranchisement, and justice for all.[4] All of the world's value
and meaning—from the intimate sighs of love to the universal symbols of mathematics—stands or falls on the shoulders of these very
pressing historically concrete responsibilities.

Václav Havel, former President of the Czech Republic, understood
this, and understood its inner relation to the spirit of Europe as the
integral heir of both Athens and Jerusalem, when he spoke the following words to the French Senate in Paris, in an address delivered
on March 3, 1999:

> Four years ago a Lithuanian Jew died who had studied in Germany
> to eventually become a renowned French philosopher. His name was
> Emmanuel Levinas. Guided by the spirit of the oldest European tradi-
> tions, apparently most of all by Jewish traditions, he taught that the
> sense of responsibility for the world is born in us with a look into the
> face of a fellow human being.[5]

The face of the other person is not a mask for a hidden God. The
specificity of each other is not a flaw or failure in being to be sublated.
Rather, in the particular responsibilities and obligations—and the
justice—a face calls forth, in the giving that each face, each person
in his or her particularity, elicits, what arises is the very inspiration,
the very elevation, the very epiphany of God on earth. In the face of
the other, in each other's irreducible alterity, encountered ethically,
better than being, there is traced on earth precisely the "image and
likeness of God."

TWELVE

Uncovering the "Difficult Universality" of the Face-to-Face

Torah or divine teaching, but also prophetic word, is expressed in Judaism, the wisdom of the commentary of the masters in which it is renewed, and in the justice of the laws which are always regulated by the love in which no one's uniqueness can be forgotten. Difficult universality. In the fraternity necessary for the "logical extension" of a genre such as that of Humankind.

—Emmanuel Levinas, *In the Time of the Nations*

Our task: to create universality or at least universal values. Win for man his catholicity.

—Albert Camus, *Notebooks, 1942–1951*, November 1945

NEITHER TRUTH NOR POWER

The invisible but compelling force that commences discourse is moral (*TI* 201). Prior to any agreement or measure one has already heard too much and responded too little. To be human is to be inordinately obligated, responsible for the suffering of others, and at the same time, because that suffering is oceanic, infinite, one has already failed to respond adequately, indeed one has failed inordinately. In this sense the Jewish declaration of trust in God, the *Sh'ma Yisroel*—which may take a variety of verbal forms, such as "I love you"—is not only the last word of the last breath of the Jew; it is also the very first word of the first breath of life, the unwritten *aleph* before the *bet* of *Bereishis* ("In the beginning").

Discourse derives from the encounter of two singular beings conjoined in what Levinas calls the "face to face." There is, first, the singularity of the other person who as a mortal being of flesh and blood suffers and commands aid. The face of the other signifies "Do not murder me," as its condition of possibility, but this ultimate imperative produces more concrete imperatives: "You shall feed me, shelter me, care for me and my things, accompany me, etc." There is, second, the singularity of the moral subject who responds in a responsibility beholden to the face of the other and, built upon this primordial response, responds to all others in the call to justice. But whatever measure of equality it must establish in the name of justice, morality — the good, kindness — begins in the priority of the singular height of the other over all the horizons of the self. It is, as we shall see, an exorbitant height which calls forth an extreme humility. What is best, most excellent, highest, is therefore not a function of the self-assured, dynamic but solitary height of a Renaissance or Nietzschean egoism overfull with its own vitality. Nor is it found in the brilliance and ponderousness of that Olympian conversation of "great" philosophers which echoes in the thought of a Hegel and a Heidegger. Rather, more glorious but without the least publicity, morality commences in the incomparably higher elevation and singularity of the other who faces, and in the singularity of an all consuming self-sacrifice, a holocaust, beholden to the infinite demands of the other person, the one who in piercing the self deepest is always nearest, the neighbor.

These are familiar Levinasian themes. The central issue of this chapter, however, is not singularity but universality. Even more specifically it is the alleged universality of a moral agency which occurs as an election to a unique or nonsubstitutable responsibility for the other. This universality proper to morality and to the ethical discourse of morality must not be conflated or confused with the universality proper to knowledge or to power, because unlike their forms of universality it is paradoxically based on no identity, indeed on no commonality whatsoever between self and other. And yet election to moral responsibility is what Levinas nevertheless insists on calling the "humanity of the human." In what sense, then, if at all, and without eventual or surreptitious recourse to representation or to repression, can we speak of the universality of a morality and ethical discourse rooted in and glorifying absolute singularity? Here, where subjectivity can no longer be conceived in terms of power or truth, and where also, and perhaps even more radically, truth is conceived neither as power nor as subjectivity,[1] where in this conception of moral responsibility is there room for universality?

LEARNING FROM *POIESIS*

To broach this subject, and mindful in particular of the exceptional status—in "method" and "substance"—for Levinas not only of descriptive phenomenology but also and especially of *aggadah* (literally "story" or "narrative") coupled with rabbinic and talmudic exegesis, let us begin by considering the meaning of "poetry," for *poiesis* in its original or etymological sense means a "creative making," and morality in its own way is also a creative making. More specifically we will follow the hint given by Aristotle in his *Poetics* when he claims that "poetry is something more philosophic and of graver import than history" because the enunciations of poetry are *universal* while those of history are not:

> The distinction between historian and poet is not in the one writing prose and the other verse—you might put the work of Herodotus into verse, and it would still be a species of history; it consists really in this, that the one describes the thing that has been, and the other a kind of thing that might be. Hence poetry is something more philosophic and of graver import than history, since its statements are of the nature rather of universals, whereas those of history are particulars.[2]

History reports the past, what is done and finished. These reports are not merely antiquarian curiosities. To the extent that our present remains in continuity with the past, whether because linked by the commonality of "the human condition" or by historical proximity, they also inform us of what is "possible" today because it was actual yesterday.

Poetry, in contrast, speaks of "a kind of thing that might be," what has not yet happened. Its condition is the novelty and unpredictability of the future. Whatever we plan, expect, think or imagine, may turn out completely otherwise. Poetry is universal because in contrast to history it can describe the human condition not limited or constricted to what has already occurred, what has irrevocably transpired. We say it is "fiction," but this takes nothing of its seriousness away when we remember that all the future is today only fiction. And if here, in addition, one is tempted to hold up contemporary hermeneutic theory against Aristotle, to say along with Hans Georg Gadamer and others that history too deals in what is only possible insofar as the meaning of what has happened depends on present and future developments and interpretations, such an objection would really only confirm the philosophical priority and greater gravity of poetry, because history would thus depend on poetry for its meaning.

To sharpen this contrast, let us continue reading from the *Poetics* to see how Aristotle defines and distinguishes the universality of the poetic statement from the particularity of the historical statement.

> By a universal statement I mean one as to what such or such a kind of man will probably or necessarily say or do—which is the aim of poetry, though it affixes proper names to the characters; by a particular statement, one as to what, say, Alcibiades did or had done to him....now whereas we are not yet sure as to the possibility of that which has not happened, that which has happened is manifestly possible, else it would not have come to pass.[3]

The difference between poetic universality and historic particularity, then, which depends on the irreducible difference between the past, the actualized possibility, what real individuals have really done, and the future, the unrealized, what is not yet even a "possibility," has at once to do with time and with freedom. We are already engaged in Bergsonian temporality, then, in duration, where the past and future, contrary to the so-called classical conception of time, are not mirror images of one another, but where the future, unlike the past, is novel, unpredictable, hence a function of freedom. And thus, as Levinas realized even more profoundly than Bergson, we are also engaged in the realm of the human, the domain of transcendence and freedom.

The future stands to the past not in the continuity of an inexorable extrapolation of a causal or deductive series, necessarily determined, as the philosophers would say, or absolutely predestined, as the theologians would say. But for this to be so, for the future to be different from the past and not its mirror's image, there must be the intervention of absolute novelty, initiative *causa sui*, free will.[4] The time of being or the being of time must itself be a creative making. Bergson, for his part, conceived this concatenation of being, time and freedom as "duration," whereby the cosmos itself was unfolding creatively, was a "machine for the making of gods."[5] But such an account would in truth only be a representation of being, time and freedom, as if—*per impossible*—one would be in and of duration and yet at the same time retain the privilege of somehow stepping outside of duration to characterize it as a whole. Levinas, in contrast, will teach that being, time and freedom as creative making requires adhesion to the significance of direct encounter with the transcendence or novelty of the future, transcendence or novelty encountered exclusively—such is his original thesis—in facing the face of the other as moral imperative. For the moment, however, we are approaching Levinas's ethical thought by means of the light shed by Aristotle's understanding of the gravity and universality of *poiesis*.

Here the connection has to do with the free imagination in contrast to perception, representation and, for that matter, conception. The gift of the poet, the wings of the poet's words, as it were, is to imaginatively transport us beyond the past and present, beyond the logic of things and ideas, to suggest what is not yet even a possibility, what might be despite the fact that no one can know beforehand what will be. Possibility, which is only discovered retrospectively, does not determine or frame actuality, since the real is created rather than caused. The poet's discourse is universal, therefore, because it breaks with the actual, and imagines what anyone, any human being—of a certain type or as such—might or might not do or be. For the poet the human is itself an unfinished artwork. All has not been said or done. The art of the poet, whether to make us laugh or cry, is to convince us—indeed, to enchant and seduce us—regarding the probability of what may become a possibility for humans because the poet has imagined it ahead of time. In this capacity poets are indeed the "unacknowledged legislators of the world."[6] Or—to begin to widen our horizon to include morality and ethical discourse—we might say that *poiesis* is an experimental prophecy, neither reporting a future already predestined nor fated as if it were in truth a past that has simply not yet arrived, but creatively imagining possibilities, and in this way suggesting, proposing and delineating specific futures for consideration and possible selection.

We can begin to glimpse, then, how poetic imagination may be related to an ethical universality initiated in the radical singular agency of the moral subject in the face-to-face, a universality which precisely as singular underlies the always relatively more abstract universalities of knowledge and power. It seems to me that what Aristotle is calling the poetic universality, a more or less convincing imagined future humanity, is similar precisely to the dimension of openness that Levinas invokes both as a dimension of the morality to which he points and as an element of his own ethical discourse, which aims to *persuade and impress* its readers with a certain moral correctness and in so doing to go beyond any straightforward epistemological justification. What this means from the side of his phenomenology, is that Levinas uses descriptive phenomenology as far as it can go, as far as the transcendental, and then beyond its horizon he indicates the transcendent moment of moral demand and responsibility. His phenomenology, in other words, is ruptured, overloaded, exceeded by ethics—to use the term of Jean-Luc Marion, it is "saturated."[7] Its positivity bursts with the "ultra-positivity" of moral imperative.[8] Just as the poet's imaginatively possible human way of being must be presented with convincing probability, but all the same remains punctured or diaphanous, a text permeated throughout by the gaping unknown of futurity, so, too, but in a self-consciously ethical register—as what *ought* to be—Levinas's discourse presents an account of humanity ruptured by the imperatives of unfulfilled moral obligations and responsibilities. Just as the poet's future may not be believed, may not be convincing, on the ethical plane the *ought* not only may be refused outright, but even in attempting to accomplish it, even in "being good," it remains unfulfilled, overloaded with greater demands. To accomplish the desire for the most Desirable is to increase rather than to diminish desire (cf. *TI* 23, 50). The face always remains an "enigma" rather than a "phenomenon," its demands unmet even while being met (Cf. *CPP* 61–73). Morality is never done, never enough, not a present but an "already passed" and a "not-yet," a "more" in the "less."

MORALIZING MORALITY

Ethical discourse, for its part, is never done because morality is never done. To think morality done is not neutral but to become complacent, indifferent, and immoral. It is to rely upon and succumb to a rhetoric emptied of sincerity and a politics devoid of justice. The discourse of ethics, too, is not simply about morality, morality as a topic, morality "at a distance," as it were, for it is permeated by the morality it elucidates. Morality occurs in an exorbitant proximity, immediacy without escape, without excuse, without the self-sufficient refuge of substance or identity. Ethical discourse is itself morally obligated in its own speaking by the same obligations and responsibilities about which it speaks. Ethics has its own "reflexivity"; it must be moral as well as just.[9] Thus its saying leads necessarily to an unsaying and a resaying, in a process of infinite refinement—a process Levinas will call "exegesis," "commentary," and "commentary on commentary" (*ITN* 112).

Poetry—creative making, art—taken this way is idealistic, inspirational, without sacrificing its realism, its probability, its "truth." As Aristotle emphasizes, it displays humans both comically worse and tragically better than we commonly are. The force of its discourse is similar, then, at least formally if not in intention, to the demanding imperatives driving Levinas's ethical philosophy and the intricate and subtle discussions of the talmudic rabbis (or "doctors" as Levinas prefers to call them). In its appeal and inspiration, then, it is not so distant from Levinas's understanding of "ethics as first philosophy," or what in his preface to the Italian translation of *Beyond the Verse*, Levinas called a "difficult universality" (*ITN* 113). In the openness of their future, *poiesis*, morality, and ethics stand in stark contrast to *techne*, the technical know-how whose "creativity" consists rather in a fastidious conformity to the order of a preestablished plan or recipe.

We can understand why Aristotle recommends that the tragedian, in contrast to the comedian, take advantage of "historic names,"[10] creating characters based on real historical figures, insofar as the tragic protagonist, who must appeal to our better selves, needs greater credibility as a fictional character than the comic figure whose credibility plays upon our baser selves. The Talmud, as we know, is quite careful to attach historic names, authors, to its statements, even making of the respect shown by this attribution a requirement of piety. "Rav Shmuel bar Yehudah said..." "Rav Yehudah has said in the name of Shmuel..." "Rabbi Yossi ben Abin, and, according to others, Rabbi Yossi ben Zevida, objected..."—the Talmud, so succinct, so parsimonious, laconic to the point of being cryptic, is nevertheless full of these attributions. Furthermore, the hosts of rabbis who appear and speak in the Talmud, even more than the "historic names" recommended by Aristotle, are real. These are rabbis who lived and breathed in ancient Israel and Babylonia, who can be situated historically, whose tombs are revered and are still being uncovered to this day in modern Israel. At the same time and no doubt more importantly, they are ideal figures, larger than life exemplars, the stuff of hagiography, inspirations.

Each other, each person, is, as the Talmud says, "a whole world."[11] Not the enclosed self-referential world of the work of art, but an interlocutor in an unfinished human community, a unique source of unpredictable meaning within an ongoing moral and juridical covenant with the past and the future. Even to embarrass another person is tantamount to murder, which in no way turns talmudic discussion into a Tartuffery of good manners or politeness—quite to the contrary: "for the sake of heaven" every word is examined, criticized, sifted, suspected, turned inside out, in a most skeptical sobriety which is at once the very spirituality of Judaism. Here, as Nietzsche said of the Old Testament, real people speak. One senses a reverberation of the talmudic respect for persons in the title Levinas chose for one of his collections: *Proper Names.* But we must never confuse the singularity of the other person and the moral self with the particularity that distinguishes all spatial-temporal things, like fingerprints or birthdates. The singularity or face of the other person, unlike that of the thing, far from being a unique node within a differential system is rather an explosion of context, an excessive "nudity," as Levinas calls it, "disincarnate" (*TI* 79), beyond the nudity of the skin, a "total alterity" (192), an "absolute difference" (194) that transcends even the color of his or her eyes. The eyes of the other are like metaphysical holes in the universe. They do not reveal another world, but the "otherwise than being or beyond essence," a call to moral attention. Likewise, the moral self responsible for the other is disturbed to its core, de-substantiated, "without identity" (*HO* 58). Moral proximity bursts the historical present and its re-presentations, overcharging the ambiguities and ambivalences of the present with what is greater than an absence: obligations and responsibilities. If we are right in our understanding of Aristotle, we can appreciate that far from highlighting a purely aesthetic or purely formal brilliance, his vision of comedy and tragedy is a moral one, just as theatre, music, and ritual were explicitly moral arts for Confucius.

SOBERING ART

It is precisely the alternative conception of art and poetry so popular today, known as "art for art's sake," as exemplified, say, in the theories of poetry (if not also in the poetry) of Mallarmé and Wallace Stevens,[12] which explicitly denies the moral dimension in art and celebrates its independence and freedom. Picasso's "Guernica," then, like "Whistler's Mother," would be an arrangement in grey and black. It is this conception of art, too, that Levinas severely criticizes in the one article he entirely dedicated to art, "Reality and its Shadow" (*LR* 130–43). It is the responsibility of criticism, he argues there, not only to enter sensitively into the inner world of the work of art but also no less, indeed of far greater importance, to locate it within a broader social context. For Levinas the work of art has an inner tendency toward self-closure, to become an exclusive and miniature world unto itself, what in "Reality and its Shadow" he calls "a dimension of evasion," or more precisely, "an evasion of responsibility" (141). At the same time, however, and because of the actual nonindependence of the work of art, its engagement with the larger world, it contains a "call for exegesis" (*OB* 41). It is to this call the critic responds. What the artwork evades, and what the critic reaffirms, are the difficult but unambiguous imperatives deriving from the larger interhuman and moral context that inevitably permeates the artwork despite itself, what Irving Massey, using a term borrowed from psychology, has called "the permanent anxiety beneath all fiction that drives it to resume even before it is finished."[13] The sincerity of the face, expression, "saying" (*dire*), always a moral significance, drives the significations "said" (*dit*) in language, at once sustaining and rupturing the formation of self-contained artworks. In this sense there are no dead languages, for meaning is already and always a living human endeavor. Art, however, left to its own devices, evades the moral responsibility that makes it possible, opting for an alternative so-called "responsibility," alleged to be higher and more refined, but caring uniquely for itself alone, for the artificial and ambiguous atmosphere of its own mini-world, an ersatz-world, a "shadow" world of ever shifting significations. But this dream of a "completed art" "is false," Levinas writes, "inasmuch as it situates art above reality and recognizes no master for it, and it is immoral inasmuch as it liberates the artist from his duties as a man and assures him of a pretentious and facile nobility" (*LR* 131).

Without the critic the artwork sinks of its own weight into myth, into irresolvable ambiguities and equivocations, producing in those who fall under its sway "a state of hypnotic inertia" (*LR* 131). Without criticism the work of art, unable to speak for itself, "manifests itself in its stupidity as an idol" (137) devolves into the enchanted world Cynthia Ozick has evoked so beautifully in her short story, "The Pagan Rabbi."[14] There she traces the art-world's sensual allure and the concomitant religious dissolution and suicide of (the fictional) Rabbi Isaac Kornfield who becomes enthralled by it. Rabbi Kornfield's is a movement of descent which Levinas would characterize as that from the "holy" to the "sacred," from the height of Jewish transcendence to the sump of pagan immanence, reversing the properly ascendant order which rises from primitive participatory ecstasies to the responsibilities of adult religion, as indicated by the title of Levinas's second collection of talmudic readings, *Du sacré au saint*.[15] The "sacredness" of art, its idolatry, seduces in a compensatory and diverting "bad" infinity of over-refinement, the vain complacency of culture enraptured with and morally anesthetized by the *frissons* of its own sophistication. It excites itself with multiple and never ending stories, tales without parable, fables without moral. It is "[t]he literature of the novel as the prerogative of culture," Levinas acknowledges, "but without doubt," he adds, "at the antipodes from the Torah which is the order of the non-equivocal" (*NTR* 119).

It is the escapism of this self-absorbed enchantment that Levinas finds fundamentally irresponsible and dangerous about the entire "poetic thinking" of the later Heidegger.[16] Heidegger delivers his thought over to the immanence or self-referential tendency of poetry, under the ponderous rhetorical guise of an alleged "generosity" or "giving" of "epochal being," the essence, thereby linguistically tapping into all the prestige of philosophy and its long history. Yet such "thinking as thanking" occurs at the hidden expense—a very great expense, a grave expense—of an allegedly superior blindness and deafness to the cries and suffering of a humanity still tortured by the outrages of injustice. The tasks of a difficult critical judgment upon history, the judging of history, are here once again subordinated and sacrificed to history's judgment, which can be nothing else than the judgment of power, of victors, the judgment of success. Heidegger's voice, his person, the flesh and blood man, cannot be wholly effaced (or "erased," Derrida will later say) in an impossible ventriloquism claiming to speak for being itself, no matter how alluring its "pretentious and facile nobility."[17]

Of course the discourse of ethical metaphysics, the Talmud and all the world's great literature is violated by a reduction to poetry in this immanent, equivocal and escapist sense. Discourse contains another intention, a higher significance, than the play of language with itself. The rabbis of the Talmud, like the characters Aristotle envisions in tragedies, are neither signs nor facts. They are neither entirely fictive, pure inventions or placeholders dependent upon a differential system of signs, nor entirely historical, if by the latter we mean personages buried in the past like artifacts or manuscripts subject only to carbon dating, or to historical or form criticism. No doubt such reductions are possible, but their price is steep. Instead, just as the poetic is higher than the historical, and in its singularity opens to the universal, ethical metaphysics and the Talmud are discourses not only initiated by moral imperatives but ones whose moral inspiration, because it is a moral inspiration, can and must continually renew those persons who engage in them and are engaged by them today.[18]

The keen and exquisitely nuanced dramatic and interrogative structure of the Talmud (an interrogation doubled by the manner in which it is traditionally learned by paired study partners) ensures that the moral dimension of its discourse cannot easily be forgotten, reduced or underestimated. To insult such discussions as "hair splitting" is to admit only one's own intellectual dullness and moral complacency. The rabbis, their discourses and dramas are *paradigmatic,* the universal in the singular, the universal enacted, alive, concrete. Levinas laments of this procedure of adherence to the concrete, this reading of the spirit in the letter, this living of ideas, that "this is never made explicit enough, which risks perpetuating the impression of a primitive or outdated formalism—this *paradigmatic conceptualism* is a theoretical procedure for comprehending the Real" (*NTR* 56; my italics). Here persons, sayings, and lives are not simply *examples* of a preestablished or preconceived order of meaning, but novel irruptions of meaning disrupting, refining and hence continually reordering the forever inadequate moral significance of the established order of meaning. More than examples or the exemplary, what transpires and what one learns is a creative making, which is the literal meaning of the Greek term *poiesis*, and hence justifies the expression "talmudic poetry." Here, contrary to the facile rhetoric of so much external criticism of monotheism, the "Eternal" and the "changing" combine. Here, indeed, the Eternal can only become manifest in and as the ongoing refinement of a moral covenant. The bush is burning even if and precisely because it can never be consumed. "The essence of the Torah," Rabbi Joseph B. Soloveitchik has written in his book *Halakhic Man*, "is intellectual creativity."[19] Michael Fishbane names the same ethical juncture of tradition and interpretive daring "the exegetical imagination."[20] In such paradigmatic life and thought the past does not paralyze the present, but neither does the future overthrow it. Rather, the present is lived as a covenant, a moral commitment and hope, a moral discipline bound to a tradition which limits but at the same time is continually open to and opened by the unmet imperatives of the future. Everything about these persons and what they say, everything about this "narrative" or "*aggadah*" is not only open to but strictly requires the dynamic interpretive movement and discipline of "ethical exegesis."

ELECTION IS NOT EGOISM

Let us return to our guiding question, the difficult question of what exactly is the universal dimension of morality as conceived by Levinas. We know what it is not. It is not the universality proper to representational and objective knowledge, the "all" of propositional logic. Hence it is not the universality of law found in Kant's first formulation of the "categorical imperative" of the "absolutely good will," namely, to: "Always act according to that maxim whose universality as a law you can at the same time will."[21] Because the transcendence of the other and the initiative of the self are both absolute, without commonality and hence incommensurate, law derives from but cannot therefore inaugurate morality. Morality emerges, paradoxically, across an unbridgeable proximity, a "relation without relation" (*TI* 80): the other's inordinate command and the shamed self's responsiveness, its for-the-other. So our question becomes: what is universal about the morality of the face-to-face, about the commanding alterity of the unique one who faces and the first person singular responsibility of the moral self? It is not an easy question insofar as the singularity of the face and the singularity of responsibility seem to preclude the very possibility of universality and universalization, or are rather, so Levinas claims, their condition.

Indeed, Levinas explicitly insists on the emphatic "*as for me*" when he speaks of the subject's self-constitutional responsibility for-the-other. Is he not therefore perforce referring to no more (and no less) than *his own* moral responsibility? While the ego, or rather while I am responsible, "me, myself," in the first person singular, it seems that for precisely this reason I cannot *in principle* insist on *your* responsibility or on the responsibility of anyone other than myself. Though I take the whole world's troubles on my shoulders, your responsibility presumably remains entirely up to you. And there's the rub. Even if I am, as Levinas says "responsible for his responsibility" (*LR* 180), how can I make or force or demand a morality, which derives from the absolute singularity of the first person singular, from the other? At the level of morality, though not of justice, with nothing in common between I and you, with no reciprocity or "mutuality"—for it is precisely on this point that Levinas rejects Buber[22]—in what way does morality have anything to do with universality? Indeed, in what way can one even speak of morality, of an imperative, say, for humans to be good, rather than of *my responsibility*, bearing upon me alone, for myself and no one else? By heightening the transcendence of the other to an absolute, and by concomitantly deepening the independence of the self, has not Levinas trapped himself, despite his allegedly good intentions, in a solipsism or monadicism which in name only can be called "responsible"? Is not—irony of ironies—Levinas's moral self responsible only for itself, and hence the greatest egoism? Such an entirely preposterous outcome seems to follow logically, and especially upon reflection. And if it does, putting aside our astonishment, it is not only ethics and morality that collapse. So too does the very possibility of communication and language. Does not Levinas's ethical metaphysics indeed lead to the violence about which Derrida was the first to warn and awaken us?[23]

The answer to these challenges lies in the superlative immediacy of the face-to-face, in the unique directness, straightforwardness or proximity of interlocutors, in the *suffering* embodied transcending command of the other, the "face," and in the *shame* and *humility* of a self giving to and giving itself to the other though nevertheless never sufficiently for-the-other—a proximity whose primordial "curvature" is always already moral—kindness, compassion, self-sacrifice—prior even to the ethics which best articulates this excess. For Levinas morality begins in the height of the face of the other, which is to say, in the other person's mortality and suffering, which impinge upon the self, upsetting and challenging the self's natural vitality, shaming the self, converting it to a responsiveness which is moral responsibility, a responsibility for the suffering of the other. There is nothing abstract about the universality Levinas sees as the very beginning of morality. We should all behave responsibly—certainly. We should all love our neighbors—absolutely. We should all honor our parents and honor our teachers—no doubt. Nevertheless, despite the universality of the "all," responsibility inexorably can only begin with *each* self in its "me, myself," with an ego, that is to say, continually and never adequately denucleated of its own spontaneous vitality for the sake of a responsibility—which can always be greater, and hence which is never enough—for the other's needs before one's own.

What is universal in morality, then, is what is paradoxically most singular at the same time, what is least universalizable in the Kantian or formal sense: one's own unique and irreplaceable responsibility for the other person. It is what Levinas calls "election," invoking a specifically Jewish religious language, but without in any way diminishing its universality. "The notion of Israel," Levinas has written, "in the Talmud, as my master had taught me, must be separated from all particularism, except for that of election. But election means a surplus of duties."[24] Such is the "humanity of the human" in *each* of us, starting with myself. It is the imperative to be oneself by being-beyond-oneself, for-the-other despite and before oneself. It is only by creating one's own humanity, where an individual rises to his or her irreplaceably singular responsibility in the face of the other, loving the neighbor before oneself, that one acts in the unsurpassable dignity the Bible dares to call "in the image and likeness of God."

THE HOLINESS OF HUMILITY

In being-for-the-other the self is its "higher self," its "human" self. One cannot confuse being-for-the-other with being-for-oneself because the former begins with the other while the latter begins with the self. The former, the human self, is the self "put into question" by the other, while the latter, the selfish self, is the self projected upon the world. One must step down or away from the formal level of representation—a step somehow invisible to Derrida for all his brilliance—in order to appreciate the universality of the *each* in its for-the-other. I would like here to invoke a very brief biblical commentary of Rabbi Eli Munk to better understand this point. We all know that Levinas's famous expression "face-to-face" is taken from Genesis 32:31, where, after having fought an angel all night, it is written: "And Jacob called the name of the place Peniel: for I have seen God face to face, and my life is preserved." The place name "Peniel" (Pey-Nun-Yud-Aleph-Lamed) broken into two words, Pey-Nun-Yud and Aleph-Lamed, means "face of God." But in the very next verse "Peniel" is spelt "Penuel" (Pey-Nun-Vov-Aleph-Lamed), a Vov instead of a Yud in the middle of the word.[25] Rabbi Munk notes that here the word broken into two parts, Pey-Nun-Vov and Aleph-Lamed, means instead "turn to God." It is precisely an expression of the universality of morality in the singularity of the responsible person: "face of God" is for Jacob, who has overcome the angel of evil (the rabbis understand the angel to be Esau's angel); and at the same time Jacob's wrestling is also a movement for others in future generations to maintain and develop, for they too should "turn to God." "Face-to-face": "Peniel," *as for me,* the humanity of the human; "Penuel," a "difficult universality," also—and together with the first—the humanity of the human. Perhaps on this basis, too, we can better understand the gloss on a verse coming just a few verses after, when Jacob actually meets with his brother Esau and says to him: "I have seen your face, which is like seeing the face of a Divine being" (Gen. 33:10). The human self is the self rising to the height of the other as toward the transcendence of God, elected, insufficient, required always to do more, and in this excess paradigmatic.

Such moral nobility, the self "turned inside out" for-the-other-before-oneself, is universal in what Levinas has named a "difficult universality," recalling or rephrasing, really, his more famous notion of a "difficult freedom." In a certain sense the moral self, unique in its relation to the other, is singular to the point of exceeding even the already high contagion of the exemplary. Morality is ultimately like a marriage: experienced exclusively from within. About this intimacy

Ecclesiastes (7:2) recommends that "it is better to go to the house of mourning than to go to a house of feasting," if one can attend only one, because, so the rabbis comment, it is only after the death of a person that one can learn a modicum of his or her true moral greatness. When, that is to say, those who were in proximity with that person can speak for the first time about the person (to eulogize) without speaking to the person. At the same time, in its election and only in its election, rising toward a height it can never reach, is the self worthy—in its worthy unworthiness, if we may say this—of the humanity which is each and everyone's nobility.

Levinas has written an entire article about this extreme goodness linked to extreme humility, and its relation to God, entitled "Judaism and Kenosis" (*ITN* 114–32). I cannot recommend it too highly. To understand the conjunction of singularity and universality in moral humility, I will turn elsewhere, however, to Moses Maimonides' celebrated eightfold hierarchy of righteousness (*tzedakah*), which in English is usually named "charity," found in his great work, the *Mishnei Torah.*[26]

This hierarchy, it seems to me, is ordered according to a very specific principle of humility or invisibility appropriate to the moral dimension of human fraternity, that is, to the height and depth of the other's transcendence penetrating into the self, or, to say the same thing differently, to the self's ever increasing denucleating or self-sacrifice for-the-other. The eighth and lowest form of *tzedakah*—which, however, let us not forget, is better than no *tzedakah* at all—is to give to others, but to do so sourly or begrudgingly. Here the donor asserts selfishness even in the selfless act. The seventh highest form of *tzedakah* is to give, but not to give enough. Again, the needs of the other person count, but only to the measure of the donor's needs. The sixth highest level is to give after being asked, as if the alterity of the other were not the very definition of the self but a mere contingency, an accident. In all these lower levels of charity the self, despite the praiseworthy fact and nobility of its giving, continues to assert itself, its own needs, its ownness, its *Eigenlichkeit,* over the needs of the other.

The fifth highest level represents a break. It is to give before being asked. In this case the other is already in the self as the self. All the subsequent levels of *tzedakah* will further refine this interiority of the other in the self. The fourth highest level of *tzedakah* is to give in such a way that the receiver is unknown to the donor, although the donor is known to the receiver. Here the donor responds in part to the asymmetrical, noneconomic or one-way direction of moral responsibility, by sparing himself or herself of even the hint of reciprocity. I do not know who the other to whom I give is, so I cannot ask for anything in return. An objective check is put on my selfishness. So, too, then, can we understand why the next level of *tzedakah* is higher, indeed, the third highest. Here it is the receiver who is spared knowing the donor. So the feelings of the poorer, the one who receives, the one who would therefore feel beholden, take precedence over the giver. The other is spared humiliation, but I the giver nevertheless still know who has received. Higher still, indeed, the second highest level of *tzedakah*, is when both parties are unknown to one another, sparing both giver and receiver of even the hint of a demand for reciprocity. In the anonymity, in the pure disinterestedness and completely noneconomic character of this giving and receiving lay the true essence of moral responsibility, the full weight of a responsibility which bears upon oneself above all and at the same time is the humanity of all and for all. In such a situation the other penetrates into the self as the self and without limit, even if for all that the giving remains inadequate.

Which leads finally to the uppermost and highest level of *tzedakah*: not only anonymous for both persons, but a providing for the other person before the other person needs help. It is to anticipate the needs of the other as if the other's needs were one's own. It is therefore to give as if there were neither giving nor receiving. It is therefore to spare the other from being poor, from being a receiver, from being beholden, hence to spare the other person of even the slightest embarrassment to his or her dignity. The expression "Love your neighbor as yourself," Levinas writes, means that loving your neighbor *is* yourself (*ITN* 110). What this "responsibility for the other's responsibility" means concretely is to have prevision and make provision for the other's employment and enjoyment. At this level of *tzedakah* moral agency is completely invisible, as if not needs and destitution but plenitude and desires alone were at play, as if, that is to say, there were no *tzedakah* at all. It is, we can say, a *Purim of morality*, not, of course because the "curse of Haman" and the "blessing of Mordechai" would be indistinguishable, but so much the reverse because as in the Scroll of Esther the name of God, or in this case, the imperatives of morality, would be commanding effectively but completely invisibly. Each person, regardless of relative wealth and worldly success, would be treated "in the image and likeness of God."

I would like to suggest, too, that beyond all quaint and rustic and sometimes even mythological storytelling, this level of *tzedakah,* this completely invisible righteousness, is yet another way to understand the extraordinary humility of the famous 36 "Lamed-Vovniks," the hidden masters upon whose unrecognized shoulders, according to the Jewish tradition, the very existence of this and all worlds depend. Along a similar line, Rabbi Judah Zvi of Stretin noted: "The [Hebrew] word *ani* [Hebrew spelling: Aleph-Nun-Yud], "I," which denotes the proud and haughty person, and *ain* [Hebrew spelling: Aleph-Yud-Nun], "nothing," which denotes the meek and humble one, have the same letters. But in the first word, the *Yud* [= *Yid* = Jew] is on the outside, while in the second word, it is inside."[27] This is not to teach, of course, that one must "be a Jew at home and a good citizen outside," but rather that, like Moses, "the humblest of men," the Jew, the moral being, must be and in the highest sense can only be moral regardless of and indifferent to all fanfare or worldly recognition.

In conclusion: the universality proper to morality and ethics is a universality which is at the same time a singularity: that of the "each" rather than that of the "all." The other person as other is the one encountered in proximity, in height, the unique one, as moral command to me. Here universality is singular "deformalization," denudation, rupture, absolute difference from the differential context. The moral self is universal in its singular election, its nonsubstitutability, its "passivity greater than all receptivity" (*CPP* 114), its Atlas-like responsibility in which despite itself each one on his or her own is responsible for all, and as such paradigmatic. It is this peculiar juncture of universality, the humanity in everyone, and singularity, where I and I alone am called, that moves Levinas's thought beyond the confines of a secular humanism to what he calls a "biblical humanism" (*NTR* 117). At the same time, in precisely this exceptional universality which arises in the singularity of the face-to-face lies the most central and enigmatic of all *religious* notions: "holiness" (*kedushah*), the paradox of absolute separation and absolute proximity.[28]

"To be holy," hence to take up one's election, is a difficult because paradoxical command. Universal, it is incumbent on all human beings. Singular, it is impossible to command. This paradox takes its concrete significance, however, in the creative and unfinished inter-human world whose ultimate significance—however hidden from objective calculation—arises in the supreme integrity of sacrifice for the dignity of the other. Such responsibility, a "difficult universality," is thus also holiness, holy in the sense that the Bible, in its exceptional linguistic and semantic audacity, gives voice in the incomparable for-mula—Leviticus 11:45: "You shall be holy, for I am holy" (*kedosheem tehiyu ke kedosh*).[29] Infinite alterity, infinite responsibility, superlative humility: "It is," Levinas writes, "the 'as-for-oneself' which discovers itself as 'as-for-the-other,' presentiment of holiness" (*NTR* 122).

THIRTEEN

Singularity
The Universality of Jewish
Particularism — Benamozegh and Levinas

INTRODUCTION

A flame needs a candle as much as a candle needs a flame. Judaism finds the universal, the holy—the "image and likeness" of God—not in another world, a heaven hovering above or a "soul" or "spirit" detached from matter here below. Rather holiness is found here and now in the unending divine-human partnership of *sanctification.* The world's ascent is God descent, or rather his ascent too. To sanctify is to make the profane holy. Passion becomes compassion. "The so-called profane," Martin Buber has said, "is only the not yet holy." The Hebrew term usually translated as "law" (*halakhah*) in fact means "walk," "path," or "way." The Jewish path creates, nurtures, enhances, and preserves the holy on earth.

Thus Judaism is a religion of *incarnation,* holiness on earth, the sanctification of life and all of creation. While Jews know the heights of personal salvation, they prefer the collective endeavor of universal redemption. Holiness is separation—the pure from the impure, the sacred from the profane, the clean from the unclean, the refined from the vulgar—but it is not exclusion. Everything—from birth to death to mourning, from morning to night, from work to rest, from the bathroom, kitchen, dining room, bedroom, office, farm, factory, dance, song, government, and army, to school, science, synagogue, and Temple—is to be transfigured and made holy. Transcendence and immanence meet in the refinement of a covenant exclusive of nothing. Judaism is thus one—not the only one, but unique—expression of the religious paradox of humanity cocreating God's created universe.

Judaism is not a religion, however, if by religion one means a compartment of life dedicated to God in contrast to other compartments of life with other devotions. Rather, like being a Hindu, or being Chinese, to be a Jew is to participate in a vast and ancient civilization. It is a civilization as old as civilization itself, and for much of its history, it has been as dispersed as the globe itself. Like any civilization, then, it is far more than a rational "system" or a consistent "worldview." It cannot without distortion be reduced to a simple formula, a principle, a thesis, or even a set of basic concepts. Its coherence is less the unity of a philosophical or theological system, than the integrity of a history, a narrative, or a life. Judaism, like any civilization, cannot without distortion be summed up or boiled down. Knowing Judaism—whether for the first time or after a long time, whether from inside its vast precincts or outside—is always a matter of highlighting, emphasizing, choosing an angle or perspective, and selecting from a multiplicity of foci that flow from and feed into one another. Neither an artificial unity nor a set of unrelated fragments, the coherence of the Jew and of Judaism is the variform integrity of life itself: unique individuals joined together as a unique people growing organically—in complexes of actions, with reactions at once internal and external—across historical time.

JEWISH UNIVERSALISM IN ELIJAH BENAMOZEGH AND EMMANUEL LEVINAS

With this overview in mind, the thesis of this chapter is that Judaism is a universal religion. This thesis strongly contrasts with and contests the perennial Christian misrepresentations of Judaism as a merely carnal, tribal, or nationalist cult. Even more profoundly, it strongly contrasts with and contests certain modern, and often Jewish, misrepresentations of Judaism that would relegate most of historical Judaism to the same small teapot of parochialism. The thesis of this chapter, in other words, is that old-fashioned, unregenerate, as it were, traditional, rabbinic, or talmudic Judaism—label it "orthodox Judaism," if you will—is a universal religion.

This claim could be justified on the basis of many Jewish thinkers, past and present. One could go all the way back to the Hebrew prophets, and farther still. Here, however, this claim will be approached through the works of two outstanding modern Jewish thinkers: Rabbi Elijah Benamozegh (1823–1900), of Livorno, Italy, and Emmanuel Levinas (1906–1995), born in Kavnas, Lithuania, a Parisian by choice.

It may seem odd to juxtapose two thinkers who, although both Jewish and philosophically minded, flourished in different centuries, hailed from very different parts of Europe (and even more so from "Jewish Europe"), and lived in quite different social and cultural milieus. If these differences do not seem divisive enough, consider also that Benamozegh served as a community rabbi, and was both a Talmudist and a Kabbalist,[1] while Levinas was qualified in none of these ways.[2] Levinas, for his part, quite unlike Benamozegh, studied under two of the most influential philosophers of the twentieth century, earned advanced academic degrees in philosophy from two French universities, and became a professor of philosophy at three. Benamozegh, in contrast, had none of these academic attainments. These are all surely significant differences. In addition, the thought of Levinas is fairly well known, while that of Benamozegh is almost unknown.

What links these two thinkers, however, is far more profound and consequential. I will briefly mention some factors of particular relevance to the concerns of the present chapter, without delving into nuances or eventual qualifications. First, the level or rank of their achievement distinguishes them. Both were privileged to articulate profound, comprehensive, and original philosophies. Second, both were fully engaged with Western civilization as a whole. Their respective philosophies are not only concerned with Western civilization but are written in its idiom; they have, thus, appropriated and engaged the great texts and spiritual creations of Western civilization. Third, and without contradicting the previous point, both Benamozegh and Levinas were faithful to Jewish traditional sources, to the Talmud above all. Fourth, both found the heart and soul of Judaism in its commitment to morality and justice for all. Both understood that Judaism's elevated and elevating commitment to holiness demands a redemptive praxis oriented by the divine commands of morality and justice. In sum, both Benamozegh and Levinas acceded to the authority of Jewish tradition by creating original ethical philosophies in dialogue with Western civilization as a whole. Both thinkers gave voice to the Hebrew spirit in Greek letters.

Benamozegh and Levinas both understood that the ancient and perennial Jewish concern for morality and justice is pivotal for Jews in relation to their own Jewish life, to be sure. But they also recognized that this concern to be pivotal in the relation of Jews and Judaism to humankind. And, even beyond that, they understood that the redemptive enterprise, as understood by normative Judaism, remains critical to the relation of Jews and Judaism to the cosmos as a whole, to all of God's creation. From these preliminary considerations alone, it should be clear that the universal morality and justice—dismissed by today's sophisticated cynics as illusion, ideology, super-structure, willful and constructed products of "modern," "Enlightenment," or "humanist" subjectivism—are, for these two thinkers inextricably bound at once to Judaism's unique experience and to the highest hopes of a pluralist humanity.

It is particularly important, in the often imperial and usually missionary environment—subtle yet crude—of Christendom, to underline the universality and the pluralism of Judaism's holy mission. The ethical zeal to make the world a better place, a zeal that inspires Levinas and Benamozegh in their Judaism, is the very same zeal that inspires them to insist upon the multiplicity of paths that can lead to the fulfillment of the commands of an infinite God. Faithful to their own tradition, hence faithful to the One God of all humanity, neither thinker is limited by an exclusionary imperialism that would require the conversion of everyone to Judaism in the manner that Christian evangelizing aims to convert the world. Many genuine paths—each one absolute and authoritative for the believer—lead to the infinite God. Chosen by such a God, Judaism is a religion not merely of tolerance, if by tolerance one means that one grits one's teeth and provisionally endures alternatives. Rather, it is a religion of tolerance whose divinely revealed teachings of universal morality and justice aim to produce not a mirror image of itself, but a righteous humanity, whatever the denominational affiliations of that humanity. With the same breath with which Benamozegh and Levinas insist upon the fundamental and irreducible relevance of Judaism for Jews as Jews,

they also insist, to the same Jews—without any diminution, condescension or duplicity—on the irreducible relevance, the universality,
of Judaism for all of humanity. To be chosen is to be responsible
for each and everyone, Jew and non-Jew alike, "widow, orphan, and
stranger."

Both refuse the cynical ideologies of secular modernity.[3] For neither thinker is Judaism conceived as a "religion" in the narrow sense,
that is, a restricted "ecclesiastical" zone or compartment of life.[4]
One is not French, Italian, or American first, and Jew second. One is
French, Italian, or American as a Jew. That is to say, contra Spinoza,
but in line with America's "founding fathers," what France, Italy, and
America do must measure up to the high moral standards of Judaism,
must be judged according to an "inalienable" right and not merely
according to the passing demands of power, success or popularity.
Not a "religion," Judaism is a way of life. It is manifest in denominational forms of piety such as prayer and communal worship services,
to be sure, but also and no less authoritatively is it manifest in the
so-called "secular" dimensions of life, in the familial, social, civic, economic, and political aspects of life.[5] In this way, too, for both Levinas
and Benamozegh, the particularity of one's own tradition and the
universality of morality and justice need not stand in conflict with
one another. Indeed, the reverse is true. The elevation demanded
by ethical universality is rooted in the particular, just as the aspiration of particularity requires and demands universality. Such is Jewish
singularity, the Jewish notion of election. Each is elected for all. The
universality of Judaism is no less universal for being Jewish and no
less Jewish for being universal. Or, in the words of Benamozegh: "the
voice from Sinai addresses all humanity."[6] Embracing and guiding
Jews, but also humanity and all of creation, these thinkers see in the
most specifically Jewish conception of universality rooted in particularity, or the most specifically Jewish concpetion of particularity rising
to universality, "the highest conceivable form of universalism."[7]

In contrast to modern Enlightenment notions of universality,
based ultimately in a mathematical conception of truth (as is evident
in Descartes), the ethico-metaphysical universalism of Judaism retains
it universality without sacrificing the particular, singular, or unique.
Indeed, standing against modern objectified forms of universality, and
for an older tradition sensitive to the humanity of the human, Judaism

demands precisely the reverse: respect for the unique, the singular, the particular. The identity of the unique, which requires pluralism, and the identity of unity, which eraces difference, are not reducible to one another. Faithfulness to the orthodoxy of traditional Judaism requires the recognition, in Benamozegh's words, "that God's face assumed many expressions at Sinai."[8] The universality espoused by Benamozegh and Levinas is wedded to the historical particularity of texts, rituals, legislation, customs, and traditions, which have been handed down and developed as the heritage of a long Jewish history. Paradoxical as it may seem, it is not despite its universality but rather because of it that Judaism remains fully Jewish. This universality joins the Judaism of today to its long history and ancient traditions, promulgating neither a denatured or abstract universality, as did the Enlightenment reformers of Judaism, nor a triumphant and exclusionary universality, as did the Church, but rather producing what Levinas names a "Jewish humanism" or "biblical humanism" (*DF* 275).[9]

This route, via the concrete universality of tradition, however, and paradoxically at first glance, claims to be more enlightened than the Enlightenment. Benamozegh and Levinas confront modernity and modern Reform Judaism in precisely those terms, and on precisely those grounds—ethics and universalism—that the modern enlightenment perspective used in its attempt to critique and overthrow traditional Judaism. But they show, contrary to the Enlightenment and contrary to the Reformers, that "positive religion"—religion in its particularity, that is to say, in its history, its texts, its traditions, and so on—is indeed positive, the ground and source of a universal humanity.

For almost two centuries, it has been standard fare in the history of ideas—in Jewish studies a history dominated by the unacknowledged biases of German *Wissenshaft* Judaism—that the central conflict within modern Judaism is (as within all modernity) the struggle between the particular and the universal, between the "positive" and the "natural" or "rational." According to this narrative, the forces of the particular would be fragmenting and hence reactionary expressions of a narrow-mindedness, of the merely partisan and parochial, throwbacks to the merely national or ethnic. Orthodoxy and particularity in this negative sense would be equated—in order to be combated, by self-proclaimed enlightened or liberated universalism. In this narrative, the "good guys" would of course be the Reformers. They would be the enlightened, cultured, fraternal bearers of the illuminating, liberating, and hence progressive forces of the *universal,* or reason, guided by the ideal of humanity united under reason.[10] But the truth is, in fact, otherwise.

All forms of Judaism, with a few minor exceptions, have always defended an ethical universalism. And all forms of Judaism, again with minor exceptions, have opposed particularism. My thesis, then, made in the name of Benamozegh and Levinas, is that the central conflict in modern Judaism is not a struggle between particularity and universality, nationalism versus humanism, ethic versus ethnic, but rather, and more deeply, *a struggle between different versions of Jewish universalism.* To make this thesis clear, I distinguish and locate Benamozegh and Levinas within a typology of three versions of universalism. Let me also say, that useful as I think this typology is—indeed I think it is of sufficient heuristic value to grasp and contextualize the essential character of Benamozegh's and Levinas's Jewish universalism—it is not perfect. It requires further refinement and qualification.[11] That being said, philosophy and wisdom must make distinctions. It is important to recognize, first, that there *are* different types of universalism, and, second, to be clear about their differences.

PARTICULARITY AND THREE TYPES OF UNIVERSALITY

It seems to me that an appropriate name for the universality promoted by Benamozegh and Levinas is *concrete universalism,* because it remains tied to particularity. Or one could call it, compressing the title of this chapter, "universal particularism." The universality of the Reformers, and of an enlightened modernity more generally, I name *abstract universalism,* because Benamozegh and Levinas will criticize it—in contrast to the concrete universalism they identify with traditional talmudic/rabbinic Judaism—precisely for its abstractness. The third kind of universalism, which is prevalent in Christianity triumphalism and in all imperial politics, but is also occasionally present in Judaism, I name *exclusive universalism,* because Benamozegh and Levinas criticize it for its exclusivity, again in contrast to the genuine or nonexclusive universalism of traditional talmudic/rabbinic

Judaism. Finally, it almost goes without saying, all forms of universality must be distinguished from the perspective—or nonperspec-
tive—of brute particularity.

Particularity

The perspective of a brute particularity is difficult to define precisely
because particularity resists the universality inherent in definition itself.
Definition works by specification within a genus. But particularity is
precisely what defies genera and generalization. Defined negatively,
then, we can say that particularity is an indifference to the universal.
It is an original fragmentation without possible cohesion, an original
pluralism without possible unity, the exception without a rule. It is
constituted, one might also say, as an indeterminable set of monads
without windows. Pure particularity is incommunicable and hence
unintelligible. Even a bump or a groan in the night, to the extent that
such events, however radically *hic et nunc,* would establish a communication, a contact, a commonality, however minimal, they would
thus already undermine the purity or absoluteness of brute particularity. Such was Hegel's enduring insight articulated at the start of both
his *Phenomenology* and his *Logic.* Particularity, then, is an ideal limit,
but as the reverse side of all idealism, the dark side.

All forms of Judaism, and not just Reform Judaism, oppose the
outlook of particularity. It is the outlook—or the tendency supported
by the outlook—Levinas identifies with idolatry and mythology, and
sees as Judaism's fundamental and implacable enemy. Indeed, the very
mission of Israel is to destroy the perspective of—or to reverse any
dereliction into—particularity. "Judaism," Levinas writes, "appeals
to a humanity devoid of myths—not because the marvelous is repug-
nant to its narrow soul but because myth, albeit sublime, introduces
into the soul that troubled element, that impure element of magic
and sorcery and that drunkenness of the Sacred and war, that prolong
the animal within the civilized" (*DF* 49). Or, more succinctly and
emphatically, he calls "the Torah itself, the book of anti-idolatry, the
absolute opposite of idolatry!" (*ITN* 58–59). Benamozegh, because
he is a Kabbalist who subscribes to the cosmological doctrines of the
"broken vessels" and the "retrieval of the sparks," finds holiness in all
things. But this perspective is not equivalent to antinomianism, and
in no way means that he sanctions or condones evil. Benamozegh,

like Levinas, opposes the particularity or polytheism of paganism precisely because, and to the extent that, it does not rise to the ethical universality of either "Mosaism" (Judaism) or "Noachism" (the minimum standard of righteousness for all nations). In his great work *Israel and Humanity*, he recalls the following words of the talmudic rabbis: " 'Whoever renounces idolatry is a true Jew,' and 'Whoever renounces polytheism thereby affirms the entire Law.' "[12]

Universality

In contrast to the particularity—noise, and ultimately silence—of pagan idol worship, polytheism, and mythology, Judaism is in all its historical forms an ethical monotheism, and on this basis it espouses universality.

Most broadly, "universality"—what logicians today call a "universal quantifier"—is the reference made by the "all": that which unifies and applies to all members of a particular set. Whether it is function of language alone, as nominalists claim to believe, or whether it has to do with the essence or nature of the real, as realists think, or whether it is some combination of the two, in every case universality is that which is the same in difference. For example, when the Greek philosopher decides that "Man is a rational animal," or when the Bible declares that man was "created in the image and likeness of God," both are making what are formally universal claims. Whether true or false, both claims identify something that is the case for all those beings and only those beings that are (in this way defined as) "human."

In religion, more specifically, the issue of universality applies primarily to relations between God and individual human beings and between God and individual organized religions. This is because individuals, whether humans or religions, differ from one another. Do God's love and providence apply to everyone and all groups equally, or to some more than others? Are God's revelation, redemption and salvation, meant for all humans equally, or for some more than others? And if the latter, is this because God's revelation, redemption, and salvation are already given (such as grace, predestination, or reincarnation) or subsequent to some chosen activity (faith, morality, repentance, or enlightenment)? Regarding the various institutionalized religions, is only one, or are only some, or are all religions equally linked to God? What I am calling "exclusive," "abstract" and "concrete" universality are three distinctive but all universal answers to these fundamental religious questions.

Exclusive Universality

The term "exclusive universality" appears to be an oxymoron, since "exclusive" and "universal" seem to exclude one another. But precisely this exclusion is what makes for this type of universality. It is the perspective of a part—a partisan—that, in its partiality, takes itself to be the whole. Maintaining itself in partiality, hence in the opacity of matter or body rather than in thought or spirit, it is the effort to achieve universality by physically or violently excluding everything else other than itself. It is the "one for all," where the one alone counts instead of all others. Its exclusiveness and its universality, then, are inseparable. This is because its universality is achieved only by excluding or negating difference. Thus it is an imperial and totalitarian universalism, because a part, as a part, takes itself to be the whole, which can only mean that it must take the place of the whole. By annihilating all difference, whether by violent obliteration or sweet conversion, whether with or without the consent of the (merely provisional) other, here a part becomes the whole, and hence the "all," the universal.

One religious version of "exclusive" universality occurs in Christian triumphalism. It appears in a Roman Catholic version, in the doctrine of "salvation through the Church alone," and in a Protestant version, the doctrine that salvation can be achieved solely through faith in Jesus Christ. It explains the otherwise paradoxical militancy of Christian missionary fervor in the name of love that will only be satisfied when it has forever eliminated all other paths to God. This form of universality has never been normative for Judaism, though it has nonetheless been found there. Whether true to authorial intention or not, one might find instances of it in the *Kuzari* of Yehuda Halevi; in certain commentaries of Nachmanides (e.g. to Deut. 18:19, that prophecy would be limited to the Land of Israel and to Jews only); in the Zionism of Rabbi Tzvi Yehuda Kook (1891–1982);[13] and in the mystical ideology of contemporary Chabad Chassidism.[14]

Benamozegh, Levinas, and Reform Judaism especially, criticize all forms of this universalism—in Judaism, in Christianity, in politics, and elsewhere—as merely particularism in disguise. Because its universalism can only be achieved by totalizing a part, hence by means of totalitarianism more or less masked, its elimination of alternative paths is inevitably achieved, according to these critics, unjustifiably and hence violently. While one must admit, in principle, that is to say, according to an abstract logic or theo-logic, that an infinite God can do whatever he wants, and hence could have provided all of humanity only one very specific path to salvation, a path known and proclaimed by only one religion, such a view, when approached from a slightly less abstract perspective, is fraught with insuperable difficulties. For one, its distribution of the damned and the saved, even from very simple chronological and geographical points of view, contradict any intuitively obvious sense of God's benevolence. Further, such a view challenges not only belief in God's goodness, but also belief in the reasonableness of his very act of creation, that is to say, the act of producing a multiple world. Finally, the logic of exclusive universality contradicts the express views of God's own revealed and hence sacred scriptures, which—without transparently self-serving interpretive gymnastics—nowhere set such limits to God's approachability.

Critics of exclusive universality see in its efforts to eliminate all other paths to God the violence of a leveling that is really nothing other than another expression of the intolerance of all parochialism, however rhetorically dressed up in a cloak of (*post facto* and hence imaginary) universality. I cite Benamozegh, referring not to Christian or Jewish exclusivism, but to one of its political manifestations in ancient Roman imperialism:

> The establishment of *jus gentium* ["law of the nations," or "international law"] has been credited to the Romans, but incorrectly, for the Romans regarded their empire as co-extensive with the world. The truth is that historically, Moses was the first to affirm its essential principle, and from a philosophical standpoint, it is clear that the very doctrine of universal Providence contained the germ of *jus gentium;* for if God rules the peoples of the world according to inviolable laws, nothing could be more natural or more just than that the peoples in their mutual relations should themselves be held responsible for the observance of these laws.[15]

Or, to take second example from one of the many he finds of Christian exclusivity, Benamozegh writes that for Judaism, as seen by the

Kabbalists, "the work of redemption is assigned not to a single individual, even a man-god, but to all humankind."[16]

Reform Judaism went further than Benamozegh or Levinas. It saw not only in Christian triumphalism and political totalitarianism, but also in traditional Judaism itself nothing less than the same anti-humanism of a parochial exclusivity. Thus it attacked talmudic and rabbinic Judaism for its particularism. And thus, in its stead, Reform Judaism proposed an enlightened, rationally purified, progressive, humanist, universalist Judaism.

Abstract Universality

Enlightened, rational, or, as I call it, "abstract" universality, in contrast to exclusive universality, is the "all for one," where the *all* takes the place of the one. Truth or value lies not in what is singular or unique, but in what is common and the same. Causality replaces casuistry. Principles replace principals. What counts is the essence at the expense of existence, the law or rule rather than the instance or the circumstance. The particular therefore lacks significance. The enlightened universal, then, is the perspective of thought or spirit independent of extension and body. It is the universalism of modern science, of logical and mathematical relations, the perspective of reason, of non-contradictory and objective knowledge. Such a universalism tends naturally and necessarily toward the unified coherence of a system, the system, *mathesis universalis*.

Like all the forms of universalism, abstract universalism is also dynamic. Because it is not based in the divisibility of extension, however, its dynamism is not manifest as overt violence, the war of one part against all other parts. Rather its effort is to eliminate particularity and partisanship altogether, but to do so rationally, through intellectual agreement. Since only the universal is real, true, and valuable, particularity can only be unreal, untrue, and worthless. Hence partisanship of any kind (except—inexplicably—that in favor of the universal!) can only be parochial, special pleading, mere privilege. Here is the universal of Spinozism, Hegelianism, and Marxist dialectic, as well as of all assimilationist ecumenicalism in religion. It is also the universalism of Paul, writing to the Galatians: "There is neither Jew nor Greek, there is neither slave nor freeman, there is neither male and female; for you are all one in Christ Jesus" (Gal. 3:28).[17]

Reformers of Judaism, of course, did not deny Jewish tradition in the name of Jesus, but rather in the name of a universal ethics, that is to say, ethics rationally purified of all particularity.[18]

Benamozegh and Levinas reject this type of universalism precisely because it is abstract and therefore reductive. Very simply, it reduces away not the partiality of the particular, as it thought, but the uniqueness of the singular, the singularity, for example, of family, community, nation, and tradition. For a genuine humanism, these are not simply the manifestation of a more primitive ignorance and unjustifiable special pleading. The particular is not an obstacle to a genuine humanity, but a necessary and irreducible dimension of its expression.[19] Ethics, both Benamozegh and Levinas insist, can never be efficacious if its idealism is merely angelic, a spiritualism divorced from the flesh and blood concerns and commitments of real people. Humans and humanity are not constituted by abstract essences alone, but in the sociality of families, communities, nations, and the like.

Benamozegh makes a powerful and deep observation: "Variety is not arbitrary or accidental, but something necessary and organic, with roots in the depths of human nature."[20] Variety is not some sort of ontological error, an affront to philosophers. It is the real, indeed, it is more real than the simplifications of a coherent thought. Benamozegh could have learned this from Vico, to be sure, but no less did he experience it daily as a rabbi, a Talmudist, a community leader, and a Kabbalist—*and,* let us add, as a son, a father, and a grandfather. Social life and its requirements of love, morality, and justice does not fit neatly into tidy intellectual categories. Referring to a pagan philosopher's observation that there are many paths to the divine, Benamozegh comments: "Nothing could be more true or profound. Monotheism can become universal only with this understanding: unity in diversity, diversity in unity."[21] Elsewhere, in a statement that surely is meant as an attack on Kantian ethics, he sums up the Jewish ethical position vis-à-vis partiality and universality: "two parts of a single system.... *Interest by way of virtue and virtue by way of interest:* this is the teleological formula of society."[22]

Levinas, for his part, has devoted long and careful philosophical analyses—in his two major works, *Totality and Infinity* and *Otherwise than Being,* and in many other shorter works—as well as in the analyses of his no less subtle and penetrating exegetical writings—his many talmudic readings, and his many "Essays on Judaism"—to show at the closest quarters that the transcendence of a genuine ethics is repressed in the tyranny of an abstract intellectualized totality. Thus, for a seductive cognitive abstractness, he will criticize the rationalism of Spinoza's metaphysics, the conceptualism of Hegel's philosophical history, and the representational prejudice of Husserl's phenomenology. No less will he criticize the totalitarian tendency of their alleged reversals, which tend toward the exclusivity of the particular: Nietzsche's fragmenting will to power, Heidegger's fundamental ontology, and Derrida's semiotic deconstruction. In the space allotted, I can do little more than recommend to the reader Levinas's masterful critiques of the imperial totalizing not only of the exclusive universal, in its opaque brutality, but also of the more subtle and sophisticated violence perpetrated intellectually and spiritually in the name of the abstract universal.

Concrete Universality

In contrast to the "one for all" of exclusive univeralism (the one instead of the all), and the "all for one" of abstract universalism (the all instead of the one), concrete universality is the "one and all": the all integrally united with the one. Here the universal and particular—mind and body, spirit and letter—are inextricably bound to one another. Universalism is achieved neither by one part masquerading as a whole, while in fact violently eliminating alternative parts, nor by a universal pretending to angelically surpass particularity, while in fact ignoring or suppressing its own material conditions. Rather, from the integral perspective of the concrete universal, the exclusive and abstract forms of universality are revealed as based upon and reproducing a constructed dualism—whether political or epistemological—of mind and body, spirit and letter, apart from one another and hence only artificially linked.

Based neither in mind nor in body abstracted from one another, the concrete universal is rooted in the integral unity of moral praxis, lived as a temporal existence penetrated by the obligations and responsibilities of a pluralist (familial, communal, social, political, economic), multivalent, and historical world. The *all* of the exclusive universal is the *only;* the *all* of the abstract universal is the *every;* the *all* of concrete universal is the *each.* Neither purely subjective, the part taking the place of whole, nor purely objective, the whole annihilating the part, its meaningfulness—and the meaningfulness of Judaism—is always already *in media res,* a present always already the product of a past and always projecting toward an unforeseeable future. Genuine universality depends on and requires particularity. In Levinas's words: "Its truth is universal like reason; its rule and moral institutions, Judaism's particular support, preserve this truth from corruption" (*DF* 274). Both Benamozegh and Levinas understand Judaism in terms of concrete universality, and what they criticize in alternative interpretations of Judaism (and in Christianity) is precisely exclusivity and/or abstractness. Of course, too, they also both attack particularism.

For talmudic or rabbinic Judaism, God, creation, and humanity are interwoven. To use Benamozegh's expression, humanity is in "partnership" with God, just as God is in "partnership" with humanity. To be sure, the relation is asymmetrical: God is above, and humanity moves upward, but true humanity and true divinity lies in, and not elsewhere than, these relations. For both thinkers, humanity's partnership with God is constituted in an interpersonal morality and social justice that are together the *holy* work of redemption. Religious life for Judaism lies neither in an "other world" that will be, nor in "this world" as it is. Hence it requires neither a blind and blinding faith nor a false and falsifying contentment with being. Rather, Judaism lives in the positive work of transforming the real into the good—the work of sanctification. In the concrete everyday labors and details that conserve and develop morality and justice on earth—hence in a piety that is equivalent to righteousness—lies the path of the divine. "The vision of God," Levinas writes, "is a moral act" (*DF* 275). What Levinas calls a "biblical" or "Jewish humanism," as one instance of the "wisdom of love" (*OB* 162), is "a difficult wisdom concerned with truths that correlate to virtues" (*DF* 275).[23] Or, as Benamozegh expresses the biblical and rabbinic perspective: "They call just men *partners* of holy God."[24] "The just person," he continues, "whom the Talmud proclaims to be greater than the heaven and earth, and the saint, whom the rabbis call the partner of God, are superior not only to nature but also to the angels and the gods."[25]

Concreteness thus means never to neglect the neighbor for the sake of the true or the spiritual. It is not God in the other that one respects, and through this respect makes one's relationship "religious," but rather because one respects the other—through moral and juridical service—one is aiming at the divine. The good—the prescriptive—is the ground of the real and the true. The good is found neither in the sky nor in the mind, but in the transcendence of the face-to-face relation and, no less, then, in the plurality of social and interpersonal relations. That is to say, goodness is found—concretely lived—in moral kindness and just institutions. This is what Benamozegh will call "Hebraic cosmopolitanism,"[26] one that takes into account the individuality of the individual, the specificity of the community and nation, as well as the importance of time and place, without, for all that, relativizing either God or the transcendent ideality of the good. Speaking of Divine providence and referring to Paul's letter to the Galatians, Benamozegh writes these remarkable words: "Unlike Paul, we do not say of this Providence that it knows neither Jews nor Greeks, for that implies an inadmissible leveling of differences, a suppression of all nationality. We affirm, rather, that Providence recognizes equally Jews, Greeks, and Barbarians—in a word, all races and peoples, who ought to be perceived as one though without losing their individual identities."[27] Jew is not Greek and Greek is not Jew, nor, even is one Jew another Jew, or one Greek another Greek, yet *each* Jew and all Jews, just as *each* Greek and all Greeks, are beholden to the same imperatives of morality and justice. "For the Jews," Benamozegh writes, "national feeling is never separated from their commitment to mankind....[Judaism] affirms that Divine Providence extends without distinction over all of mankind, that God is the universal judge of nations as well as of individuals."[28] Thus Benamozegh's stunning and fundamentally pluralist proposition: "variety is not arbitrary or accidental, but something necessary and organic, with roots in the depths of human nature."[29] The virtue of variety, indeed, the necessity of variety—of the difference between one and another—for virtue, is precisely what the Reformers of Judaism, in their zeal for the abstract universal, did not grasp, or refused to grasp. Needless to say, defenders of exclusive universality are also blind to the fundamental virtue of pluralism.

But let us ask how, more specifically, do Benamozegh and Levinas find in Jewish concreteness—in specific rituals, prayers, history, books, traditions, and so on—and not only in its universally recognized moral legislation, such as most of the Ten Commandments—*how specifically do they find universality in Jewish concreteness?* They both find the unity of the particular and the universal in morality and justice. But their approaches nonetheless differ, because Benamozegh and Levinas differ, in background, family, language, training, social environment, audience, and immediate spiritual context.

No doubt in part because of his university training, his devotion to philosophy, and the fact that most of his writings were published for an educated and cultured but non-Jewish audience, Levinas will often characterize Judaism's concrete universalism in terms of method. More specifically, he contrasts the ethical orientation of rabbinical exegesis, as found in the Talmud, and in his own exegetical writings, to the epistemological and ontological orientation of abstract rationality. That is, he finds in Judaism's talmudic and rabbinic hermeneutics—in its attention to both the letter and the spirit of texts to discover the sacred, and to discover it in a moral and juridical social context—the meeting place of the concrete and the universal. I cite Levinas:

> I wish to speak of the Torah as desirous of being a force warding off idolatry by its essence as Book, that is, by its very writing, signifying precisely prescription and by the permanent reading it calls for—permanent reading or interpretation and reinterpretation or study; a book thus destined from the start for its Talmudic life. A book that is also by that very fact foreign to any blind commitment that might think itself virtuous because of its decisiveness or stubbornness.... The Talmudic life and destiny of the Torah, which is also an endless return, in its interpretation of several degrees, to particular cases, to the concreteness of reality, to analyses that never lose themselves in generalities but return to examples—resisting invariable conceptual entities...renewing, though continual exegesis—and exegesis of that exegesis—the immutable letters and hearing the breath of the living God in them. A liturgy of study as lofty as the obedience to the commandments that fulfills the study. (*ITN* 58–59)

For Levinas, it is "through continual exegesis—and exegesis of exegesis," that Judaism finds spirit in letter, in all registers, no matter how particular they may seem—in prayer, family life, eating habits, manners, holidays, tradition, and so on. For it is in the concrete that an ethical universal finds its genuine if never final manifestation. Such is the universal and u-topian vision of Judaism.[30]

Benamozegh, in contrast, explicates the indissoluble integrity of particular and universal in rabbinic and kabbalistic terms, in terms of Jewish priesthood and the two dimensions/orientations of Mosaism

and Noachism. Benamozegh affirms the unity of God, of humanity, and of Providence, but rejects an abstract universalist account
of them, because "we would have an apparently universal religion,
but one whose very constitution would tend to preclude Jewish
individuality."[31] Rather, Benamozegh affirms, "a religion of truly universal character [which] would embrace all of mankind, even while
preserving Jewish individuality," and he continues, rejecting exclusive universality, by adding: "nor would this be an Israel to whom
all the other peoples were subordinated."[32] The bond that unites the
particular and the universal in Judaism is the bond that unites its
Mosaic and the Noachide dimensions globally, namely, "the hier-
archical organization of the human race into priests and laymen."[33]
That is to say, the particular is harmonized with the universal when
the particular, like the priest in relation to the layman, *serves* the universal. Thus, like Levinas, ethical monotheism—service to and for
the other, the other before the self—lies at the basis of a concrete or
Jewish universalism.

I conclude with a striking citation from Benamozegh's *Israel and
Humanity,* in which he highlights a rabbinical commentary on the
praise and priority Jews give to Israel, the chosen land—so seemingly
particularist—in universalist terms. Benamozegh writes:

> It seems to us that the strikingly universalist idea which the sages derive
> from this text, which is apparently so exclusive in its implication, beau-
> tifully characterizes the authentic spirit of Judaism. A country which
> finds itself chosen to be a means of grace and blessing for the entire
> world, but is in no way licensed to hold others in contempt: This is
> the dominating concept of the entire Law, written and oral, beginning
> with Abraham, in whom all races should be blessed, and finishing with
> the Messiah, who will bring both deliverance for Israel and the knowl-
> edge of truth for all peoples.[34]

The universal is thus found not outside the particular, or despite the
particular, but precisely because of, and in view of the particular. It
is found neither in an epistemological nor in an aesthetic rigor, but
in the stringency of an ethics through which humanity is constituted:
in the moral obligations and responsibilities of one for another,
and in the demand for justice that these obligations and responsibilities exert on each for all.

FOURTEEN

Levinas and Rosenzweig

Proximities and Distances

INTRODUCTION

"We were impressed by the opposition to the idea of totality in Franz Rosenzweig's *Stern der Erlosung,* a work too often present in this book to be cited" (*TI* 28), Levinas wrote in the preface to *Totality and Infinity*. It is an extraordinary acknowledgment, made the more so because the title of Levinas's book announces and its contents show that the *critical* object of Levinas's entire endeavor is precisely an "opposition to the idea of totality." "But," Levinas continues in the next sentence, "the presentation and the development of the notions employed owe everything to the phenomenological method" (28).[1] With this qualification Levinas indicates that his method, phenomenology, following Husserl and Heidegger, is what decisively separates his thought from *The Star of Redemption,* whose method, in contrast and according to Rosenzweig's own words, is a "*system* of philosophy,"[2] a system following and indebted to the later Schelling.

I have elsewhere examined the core inspiration which guides the thought of both Rosenzweig and Levinas: the primacy of "non-indifference," the peculiar proximity of one person both in and out of relation to another, the nonindifference of the self in its first person singularity to the other person who faces in his or her singularity. It is an inspiration enabling both thinkers to oppose totality in the name of irreducible transcendence, even if from the side of the surplus of that transcendence they oppose totality quite differently.[3]

The aim of the present essay is more specific. Its first part sketches out several of the original and positive ideas in Rosenzweig's *Star* that also appear in Levinas. Despite their methodological differences, Levinas has indeed appropriated much from Rosenzweig. The second part sketches out several key ways in which Levinas differs from Rosenzweig. I admit readily that the treatment in both parts is too brief. I aim nevertheless not only to indicate fundamental similarities and differences, but also to open up possible lines of further research.

ROSENZWEIG: TEACHER OF LEVINAS

Let us say right away that "influence" is often obscure and hard to trace, even when an author admits to it or when the ideas of two thinkers are nearly the same. Certain "original" ideas are at any time "in the air," as it were. Thus Rosenzweig and Levinas join all their contemporaries in taking seriously — as primary rather than derivative structures — time, change, worldliness, language, and subjectivity. To be sure, each thinker will understand these and other phenomena in his or her own distinctive way. Accordingly, the work here is not that of a detective seeking confessions, but rather that of a scholar uncovering linkages and divergences. One must keep in mind, too, that Levinas's concordances with Rosenzweig come at varying levels of generality, so that agreement at one level will not preclude disagreement over the "same idea" at another.

Temporality

Bergson's notion of "duration" was a turning point in Western thought, inaugurating contemporary philosophical discourse: it solved Zeno's paradoxes and justified human freedom by making the flow or passage of time primary instead of its measurement based on stoppages which would henceforth be conceived as practical or theoretical derivatives. Following Bergson, Husserl formally and Heidegger existentially elaborated the "ecstatic" structure of temporality, the extensive presence of the present as a synthesizing of past and future.

What Rosenzweig emphasizes, and what we find also in Levinas, are two additional elements of time: (1) its "sequence" (*Reihe*),[4] irreversible and uni-directional, which Levinas will later call its "one-way" movement from past to present to future, expérienced in the aging[5] of a subjectivity independent of history; and (2) the nonsynthesizable transcendence of time's dimensions relative to one another: the irreducible "pastness" of the past, observed in Rosenzweig's "Creation" and Levinas's "immemorial past which was never present," and the ungraspable "futurity" of the future, Rosenzweig's "Redemption" or "Truth" of Part Three of *The Star* and Levinas's "messianic" time of justice, rupturing the self-presence of ecstatic temporality. These are profound and revolutionary advances in our understanding of time. Given their different methodological starting points, for Rosenzweig the transcendence of time's dimensions is that which exceeds and is unknown to the reductive identity sought by idealist representation and its specious present of simultaneity for which the sequence of real time has no place. For Levinas, in contrast, the transcendence of time's dimensions overloads and disrupts with moral and juridical exigencies the unifying synthesis of ecstatic temporality as both Husserl and Heidegger had conceived it. These two elements—irreversibility and the nonsynthesizable transcendence of past and future—are remarkable and original insights regarding the nature of genuine time, already at work in Rosenzweig and later taken up by Levinas.

The structure of Rosenzweig's *Star* as a text and the structure of the "new thinking" this text conveys reflect this new appreciation of and status given to real time. Part One of *The Star,* shows the failure of reason which, in an essential idealism upholding the ancient equation of thought and being, attempts to posit all of being from out of thought itself. This failure, however, which is entirely negative, finds its true ground and gains a positive sense in Part Two of *The Star* as "Revelation," as divine-human "love" and human-human "love," which Rosenzweig presents as a uniquely constitutive relation. In it the absolute "origin" of reason discovers itself—*per impossible*—*second* to the "beginning" of subjectivity in its always-tardy relation to God. The past, now understood as independent "creation," precedes reason's allegedly absolute self-positing. The future, too, as the futurity of Redemption and Truth, exceeds reason's alleged comprehensive grasp. This peculiar structure, which gives priority to what is more concrete and more pressing than reason, is central also to Levinas's thought. In *Totality and Infinity* he writes: "The posteriority of the anterior—an inversion logically absurd—is produced, one would say, only by memory or thought" (*TI* 54). What is "anterior" is that which has priority, a relation to transcendence, but a relation for which reason is forever too narrow and therefore can only judge it to be "logically absurd." In his later thought Levinas will call this new and ultimate time structure "diachrony," discovering in it the very singularity of a self responsible for-the-other before its own for-itself.

Language

That the texture of language is an essential part of signification, that spirit and letter are inseparable, that ideas, reason, and truth are therefore not "pure" of their symbolic expression and historical context, these notions determine all of contemporary thought and hence the thought of Rosenzweig and Levinas as well. "Mathematical science," Rosenzweig writes, "must be replaced by the morphology of words, by grammar."[6] No doubt because he is writing earlier in the century, thus closer to the novelty of these notions in their opposition to prior philosophizing, Rosenzweig celebrates them with greater enthusiasm than Levinas. He labels his philosophy a "new thinking" and, following Eugen Rosenstock-Huessy, identifies its central innovation to be a "grammatical" or "speech" thinking. In Book Two of Part Two of *The Star*—its center in every way—this means that revelation is understood as "narrative" in contrast to the disembodied ideas sought by the idealism criticized in Part One. "The language of revelation speaks."[7] "For in the world of revelation everything becomes word, and what cannot become word is either prior or posterior to this world."[8] "This," Rosenzweig adds, "accords with the wholly real employment of language, the center-piece as it were of this entire book."[9] Ideas follow speaking and language and remain colored by them. The discursive world of meaning is not merely the dark cave or failure of a pure world of Ideas.

The same perspective is adopted by Levinas as a matter of course, though he too emphasizes the inextricable bond between text and interpretation when it comes to scriptures and sacred texts, recalling Rabbi Leo Baeck's criticism of Christianity as a "spiritual" religion too "romantic" and "sentimental" for the concrete realities of human finitude and the historical world. (And no doubt Christianity, historically and theologically, far more than Judaism in any event, has strong tendencies toward gnostic otherworldliness.)[10]

Certainly the appreciation for the irreducibility of language, narration and rhetoric was the central critical insight of the "new science" of Giambattista Vico centuries earlier. It is operative indirectly far earlier in the innovative literary-philosophical form of Plato's *dialogues*. It is of course a central element of Schelling's later thinking. It is in Nietzsche, an insight central to Heidegger, Gadamer, Wittgenstein, Merleau-Ponty, and all other significant twentieth century thinkers. The particular twist that both Rosenzweig and Levinas discover in this notion, however, comes—influenced by Buber's *I and Thou*—from their elevation of the sociality of *dialogue* over the egoism of *monologue*.[11]

Dialogue

Thus at the center of *The Star* Rosenzweig insists that what is new in his "grammatical" thinking is the elevation of dialogue between people over the idealist monologue of the mind with itself. "Only in the discovery of a Thou is it possible to hear an actual I, an I that is not self-evident but emphatic and underlined."[12] "In actual conversation," Rosenzweig writes in "The New Thinking," "something happens; I do not know in advance what the other will say to me because I myself do not even know what I am going to say."[13] And in the final book of Part Three of *The Star*, Rosenzweig proposes a new form of truth, not as a set of validated propositions but as a subjective internalization, a "verification," the subjective appropriation of truth as the very truth of truth. One thinks here of Kierkegaard's dictum that "Truth is subjectivity." Thus for Rosenzweig—as for Levinas—time, language, subjectivity and dialogue are themselves intimately and intricately linked and stand as the unsurpassable beginning and end of signification. "Better than comprehension, *discourse* relates with what remains essentially transcendent," Levinas writes (*TI* 195).

Levinas articulates the primacy of "saying" (*dire*) over the "said" (*dit*), the primacy, as he understands it, of the moral imperative of conversation or "proximity" over contents proposed. "Saying makes signs to the other, but in this sign signifies the very giving of signs. Saying opens me to the other before saying what is said, before the said uttered in this sincerity forms a screen between me and the other"

(*LR* 183). Rosenzweig speaks of the self "emphatic and underlined" in dialogue with the other. That transcendence transpires across morality, in responsibility as *response* to the other person, in the exceptional nonintentional passivity or "difficult freedom" of a self elected to its moral obligations, is perhaps the central inspiration of all of Levinas's thought. "Signification as proximity," Levinas writes, "is thus the latent birth of the subject" (*OB* 139). "This being torn up from oneself in the core of one's unity, this absolute non-coinciding, this diachrony of the instant, signifies in the form of one-penetrated-by-the-other" (49). Levinas devotes many pages to the responsible self, torn from its immanence to a for-the-other, "put into question" by the other, "an-archic," "without identity," "hostage" to the other, responsible even for the other's responsibility, all the way to the point of dying for-the-other. The elected self, he writes, arises in the "accusative" (*OB* 112)—what better illustration could there be of Rosenzweig's "grammatical" and dialogical thinking?

Religion

No reader of Rosenzweig and Levinas can fail to note their free use of overt religious language, their positive attitude toward concrete or positive religions, with their scriptures, prayers, rituals, communities, and so on. But for neither thinker is this recourse meant as a retreat into the merely parochial and exclusive. This is because what they find in religious language and religious life is the expression of precisely the transcendence that escapes the immanence of philosophy's equation of being and thinking. For neither is religion a faith or dogma opposed to reason, but rather the articulation of a greater concreteness, a more intense singularity, and an appreciation for a higher transcendence than reason would otherwise admit.

Rosenzweig—perhaps still overly influenced by Hegel—finds genuine transcendence in two religions only: Judaism and Christianity. It has often been remarked that Rosenzweig is perhaps the first Jewish thinker to find for Christianity an independent and positive role both necessary and complimentary to Judaism in holy history. On the other hand, it has been no less noted that Rosenzweig has little positive to say about all other world religions, and much negative to say about Islam. Nevertheless, we must not lose sight of the fact that Rosenzweig has understood religion is not the handmaid of philosophy, reducible to its idealist tendency, but rather lies closer to the real, hence closer to the "truth"—what Rosenzweig often calls "life"—which lies beyond propositions and their differential coordination.

Levinas will often tease out the "saying" of the "said" in careful "talmudic readings," in which he comments on the Oral Torah, the Talmud, which itself breathes life into the Written Torah, the Hebrew Bible. These and other "confessional" writings, however, teach the same ethics—the same morality of the face-to-face, the same call to justice as a divine call—that is found in his nonconfessional or "philosophical" writings. There is no split in Levinas between philosophy and religion, because both are founded on ethical transcendence (*ITN* 170).[14] So, too, then, Levinas can find in literature, in Shakespeare, Dostoyevsky and Celan, for instance, the same ethical transcendence that inspires his meditations on religion and all his philosophical speculations. The point here, however, is that like Rosenzweig, Levinas finds in Judaism, in so-called Jewish "particularism," in its treasured texts, its rituals, its customs, in the Judaism of the rabbis, the Judaism lived by the Jewish community yesterday and today—truths for all humankind and not not only for Jews. Without in any way promoting Jewish exclusivism or conversion to Judaism, he can nevertheless declare, "The authentically human is the being-Jewish in all men" (164).[15] This is because the universalism of Judaism does not come from abstracting away and discarding its particularity but lies precisely in the moral singularity that its particularism—at its best—promotes, and in the justice that such moral singularity requires. The Hindu as a Hindu, the Muslim as a Muslim, the Confucian as a Confucian, lives the "difficult freedom" that is human. "Religion," Levinas writes—and here one sees the broad inclusive sense which this term has for him, "is the excellence proper to sociality with the Absolute, or, if you will, in the positive sense of the expression, Peace with the other" (171).

Paganism

Despite their commitments to monotheism and to Judaism (or to specific religion), both Rosenzweig and Levinas nevertheless admit the perennial and ineradicable status of paganism (or what Levinas calls "atheism"), especially and essentially with regard to the independence of the religious or ethical self. Indeed, for Levinas "the risk of atheism" is an essential positive moment of genuine religion (*DF* 15)! Only a self having the internal resources, the independence of its separation from anonymous being, is able to refuse transcendence and remain for-itself. Only such a self can be responsible, hence pious. Religion and ethics are not necessary like the laws of nature. The "force" of the other's alterity, in other words, is not ontological; it is a nonviolent force. Levinas writes, "Only an atheist being can relate himself to the other and already *absolve himself* from this relation" (*TI* 77; cf. 53–60). Ethics and religion are not slavery, but neither are they simply the abstract freedom of consciousness. Freedom is difficult. The "risk of atheism" is at the same time essential to a selfhood which is able to respond to the other, able to enter into relation with another person and not be obliterated or reduced away by that relation. The self must have an unsurpassable independence—Rosenzweig calls it pagan; Levinas calls it atheist—to be able to take upon itself what exceeds itself, not as a robot, however, forced, compelled, necessitated, and hence no longer a loving or moral being acting upon love or a moral obligation. To be a moral being means also the possibility of acting immorally, refusing the alterity of the other, harming and violating the other, remaining indifferent to the other's pain and suffering. Religion and ethics are risks—fine risks. Paganism, atheism, the independence of the human in the world, is not only a downward path to sensualist and egoist pleasure seeking, which it can certainly be, but also nothing less than the condition for human freedom.

Rosenzweig will recognize the same equivocation and positivity in the self to which revelation is revealed as *love*. "Here is the I, the individual human I, as yet wholly receptive, as yet only unlocked, only empty, without content, without nature, pure readiness, pure obedience, all ears."[16] For this openness to the other, Levinas will use the biblical term *hineni*, "here I am" (a term Rosenzweig reserves for the becoming-Jewish of the Jew).[17] In Part One of *The Star*, the "factuality" which cannot be reduced to thought, that against which the intentions of such thought fails, can stand by itself, and when it does so it is caught up in what Rosenzweig calls "paganism." Such paganism, however, remains outside of the "wholeness" and "visibility," which Rosenzweig finds in loving revelation, to be sure, but it nevertheless has the resources—like Levinas's "separated" being—to stand on its own. "Paganism," Rosenzweig writes, "is therefore in no way a mere religio-philosophical child's bogeyman for adults.... Rather, it is—no more and no less than the truth. The truth, indeed, in its elemental, invisible, unrevealed form."[18] Indeed, the all-embracing poet Goethe—"the great heathen"—serves Rosenzweig as an example of a modern pagan. "In the prayer to his own fate, man is at one and the same time wholly domiciled within his Self and—by virtue of that very fact—also entirely at home in the world."[19] The pagan self, "solitary" or "tragic," as Rosenzweig calls it, like the separate, independent atheist self of Levinas, "lacks all bridges and connections; it is turned in upon itself exclusively."[20] It lives in a silent mythic pluralist world. And yet for this same reason it is liable to revelation, as a self that can be transfigured without being annihilated. Thus Goethe is "the great heathen and the great Christian at one and the same time,"[21] though he "in particular remained a pagan all his life."[22]

It is only starting out as pagan, as atheist, as independent, that one can encounter—and remain in encounter with, in "proximity" with—radical alterity. This all-important notion of the "factual," inarticulate or embodied independence of the self as a condition for the self's transformative relation to transcendence—love or goodness—is shared by both Rosenzweig and Levinas. It breaks with the idealist notion of the self as nothing more than a node of relations, and yet does not result in "windowless" monads isolated in their individuality. The singular self, in love or in goodness, remains at once in relation to the other and out of relation—nonindifferent.

Levinas contra Rosenzweig

However much Levinas learned from Rosenzweig, including their shared commitment to transcendence in opposition to totality, and however much their thoughts agree regarding various aspects of temporality, language and religion, Levinas's thought is of a fundamentally different character than Rosenzweig's, separated from it by the abyss that separates, as Levinas indicates at the start of *Totality and Infinity,* the systematic organization of prephenomenological philosophy from the rigorous descriptive science of postphenomenological philosophy. And beyond this, there is the even greater abyss that separates Rosenzweig's essentially romantic or aesthetic outlook from the harsher moral and juridical imperatives that drive the ethics of Levinas. Of course there is an appeal to ethics in Rosenzweig, as there is a phenomenology of *eros* in Levinas, but that notwithstanding, their visions of ultimate exigencies are divided on this score.

Phenomenology Versus System

As we have seen, both Rosenzweig and Levinas criticize science in its Parmenidean pretensions to totality. But Levinas is no despiser of science. Indeed, he utilizes the science of phenomenology, presenting insightful phenomenological descriptions of human self-constitution and sociality, as far as such descriptions are able to go before reaching their breaking point in the imperatives of ethics. He also understands that science, and the technology that follows from and supports science, is necessary to create a just world, a world in which material plenty and equal distribution are made possible by objective knowledge. Rosenzweig, in contrast, after having criticized science in part one of *The Star* appears to leave it behind for what he proposes as an alternative and higher mode of sense altogether: God's love of each human in his or her singularity, and each human's love for the neighbor, a love which takes one of two communal directions, the perfected or "eternal" community of Judaism, or the spread or building toward perfection or eternity of Christianity. It is unclear, or Rosenzweig leaves unspecified, what role science plays in these individual and communal projects.

Because his positive thought seems to stand outside of science, whether natural-quantitative or phenomenological-descriptive, Rosenzweig gives epistemological flesh to his thought by means of a highly idiosyncratic system: the three points of independent transcendence—God, Humankind, and World—joined by three exceptional relations—Revelation, Creation, and Redemption. Whether these two sets of threes, figured as two overlapping triangles, are meant to conform to the Star of David or to serve as its inner truth cannot be decided, nor, in any event, can one find a convincing justification for these and only these three points and their relations. Thus there is something strangely arbitrary and therefore disconcerting in the very framing of Rosenzweig's thought, despite its many brilliant insights. Certainly, too, Rosenzweig's triadic framing leads to distortions in the content of his thought, for instance finding room only for Judaism and Christianity as legitimate religions, or their sublation in *The Star* in a post-Jewish and post-Christian absolute "Truth." Like the ambivalence found in the later Schelling, about whether human-kind's project of Redemption is a genuine mediation of God or sim-ply the return of an already perfect God to himself, it is unclear for the very same reason what Rosenzweig means by the absolute Truth with which he concludes his "system of philosophy" in *The Star*.[23] This ambivalence—the exclusive privileging of Judaism and Christianity, the unclear meaning of truth as verification, the procrustean triadic system—perhaps all these questionable dimensions of Rosenzweig's thought stem from a too hasty disregard for science and an overly enthusiastic defense of faith. In any event, they are not convincing.

Levinas's use of phenomenology, on the contrary, means that the strictly epistemological aspects of his thought, his many descrip-tive claims, remain verifiable and at the same time open to revision. Indeed, each of his phenomenological analyses—of death, enjoy-ment, work, time, language, and worldliness—correct and displace the earlier and now inadequate analyses of Heidegger in *Being and Time*. This is the very way of science: to be self-correcting, to develop, to follow the evidence rather than impose—or presuppose—an arti-ficial system, structure, or idea. This is precisely what Husserl meant by his motto "to the things themselves"—that philosophy, presup-positionless science, must be based in evidence and forever tested against evidence. To be sure, Levinas does not end with phenom-enology and shows its limits in ethics. Though he is certainly one of the great phenomenologists of the twentieth century, he utilizes this method precisely because it is scientific in the strictest sense. By push-ing his analyses to their limit and showing at what precise point they are inadequate to the imperatives of ethics and yet presuppose these imperatives, he *justifies* his thought. The genius of Levinas's philoso-phy is that unlike his philosophical predecessors who merely assume or presuppose the worth of reason in rhetorical circularity, it is able to justify science in ethics. Philosophy, which has so prided itself in justification, in opposing "opinion" with "knowledge," finally finds its genuine justification, albeit in ethics—in justice—rather than in knowledge and epistemology by themselves. It is an enormous step forward for thought.

Thus Rosenzweig, who begins his "new thinking" with an aesthetic faith outside of and beyond science, ironically remains in step
with the *romantic* overstepping of Kantian rationalism intended by
the very idealists he most severely criticizes, even if he does prefer the
later Schelling to Fichte, Hegel, and the early Schelling. Levinas, on
the other hand, adheres to science and pushes it to its limits, forcing
science itself to admit its indebtedness—*per impossible* by its own
standards—to the demands of ethics, and finding for science a necessary role within the project of justice which morality itself requires.

Ethic Versus Aesthetic

It is no wonder, then, that the deepest divide separating Levinas
from Rosenzweig is that between ethics and aesthetics. For Levinas,
monotheism and Judaism and the limits of science put into play the
demythologizing and pacific imperatives of ethics, whereas Rosenzweig's thought, again following the later Schelling, institutes a remy-
thologizing in the name of Redemption, a fidelity to God based in
what he names "love." God loves each person . . . but we must ask what
does this mean and upon what basis is this assertion justified? As we
have seen, in his desire to escape the abstract intellectualist self-positing of idealism Rosenzweig seems to leap into faith, and in this sense
his "system of philosophy" seems more a personal *witnessing*—however beautiful and inspiring—than a philosophy. Or is Rosenzweig
perhaps defending a more liberal and intelligible view, namely, that
when one flesh and blood person is loved by another flesh and blood
person, then that person knows—by analogy, or perhaps as best as
a human can know—God's love? In this case his philosophy, like
Levinas's, would be a transcendental thought, accepting love as
a given, just as Levinas accepts acts of kindness as given. But it is
unclear, at best, if this is Rosenzweig's tack.

What is clear, however, is that Rosenzweig follows the Buber of *I
and Thou* (as Levinas understood this work, as a philosophy of *eros*)
in characterizing the central transcendent moment of his thought on
the model of erotic love—something which Levinas clearly rejects
in the name of the harsher imperatives of ethics. For Levinas, contra
Rosenzweig, "love of the neighbor" is an ethical relation, one in which
the moral imperative comes from the other person and singularizes

the responsible self as obligated to aid that other: "It is an original obligation to which I am, in guise of *me*, devoted and elected, I am ordered *me*. 'Thou shalt love thy neighbor as thyself,' or 'Thou shalt love thy neighbor, that is what thyself is'" (*ITN* 110). As for love, Levinas devotes several subsections of *Totality and Infinity* to a phenomenology of *eros* (*TI* 256–73), and even discovers an "infinity" within *eros* in terms of the futurity of procreation, the futurity of the child. He will also in his later thought speak of the responsible self's being-for-the-other as a "maternal" relation in which the other is "in" me—borne by me—more than my own natural self. Nevertheless, Levinas never takes love to be the basic model of transcendence. The self's moral obligation to the other person, impossible to completely fulfill, is the transcendent moment, transcending being itself as the "ought" transcends the "is."

No wonder, then, that Rosenzweig will speak of his system of God, man, world, creation, revelation, and redemption, as the "great world poem,"[24] and devote many pages in *The Star* to the biblical "Song of Songs" and to the world as narration. Although he once characterized his method as "absolute empiricism,"[25] it seems more like a cosmic tale, not empirical but rather absolute in the speculative sense Kant forbade. Levinas, in contrast, is perfectly clear that the true depends on the good, just as the good requires the real—the science of being—to be effective. Because his thought is based in a universal ethics which is itself always particularized in the singularity of the responsible self and in the concrete, historically specific and difficult freedom of the call to social justice, Levinas is not susceptible, as is Rosenzweig, to romantic illusions about love or the special status of Christianity and Judaism in a cosmic drama, nor, for that matter, does he have illusions about organized religions—even in Rosenzweig's sense of the inspired lived-religion which kindles within organized religions—as the exclusive bearers of humanity's great task of justice.

For Levinas it is not through human love, or on the model of human love, that God and religion—and Judaism—are effective in changing the world, but through the sufferance of acts of kindness and in the hard task of establishing a just state. And thus we are able to underline the all-important differences, between Levinas and Rosenzweig, to be sure, but between science and religion as well, as also to some extent between Judaism and Christianity, and the specifically Levinasian reading, hidden in the fraternal praise for Rosenzweig which we find in an article by Levinas on Rosenzweig entitled "Between Two Worlds":

> If the Revelation is the Revelation of Redemption, it is not that Revelation *announces* to man that he will be redeemed. The Revelation *provokes* Redemption. The Revelation of God to Man, which is the love of God for Man, provokes Man's response. Man's response to God's love is the love of one's neighbor. God's Revelation therefore begins the work of Redemption which is nonetheless Man's own work. Here we have a Jewish moment in the work of Rosenzweig: Redemption is the work of Man. Man is the intermediary necessary to the Redemption of the World. (*DF* 193)

The work of redemption, however, depends not on love as a mood or sentiment, however strong (even "strong as death," as Rosenzweig insists, citing the "Song of Songs"), but on the everyday wakeful, detailed, and arduous and often dangerous, risky, and thankless work of justice. "God," Levinas writes, "rises to his supreme and ultimate presence as correlative to the justice rendered unto men" (*TI* 78).[26] And again on the same page, in a citation that marks his closeness and distance from Rosenzweig, Levinas writes:

> The ideal is not only a being superlatively being, a sublimation of the objective, or, in the solitude of love, a sublimation of a Thou. The work of justice—the uprightness of the face to face—is necessary in order that the breach that leads to God be produced—and "vision" here coincides with this work of justice. Hence metaphysics is enacted where the social relation is enacted—in our relations with men. There can be no "knowledge" of God separated from the relationship with men. (78)

And in Levinas's (so-called) "confessional" writings, in his essay "A Religion for Adults," the same vision is traced, with reference to prayer and liturgy and its allusion to the biblical prophets:

> The Justice rendered to the Other, my neighbor, gives me an unsurpassable proximity to God. It is as intimate as the prayer and the liturgy which, without justice, are nothing. God can receive nothing from hands which have committed violence. The pious man is the just man. *Justice* is the term Judaism prefers to terms more evocative of

sentiment. For love itself demands justice, and my relation with my neighbor cannot remain outside the lines which this neighbor maintains with various third parties. The third party is also my neighbor. The ritual law of Judaism constitutes the austere discipline that strives to achieve this justice. (*DF* 18)

Though Levinas is surely thinking of Christianity in this final reference to law in contrast to sentiment, he is no doubt also thinking of Rosenzweig's exaltation of love in contrast to Levinas's own vision of Judaism and monotheism — "biblical humanism" — soberly pursuing justice as its highest spiritual vocation. Our "relationship with men," whose ideal is the just society, begins in and never departs from the always singular and always inadequate responsibility which responds to the always singular and always excessive suffering of the other person who faces me. But beholden first to the one who faces, the responsible self is by extension no less beholden to all of humanity and ultimately to all of creation, to animals, to all sentient life, to the environment within which goodness and justice can be sustained.

Such is Levinas's vision of the redemptive task set before humanity at once as its "religion" and as the very "humanity of the human." It is demanding and difficult, no doubt, at once the most singular of commands and the most universal, beginning in acts of kindness and yet requiring all the complexities of mathematics, physics, chemistry, and the other sciences, as well as technology, government, courts, police, education, social services, and so on, but nothing in the world or beyond the world is nobler or greater.

FIFTEEN

Virtue Embodied
Bris Mila, Desire, and Levinas

On the eighth day of Chanukah, 5756 (December 25, 1995), Emmanuel Levinas was taken from this world. That his passing occurred during Chanukah, which recalls and celebrates the superiority of the light of Jerusalem over the light of Athens, is certainly fitting. That it occurred on the eighth day is particularly striking for a number of reasons. For Judaism eight represents a transcendence even beyond, if one can say this, the transcendence of the Sabbath, the seventh day, whose perfection is relative to the imperfection of the six workdays with which it alternates. And for our purposes, eight is of course the day of *bris mila.*

Immediately we sense the peculiar temporality of *bris mila:* it has a future beyond Abraham's will. It binds every Jew thereafter. Furthermore, performed upon an eight day old infant, there can be no question of the child's consent, however passive, as at Sinai, or even of recognition. It is done before one knows it, and in some sense even before there is a one to feel it. When a Jewish male becomes aware of his body, it is always already circumcised. Furthermore, *bris mila* also links descendants to a long dead relative, to a distant always personally unknown and unknowable progenitor, a beginning before one's origin. Here consciousness and will, and hence freedom, are quintessentially "too late," exceeded but marked by an "immemorial past." But a nagging question keeps returning: are not these temporal distortions, a future and a past beyond choice, beyond but impinging

288

upon consciousness, évidences of the *primitive* status of *bris mila*, its unbridgeable distance from morality and from the individual autonomy and social justice demanded by morality?

To add to this question, there is unavoidably also the complex and perplexing question of gender: *Bris mila* is for males only. No parallel or equivalent gender ritual exists for Jewish females. Thus *bris mila* heightens and underscores the gender difference. What has gender difference to do with ethics? Or more generally, as we are prone to ask today, what has gender difference to do with anything? And there is another consideration: *Bris mila* is a mutilation of the male body, a refusal to accept it in its natural state. It is not merely a cut with a knife, but an excision of flesh. And not just any flesh: the removal of the foreskin of the penis, male organ of urination and generation. Furthermore, *bris mila* is a refusal by the parents to allow the child to decide, basing its decision on the natural body which it will never have, and which the father never had. For thousands of years, forming a long tradition, circumcised males have been circumcising other males. From Abraham on there is no longer any room for radical decision. Rather, decision is now carved physically within the space of circumcised bodies. Here, I think, we sense an echo of Levinas's notion of "difficult freedom," a specifically "religious" conception of freedom: freedom already committed within the space of its free choices, and hence a freedom different from the unruly freedom for so long touted by philosophers.

Each of these dimensions of *bris mila* — Jews only, males only, babies, body, penis — seem more troublesome for a universal ethics than the next. They are without doubt troublesome for a clear consciousness. But consciousness is naturally curious, fascinated by all things, already in Homer's day fascinated by the spectacle of dead bodies, and in our day of global media coverage, fascinated by far more gruesome sensationalism. More bothersome, then, these dimensions which trouble consciousness, all of these so particularizing dimensions, seem even more troublesome for an ethics whose exigencies command universally. Perhaps there is no link. But the ethics whose exigencies command universally, for Levinas, is an ethics that commands in the particular face that faces. Ethics arises not in the law behind that face, nor in the proletarian condition which produced it, nor in the psychic apparatus alleged to under gird it, nor in any of the other synthetic structures that unite self and other, but rather through the irreducible alterity of the face, pure alterity, whose purity is not in the least diminished by the particular face that faces but is rather and precisely presented and enhanced by it.

We cannot help recalling Levinas's insistence at every point, and against so many alternative views—one thinks of Christianity very broadly, or of Descartes and Kant, and also of Levinas's contemporaries Martin Buber and Leo Strauss—that there is *no* hiatus between reason and revelation, no rupture between a properly Jewish thought and the thought of humanity, a link Levinas calls "the significance of Israel in the spirituality of the Human" (*ITN* 93). Nor is there an identity—"The struggle against Rome is the preservation of Israel" (104). What, then, permits the conjunction, if not separation or identity, plurality or unity, between revelation and reason? It is the unsurpassable concreteness of singularity—moral singularity, election. And it is here, again, that we hear the echo of ethics in *bris mila*.

Levinas is in agreement here with Samson Raphael Hirsch's commentary to Genesis 17:10, that in the difference between *mila* as *bris,* that is, as actual covenant, and *mila* as *ose,* that is, as *sign* of the covenant, Judaism teaches the unity of spiritual meaning and physical act, or what is commonly known, and as Levinas knows it, as the unity of the spirit and letter. Here lies the solution to our problem, the link between *bris mila* and Levinas's ethical metaphysics: the inextricable link between letter and spirit. "There is constantly within us a struggle between our adherence to the spirit and adherence to what is called the letter...adherence to the principle is not sufficient (*BV* 78). *Bris mila,* then, like ethics, would be a form of exegesis, a symbol calling for meaning, a meaning attached to body, *bris* and *ose*—convenant and sign—at once.

Like Sabbath, which is also an eternal sign, but one of and for all of *creation,* and the rainbow, which is an eternal sign of and for the *human,* Jewish tradition designates *bris mila* as a sign of God's *covenant* with His chosen people.[1] What seems so primitive, so recidivist, like tattoos or ear loops on aborigines, it is carved on the body, like a insufficiently repressed oedipal complex. Ethics seems so far away from this. What have high sentiments and noble responsibilities to do with knife cuts to the foreskin, scars on a penis, males exclusivity, one nation rather than a united humanity? But perhaps it is precisely the sentimentality of such high sentiments, the spiritualization of the hard task of morality, that the Jewish conception of ethics resists, and that *bris mila* unmistakably marks. Surely Levinas teaches that morality and materiality are bound up with one another. Levinas is fond of quoting Rabbi Israel Salanter: "The material needs of my neighbor are my spiritual needs" (*NT* 99). The answer to our inquiry, it seems to me, lies in the distinctions Levinas makes between need (*besoin*) and desire (*desire*), between will (*volonte*) and reason (*raison*), and finally between desire and the most Desirable.

"Corporeity," Levinas writes already in *Totality and Infinity*, "describes the ontological regime of a primary self-alienation" (*TI* 226). The body is at once my body and a thing in the world for others. "The body in its very activity, in its for itself, inverts into a thing to be treated as a thing" (229). Thus even when one refuses the other with all one's might, with all one's will, the self is still alienated from itself, exposed, delivered over to others through its body and through its work. The alienation of one's work—which can be bought and sold, stolen or copied—is more obvious than the alienation of one's body, but both are equally exposed to others, equally beyond the will, or, as Levinas writes, "willing escapes willing" (228).

To be embodied is thus to be at once a poetic being, productive, outside oneself, and an historical being, subject to alien judgment, threatened by others, "exposed to violence" (*TI* 229). No refusal, not even suicide, can overcome this exposure, since "Absolute dissention with a foreign will does not preclude the carrying out of his designs...does not preclude serving him by one's death" (230). To be embodied is thus to be fated with an essentially ambiguous existence, ambiguous even in one's most voluntary power, in one's will: at once for oneself and for others. Already, then, even when just considering the body and will, the mark of *bris mila* comes to make sense: the body is precisely one's inescapable insertion into the public sphere. Already, from the first, one is exposed to others, without one's permission, vulnerable regardless of one's permission, will, agreement, or contract. Such *is* embodied existence. One is already bound to others, bound to all the divisions that make up the human as opposed to a purely natural dimension of being. Hence there are moral consequences to embodiment—and not merely consequences. Levinas will write: "Responsibility for another is not an accident that happens to a subject, but precedes essence in it, has not awaited freedom, in which a commitment to another would have been made. I have not done anything and I have always been under accusation—persecuted" (*OB* 114).

Does not *bris mila* mark precisely a taking of sides in the body's fundamental ambivalence: to be human, even in one's most animal parts, that is to say, moral, even in one's most private parts—and there especially? Think of the rules of *kashrut* for eating. Or of the "laws of family purity" surrounding sexuality which, years later, include the female along with the male in the sanctification of sexual intimacy.[2] So called *natural* being for humans is *human* being, as we know from the testimony of those unfortunate children left to raise themselves in the forests, far from civilization. *Bris mila* would be the admission, then, of a truth embodied deeper than one's animality, deeper than truth and consciousness, more than a truth. *Bris mila* would be the mark of solidarity, interconnection, the human, insertion in a field of moral forces, of obligations and responsibilities, preceding and exceeding one's animal powers. It would be, as it is, the mark of a *covenant,* where the excessive futurity of a promise of eternity, and the excessive passivity of an unbreakable commitment by and with God, combine to capture this sense of being bound by an alterity deeper than a contract which can be kept or broken. Levinas writes: "But one can also understand by life precisely this limitation of the savage vitality of life—something that circumcision would symbolize, the limitation through which life awakens from its somnambulant spontaneity, sobers up from its nature... to open itself to otherness and the other" (*NTR* 60). And elsewhere: "This is a concept essential to Judaism: that the consent to a corporeal wound to be undergone—or to have one's newborn son undergo—places us beyond all pious rhetoric and outside the pure 'inner realm' in which ambiguity, amidst unverifiable 'mysteries,' always finds a convenient shelter" (*ITN* 63).

But it is not only because an embodied being is one body among others, one living organism in a complex and varied biosphere, that the will is ambiguous: it is ambiguous in its very being, "in its mortality" (*TI* 232). To will one's own will and one's own will alone is still, contrary to Max Stirner's defiant dream, to be subject to the will of others. Willing contains within itself the possibility of its own betrayal. This is not only a matter of choosing slavery, submission, abject being. Even as I strive to will only my own will, I may will an alien will. More deeply, I cannot control the meaning of my willing for others, or at least I cannot guarantee the success of my willing the meaning of my willing for others. And death finally gives the meaning of all my willing, however careful, over to others, survivors, forever beyond the reach of my will. Hence my willing, because embodied, hence exposed, contains its own betrayal.

This does not mean, however, and contrary to certain religious traditions outside of Judaism, that the body or the will are evil. Rather, they are exposed, vulnerable, ambiguous, not wholly subject to the subject nor, for that matter, wholly subject to the object either. Embodiment is not simply need, not simply natural being, a dog that eats when it is hungry and sleeps when it is tired, a leaf bent to the sun, a rock inert in its inertia. Rather, the human body is desire, needs converted to wants, hunger become taste, cold not only warmed by but from the start enjoying the sun's warmth, exposure and territoriality become comfort and home. The human, in other words, cannot escape human signification, cannot escape what we call civilization, interhumanity. And interhumanity is not given as natural being, rather the reverse. It unravels between will and betrayal of will, recognition and betrayal of recognition, inside turned inside out, and outside penetrating inward. "The self is a *sub-jectum;* it is under the weight of the universe, responsible for everything" (*OB* 116). The deepest most hidden precincts of the self are the erotic, the outside inside the inside, male inside female, inside outside the outside, female encompassing male. Is it any surprise, then, that Judaism marks this greatest depth of humanity in animality, the very privacy of the private, the intimacy of the intimate, as the holy of holies—that it marks this encounter of flesh with flesh, soul with soul, with the sign of God's covenant?

We know the Jewish response to this situation of ambiguity: *sanctification,* the project of redemption, the task of saving the world, drawing it up into God's path. And this task, as Levinas understands it, is to wipe out mythology and mythological thinking. To sanctify—this is the meaning of Jewish existence. This is the category of being Levinas calls Israel. A world divided between integrity and betrayal, reality and appearance, truth and lie, morality and mythology, is transformed in Judaism into a world struggling between the holy and the profane, or, as Buber taught, between the holy and "the not yet holy." It is a world not built on an *arche,* and hence not unmasked through *archaeology,* but rather a world built upon *hierarchy* and the *hieratic,* calling for elevation. To elevate the not yet holy to the holy, concretely enacted as the struggle for morality and justice, that is the Jewish task, a task in the service not of Jews or Judaism alone, but in the service of humanity. "[*E*]*thics* is not determined in its elevation by the pure height of the starry sky;...all height takes on its transcendent meaning only through ethics" (*BV* 111).

Responding to this service, the Talmud calls *bris mila* the *makah tam,* the "wound of perfection" (*Sotah* 10b). It is an expression neither more nor less paradoxical than Levinas's expression "difficult freedom." It relates to God's words to Abraham, in Genesis 17:1: "Walk before me and be perfect." *Bris mila* is a "wound of perfection" in the sense that it is a call, a cry, as is any wound, to rectification. Humans, created in God's image, must, like God, love perfection. This means that they must strive to perfect creation, to make it more perfect, to bring it back to God. *Bris mila,* then, far from being a violation of the flesh, or a mutilation, a wound pure and simple, is an uplifting, a perfecting of the flesh itself. This is no doubt why Benamozegh, whose thought is no less universal than Levinas's, will think of it in kabbalistic terms, as a retrieval of sparks, of the heights found in the depths, and the depths that must be brought to their proper height. In his great work *Israel and Humanity* he relates the following *midrash* from *Genesis Rabbah* (11:6): When a Roman official, some say a philosopher, asked Rabbi Oshaya why God had not made man circumcised as He wanted him, Rabbi Oshaya replied, "All that was created during the six days requires perfecting, and man too needs to be perfected."[3]

In Judaism, Levinas teaches again and again, the task of perfection is not treated as an abstraction. The *tzitzis,* also a reminder of God's commandments, surround a man's loins because it is there, apart from any falsely angelic picture of human virtue, that much moral trouble originates;[4] the *bris mila,* even more so, prints the sign of God's covenant on the penis itself. "Adherence to principle," Levinas writes, "is not sufficient" (*BV* 78). It is precisely a *mitzvah,* a commandment, an essentially good deed, such as circumcision that "places us beyond all pious rhetoric and outside the pure 'inner realm' in which ambiguity...always find a convenient shelter" (*ITN* 63).

Bris mila, then, would not be a primitive rite, but rather a primitive protection, a basic sanctification. It would be appropriate for an ethics whose "ought" remains tied to the "is" of an ambiguous human condition. Commenting on the rabbis' commentary on the meaning of calling the Sanhedrin, the ancient Jewish court of law, the "navel of the universe," referring to its significance as a universal vision of justice, Levinas will again indicate the link between justice, passion, and the concreteness of *mitzvot:*

> Perhaps justice is founded on the mastery of passion. The justice through which the world subsists is founded on the most equivocal order, but also on the domination exerted at every moment over this order, or this disorder. This order, the equivocal *par excellence,* is precisely the order of the erotic, the realm of the sexual. (*NTR* 76)

How does one close the gap between the public and the private sphere? How does one produce a just humanity, that is to say, how does one sanctify and redeem the world? And what is Israel's role in this most noble enterprise? Levinas writes:

> How do such men become reality? By means of *mitzvot*. The originality of Judaism consists in confining itself to the manner of being where...in the least practical endeavor, there is a pause between us and nature through the fulfillment of a *mitzvah*, a commandment. The privilege of Israel resides not in its race but in the *mitzvot* which educate it....Nothing is more foreign to me than the other; nothing is more intimate to me than myself. Israel would teach that the greatest intimacy of me to myself consists in being at every moment responsible for the other, the hostage of others. (*NTR* 83, 84, 85)

Hence the event and sign of *bris mila* serves to direct the passions of men and women, via *mitzvah,* to remind humanity that the most private privacy, the most intimate intimacy, is also a place of holiness, indeed, the holy of holies.

Sixteen

Against Theology
"The Devotion of a Theology Without Theodicy"

The sentence in which God gets mixed in with words is not "I believe in God." The religious discourse that precedes all religious discourse is not dialogue. It is the "here I am" said to a neighbor to whom I am given over, by which I announce peace, that is, my responsibility for the other.

—Emmanuel Levinas, "God and Philosophy"

This obligation is the first word of God. For me, theology begins in the face of the neighbor.... To recognize God is to hear his command-ment "thou shalt not kill, which is not only a prohibition against mur-der, but a call to an incessant responsibility with regard to the other.

—Emmanuel Levinas, Interview with Bertrand Revillon

The doctrines which flowed from the lips of Jesus himself are within the comprehension of a child; but thousands of volumes have not yet explained the Platonisms engrafted on them; and for this obvious rea-son, that nonsense can never be explained.

—Thomas Jefferson, Letter to John Adams

INTRODUCTION

"Theology" is a notoriously difficult term to define, owing both to the depth of its meaning and its long and varied usage in the West. Etymologically, the term is a combination of two classical Greek words: *theos,* referring to the divine, and *logos,* referring to word, speech, manifestation, reason, science, or logic. Both of these words are perhaps no less difficult to define. We can nevertheless say that the term "theology" is commonly used to mean a reasoned speech about God. In this way it is a term akin to such words as "biology," "anthropology," and "etymology," except that common sense also understands that the term "theology," unlike these scientific terms, usually includes an aspect of special pleading or apology.

For the most part, Levinas usually uses the term "theology" in three different senses, two of them strict and one of them relatively loose.[1] The loose sense is as a synonym for religiosity (as in the second epigraph above) or, somewhat more narrowly, for the intellectual or discursive dimension of religion or spirituality, as when he speaks of "rabbinic theology" or "Jewish theology." What it refers to varies according to context and Levinas attaches no strong evaluative judgment to it. For obvious reasons, this loose usage is not our concern.[2]

The first and broader of the strict senses in which Levinas uses the term "theology" refers to "formulations of articles of faith" (*BV* 139). Here he has in mind a person's or an organized religion's *representations* of God, whether as testimony, prescription, description or dogma. Here theology means *discursive truths* articulating belief or faith in God.

The second strict sense in which Levinas uses the term is actually a subset of the first, but, as we shall see, we must treat it separately according to its specific difference. By "theology" here, he will refer specifically to Christian dogmas and doctrines, that is to say, Christian representations articulating, expressing and, above all, *performatively* actualizing faith in God.[3] Theology as performative utterance, in this instance, occurs when a Christian verbally professes his or her articles of faith. Here, to verbally express one's faith is to have faith, to have proven it, to bear witness to its reality. To say "I believe in God" or to say "I acknowledge Jesus as my Lord and Savior" is to be a believer and to be saved by Jesus. And it is only in the saying of these statements, in *using* them and not merely *mentioning* them, that these testimonials become true. Since no other human (but only God) can verify the sincerity with which one enunciates such theological formulations, the issue of whether one means it or not, in contrast to the question of whether one is using or mentioning these dogmas, is *objectively* not at stake. Theology in this narrower but still strict sense, and regardless of the degree of its intellectual sophistication—from the magisterial *Summa Theologica* of Thomas Aquinas, on the one hand, to the emotionally charged outpourings of a simple American Southern Baptist, say, on the other—is both witness and apology, that is to say, performatively self-justified Christianity. To declare one's faith in God is to be faithful to God.

Regarding both of these versions of theology—*doctrinal representation* of religion and *verbal performance* of Christianity—Levinas boldly criticizes them as essentially inadequate, as approaches unfaithful, indeed traitorous to the very religious dimension they claim to discursively enunciate. Theological formulations eclipse rather than express true religion. Furthermore and of utmost importance, the critique of theology, the putting into question of theology, is itself a constituent moment of a genuine religious consciousness. Theology, in other words, is not an accidental aberration of religion, but one of its permanent if pernicious and dangerous temptations. The subversion of theology, then, is not merely a negative enterprise but is in fact a necessary and ever to be renewed positive component of true religion. The critique of theology aims to puncture the pretensions of theology precisely in order to awaken theology from its slumbers, to awaken theology to religion.

It is with the two strict meanings of the term "theology," and with the reasons for Levinas's rejection of them, that this chapter is concerned. Nevertheless, I underline that its aim remains primarily positive rather than negative. It is only by seeing why theology is inadequate, where precisely it fails, that we can glimpse what for Levinas is the genuine core of religion. Levinas opposes theology not by rehearsing the usual enlightened attacks that prove it's internal inconsistencies and hence its basic incoherence, which is no doubt the case.[4] But rather and more essentially, he opposes theology because it is a compelling but nevertheless inadequate means to grasp the religious dimension which he defends. In sum, Levinas is against theology not because he is against religion but because he is for it.

Excursus: The Sacred and the Holy

Before turning to theology, however, let us first clarify the place of Levinas's critique within the broader architecture of his thought. This is important for our purposes because we must distinguish his critique of theology from his critique of the sacred.[5] Levinas opposes the "holy" to the sacred, and rejects the latter because it interprets religion in terms of participation, ecstasy, rapture, enthusiasm (Greek: *en-theos*), and the dissipation of the self that these states induce. Indeed, Levinas entitled the second collection of his annual talmudic readings, *From the Sacred to the Holy* (*Du sacre au saint*) (*NT* 91–197).

Briefly, for Levinas "holiness" (which is expressed in Hebrew by the term *kedushah*, whose noun form is *kadosh*, "holy,"[6] and which is another notoriously difficult term to define in any language) means "separation or purity" (*NT* 141). Here Levinas is following the classic definition of this term given by the great Jewish French medieval commentator, Rabbi Solomon ben Isaac (1220–1293), better known by his Hebrew acronym "Rashi." The holy is that which is separated from the profane, the vulgar, the ignoble, the "unclean," the forbidden, and certainly from evil and injustice. As for the "sacred," which in this particular talmudic reading Levinas discusses in terms of "sorcery" and "magic," the exegesis is complex, but the heart of the matter lies in it manifesting a loss of identity. Characteristically referring both to the ancient and the contemporary at once, Levinas writes: "Nothing is identical to itself any longer. That is what sorcery is: the modern world; nothing is identical to itself; no one is identical to himself; nothing gets said for no word has its own meaning; all speech is magical whisper; no one listens to what you say; everyone suspects behind your words a not-said, a conditioning, an ideology" (152).[7] The sacred, then, in this sense, is the loss of the sincerity of meaning ("saying") and the initiative of selfhood ("responsibility") through the "proliferation" of anonymous significations and personae (152). In *Totality and Infinity,* Levinas called this loss of identity the war, violence or violation effected by "totality," ending ultimately in the totalitarian State (*TI* 21–30). To refer only to the dissipation of meaning and identity, however, is too broad a way to specify what Levinas means by the sacred in contrast to the holy. For our purposes, then, we will limit the meaning of the sacred to pagan idolatry, that is to say, to the loss of the identity of both meaning and selfhood through a proliferation which occurs at the levels of sensations and praxis in a dizzying paroxysm, effusion, or enthusiasm of ecstatic participation. In a word, it is Dionysian frenzy—carnal intoxication, enchantment, mystification in speech and action.

The overall point of bringing up the opposition of the sacred and the holy is to distinguish Levinas's critique of theology from his opposition to the sacred in terms of the levels at which each occurs within the architecture of his thought. His rejection of the sacred opposes totality from "the bottom," as it were, at the level of sensations and praxis, where Levinas rejects the lure of sensuous or sentimental dissipation of identity into the dark anonymity of the "there is," an existence without existents. His critique of theology, in contrast, as we are about to see, opposes totality from "the top," at it were, at the level of representation and knowledge. So, if we distinguish, as I think is appropriate, three levels in Levinas's phenomenological analysis of meaning and selfhood, namely, the sensational, the practical, and the theoretical, the sacred operates primarily at the level of the sensational, as the sensuous seduction to succumb or lose oneself to the "there is," while theology operates at the level of the theoretical, as the intellectual seduction to remain or lose oneself at the cognitive level. Worship as the sacred and worship as theology both have broad practical consequences, to be sure, but their primary locus of operation lies in sensations and contemplation respectively. Notice that I do not say that the holy, like the sacred, operates primarily at the level of sensation. There is no simple symmetry here. Levinas opposes the holy to both the sacred and to theology. With these distinctions in mind, we are now better able to take a closer look at Levinas's critique of theology.

THEOLOGY AS REPRESENTATION

Like all other contemporary philosophers, Levinas began his intellectual career with a critique of representation, although in his case this means a critique of the contemporary phenomenology of Husserl! On the concluding pages of his celebrated expository book of 1930, *The Theory of Intuition in Husserl's Phenomenology,* which introduced Husserlian phenomenology to France, after having shown the nature and centrality of intuition as the key to the phenomenological method, Levinas argues that Husserl, despite himself, continues to privilege representation and theory. "This admission of representation as the basis of all acts of consciousness," Levinas writes, "undermines the historicity of consciousness and gives intuition an intellectualist character" (*TTI* 157). Here, in speaking of "the historicity of consciousness," Levinas is not at all reverting to the historicist relativism Husserl had refuted so definitively in the "Prologomena" to the *Logical Investigations,* but rather to Heidegger's account of the temporality and historicity of Dasein published a few years earlier in *Being and Time* (156). But Levinas is far from being a Heideggerian or even following Heidegger.

His critique of Husserl in *The Theory of Intuition* continues by invoking the "phenomenological reduction" which is meant to neutralize humanity's naive realism and is for Husserl the very beginning of the "presuppositionless" or disinterested quest for truth which is the mark of philosophy. Levinas writes: "by virtue of the primacy of theory, Husserl does not wonder how this 'neutralization' of our life, which nevertheless is still an act of our life, has its foundation in life" (*TTI* 157). The issue raised in these few seemingly obscure and apparently abstract words about method is the fundamental question of the origin of philosophy. Levinas is asking how in beings such as humans the disinterested quest for truth begins. He is asking what it is that jolts a person from his or her self-interests, desires, and prejudices, in order to engage in the quest for truth. It is a fundamental question, one that all philosophers must and do answer, whether implicitly or explicitly. If Husserl did not provide a precise or clear account of the origin of the phenomenological reduction, his students, by contrast, did, and they differed from Husserl and from one another about what precisely shocks or disabuses the naive individual from his or her naivete. In addressing this issue Levinas joins Heidegger and all of contemporary philosophy by seeking and discovering a nonrepresentational and nontheoretical ground for representation and theory. But quite unlike Heidegger, whose answer lay in the historicity of "fundamental ontology," and hence, more generally, in the same aesthetic path already trodden by Bergson and Nietzsche, among others, Levinas, beginning in 1930, but even more originally in 1935 and continuing throughout his subsequent intellectual career, will answer this question by turning to the unique significance of the impact of the other person. That is to say, he will turn to the primacy not of the world of things but of the world of people, of intersubjectivity, and there, even more importantly, he will discover that intersubjectivity is from the first not a derivative aesthetic event, an event of being (as is

Heidegger's *Mitsein*), will, or history, but an irreducibly *moral* event, and hence that first philosophy must be ethics.

To return more directly to our topic, theology, we leave behind Levinas's first book and turn to his last, *Otherwise than Being,* published in 1974. The "germ" of this entire book, as Levinas calls it, is chapter four, entitled "Substitution," which is a modified version of a paper Levinas gave in 1967. As he had been doing with an ever more refined precision since the 1930s, Levinas is once again addressing the topic of the unique encounter with the other person in moral proximity. Once again, too, he is discussing phenomenology and its limitations. The link between these two topics—the surplus of morality and the limitations of phenomenology—parallels the link that joins and separates what is positive and what is negative in Levinas's critique of theology. Of the moral encounter with the other person, Levinas writes: "Here there is proximity and not truth about proximity, not certainty about the presence of the other, but responsibility for him without deliberation, and without the compulsion of truths in which commitments arise, without certainty" (*OB* 120). Though truth, deliberation, certitude, commitments—representations—do arise in the need for justice, here Levinas is discussing their condition and justification, namely, morality. Morality, for Levinas, is a function of an inalienable responsibility, of selfhood in the first person singular—me, myself—responsible for-the-other prior to self-interest and self-esteem. The rhetorical effort of Levinas's argument is to *intimate and emphasize* not only the prerepresentative or precontractual character of this responsibility: "proximity and not truth about proximity," but also, related and no less importantly, its preactive, presynthetic, preintentional, character, what Levinas calls "the absolute passivity of the self...more passive than any inertia" (121). The latter, the exceptional passivity of a moral self, its extreme receptiveness, Levinas describes in social-moral terms as "accusation, persecution, and responsibility for the other," or, borrowing from psychology, the self's "obsession" with and "insomnia" over the other, the other whose very alterity "traumatizes" the self (121). The surplus of the other short-circuits and overloads the reflexive intrigues of a self-interested selfhood. It "denucleates" the self, to use another Levinasian expression, so that the self is without its own principle, is an-archic, for-the-other before itself, turned "inside out" for the other, and yet is not lost in or annihilated by the other (64).

Regarding the exceptional passivity of the moral self accused and responsible in moral proximity to and for the other, and regarding the danger of representation to this responsibility, Levinas writes: "To thematize this relation is already to lose it, to leave the absolute passivity of the self" (*OB* 121). Accordingly, must we not ask if Levinas (and I myself, right now), as a philosopher and author of books, thematizes morality? The answer is yes and no. Yes, as the author of a book of ethics, a book about morality, one indeed presents an exposition, a thematization, a propositional representation of morality. But no, too, because the four-dimensional nature of morality as Levinas conceives it—the irreducible transcendence of the other, the inordinate proximity of I and you, my infinite responsibility, and the exceptional passivity of the moral self—is that which occurs outside of thematization, outside of representation, indeed, more deeply (or, one can also say, "higher" or "more nobly") than the freedom of thought or action. This "excess" is in no way "guilty" of an unjustified and unjustifiable "empiricism" (or "external relations"), for such a charge comes only from a philosophical idealism (Hegelian or deconstructive) no less naive (or adamant, or ingenuous) about its own totalizing presuppositions. Moral proximity makes thematization possible and not the other way around. Writing, like speaking, is already an act of communication, and hence already a moral response to others. Thus even to represent is, as Levinas once put it, "the ruin of representation" (*DEH* 111–21), that is, a deposing of representation's sovereign pretensions, an infusing of representation with the trace of morality's proper authority—a "saying" and not merely a "said."

The matter is complex. To thematize, and thereby to misrepresent morality, is also to bring into play—to trace—a moral proximity beyond thematization. But thematization tends, by virtue of its own temporal structure of representing—which places the anterior posterior, or the prior later, or the philosopher before the prophet (*TI* 24, 54)—to deny this "beyond." To take the position (or, more precisely, the nonposition, because it is "de-posed") of the moral self ("proximity and not truth about proximity"), there, in that first person singularity, there where alone morality occurs and nowhere else, thematization would be inappropriate to the morality, to the obligations and responsibilities of the moral relation undergone. Morality is not stupefying, one does not become an idiot, not at all; but its imperative is not initially an intellectual representation of what one "ought to do." Therefore, what Levinas thematizes in his ethical writings is a morality that precedes, traumatizes and subtends representation, but at the same time it is a thematization that also shows how morality in requiring justice (equality) also requires thematization—including an ethical account of morality. In this sense Levinas's writings are at once concrete works of justice, products of the quest for truth, and "transcendental" writings, exceeding their propositional statements, even though in the latter function they point to a condition—moral proximity—that is a noncondition, indeed a nontruth, because it transcends, disrupts, exceeds what it nevertheless makes possible, including truth. Moral "saying," from the other, or from my own mouth, is only "traced" in any ethical thematization, in what is "said."[8] But far from making ethical thematizing worthless, precisely this—requiring an unsaying and resaying of whatever is said ("exegesis of exegesis"), animating a saying that alone makes the said significant—is what makes such thematizing imperative.

The contrast with Kantian morality is instructive. For Kant, to be moral the self must indeed thematize, must ask itself if its potential actions are following maxims (rules) that can be universalized. Only maxims that can be universalized, and in this way be thematized, can be good. Universalization is indeed the standard by which the moral agent determines which maxims are moral rules and which are not. The good is therefore subordinated to rationality, must pass the test of rationality in order for it to be good in the first place. Levinas is rejecting this priority, whether explicit or implicit, given to knowledge (and hence, in philosophy, to epistemology), despite the long and venerated Western tradition of giving priority to intellect in all things.

What has this to do with theology? Theology, as I have indicated, is first of all a rational account of God, or, more specifically, since theology, unlike philosophy, is apologetic (the committed defense of a particular religion's vision of God), it is always a particular religion's rational defense of God. Reason, in this instance, serves as the handmaiden of religion, as a tool to coordinate, bolster, and render convincing its beliefs. In a word, it is "monstration," an obsolete term in English which is defined as "the act of demonstrating proofs of an asserted conclusion." The term "monstration" derives from the same Latin root as the word "monstrance," which is the receptacle, usually made of gold or silver, in which the consecrated host is publicly exposed for adoration during Mass in the Roman Catholic communion (and curiously, too, so does the word "monster"). With this in mind we turn to another citation (and a footnote) from the same section of *Otherwise than Being* we have been examining. Having explained that phenomenology, which aims at descriptive rather than deductive disclosure, necessarily requires and yet is exceeded by ethics, because only the latter, beyond thematization, is able to point to the trace or surplus of moral proximity, Levinas writes:

> This trace is significant for behavior, and one would be wrong to forget its anarchic insinuation by confusing it with an indication, with the monstration of the signified in the signifier. For that is the itinerary by which theological and edifying thought too quickly deduces the truths of faith. Then obsession is subordinated to a principle that is stated in a theme, which annuls the very anarchy of its movement. (*OB* 155)

To this, he appends the following footnote: "Thus theological language destroys the religious situation of transcendence. The infinite 'presents' itself anarchically, but thematization loses the anarchy that alone can accredit it. Language about God rings false or becomes mythic, that is, can never be taken literally" (*OB* 197).

Here we see Levinas's critique of theology. Theology, because it is monstration, interprets the trace of the other as a relationship of signifier to signified, as a kind of "proof" by "witness," as if the terms of moral proximity were amenable to thematization. But it is precisely because they are not amenable to thematization that the one-for-the-other relationship is a moral relationship in the first place, a relationship of command and responsibility, an asymmetric relationship whose terms exceed their relationship while maintaining a relation. Such a peculiar relationship, neither wholly external nor wholly internal, nor a dialectical relationship, can only make "sense" in moral terms. And it is this relation that Levinas, in *Totality and Infinity*, calls "religion" (*TI* 40).

One cannot reason or even speak about God in a religiously genuine way because God is not a subject-matter, not a "signified," and least of all is he (or what Levinas calls "illeity," the third person) the conclusion of a demonstrative proof. Transcendence—which always absents or absolves itself—can only be pointed to, hinted at, indirectly in thematization. And this can only been done by an ethical discourse, which points to the situation of moral proximity wherein absolute alterity transpires as the irreducible otherness (transcendence) of the other person; the inexhaustible passivity of the self ("here I am"), the inescapable exigency of the other's commanding destitution (mortality, suffering), and the non-substitutability (election) of the self's responsibility for the other person. This relation, and not by any deduction, demonstration, manifestation, revelation, or disclosure, is the "way" in which transcendence transpires on earth. "There is only His word in the face of the Other" Levinas said in an interview with Edith Wyschogrod about theology, "...the essential thing is not to appear, not to show itself, not to be thought, not to be witnessed. It is to go toward the other human being who is God's divinity."[9] Theology, by reducing transcendence to a theme, even if a *via negativa,* even if a creedal witnessing, by its very nature as thematization occludes the genuine and prior transcendence which marks the interhuman proximity that requires a going toward the other, giving to the other, kindness.

CHRISTIAN THEOLOGY

Before turning to Levinas's critique of Christian theology, let us mention several positive aspects of Christianity he has noted. First and at the personal level, it is well known that his wife and daughter were hidden in a convent of the Sisters of Saint Vincent outside Orleans during the Vichy-Nazi persecution of Jews in France, and that Levinas, in addition to being grateful to them, has expressed his gratitude to the many priests and clergy who at risk to their own lives provided safety for Jews throughout the Nazi period. Second, more broadly, and reflecting the traditional Jewish perspective on this matter, Levinas acknowledges the virtue of Christianity as a monotheistic religion for the Gentiles. Third, Levinas's thought, like all modern European thought, is permeated by references to Europe's Christian heritage, from citations taken from Pascal to the appropriation and reinterpretation of religious terminology now usually associated with Christianity such as "kenosis," "parousia," and "the passion." Of course, much of Christianity is itself permeated by the influence of its Jewish origins, and often Levinas is simply reminding Christianity of, or attempting to reinvigorate it with forgotten Jewish significations. Finally, independent of Christian theology, Levinas has expressed his closeness to many of the teachings of the Gospels, for instance Matthew 25, "where," Levinas writes, "people are quite astonished to learn that they have abandoned or persecuted God, and are told that when they turned away the poor who knocked on their doors, it was really God in person they were shutting out" (*ITN* 162).[10]

Of course, too, Levinas also has several important reservations regarding Christianity. It is clear, and again in keeping with Jewish tradition, Levinas has no sympathy whatsoever with Christianity's claim to have superseded Judaism. Jews and Judaism are full-fledged contemporaries and not simply antiquated ancestors of Christians and Christianity.[11] Second, Levinas, along with everyone else who is not Christian, does not accept Christianity's hubristic claim to be the exclusive path of salvation. *Extra Ecclesiam nulla salus:* "Outside the Church there is no salvation."[12] For Judaism, in contrast, the path to salvation is open to "the righteous of all nations." For Islam (excepting, apparently, Wahabi Islam, which is also exclusivist) it is open to all monotheists. For Hindus it is open to all spiritual seekers. Indeed, no other world religion outside of Christianity, however deeply attached to its own spirituality, takes itself to be an exclusive path to God. Or, as I tell my students, Christianity is the only religion that thinks it is the only religion.[13] Finally, Levinas holds European Christendom culpable for not having had the moral fiber during the long and dark years of persecution and Holocaust to "love your neighbor as yourself" (Levi. 19:18). We can think back to the Inquisition, the Crusades, and more recently to the Holocaust, and really to so much else, to understand why Levinas is disturbed by "the fact that, properly speaking, the world was not changed by the Christian sacrifice" (*ITN* 162). This colossal failure, this Himalayan lack of love, which has yet to be fully acknowledged let alone rectified, along with Christian exclusivism, furthermore, is directly related to Levinas's critique of Christian theology, to which we now turn.

The moral failure of Christianity has everything to do with theology, with the place held by theology within Christian spirituality. We must realize that it is no accident that theology and Christianity in particular are intimately entwined if not synonymous. Indeed, in the final account, one can say that Christianity does not simply *have* a theology, but *is* a theology. Christianity, in any event, is the theological religion par excellence. What this means is that Christianity is based on right adherence to doctrine or what the Church explicitly calls "dogma." Its "faith" is "creedal," the affirmation of correct doctrine. This, as I indicated earlier, is religion as theology, theology as performative utterance: To declare one's faith in Christ is to be faithful to Christ and hence the very accomplishment of personal salvation. While Jews are a "people" or "the children of Israel," Christians are "believers" or "the faithful," and their clergy are one and all "theologians." Christians are in this sense, whether explicitly, as with clergy, or implicitly, as with laypersons, all theologians. For Levinas, however, because he takes the ethical redemption of the world to be religion's first priority, "personal perfection and personal salvation are, despite their nobility, still selfishness" (*NT* 87). It is a strong statement, to be sure, but it needs to be said. Personal salvation permits him or her who is saved to opt out of the larger redemptive enterprise, regardless of the state of the world, regardless of immorality and injustice, regardless of the suffering of the "widow, the orphan, the stranger."

Although Heidegger claims to be a philosopher and not a theologian, he has, however, articulated the theological essence of Christianity. He is also Levinas's great protagonist. In his lectures of 1937–1938, entitled "Phenomenology and Theology," he summed up the intimate relation between Christianity and theology as follows:

> For the "Christian" faith, that which is primarily revealed to faith, and only to it, and which, as revelation, first gives rise to faith, is Christ, the crucified God. The relationship of faith to the cross, determined in this way by Christ, is a Christian one. The crucifixion, however, and all that belongs to it is an historical event, and indeed this event gives testimony to its specifically historical character only in the scriptures. One "knows" about this fact only *by believing*....The occurrence of revelation, which is passed down to faith and which accordingly occurs only through faithfulness itself, discloses itself only to faith....*Presupposing* that theology is enjoined on faith, out of faith,

and for faith, and *presupposing* that science is a *freely* performed, conceptual disclosure and objectification; theology is constituted by thematizing faith and that which is disclosed through faith, that which is revealed....Insofar as theology is enjoined upon faith, it can find sufficient motivation for itself only through faith.[14]

The fundamentally "Barthean" elements of this description of theology are, of course, its grounding of theology in faith and faith alone, and then, even more specifically, its grounding of faith in scripture and scripture alone, meaning, of course, the *New Testament,* as supplemented by the *Old Testament.*

The "Heideggerian" element of the description, on the other hand, is not especially evident in this citation, but it is alluded to in Heidegger's use of the term "science." For Heidegger, theology is an "ontic" science, an account of beings (and not of the being of beings), what Heidegger calls an "onto-theology," and as such it stands in contrast to and remains ultimately determined by and dependent upon "fundamental ontology," which does raise the "question of being" (*Seinsfrage*). Insofar as theology sees itself as fundamental, however, Heidegger's recontextualization cannot be satisfying to Christian theologians. Nevertheless, there are theologians (most notably the Heidegger scholar, Jesuit priest, professor and psychoanalyst, William Richardson)[15] who believe that Heidegger's notion of "fundamental ontology" is itself more theologically satisfying than the ontic notions of theology it displaces.

For Levinas, however, whether one takes fundamental ontology to be a better expression of Christian theology than what Heidegger considers its ontic and merely onto-theological expressions, as Levinas agrees,[16] or whether one believes that onto-theology is more deeply rooted than Heidegger takes it to be, in either case what disturbs Levinas is that in the equation of Christianity and theology, religion in both cases is reduced to *disclosure.* For Levinas, as we know, the domain of the divine is morality and justice, not disclosure, or, to the extent that it is disclosure, it is disclosure serving justice, "the love of wisdom in the service of the wisdom of love."[17]

One can see the centrality of disclosure in Christian theology in the thought of Jean-Luc Marion, who while acknowledging Levinas's great influence on his thought remains, in the end, a Catholic philosopher-theologian in the very sense that Levinas rejects. Marion continues to make *logos* and its disclosure the highpoint, indeed, the very essence of Christianity. In his book, *God Without Being,* despite its title, he goes so far as to characterize the central and defining moment of Christianity—in this case Roman Catholic Christianity—as an "absolute hermeneutic," one that "culminates in the Eucharist," a Eucharist that itself culminates in theology. "The theologian," he writes, "finds his place in the Eucharist because the Eucharist itself offers itself as the place for a hermeneutic. . . . This place—in Christ in the Word—is opened for an absolute hermeneutic, a *theo*logy."[18] Monstrance becomes monstration. Marion's "beyond being" remains within the orbit of Heidegger's ontological hermeneutics; and let us remember that Heidegger too, in his later thought, also (and literally) crossed out being without thereby departing from the question of being.[19] Again we see confirmed Levinas's contention that at the heart of Christianity is theology, and that the significance of the centrality of theology is the centrality of disclosure, understanding, hermeneutics, and comprehension as the key to religious consciousness. It is precisely this, of course, that Levinas contests. Keeping alive the surplus trace, the an-archy of morality through discourse—the ever renewed exegetical resaying of the said—however tempted by knowledge, is never reducible to the disclosure of knowledge, conceptual, or hermeneutic.

Early in his career, and in reference to Heidegger, Levinas had challenged the Christian equation of religion and theology/disclosure in an article of 1951 entitled "Is Ontology Fundamental?" There he first shows that far from contesting philosophy's traditional predilection for knowledge, truth and intellection, the existential or ontological analysis that Heidegger proposes in contrast to onto-theology merely deepens it. "Understanding," he writes of Heidegger's account of Dasein and fundamental ontology, "is the very event that existence articulates. All incomprehension is only a deficient mode of comprehension. It turns out that the analysis of existence and of what is called is *haecceity* (*Da*) is only the description of the essence of truth, of the condition of the very understanding of being" (*BPW* 5). If anyone has the slightest doubt that Heidegger's analyses of Dasein and fundamental ontology lead to the comprehension of being as the truth of being, consider his 1930 lecture entitled "On the Essence of Truth," where this connection can hardly be made clearer.[20] For

Levinas, in contrast, religion is not ultimately a matter of being or — since being is equivalent to the disclosure of being — of disclosure, whether ontic or ontological, but rather of the transcendence which transpires in the relationship of *beings as beings to other beings*, a relation whose adequate expression is found in morality and justice rather than ontology or theology. In this way, as I have indicated, Levinas takes seriously the notion of creation, not as an illusory or provisional phenomenon, but as the irreducibly multiple scene of a "Divine Comedy"[21] lived in all the seriousness of the first person singular, in responsibility for the other and for all others, or, to recall the subtitle of this chapter, lived in "the devotion to a theology without theodicy" (*TO* 120).[22]

The transcendence proper to religion, for Levinas, is not that of *logos*, which is always reducible to immanence, whether personal and existential or world-historical and ontological, but rather the otherness of the other person encountered morally. Indeed, the otherness of the other person, hence irreducible transcendence, is only encountered when encountered morally. Morality, in other words, is not added to intersubjective relations as a gloss or luxury or bonus. It is what first makes intersubjectivity possible, or, more precisely, morality is the first significance by which such a relation occurs. It is for this reason, because religion is relation with absolute transcendence, that Levinas locates religion within the proximity of moral intersubjectivity rather than in any form of the disclosure of self-understanding, which is a product and not the source of the original significance of moral proximity.

After showing Heidegger's conformity to philosophy's and theology's time worn privileging of ontology and knowledge, Levinas writes: "Religion is the relation with a being as a being" (*BPW* 8). Of course, as I have already indicated, in *Totality and Infinity*, thirteen years later, Levinas defines religion in the same basic way, as "the bond that is established between the same and the other without constituting a totality" (*TI* 40). In his 1951 article, Levinas writes of his choice of the word "religion" that

> in choosing the term *religion* — without having pronounced the word *God* or the word *sacred*, nothing theological, nothing mystical, lies hidden behind the analysis that we have just given of the encounter with the other...the object of the encounter is at once given to us and

in *society* with us; but we cannot reduce this event of sociality to some property revealed in the given, and knowledge cannot take precedence over sociality. If the word *religion* should, however, announce that the relation with human beings, irreducible to comprehension, is itself thereby distanced from the exercise of power, whereby it rejoins the Infinite in human faces, then we accept the ethical resonance of that word. (*BPW* 8)

And earlier in the same article: "this tie to the other, which does not reduce itself to the representation of the Other but rather to his invocation, where invocation is not preceded by comprehension, we call *religion*" (7).

In his early writings Levinas associates religious consciousness with morality, the face-to-face relation, the responsibility of one-for-the-other. In his later writings, in contrast, he links the "presence" of God more specifically to justice, which is to say, to the laws, to legislative, judicial and executive institutions, to courts, police, army, and schools which are required in society by morality. Regarding the theological implications, Levinas once declared, with a certain irony and constructive honesty: "The direct encounter with God, *this* is a Christian concept. As Jews, we are always a threesome: I and you and the Third [the call for justice] who is in our midst. And only as a Third does He reveal Himself" (*LR* 247). This comment, which recalls Buber's critique of Kierkegaard, was made at an academic conference, held in Israel in July of 1972. Levinas was responding — in Hebrew — to what he called "a fundamental question," asked by Jacob Petuchowski (1925–1991). Professor Petuchowski had wondered, in Levinas's words, why or how Levinas passes "from ethics to divinity," and had raised the question: "Is morality possible without God?" Levinas responded (again, with some humor and much profundity): "I answer with a question: Is divinity possible without relation to a human Other? Is such a thing possible in Judaism? Consider Jeremiah 22, or Isaiah 58:7: 'to bring to your house the poor who are outcast.'" It is then that Levinas made the statement just cited about direct encounter with God being a Christian concept, in contrast to the prophetic idea that only in justice does God reveal Himself. Jeremiah, in fact, is far braver than Levinas who is speaking to fellow academics. In the text to which Levinas refers, Jeremiah is castigating the king of Judah and the throne of David, as well as their servants and the people Israel, in the name of God: "Execute judgment and righteousness, and deliver the robbed out of the hand of the oppressor, and do no wrong, do no violence to the stranger, the fatherless, or the widow, neither shed innocent blood in this place" (Jeremiah 22:2–3). And, as is characteristic of Jeremiah, he threatens dire consequences if these things are not done.

For Levinas, God is found in morality and justice, in what little there is of both in our world, rather than in theology, whose representations, even with the best of good will, obscure and deflect the imperatives of God's love. Levinas has written:

> Religion is the excellence proper to sociality with the Absolute, or, if you will, in the positive sense of the expression, Peace with the Other.... The obligation of responding to the unique, and thus of *loving*.... The love of God in the love of one's neighbor. This original ethical signifying of the face would thus signify—without any metaphor or figure of speech, in its rigorously proper meaning—the transcendence of God not objectified in the face in which he speaks; a God who does not "take on body," but who approaches precisely through this relay to the neighbor—binding men among one another with obligation, each one answering for the lives of all the others. (*ITN* 171)

Religion, prior to knowing and yet as the support of knowledge, is an ethical service, a devotion to others in what Levinas has called the "wisdom of love." It is by serving the imperatives of the wisdom of love that the propositions of the "love of wisdom"—philosophy, science, theology—emerge and find their true significance.

SEVENTEEN

Theodicy After the Shoah
Levinas on Suffering and Evil

A religion that insists that the earth is a passage and the future life a definitive dwelling ends up surrendering the world to the strong and the bold.

— Manuel Gonzalez Prada, "Catholic Eduction"

Evil is not a mystical principle that can be effaced by a ritual, it is an offence perpetrated on man by man. No one, not even God, can substitute himself for the victim. The world in which pardon is all-powerful becomes inhuman.

— Emmanuel Levinas, *Difficult Freedom*

THEODICY: GOD AND EVIL

What about evil? If the human self is meant to be good, to be "for-the-other," then what sense can be made of the countervailing weight of being, being-for-oneself, selfishness, refusal of the other, the "as for me," the "me first"? Even if we cannot have a good conscience after all the horrors of the twentieth century, can we continue to take any ethico-religious tradition seriously? After all, did not the Shoah take place in the most Christian part of the world? And even if, to explain the failure of Christians and Christian Churches, one were to offer explanations based on contingent events, fear, Nazi power, or intimidation, would one not, with the best of good wills, still be trapped by a theo-logic incapable of accounting for evil, and then—built on this incapacity and worse—also incapable of standing up to evil?

The theological explanation for evil—theodicy—is that evil is willed by God, willed by an absolute God, an absolutely benevolent God. The logic may be painful, in the sense that it outrages moral reason, but it remains logical for all that. Since God wills all things, God willed the Shoah. Because all things willed by God are good, the Shoah too was good. Not just that good comes from the Shoah, but that the Shoah itself was good, as repentance, sacrifice, purification, sign, redemption, punishment, perhaps all of these, but ultimately good in itself. Not only do such scandalous conclusions necessarily follow from the logic of a philosophical God, from an absolute omnipotence, omniscience, omnipresence, and benevolence, but even more painfully and intimately, they follow from the personal God of Abraham, Isaac, and Jacob, from his special covenant with the Jews, and in our day with "Israel, in its Passion under Adolph Hitler."[1] Part of holy history (*Heilsgeschichte*), the Shoah above all—where the Jews once again take center stage, not only in the locale of the Middle East, or of Europe, but globally—would have been willed by God, and thus would be good. It would have to be good, or it would be meaningless, and the Jews forsaken. As we know, this very line of thought, enunciated in 1961 by a leading German cleric whose moral heroism had earlier been proven saving Jews during the Nazi period, so shocked Richard Rubenstein that he rejected altogether any belief in the special election of Israel.[2] As we know, too, in the name of this same logic certain Jewish "pietists" have blamed the "impiety" of the German Jewish reformers, the Zionists, or more usually, or themselves, the most scrupulously observant of Jews, to "explain" the Shoah as the will of God.[3] Levinas too is shocked by this sound but appalling logic. Like Rubenstein, he too rejects theodicy, the vindication of evil in terms of divine justice. But he rejects neither God nor the idea of Jewish election.

How can one affirm God, Israel's election, and ethics after the Shoah? We are challenged to ask anew what sense, if any, do religion and morality have if human affairs are divorced from divine transcendence and divine justice. Is a God who hides His face[4] or is eclipsed any different than no God at all? Have the faithful now become no different than the "agnostics" whose mendaciousness Nietzsche derides because "they now worship the *question mark itself* as God"?[5] If the rejection of theodicy leaves those for whom God is still meaningful no more than a numbing astonishment in view of a *tremendum*,[6] is it really more than a clouding of consciousness, an elliptical but disingenuous gesture, or a brave but opaque stubbornness? Levinas answers in the negative. After the Shoah, to be sure, he rejects theodicy. But for Levinas the "meaning"—or meaninglessness—of the Shoah is to be found neither in a deviously disguised agnosticism or atheism nor in the fetishization of dumb astonishment. Rather, it is found precisely in the "end of theodicy." "The most revolutionary fact of our twentieth century," Levinas writes, "is that of the destruction of all balance between...theodicy...and the forms which suffering and evil take" (US 161). "The Holocaust of the Jewish people," he continues, is the "paradigm of gratuitous human suffering, where evil appears in all its horror" (162). "Auschwitz:" he writes, "the radical rupture between evil and mercy, between evil and sense" (SE 16). The negative lesson of the Shoah is thus precisely the end of theodicy. And its positive meaning? The answer lies in suffering.

To approach this positive meaning we must return to the question of evil. For above all the Shoah was evil (whether the greatest evil or a very great evil, that is not the issue; the issue is the question of evil). This most questionable question, older than Job, is in fact newly deepened, newly sharpened, radicalized by the Shoah. Job, after all, was restored; the Jewish people remain truncated and traumatized while today Germany thrives. And even as the Jews recover—nothing, not recovery, not forgiveness, not retribution, not even a justice which did not in fact occur, can undo the horrors, the unutterable horrors, the murders, the slow starvation, the slave labor, the tortures, the degradations, the vast theft of property, suffered by millions of innocents abandoned to the darkest of dark agonies. The world's leaders knew and the whole world knew, for it was reported in all the major newspapers. Levinas faces the question squarely; he does not shirk from asking: What can suffering mean when suffering is rendered so obviously "useless" [*inutile*], useless to its core? What can suffering mean when it is "for nothing," when it heralds and leads only to death and is intended only for obliteration? Jews were tortured and murdered for no other reason than that they were born Jewish—how else "explain" the torture and murder of one million Jewish babies and small children? What had they done? What can suffering possibly mean, what sense can it make, when it is rendered meaningless?

Friedrich Nietzsche was also troubled by "the meaninglessness of suffering."[7] Like Levinas, but of course decades before the Shoah, he too rejects as false and self-deceptive all the justifications of suffering provided by theodicy, for example, punishment for sin, or a necessary piece of a hidden but divinely ordained whole. But with the same stroke, with the same hammer blow, Nietzsche rejects all interpretations whatsoever for suffering. His readers are acutely aware of the provocation which concludes the third book of *On the Genealogy of Morals,* where after having masterfully tracked down and categorically rejected the self-deceptions of the "ascetic ideal," including theodicy in all its multifarious forms, both gross and subtle, Nietzsche challenges himself and his readers with the regretful admission that fundamentally no other interpretation of suffering has existed hitherto: "It was the only meaning offered so far."[8] For himself, Nietzsche answers with a brave but empty and fantastic heralding of the coming of yet another messiah: Zarathustra heralding the Overman. In agreement with the rejection of theodicy, Levinas takes up Nietzsche's challenge, the stigma of the meaninglessness of suffering, but he articulates another response, where suffering and evil, without losing and without denying their essentially useless character, nonetheless retain a meaning—"the only meaning" (US 159)—for religion and morality.

Levinas takes up the interwoven topics of evil and suffering, the end of theodicy, and a "new modality of faith today" (US 164n16), that is to say, the topic of ethics after the Shoah, in three short articles, comprising 24 pages in all, published at four-year intervals in 1978, 1982, and 1986. The first is entitled "Transcendence and Evil" (*CPP* 175–86). It is a creative review of Philippe Nemo's book, *Job and the Excess of Evil,* also published in 1978. The second article, entitled "Useless Suffering" (US 156–67), and the third, under the heading "*Le Scandale du mal*" (SE 15–17), invoke the Shoah and Emil Fackenheim's book, *God's Presence in History,* which appeared in French translation in 1980. The third article concludes, as we will also, by referring back to another short article, published in 1955, entitled "Loving the Torah More than God" (*DF* 142–45),[9] comprising Levinas's thoughts on evil and suffering one decade after the Shoah.

The three articles of 1978, 1982 and 1986 unfold as do most of Levinas's writings, by progressively building on original phenomenological and ethical insights, reviewing and elaborating them, circling back to retrieve, extrapolate, and amplify original intuitions. Each article and the set of three articles taken together develop as an ever-deepening commentary upon basic insights, like talmudic exegesis, resaying its own said—like *musar* (ethical self-development) training, as Rabbi Ira Stone[10] has pointed out. The three articles are each structured, in different proportions and depth, along the same basic lines: (1) they begin with a phenomenology of evil and suffering, (2) they turn to ethics to negatively criticize theodicy, and finally, (3) they propose a positive ethical alternative, which is Levinas's answer to the problem of evil. In the following, relying on all three articles at once, I will trace this same route, beginning with suffering and evil, and concluding with Levinas's positive religico-ethical alternative to theodicy.

PHENOMENOLOGY OF SUFFERING AND EVIL

Owing to the originality and greatness of his ethics, it is too often forgotten that Levinas was also one of the greatest and most original phenomenologists of the twentieth century. Thus Levinas begins his inquiry as a scientist, closely examining and uncovering the two primary (and related) dimensions of the phenomenon of suffering: (1) excess or transcendence, and (2) meaninglessness. These two essential aspects of suffering are fundamental, and by means of them Levinas links suffering with evil, both in oneself and in the other.

Suffering appears in and as an "extreme passivity" (SE 15), a passivity "more passive than receptivity," "an ordeal more passive than experience" (US 157). The passivity of suffering is extreme or excessive because of its quality of "unassumability" (15), "non-integratability" (*CPP* 180). This quality of "excess" or "transcendence," which makes up its essence, cannot be understood quantitatively (179–81; cf. US 156). Little and great suffering are both suffering. The "too much" of pain is its very essence, "manner," or "quiddity" (*CPP* 180). Suffering, that is to say, is not only a suffering from something, as Husserl's commitment to intentional analysis would suggest, but also at the same time it is a suffering from suffering itself, a redoubling of suffering. Thus all suffering, regardless of its quantitative measure, and regardless of whether it is endured voluntarily or not, is unwanted, insupportable, unbearable of itself.[11] Just as a bodily being enjoys enjoying, it suffers suffering (*TI* 110–21). The unwanted and at the same time inescapable character of pained corporeal reflexivity is what distinguishes the phenomenon of suffering: one suffers from suffering itself. One can turn to an abundant autobiographical literature from those who underwent the Shoah for corroborating testimonies.

Shortly after the Shoah, in 1947, and thus also shortly after his own wartime internment in Germany, Levinas had already described the over-determination of suffering in *Time and the Other*. There, describing "the pain lightly called physical"—which he distinguishes from "moral pain" in which "one can preserve an attitude of dignity and compunction" (*TO* 69)—he writes:

> Physical suffering in all its degrees entails the impossibility of detaching oneself from the instant of existence. It is the very irremissibility of being. The content of suffering merges with the impossibility of detaching oneself from suffering. And this is not to define suffering by suffering, but to insist on the *sui generis* implication that constitutes its essence. In suffering there is an absence of all refuge. It is the fact of being directly exposed to being. It is made up of the impossibility of fleeing or retreating. The whole acuity of suffering lies in the impossibility of retreat. It is the fact of being backed up against life and being. In this sense suffering is the impossibility of nothingness. (69)

Thus the notion that suffering involves an inescapable suffering from suffering itself is therefore a relatively early notion in Levinas's thought.

In the inherent excess of suffering we glimpse also its second characteristic and its link to evil: meaninglessness. Despite a variety of possible *post facto* explanations or finalities—that pain serves as a biological warning, or is the price of spiritual refinement, or of social or political regeneration (US 159), and so on—the "non-sense of pain...pierces beneath reasonable forms" (160). "In its own phenomenality, intrinsically," Levinas writes of suffering, "it is useless, 'for nothing'" (157–58). As such it is "monstrosity" (*CPP* 180), "non-sense *par excellence*" (SE 15), the "absurd" (US 157; SE 15), "basic senselessness" (US 158), the "disturbing and foreign of itself" (*CPP* 181). "The evil of pain, the harm itself, is the explosion and most profound articulation of absurdity" (US 157). "The break with the normal and the normative, with order, with synthesis, with the world, already constitutes its qualitative essence" (*CPP* 180). Jean Amery, writing from his own experience with the Nazis, of having been hung up by his hands behind his back, writes in confirmation: "The tortured person never ceases to be amazed that all those things one may, according to inclination, call his soul, or his mind, or his consciousness, or his identity, are destroyed when there is that cracking and splintering in the shoulder joints."[12]

Unbearable and useless, in this way suffering is evil. Suffering is evil; evil is suffering. Together they constitute an irreducible point of nonsignificance, an *Ur-non-significance*, as it were, a dark conjunction "where the dimensions of the physical and moral are not yet separated" (SE 15). "All evil," Levinas writes, "refers to suffering" (US 157).[13] It is "not," he continues, "through passivity that evil is described, but through evil that suffering is understood" (157)—"Sickness, evil in living, aging, corruptible flesh, perishing and rotting" (*CPP* 179). Suffering and evil are names for the meaningless painfulness of pain, which is always, regardless of quantitative considerations, intrinsically excessive, unwanted, not to be accommodated. To make someone suffer is a moral evil, because to suffer is evil. The original meaning of suffering is evil: it is unwanted, meaningless.

From this character of suffering as an unwanted meaningless burden, comes Levinas's first articulation of an ethical issue: "the fundamental ethical problem which pain poses 'for nothing'" (US 158). The ethical problem is not the sufferer's, the one subject to the pain of meaningless suffering, the victim, but that of the witness in relation to the sufferer: "the inevitable and preemptory ethical problem of the medication which is my duty" (158). In the other's suffering, then, Levinas sees an "original call for aid" (158), an original call "for curative help" (158)—"where the primordial, irreducible, and ethical, anthropological category of the medical comes to impose itself—across a demand for analgesia" (158).

Earlier, in *Totality and Infinity*, Levinas had already written: "The doctor is an a priori principle of human mortality" (*TI* 234). There he contested perhaps the central claim made in Heidegger's *Being and Time:* that dying or being-toward-death (*Sein zum Tode*) isolates and individualizes human subjectivity. For Levinas, in contrast: "A social conjunction is maintained in this menace" of death, which "renders possible an appeal to the Other, to his friendship and his

medication" (234). The evil of suffering, then, meaningless for the
sufferer, would at once be an appeal to the other, "a demand for
analgesia." Suffering—mortality—already reaches out to the other,
remains a social relation, obligates.

These are Levinas's first and fundamental phenomenological and
ethical elaborations of suffering: suffering as a call to help, the lash
that gives rise to my responsibility to respond.

But what if the other's suffering is hidden, muffled and silenced?
What if it is heard but faintly across a long distance, and ignored?
Machine-gunned in the forests the sobbing, the cries, the screams, the
death rattles of tens of thousands of Jews went unheard. Crammed
into cattle cars without food or water, sent to impenetrable concentration camps without exit, millions of Jews were enslaved, brutal-
ized, starved, gassed and immolated, ascending to the empty skies as
foul smoke. The lands of Europe are still covered with their ashes, still
soaked with their blood. The tears and moans of their agonies found
no echo in the great haunting and corrosive silence, which resounds
to this day. Theologians and the faithful seek God; the philosophers
and poets seek truth—what testimony have such uplifted souls given
to these terrors, these abominations?

Shoah: the End of Theodicy

The phenomenal or intrinsic meaninglessness of suffering and evil
render them resistant to all theodicy. The enormity of the Shoah
would be the unforgettable and irrefutable historical proof, and
henceforth a paradigmatic proof, prospectively and retroactively, of
the essential disproportion between suffering and explanation. But
Levinas goes one step further. After Auschwitz *theodicy itself becomes
immorality*. The idea of theodicy may remain a consolation or a
moral challenge for the sufferer, but as an interpretation coming from
someone else it is dismissive condescension, hurtful rationalization,
the rudest flippancy and flight. Thus there are two sorts of evil: the
intrinsic evil of suffering for the sufferer, and the evil of the one who
rationalizes the other's suffering. Levinas will call the latter, because
it is the most radical form of the refusal of the dignity of the other,
"the source of all immorality." "For an ethical sensibility," Levinas
writes, "confirming itself, in the inhumanity of our time, against

this inhumanity—the justification of the neighbor's pain is certainly the source of all immorality" (US 163).[14] Theodicy is thus itself one form—the theological form—of the redoubling, the exacerbation of evil that occurs in every rationalization of another's suffering. That I can explain someone else's woes, that I can justify their tears, is to pile evil upon evil, pain upon pain.

But how, we must still ask, reflecting on the word of Levinas just cited, is it possible to retain an "ethical sensibility" beyond the non-sense of evil after the Shoah? If suffering is intrinsically meaningless, and the Shoah represents the unavoidable global proof of this mean-inglessness, the proof of the inapplicability of any explanation, then why and how can we still speak of evil and of morality and God at all? This remains a fundamental question. How can we retain an ethical sensibility? Or, as Levinas expresses this in the now famous opening sentence of *Totality and Infinity:* "Everyone will readily agree that it is of the highest important to know whether we are not duped by morality" (*TI* 21). Was Nietzsche right, is morality simply the venge-ful ideology of the weak and infirm? Why call a suffering that is mean-ingless "evil"? Why blame as "evil" a refusal to attend to the other's suffering? Should not the strong and healthy, as Nietzsche suggests, be segregated from the weak and suffering lest they too become sick, sickened with morality?

We know the many theological answers, which either explain suffering away as if it were not truly suffering or threaten the unfaith-ful and immoral with otherworldly hell and brimstone. Levinas, for his part, does not flinch from the phenomenological "fact" that suf-fering and evil are intrinsically meaningless. The inordinate suffering and evil of the Shoah make this evident not only to diligent stu-dents of phenomenology and to Nietzsche, but to the whole world, and to all the religions of the world. "The philosophical problem," Levinas writes, "which is posed by the useless pain which appears in its fundamental malignancy across the events of the twentieth cen-tury, concerns the meaning that religiosity and the human moral-ity of goodness can still retain after the end of theodicy" (US 163). Precisely this "philosophical problem" agitates the various exigencies that drive the imperatives of ethics, the "problem of evil" (its "real-ity" or ontological status), and the meaning of religion in our time. What is Levinas's answer?

To Suffer Another's Suffering

Deepening his earlier formulations regarding the "category of the medical," and the "a priori principle" of the doctor, by holding fast to the phenomenon of suffering itself, Levinas's entire answer regarding the ethico-religious meaning of suffering, can be summed up in a simple but powerful statement: the only sense that can be made of suffering, that is to say, of evil, is to make one's own suffering into a suffering for the suffering of the other. Such is the embodied transubstantiation in which morality and religion find their home on earth. Or, to put this in one word: the only ethical meaning of suffering, indeed, "the only meaning to which suffering is susceptible" is *compassion* (US 159). Compassion begins in co-passion. In this way meaningless suffering enters into an ethical perspective.

The other person suffers — that is evil. There is no moral or religious explanation for it. Indeed, such explanations are themselves immoral, irreligious. Suffering, in short, cannot be made into an object, cannot be appreciated externally. Remember its other characteristic: the compression of suffering, its passivity, suffering as a suffering from suffering. Suffering lacks the distance of objectivity. Any attempt to to erase the suffering of the sufferer by inserting an explanatory distance between the sufferer and his/her suffering, in whatever exalted name, is not only a sham and hence futile, it is immorality itself. But I am, a being who suffers too. What Levinas is proposing, then, without any "mystical" implications, is a kind of holy, almost sublime, contagion of suffering.[15] He is proposing that morality and religion can still make sense, indeed can only make sense — after the Shoah — in "suffering elevated or deepened to a suffering-for-the-suffering-of-another-person" (SE 16). The fundamental philosophical problem of suffering, then, its evil despite its meaninglessness, its malignancy, would then become the "problem of the relationship between the suffering of the self and the suffering that a self can experience over the suffering of the other person" (*CPP* 184).

It is this empathy, this compassion, which is at once passive and active, a "difficult freedom," provoked, but provoked to a real and not merely a sentimental response, which would be the "new modality of faith today" (US 164): "that in the evil that pursues me the evil suffered by the other man affects me, that it touches me" (*CPP* 185).

To take on, in and as one's own affliction, the affliction of the other, is not simply a feeling, nor is it a mystical or vicarious action at a distance. Rather, it is a being *responsible* for the other, the self-as-responsibility, the self as "ashes and dust" before the mortality of the other, as Abraham said.[16] Morality and humanity, in other words, arise in the humility of a painful solidarity. The humanity of the human would arise — it is an elevation, an "election" — across the narrow bridge of compassion, a bridge, which despite its narrowness is linked to all and everything. "[T]he humanity of man," Levinas writes, "is fraternally solidarity," solidarity not only with all humans, but also "fraternally solidarity with creation" (*CPP* 184). Animals too suffer. Nature too suffers. But human suffering is the first portal and the primary modality through which all suffering afflicts us. This is not, then, the human defined by spiritualization or, conversely, by absorption into nature, whether nature be spirit or mother. Rather it is nature uplifted to creation, where emerging from human responsibility — "responsibility for everything and for all" (184) — no one, not the greatest and not the least, no creature whatsoever, whether animal, vegetable or mineral, is left out, ignored, dismissed, refused.[17] Levinas will call this vast empathy, this vast compassion, this vast responsibility: "theophany" and "revelation" (185). Beyond theodicy, it is compassion without concern for reward, recompense, or renumeration. It is solar love. Putting the other above oneself, converting one's own suffering into a suffering for the other's suffering, has "no other recompense than this very elevation" (185).

This "new devotion" after the Shoah, then, would be the "ultimate vocation of our people," and hence the ultimate vocation of and for humanity: "to give rather than receive, to love and make love, rather than be loved" (SE 17). Such, again, would be the nobility of Israel and humanity and, conceding nothing to Caesar,[18] it would be the "u-topian" imperative Levinas sees demanded of the State of Israel, as a paradigmatic state, *and hence of all the nations of the earth*. In requiring that after the Shoah Jews remain faithful to the uttermost depths or heights of Judaism, in the uniqueness of a singularity which always refers to the universal without ever giving up its particularity, Levinas several times invokes the demand of Fackenheim that now more than ever Jews — and in this sense everyone is a Jew (*ITN* 164) — must deny Hitler a posthumous victory.[19]

Jews must remain Jews. Christians must remain Christian. Muslims must remain Muslim. After the Shoah, in other words, humans must remain human. We must be "servants," Levinas writes, citing the talmudic tractate *Pirke Avos,* I:3, "who serve without regard to recompense" (SE 17). And this, he continues—circling back to his article of 1955—this new devotion and ultimate vocation of Israel after the Shoah is nothing other and no less than "loving Torah more than God" (SE 17).

CONCLUSION: WITH GOD WITHOUT GOD[20]

In 1955, Levinas had already written of suffering, God's absence, and the Shoah. "What," he asked then, "can this suffering of the innocent mean?" (*DF* 143). The answer is powerful and magnificent, and true beyond being. I will cite it at length:

> The God who hides his face is not, I believe, a theological abstraction or a poetic image. It is the moment in which the just individual can find no help. No institution will protect him. The consolation of divine presence to be found in infantile religious feeling is equally denied him, and the individual can prevail only through his conscience, which necessarily involves suffering. This is the specifically Jewish sense of suffering that at no stage assumes the value of a mystical atonement for the sins of the world. The condition of the victims in a disordered world—that is to say, in a world where good does not triumph—is that of suffering. This condition reveals a God Who renounces all aids to manifestation, and appeals instead to the full maturity of the responsible person. (*DF* 143)

"The suffering of the just person for a justice that has no triumph," Levinas continues, "is physically lived out as Judaism. The historical and physical Israel becomes once again a religious category" (144). It is through the Torah, then, through the Written and Oral Torah, through saying and the said, *through* law dedicated to justice, and justice bound to morality, and morality emerging out of compassion that we discover "the link between God and man" (144). Such, then, in contrast to an "infantile religious feeling," would be a mature ethics and a "religion for adults" inextricably linked, as one person is linked to another in the humanity of the human. "[O]nly the man who has recognized the hidden God," Levinas concludes, "can demand that

He show Himself" (*DF* 145). That is to say, only a humanity where each and every person has his or her own irreducible dignity and on this basis can enter into a compassionate solidarity with the mortality and suffering of others can rise to the imperatives of the divine.

"Loving the Torah more than God" would thus have two senses. And nothing is more serious than the play between them. It would mean, first of all, loving God's commands, His law, loving the redemptive work of institutionalizing justice, the u-topos of the "State of Israel" (hence of all states), which arises from and depends on the work of loving one's neighbor, on moral relations between humans, and loving all of these moral and juridical tasks more than oneself and more, even, than one's own unmediated personal relationship with God. This is Buber's rejoinder to Kierkegaard: marrying Regina, sanctifying God through the world, is not flight from purity, flight from God, the knight errant, but rather the very task God demands of humans. Morality would be revelation; justice would be redemption; redemption would be the spread of revelation. God has this much trust in His creatures.

But "Loving the Torah more than God" would also have a second sense, unavoidable after the Shoah. It would mean humans must love the work of morality and justice more, apparently, than God does. It would mean that even if God seems to have let humanity down, having hidden his face or having been eclipsed, as the barbarianisms of the twentieth century taught again and again, that now *all the more* must we, we humans, love the Torah, that is to say, "do justice and love mercy." The prophet Isaiah taught the lofty lesson that God was "afflicted by her [Israel's] afflictions" (Isaiah 63:9).[21] After the Shoah, Levinas is urging that we must take this burden upon ourselves, joining Yom Kippur[22] to Purim.[23] Regardless of God's silence or absence, indeed inspired by the responsibilities which devolve upon humanity through this silence and absence, we must be moved in our afflictions by the afflictions of our fellow humans.

Perhaps only in this way, finally, without making any demands, without expecting any rewards,[24] without reservation or reserve, without debilitating miracles, can each one of us for the first time as adults "walk humbly" with God. To help the mortal and suffering person, to aid the victim, without thought of reward for oneself, indeed, without thought of oneself, for-the-other before oneself, without any guarantees of safety and security, indifferent to compensation, this extraordinary and inordinate responsibility, this "love of the neighbor" which constitutes the moral self, and then also coupled with it the difficult and risky work of instituting a bountiful and just world where the suffering of each and everyone is minimized, are together the highest nobility of which human dignity is capable and the greatest manifestation of an impossible gratitude by which humanity elevates itself, however inadequately, toward a benevolent God. "It is up to man to save man: the divine way of relieving misery is not through God's intervention" (*UH* 117).

NOTES

Notes to Introduction to Part One

1. Husserl, *Phenomenology and the Crisis of Philosophy*, 82.
2. Plotinus, *The Enneads*, third tractate, I.3. See, also, Shestov, *In Job's Balance*, 32.
3. Once, after giving a paper in Jerusalem, in answer to a question regarding the ability of his philosophy "to solve actual ethical problems," Levinas remarked: "I have no ambition to be a preacher. I am neither a preacher nor the son of a preacher, and it is not my purpose to moralize or to improve the conduct of our generation. It is likely, in any case, that sermons have no power to raise the level of morals" (*LR* 247). Levinas's skepticism about the efficaciousness of preaching and moralizing is quite consistent both with his critique of theology and with the primacy he accords to morality and justice. His point is that morality and justice come first, and that ethics, the philosophy of morality and justice, is first philosophy precisely because it recognizes exactly this priority and not its own. It is, of course, Amos *the prophet* who said "I am neither a prophet nor am I the son of a prophet" (Amos 7:14). Far from demeaning morality by criticizing it, Levinas is trying to divert a complacency in morality that would put words above deeds.
4. See Habermas, *Knowledge and Human Interests*, whose own thought, continuing lines begun with the Frankfurt School, has always been very close to that of Levinas.
5. In "Language and Proximity," Levinas goes so far as to call this "first word," this "first saying" or "original saying," "God" (*CPP* 126). This is certainly the case, but only if we do not forget that "the true correlation between man and God depends on a relation of man to man in which man takes full responsibility, as if there were no God to count on" (*UH* 117).
6. Regarding the ubiquitous significance of "covenant," see John F. A. Taylor, *The Masks of Society*. It is a beautifully written book of which I was unfortunately unfamiliar prior to the completion of the chapters of the present volume.

Notes to Chapter 1, "The End of the World"

1. Heidegger, "The Question Concerning Technology," 4.
2. Ibid., 35: "For questioning is the piety of thinking." See also, Heidegger, *The Piety of Thinking*.
3. Hedegger, "'Only a God Can Save Us,'" 57.

4. That Heidegger's personal and intellectual attachment to nazism was anything but short-lived, accidental, forced, or the result of political naivete, and was something he never recanted, has been known for a very long time, though it has certainly also been denied or rationalized by all too many Heideggerians. It remains a very sad chapter in the history of philosophy. See Farias, *Heidegger and Nazism;* Wolin, *The Politics of Being;* Sluga, *Heidegger's Crisis;* and perhaps the most damning of all, Faye's recently translated, *Heidegger.*

5. Kant, *Critique of Pure Reason,* 29. "What we have alone been able to show...is that causality through freedom is at least *not incompatible with* nature" (479).

6. Kant, *Religion within the Limits,* 3.

7. In the *Foundations of the Metaphysics of Morals,* and elsewhere, Kant names "holy will," a will that follows the moral law not as a duty but *always and automatically*—without any countervailing force. In one sense, then, such a will and such a law are no longer *moral.* "The 'ought' is here out of place," Kant writes, "for the volition of itself is necessarily in unison with the law" (31). In another sense, however, it is purely moral in the sense that "good" is a meaningful term independent of its distinction from "evil." The latter peculiarity, a term that makes sense without contrast, parallels the manner in which God's "benevolence" stands on its own and is defined by itself and not by contrast. Certain Jewish exegetes have said that Adam had a holy will before his "fall." He was, they say, good *in truth.* Post-Adamic humanity, in contrast, now lives in "the knowledge of good *and evil.*" For Kant, the "holy will" is the unattainable but highest "regulative ideal" for human moral agents.

8. Ibid., 36.

9. Certainly I do not wish to deny that perhaps nothing is more puzzling and controversial in the whole of critical philosophy than the nature and role of imagination. That this is the case is precisely because Kant embraces Cartesian dualism. Imagination is made to function as a "third term," in an artful but ultimately unsuccessful attempt to escape the "bad infinite" which inevitably results from bridging the unbridgeable.

10. Kant, *Religion within the Limits,* 146. However, Kant had granted, that a "later Judaism," and "Mohammedans" as well as "Indians" are capable of an ethical exegesis of their holy scriptures (102). It would be instructive to discover to what extent Kant's knowledge of Judaism came from current Christian teachings about Jews and Judaism, and to what extent it derived from Moses Mendelssohn's somewhat idiosyncratic account of Judaism in *Jerusalem or On Religious Power and Judaism,* which had been published just ten years earlier in 1883.

11. Ibid., 102n4.

12. Ibid., 102.

13. Ibid., 101n: "I raise the question as to whether morality should be expounded according to the Bible or whether the Bible should not rather be expounded according to morality." Of course Kant affirms the second alternative.

14. Ibid., 162–63 for a more specific discussion and definitions of superstition and fanaticism, 163–69 for Kant's account of religious "fetishism," and 182 on "illusory faith."

15. Ibid., 158. I cannot, therefore, agree with Otfried Hoffe when he says of Kant: "It would thus be wrong to view the postulates, in a pragmatic sense, as useful fictions. For Kant, immortality and God are real objects belonging, however, not to the empirical but to the moral world." Hoffe, *Immanuel Kant,* 203.

16. Kant, *Religion within the Limits,* 136.

17. Ibid., 142.

18. Ibid., 94.

19. Translation slightly altered.

20. See, Levinas, "The Primacy of Pure Practical Reason."

21. See, Heidegger, *Kant and the Problem of Metaphysics;* Heidegger, *What Is a Thing?;* Heidegger, *Schelling's Treatise on the "Essence of Human Freedom."*

22. Kant, *Religion within the Limits,* 118.

23. See chapter 2 of this volume. On the body and death, see chapter 3.

24. Though Levinas's phenomenological explication of immanent being appears in many writings, spanning his entire career, its most mature formulations are found in *TI* 109–83.

25. Ethics is the heart and soul of Levinas's original contribution to philosophy, so there is no one text that best articulates his position; nevertheless, its most mature philosophical expression is found in *TI* 187–247 and *OB.*

26. Levinas writes about justice in too many places to cite, however *TI* 21–30, 33–105 and *OB* 131–85 are exceptionally fine texts on this topic. Also, for an excellent exposition of the whole of Levinas's philosophy, with special attention given to the role of justice, see, Burggraeve, *The Wisdom of Love in the Service of Love.*

27. *Sayings of the Fathers,* book 6, section 2. This tractate is unique in the Talmud because it is all *Mishnah* with no *Gemara,* and because it formulates no *Halacha* ("laws") but presents almost exclusively moral wisdom.

28. *Sayings of the Fathers,* 109. I have slightly altered the translation to conform to modern English usage.

29. *Sayings of the Fathers,* 108.

Notes to Chapter 2, "Being, Time, and the Ethical Body"

1. See Ernst Cassirer's early three-volume work, *The Philosophy of Symbolic Forms,* and his final book, *An Essay on Man.*

2. To give only a preliminary indication of the difference between the classical reduction of the body and the contemporary appreciation of the body, one might think of the important and influential distinction made by Max Scheler, in 1913, between the body as *Korper* ("thing-body") and the body as *Leib* ("lived-body"). See, Scheler, "Lived Body, Environment, and Ego," 159–86.

3. Kirk, Raven, & Schofield, *The Presocratic Philosophers,* 247.

4. Aristotle, *Organon*, 7–212.

5. Kandinsky, *Concerning the Spiritual*, 32.

6. Bergsonian philosophy is in no way resigned in the face of death; indeed, while recognizing the dampening power of death, it opens up a realistic struggle against it. See, Bergson, *Creative Evolution*, 294–95: "Consciousness is essentially free; it is freedom itself....All the living hold together, and all yield to the same tremendous push....The animal takes its stand on the plant, man bestrides animality, and the whole of humanity, in space and in time, is one immense army galloping beside and before and behind each of us in an overwhelming charge able to beat down every resistance and clear the formidable obstacles, perhaps even death."

7. I am thinking of the Christian theological interpretation of the incarnation as God's entrance into history, and of the German philosophical tradition of historical phenomenology from Hegel and Marx to Nietzsche and Dilthey.

8. It is interesting that this criticism, the empty formalism of Bergsonian creativity, was raised in France by Albert Camus in 1932. See Camus, "The Philosophy of the Century," 126–29.

9. Despite his general criticism of Western thought as totalization or self-sameness, Levinas will discover the peculiar temporal structure of an absolute past in several key moments in the history of philosophy, perhaps most notably in Descartes' *Third Meditation,* where the indubitable self-certainty of the *cogito* inexplicably discovers that "I have in me the notion of the infinite *earlier* than the finite" (my italics).

10. Levinas repeatedly draws this theme from Dostoyevsky: "We are all responsible for all and for everyone before all, and I more than all the others" (*The Brothers Karamozov*, 264; cf. *OB* 146; *EI* 98; *TO* 108; *LR* 182). And with no more or less sincerity, he will also utilize biblical references to illustrate this same excessive responsibility and humility, this emptying of the self for the other, this giving before receiving.

Notes to Chapter 3, "Levinas: Thinking Least About Death"

1. "A free man thinks of death least of all things, and his wisdom is a meditation of life, not of death." Spinoza, *The Ethics*, 192.

2. Heidegger's reinterpretation of Husserl's phenomenology in hermeneutic and ontological terms can be found in *BT* 36–63.

3. That Dasein *is* understandingly is of the utmost importance, as Theodore Kisiel points out in terms of Heidegger's relation to Husserl: "The displacement of categorical intuition by the understanding-of-being is in effect the transformation of Husserl's transcendental-eidetic phenomenology into Heidegger's hermeneutic phenomenology." Kisiel, *Heidegger's Way of Thought*, 175.

4. It is hardly controversial, and I am certainly not the only one to see in being-toward-death the lynchpin of Heidegger's thought. Leo Strauss contextualizes the point as follows: "Yet while according to Plato and Aristotle *to be* in the highest sense means to be *always*, Heidegger contends that *to be* in the highest

sense means *to exist*, that is to say, *to be* in the manner in which man *is*: *to be* in the highest sense is constituted by mortality." I mention this not so much for its own sake but rather to draw attention to another quite telling remark Strauss makes in the same lecture: "Only a great thinker could help us in our intellectual plight [of historicist relativism]. But here is the great trouble: the only great thinker in our time is Heidegger." Strauss, "An Introduction to Heideggerian Existentialism," 37, 29. Strauss died in 1973, so he could have read a good deal of Levinas. It is a pity that he was apparently unaware of Levinas's thought, and therefore unaware of its greatness as an alternative to Heidegger.

5. Three texts serve as our primary though certainly not as our exclusive guides to understanding the meaning of death as Levinas understands it: *Time and the Other*, *Totality and Infinity*, and a short lecture reprinted in Levinas's collection, *Entre Nous*, under the title "Dying for..." For reasons I have given at length in a book review (in *International Studies in Philosophy*, Vol. 45.2, 2003, 154–61), the much edited transcripts of student notes taken at Levinas's Sorbonne lectures of 1975–76, published under the title *God, Death, and Time*, are of only very limited use despite the pages devoted to the topic of death therein.

6. This notion of "enchainment to oneself"—"a kind of dead weight in the depths of our being" (60)—is the central theme of Levinas's article entitled, "On Escape." There already Levinas writes: "Nevertheless, death is not the exit toward which escape thrusts us. Death can only appear to it if escape reflects upon itself." (*OE* 67).

7. Here I mention Michael J. Hyde's book, *The Call of Conscience*. Because his topic is euthanasia, Hyde's approach to death in Heidegger and Levinas occurs precisely at the level of suffering, of the death that is "announced" in suffering. Hyde discovers that suffering persons who oppose euthanasia find sufficient meaning in life despite their enormous suffering. Those who support euthanasia and choose to die voluntarily, do not. They refuse to live a life hopelessly debilitated, as they see it, by enormous suffering. It is because his book is about suffering, then, and not really a philosophical debate over the ultimate significance of death, that for Hyde: "These two thinkers [Heidegger and Levinas] can (and must) go together" (254). Instead of attempting to engage or decide the Levinas-Heidegger debate in terms of the root "definition" of human subjectivity, Hyde rather *uses* their respective insights as two perspectives, which are both useful to understand concrete human responses to pain. To the extent that something is said regarding this debate, however, Hyde argues that Heidegger's notion of being-toward-death as nonrelational is by itself inadequate and dangerous (for those who suffer), and must be tempered with Levinas's account of the irreducible intersubjective and hence moral context of human mortality (7–10).

8. Marcel's Gifford Lectures of 1949–1950 at the University of Aberdeen were published in two volumes under the title *Mystery of Being* [vol. 1, *Reflection and Mystery*; vol. 2, *Faith and Reality*]. He also takes up the notion of "mystery" in his *Metaphysical Journal*. One of Marcel's efforts to provide what he calls a "definition" of the term "mystery" occurs in a volume of several of his writings

in English, which appeared under the title *The Philosophy of Existentialism*. In its first essay entitled, "On the Ontological Mystery," Marcel states: "A mystery is a problem which encroaches upon its own data, invading them, as it were, and thereby transcending itself as a simple problem." Mysterious indeed.

9. Conrad, *Youth, a Narrative,* 150. I thank Professor James Mclachlan for this reference.

10. Cited in Frankl, *From Death-Camp,* 66.

11. "The Interpretation in which the 'not yet'—and with it even the uttermost 'not-yet,' the end of Dasein—was taken in the sense of something still outstanding, has been rejected as inappropriate in that it included the ontological perversion of making Dasein something present-at-hand" (*BT* 293).

12. Keenan's *Death and Responsibility,* a book that purports to be on the topic of death and responsibility in Levinas, in fact focuses more narrowly on the time of "postponement." And even here, dealing with what is only a component of Levinas's far more complex account of death, Keenan confines himself, to the cleverness of a deconstructive "reading," influenced especially by Derrida's *The Gift of Death.* Keenen misreads Levinas's faithful descriptions of ambiguities inherent in incarnate freedom as if Levinas were naively guilty of "contradictions," as if logic ruled phenomenology. And so too does Keenan's "reading" manage to discover that Levinasian responsibility is guilty of…irresponsibility! Keenan can assert all he wants that his is "a close, careful, and detailed reading" of Levinas, "a matter of nuance." In fact it is nothing of the sort. As for Keenan's Master, Derrida, I am remindedof Levinas's comment in a 1985 interview with Angelo Bianchi: "I have often wondered, with respect to Derrida, whether the *différance* of the present which leads him to the deconstruction of notions does not attest to the prestige that eternity retains in his eyes, the 'great present,' *being,* which corresponds to the priority of the *theoretical* and the truth of the theoretical, in relation to which temporality would be failure. I wonder if time—in its very dia-chrony—isn't *better* than eternity and the order of the God itself" (*AT* 173). Also, see chapter 14, in my book, *Elevations,* 305–21.

13. Psychologists refer to the "delusion of reprieve" of persons condemned to death who just before their execution misinterpret signs in the surounding world to believe that a pardon is immanent. One thinks also of Ambrose Bierce's remarkable and jarring story, "An Occurrence at Owl Creek Bridge."

14. At the conclusion of Dostoyevsky's *The Brothers Karamazov,* it is only after he has declared to the gathered children that he wants "to suffer for all men," and only after he has taught them to love one another as a proper memorial to their dead friend, Ilusha, and only in response to a direct question put to him by one of the children, that Alyosha, "half laughing, half enthusiastic," assents to a literal and consoling interpretation of resurrection.

15. Camus, *The Rebel,* 285–86. In this book, Camus, like Levinas, defends being-against-death as the very heart of human "rebellion,"—of finite human freedom: "The consequence of rebellion…is to refuse to legitimize murder because rebellion, in principle, is a protest against death" (285).

Notes to Chapter 4, "Levinas and Buber"

1. This chapter presents part of a larger essay on Levinas and Buber which has been edited for this volume.

2. Buber, *I and Thou,* 171.

3. Buber, *Between Man and Man,* 118–205.

4. Buber, *Eclipse of God,* 63–92.

5. Buber, *I and Thou,* 172.

6. Buber, *Eclipse of God,* 78.

7. Ibid., 72.

8. Ibid., 76.

9. Ibid., 77.

10. Ibid., 77.

11. Ibid., 77.

12. Buber, *The Way of Man,* 163–65.

13. Ibid., 166.

14. Ibid., 166.

15. Ibid., 168, 172.

16. Ibid., 171.

17. Buber, *Between Man and Man,* 170–01.

18. Ibid., 170.

19. Ibid., 171.

20. Ibid., 175.

21. Ibid., 175–76.

22. Buber, *Paths and Utopia,* 134.

23. Buber, *Between Man and Man,* 175–76.

24. Buber, *Paths and Utopia,* 145.

25. Ibid., 134.

26. Buber, *Between Man and Man,* 176.

27. Munster, "De la pensée Buberienne," 61–79.

28. See Mendes-Flohr, *From Mysticism to Dialogue,* 147–48n2. Mendes-Flohr, intent on showing the influence of Nietzsche and (above all) Gustav Landauer, only considers the influence of Bergson via the analyses of Hans Kohn in *Martin Buber: Sein Werke und seine Zeit* (161–62n234). Levinas, in contrast to Mendes-Flohr, believes that "the adjective Hasidic seems inaccurate" to characterize Buber's actual insight. He writes: "Are not the instants transfigured by fervor, according to Buber (and all instants open themselves, according to him, to that natural magic to the point where one is no more privileged than another), the continually renewed springtimes of Bergson's duration?" (*OS* 10). Levinas continues, "Meetings are, for Buber, dazzling instants without continuity or content" (17).

29. Buber clearly is greatly influenced by the popular sociological work by Ferdinand Tönnies (1887), *Community and Society.* For Buber, however, genuine sociology is reduced to the intersubjective encounter of the "I-Thou." Mendes-Flohr, referring to "Buber's tendency to emasculate sociological concepts" (*From Mysticism,* 78), writes: "Buber frequently employs sociological

concepts. However, he introduces these concepts, essentially, only as rhetorical props...deprived of their sociological content....External regulation, that is, a regime of instrumental aims, is antithetic to authentic human *Gemeinschaft*, which can only define itself in the immediacy of each moment" (76–77). For Buber's pre- and post-*I and Thou* relation to Tönnies, see 76–78, 112–13.

Notes to Chapter 5, "Levinas, Plato, and Ethical Exegesis"

1. See my *Ethics, Exegesis, and Philosophy*, especially chapter 7, "Humanism and the Rights of Exegesis," 216–65.

2. Ibid., 246. Levinas's "interpretation" of rabbinic exegesis is in no way idiosyncratic, wishful thinking or invented. For a very fine account along the same lines of the living and authoritative dialectic operative in rabbinic exegesis—called "Intrinsic Inspiration" (lxv)—in contrast to both strict literalism and loose liberalism, see Loewe's introduction to *A Rabbinic Anthology*, esp. lv–lxxxi.

3. Plato, *Phaedrus*, 247c.

4. Levinas has also characterized Plato's *Phaedrus* as one of the "finest books in the history of philosophy" (*EI* 37).

5. Nussbaum, *The Fragility of Goodness*, 165–99; See Vlastos, *Platonic Studies*, 3–34.

6. For reasons indiscernible to me, Nussbaum twice notes that only Alcibiades' speech claims to be true, without mentioning the obvious counterfact that Socrates also declares before giving his encomium that instead of flattering love he will speak the truth about it.

7. Plato, *Symposium*, 211c, 211e.

8. Ibid., 210a.

9. Nussbaum, *Fragility of Goodness*, 198–99.

10. Plato, *Symposium*, 177e.

11. Plato, *Phaedrus*, 274e.

12. Ibid., 175a.

13. Ibid., 275b, 276a, 275e. Surely Derrida and his disciples have made Socrates' second point glaringly evident.

14. I have slightly revised the English translation.

15. I have analyzed this peculiar temporal structure of knowledge, which effaces its own ethical tracks, in chapter two of this work. See also in my book, *Elevations*, 133–61 and "For the Unforeseeable Future" (*UH* xi–xxv). This is not, however, to denigrate the moral wisdom of such sayings—but only if one remains alive to the human challenge, the living pedagogy, in them.

16. This is not, however, to denigrate the moral wisdom of such sayings—but only if one remains alive to the human challenge, the living pedagogy, in them.

17. I can no longer find the textual source of this citation from Levinas. A nearly identical citation—which, however, does not mention the Talmud specifically—can be found at the concluding sentence of *Time and the Other*: "Set against the cosmos that is Plato's world, is the world of the spirit (*l'esprit*)

where the implications of eros are not reduced to the logic of genus, and where the ego takes the place of the same and the *Other* [*autrui*] takes the place of the other [*autre*]" (*TO* 94).

18. Plato, *Phaedrus*, 257a.

Notes to Chapter 6, "Some Notes on the Title of Totality and Infinity"

1. I do not include Sartre's *Being and Nothingness* because, despite its subtitle and the often illuminating phenomenological descriptions it contains, its basic theses—the pure freedom of the "for-itself" and its opposition to the "in-itself"—are structured by a logic that stands closer to German Idealist philosophy (Kant, Fichte and Hegel) than to Husserlian phenomenology. Heidegger tends simply to ignore Sartre, while Levinas both phenomenologically and ethically challenges the abstractness of his purely free subjectivity.

2. Against Sartre, Levinas writes: "Existence is not in reality condemned to freedom, but is invested as freedom. To philosophize is to trace freedom back to what lies before it, to disclose the investiture that liberates freedom from the arbitrary. Knowledge as a critique, as a tracing back to what precedes freedom, can arise only in a being that has an origin prior to its origin—that is created" (*TI* 84–85). Levinas both admired and criticized Sartre; see chapter 7 of this volume.

3. For Georg Lukacs, "totality" is the very lynchpin of Marxism; see his article entitled "What is Orthodox Marxism?" Of course, Max Horkheimer and especially Theodor Adorno defended a nontotalizing Marxism and hence opposed Lukacs on precisely this point; see Buck-Morss, *The Origin of Negative Dialectics*, 45–52.

4. I cannot repeat too often the citation from Levinas: "The true problem for us Westerners is not so much to refuse violence as to question ourselves about a struggle against violence which, without blanching in nonresistance to evil, could avoid the institution of violence out of this very struggle" (*OB* 177).

5. The title of this subsection of course recalls the informal fallacy of "double question," a point to whose significance we will shortly return. This informal fallacy is also found embedded in the chapter titles of Nietzsche's intellectual autobiography, *Ecco Homo*. For Levinas's support of the human but not the rational legitimacy of skepticism's self-negating objection to objective truth, see the penultimate subsection of *Otherwise than Being*, "Skepticism and Reason" (*OB* 165–71).

6. Levinas had already described "metaphysical Desire" in his early 1935 essay, "On Escape" (cf. *OE* 49–73).

7. Often defenders of the Humanities, in their noble effort to retrieve ancient Greek wisdom in contrast to our own (the "quarrel of the Ancients and the Moderns"), remain nevertheless bound within the standards of totality—a wholeness or cosmos lost or a self-certainty and absolute knowledge to be gained—that permeates this entire tradition, forgetful of the infinity of Jerusalem. See Proctor, *Defining the Humanities*. The original title of this volume (and it seems ironic that the following title was replaced) was *Education's Great Amnesia*.

8. Ricoeur, *Oneself as Another*, 337.
9. See Burggraeve, *The Wisdom of Love.*
10. See Cohen, *Ethics, Exegesis and Philosophy,* chapter five.
11. Hegel, in rejecting Kant's distinction, does not refute or overcome it, but with great rhetorical flair, and the resuscitation of an ancient philosophical conceit repeated with great fanfare *ad nauseum* ("Thought can only think itself"), he shifts to an alternative conception of rationality instead.
12. Husserl, *Phenomenology and the Crisis of Philosophy*, 158.
13. Ibid., 162.
14. The French states,"*On conviendra aisément qu'il importe au plus haut point de savoir si l'on n'est pas dupe de la moral.*"
15. Kant, *Foundations*, 407.
16. Ibid., 407.
17. Nietzsche, *On the Genealogy*, 155.

Notes to Chapter 7, "Choosing and the Chosen"

1. On the issue of Sartre's faithfulness to the individualist existentialism of *Being and Nothingness,* see note nine below.
2. The French reads "*Essai d'ontologie phénoménologique,*" though Hazel Barnes's English translation is "*A Phenomenological Essay on Ontology.*"
3. I have heard the story that on Sartre's death a perceptive radio newscaster in Paris noted that contrary to superficial misunderstanding, Sartre had not passed from being to nothingness, but rather from nothingness to being.
4. Kearney, "Dialogue with Emmanuel Levinas," in *Face to Face,* Cohen, ed., 17: "At a personal level, I always liked Sartre."
5. Indicative of their disparate "fame" during this period, we note that Levinas's name does not occur even once in the Index to the 708 pages of commentary compiled in the 16th volume of "The Library of Living Philosophers" series devoted to Sartre: *The Philosophy of Jean-Paul Sartre.*
6. Cohen, ed., *Face to Face,* 16–17.
7. For Levinas's own comments on these sorts of similarities, see, "When Sartre Discovers Holy History" (*UH* 96–98). We know Sartre read Levinas's *Theory of Intuition* and *Time and the Other,* but beyond this there is no evidence one way or the other. I suspect Sartre read Levinas's "On Escape," and took the title of his 1938 novel, *La Nausée,* from Levinas's analysis of nausea therein (see note 34 below). It is more certain Levinas kept up with Sartre's writings, though we do not know (beyond the specific texts he comments upon, e.g., *Anti-Semite and Jew*) precisely what Levinas read or did not read. Levinas published many writings, but Sartre published far more.
8. For an even more positive "review" of *Anti-Semite and Jew,* or really of Sartre and his relation to Judaism more generally, see, "A Language Familiar to Us" (*UH* 92–95).
9. The notion of the "third" in Sartre—the others who look upon, and in some way "totalize," the for-itself in what would otherwise be its inescapable

opposition to another for-itself—is introduced in *Being and Nothingness*, but does not become central to Sartre's thought until sixteen years later in the *Critique*, where Sartre tries to develop a social theory without being unfaithful to the "existentialism" of the earlier work. Most commentators—including Ronald Aronson and Wilfrid Desan who both devoted entire books to Sartre's *Critique*, [Aronson, *Sartre's Second Critique*; Desan, *The Marxism of Jean-Paul Sartre*, Raymond Aron [*Marxism and the Existentialists*], and Thomas Flynn ["Mediated Reciprocity," in Schlipp, ed., *The Philosophy*, 345–70]—argue that Sartre fails to develop a genuine notion of sociality precisely due to his continued commitment to the oppositional dyad of the for-itself and in-itself elaborated in *Being and Nothingness*. Fredric Jameson, in contrast, argues that Sartre succeeds, and precisely because of the "third," which he calls "one of the most original notions in the *Critique*" (*Marxism and Form*, 206–305). R. D. Laing also seems to support the idea that Sartre has advanced beyond the individualist existentialism of *Being and Nothingness* in his *Critique* (Laing and Cooper, *Reason and Violence*, 93–176). For myself, without judging Laing, I think Jameson's account is brilliant, but more Jameson than Sartre. I am inclined to see in the *Critique*'s "translations" of the for-itself into "praxis," the in-itself into the "practico-inert," and being-for-others into the "third," attempts, efforts, intentions that strive mightily but fail, rather than genuine developments in establishing the social theory that forever eluded Sartre. For this reason, too, limiting this paper to the philosophy of *Being and Nothingness* does not, ultimately, exclude the philosophy of the *Critique*, and is no limitation at all.

10. Desan, *The Tragic Finale*.

11. Sartre, *Being and Nothingness*, 707, 708.

12. Sartre, "Existentialism Is a Humanism," 396. It is also found in another version under the title "The Humanism of Existentialism," 37. The version cited is an amalgam of these two translations. Sartre's essay provoked Heidegger's denunciation of humanism in his "Letter on Humanism" to Jean Beaufret, written in the same year. For a discussion of the humanism/antihumanism debate between Heidegger and Cassirer (with Levinas and Sartre standing on the side of humanism), see my introduction in *HO* vii–xliv. Let us note, also, that Sartre takes it upon himself to be the spokesperson for "Existentialism," a label more adamantly rejected by certain other "existentialist" philosophers.

13. Several commentators have mistaken Levinas's "humanism," the fact that morality begins and has its highest exigency in the face-to-face and interhumanity, with indifference for and hence an immorality toward animals and other sentient life. This is not at all the case. Hierarchy is a necessary dimension of morality, and its first "height" is precisely the height of the other person who faces. Justice, however, based in the face-to-face, based in morality, in kindness, extends beyond the other person, and this extension goes as far, as I have indicated, to include the entire universe, "all of creation."

14. *EI* 101; *OB* 146; *LR* 182; *TO* 108. The words are those of Father Zossima's consumptive and fatally ill brother, Markel. Levinas has combined two of his statements: "every one of us has sinned against all men, and I more than

any" and "everyone is really responsible to all men for all men and for everything." Dostoyevsky, *The Brothers Karamazov*, 264.

15. The "moral atlas" indicated here is therefore not the figure "petrified in the statue of Atlas" Levinas invokes as part of his critique of Jewish Enlightenment assimilation in "Means of Identity" (*DF* 51).

16. The allusion is to Heidegger, who explicitly denies to an "authentic" or "resolute" (*entschlossen*) Dasein morality in the ordinary (or "ontic") sense of the term. For Kant and Levinas, in contrast, along with most ethical thinkers of the Western tradition, there is no other morality than the so-called "ordinary" one, that is to say, the morality and justice of the Ten Commandments, "love of the neighbor," or the "Declaration of the Rights of Man."

17. Husserl, *Cartesian Meditations*, 106–31.

18. Buber, *I and Thou*. For all his respect for Buber's enormous accomplishments, Levinas, in several articles and interviews (and a letter directed to Buber himself), always rejects the mutuality or reciprocity of the I-Thou.

19. See note nine above on the failure (or one might say the success!) of Sartre's *Critique of Dialectical Reason* to establish totality.

20. Sartre, *No Exit*, 47.

21. As we shall see in the following, it is in the sections entitled "Freedom Called into Question" (82–84), "The Investiture of Freedom, or Critique" (84–90), and "Freedom Invested" (302–04), in *Totality and Infinity*, that Levinas most closely criticizes Sartre.

22. *TI* 295; my translation. Lingis's translation: "an 'unrelating relation,'" is also good.

23. Sartre, *Being and Nothingness*, xxix.

24. Ibid., 25.

25. Ibid., 23.

26. Sartre, *Being and Nothingness*, 567.

27. Sartre, "Existentialism Is a Humanism," 399.

28. On the "freedom" of "the truth of being" in Heidegger, in contrast to human freedom, see, Heidegger, "On the Essence of Truth," in *Basic Writings*, 114–141. "Freedom," Heidegger declares, "for what is opened up in an open region lets beings be the beings they are. Freedom now reveals itself as letting beings be" (127).

29. Fromm, *Escape from Freedom*, 53.

30. Cohen, ed., *Face to Face*, 17.

31. Peperzak, "Some Remarks on Hegel," in *Face to Face*, Cohen, ed., 211–12.

32. Even a Jewish thinker as committed to Judaism as Maimonides, under the influence of philosophy (Aristotle) and the primacy it gives to knowledge and intellect, declares that the "great loss" of Adam and Eve was their fall from absolute *knowledge of truth and falsehood* into a lower form of (still knowledge!) *knowledge of good and evil*. See, Maimonides, *The Guide of the Perplexed*, 23–26: "For the intellect that God made overflow unto man and that is the latter's ultimate perfection, was that which Adam had been provided with before he

disobeyed. It was because of this that it was said of him that he was created *in the image of God and in His likeness*" (24).

33. de Boer, "An Ethical Transcendental Philosophy," in *Face to Face,* Cohen, ed., 89.

34. Sartre, *Nausea,* 133, 132, 127, 130–31. Several years earlier, in 1935, in his article "On Escape," Levinas, too, wrote of "nausea" as an experience of being in its purity: "In nausea—which amounts to an impossibility of being what one is—we are at the same time riveted to ourselves, enclosed in a tight circle that smothers. We are there, and there is nothing more to be done, or anything to add to this fact that we have been entirely delivered up, that everything is consumed: *this is the very experience of pure being*" (*OE* 67). In contrast to Sartre, however, for Levinas, nausea, with its sense of powerlessness in the face of the apparent inescapability of being, is not the last word, as it were, with regard to the human relation to being. "Condemnation to be oneself" (70), is rather a spur to a deeper metaphysical desire—"a matter of getting out of being by a new path." (73) It is not the former, the "plenitude of being" (69), but the latter, desire for the beyond being, as Jacques Rolland points out in his essay of the same name ("Getting Out of Being by a New Path," *OE* 3–48), that is the key to all of Levinas's subsequent thought.

Notes to Chapter 8, "Some Reflections on Levinas and Shakespeare"

1. In French, the quotation reads, "*[I]l me semble parfois que toute la philosphie n'est qu'une meditation de Shakespeare.*"

2. "Reality and Its Shadow," published in French as "*La realite et son ombre,*" appeared in 1948 in the fourth number (November) of volume 38 of *Les Temps Modernes.* Levinas was invited to make this contribution to *Les temps modernes* by Jean-Paul Sartre, who was the principal editor of *Les Temps Modernes* at that time.

Levinas's thoughts on art are at one level a response to and criticism of Sartre's reflections on art. But to fully understand Levinas's philosophy of art as found in "Reality and Its Shadow," however, one must go beyond the more immediate conversation with Sartre to the deeper reflections on art by another philosophical interlocutor, Martin Heidegger. While Levinas is certainly a radical and trenchant critic of Sartre, because Heidegger's fundamental ontology of be-ing (*Sein*) and beings (*Seindes*) is deeper than Sartre's somewhat schematic existentialism of being (*etre*) and nothingness (*neant*), Levinas's deeper protagonist, and hence his more profound criticism, is directed against Heidegger. Heidegger's most important article on art is entitled "The Origin of the Work of Art" ("*Der Ursprung des Kunstwerkes*"). It had first been given in a short form as a public lecture in Freiburg in 1935, and again in Zurich in early 1936. In its final and longer form it was given as a series of three lectures at the end of 1936 in Frankfurt. It first appeared in print, however, only in 1950, in Heidegger's collection entitled *Holzwege* (1950), so Levinas could not have known the text, though he may well have been indirectly familiar with the lectures. Also chronologically prior to Levinas's article of 1948, is Heidegger's lecture entitled "What are Poets For?" ("*Wozu Dicther?*"), which was delivered in 1946, on the twentieth anniversary of

Rilke's death. But it was delivered to only "to a very small group," and appeared in print long after Levinas's article. Nonetheless, two of Heidegger's important shorter works on art had been published prior to Levinas's article. Heidegger's "Hölderlin and the Essence of Poetry" appeared in print in 1937, and the more important article entitled "On the Essence of Truth" (first delivered in 1930) had been published in 1943. Given these last two publication dates, there is every reason to believe that Levinas was familiar with these two pieces. But more broadly, it is safe to say that Levinas was familiar with Heidegger's thoughts on the nature and significance of art and its relation to truth. In any event, whatever the bibliographical connections, it is clear that in "Reality and Its Shadow," and in his subsequent criticisms of aesthetic philosophy, Levinas is critically responding less to the "existentialism" of Sartre than to the "fundamental ontology" of Heidegger.

3. Nietzsche, *The Anti-Christ*, 81.

4. Lionel Trilling, *A Gathering of Fugitives*, 136.

5. See, Cohen, *Ethics, Exegesis and Philosophy*.

6. Again it is enlightening to cite Nietzsche—who has in mind Wagner's appropriation of Schopenhauer (including the latter's anti-Semitism)—who denounces artists lack of independence: "They have at all times been valets of some morality, philosophy, or religion.... They always need at the very least protection, a prop, an established authority; artists never stand apart; standing alone is contrary to their deepest instincts" (Nietzsche, *On the Genealogy of Morals*, 102).

7. Bloom, *Shakespeare*, 17.

8. For his basic perspective and his high appreciation of Shakespeare, Bloom cites Thomas Carlyle's assessment: "'If called to define Shakespeare's faculty, I should say superiority of Intellect, and think I had included all under that.'" (Bloom, *Shakespeare*, 1.) Bloom distinguishes "the self as moral agent" (4), from personality: "Personality, in our sense, is a Shakespearean invention, and is not only Shakespeare's greatest originality but also the authentic cause of his perpetual pervasiveness" (4). Influenced by Leo Strauss's stark opposition between Athens and Jerusalem, what Bloom does not realize—if one can say that a critic of Bloom's great breadth and stature does not realize something—is that at the bottom of "personality," making it truly interesting—from Falstaff to Hamlet—is precisely the drama of *moral* agency. For Levinas, Athens and Jerusalem cannot be separated; hence, again, philosophy as a meditation of Shakespeare.

9. See Harbage, *Conceptions of Shakespeare*, 120–37. "[W]e are sometimes uneasily aware of a basking in the *emotion* of benevolence, detached from its practical effects [Levinas calls this detachment "the temptation of temptation."].... One thing that sends us back to Shakespeare for strength and refreshment is that his good people are incorrupt. They do not luxuriate in impulses of goodness, but act upon them within their limited sphere. The emphasis is upon achievement." (136).

10. It is interesting that in this list of 1981, while certainly making room for him in the highest order of literature, Levinas overlooks to mention the proper name of Shakespeare.

11. The indifference of nature to moral values, hence the immorality of its amorality, is perhaps the deepest philosophical point of the writings of the Marquis de Sade; the same indifference is true of art for art's sake.

12. Levinas, "*Quelques Reflexions*," 27.

13. One can argue, as did my teacher Justus Buchler, that the real, from an ontological point of view, does not admit of degree. For more on "ontological parity," see, e.g., Justus Buchler, *Metaphysics of Natural Complexes* (New York: Columbia University Press, 1966). If Buchler is right, and I think he is, then the priorities that philosophers and theologians claimed for levels of being were in truth priorities deriving from ethical rather than purely ontological imperatives.

14. Cited in Halliday, *Shakespeare and His Critics*, 86.

15. I put "phenomenological" in scare quotes because even in his early works Levinas's ethical metaphysics exceeds his phenomenological "physics."

16. Levinas, "Bad Conscience," in *Face to Face*, ed. and trans. Cohen, 40. Cf. *GCM* 172–77; *EN* 123–32).

17. Discussing the Jewish notion of Revelation, Levinas recalls the words of an (unidentified) eighteenth century Jewish scholar for whom "the slightest question put by a novice pupil to his schoolmaster constitutes an ineluctable articulation of the Revelation, which was heard at Sinai" (*BV* 134).

18. Perhaps the most celebrated case is that of Spinoza, where, despite the considerable counter evidence of his own philosophy, not to mention his probable lack of advanced talmudic study, at least a serious argument can be made, and was made by Harry Austryn Wolfson, in favor of his familiarity with Jewish sources. Probably the most recent case of this projection of vague Jewish values is the case of Jacques Derrida, where despite many attempts (perhaps beginning with Susan Handelman), I know of no serious argument that can be mounted in favor of his familiarity with—or even acquaintance with—Jewish sources.

19. Commentaries on *Sanhedrin* 99a (1960) and *Sanhedrin* 98b–99a (1961), appear in *DF;* commentaries on *Yoma* 87a (1963), *Shabbat* 99a–b (1964), *Sota* 34b–35a (1965), *Sanhedrin* 36b–37a (1966), *Baba Metsia* 83a–b (1969), *Nazir* 66a–b (1970), *Sanhedrin* 67a–68b (1971), *Berakhot* 61a (1972), and *Baba Kama* 60a–b (1975), appear in *NT;* commentaries on *Makkot* 23a–24b (1974), *Tamid* 31a–32b (1988), and *Chullin* 88b–89a (1989), appear in *NTR;* commentaries on *Menahot* 99b–110a (1976), *Makkot* 10a (1978), *Yoma* 10a (1979), *Sotah* 37a–37b (1980), *Berakhot* 33b (1980), *Makkot* 23b (1979), *Shevuot* 35a / *Temurah* 4a / *Sukkah* 53b (1969), appear in *BV;* commentaries on *Megillah* 7a (1983), *Sanhedrin* 99a–b (1984), *Berakhot* 12b–13a (1984), *Pesachim* 118b (1986), appear in *ITN*. Gibbs, in *Correlations*, 175, provides a list of the addresses and talmudic readings Levinas delivered at the annual Colloquia of French-speaking Jewish Intellectuals.

20. Theodore de Boer, one of the great Levinas scholars of our time, calls this method "ethical transcendental philosophy." See, de Boer, *The Rationality of Transcendence*. Also, see the articles on Levinas's "method" by Steven G. Smith, Charles William Reed, Jean-François Lyotard, Jan de Greef, and Robert Bernasconi, collected in *Face to Face*, ed. Cohen.

21. Camus, *The Myth of Sisyphus*.

22. Camus, *The Rebel*.

23. "Death Dont't Have No Mercy," written by Reverend Gary Davis, made famous by the Grateful Dead.

24. Wyschogrod, *Emmanuel Levinas*.

25. For an extended discussion of this idea in relation to Husserl and Spinoza, see my *Ethics, Exegesis and Philosophy*, chapter two.

26. Levinas, *Les imprevus*, 110.

27. "The same man is indeed a comic poet and a tragic poet, an ambiguity which constitutes the particular magic of poets like Gogol, Dickens, Chekov—and Molière, Cervantes, and above all, Shakespeare" (*LR* 138). And, "Modern literature, disparaged for its intellectualism (which, nonetheless goes back to Shakespeare, the Molière of *Don Juan*, Goethe, Dostoyevsky) certainly manifests a more and more clear awareness of this fundamental insufficiency of artistic idolatry" (143).

Notes to Chapter 9, "Defending Levinas"

1. Lawlor, *Thinking Through French Philosophy*, 180n14.

2. For more on Bergson and Levinas's view of time, see chapter 2 of this volume.

3. First: "Act only according to that maxim by which you can at the same time will that it should become a universal law." Third: "Act as if your maxims should serve at the same time as the universal law (of all rational beings)."

4. Cohen, ed., *Face to Face*, 1.

5. Derrida, *Writing and Difference*, 117.

6. Ibid., 117.

7. Cohen, ed., *Face to Face*, 123.

8. Lyotard, *The Postmodern Condition*, 10.

9. Cohen and Marsh, ed., *Ricoeur as Another: The Ethics of Subjectivity*, 127–60.

10. Beauvoir, *The Second Sex*, xl.

11. Irigaray, "The Fecundity," in *Face to Face*, Cohen, ed., 250; quotation modified.

12. Ibid., 237.

13. Irigaray, "Questions to Emmanuel Levinas," 180.

14. Cf. Cohen, *Elevations*, 195–222.

15. Cf. Wolfe, "In the Shadow of Wittgenstein's Lion," in *Zoontologies*, 16–17. Wolfe is actually quoting here from Llewelyn's essay, "Am I Obsessed with Bobby?"

16. Cf. Perpich, *The Ethics of Emmanuel Levinas*, 150–76.

17. Žižek more directly responds to Levinas's ethics in his essay "Neighbors and Other Monsters," in *The Neighbor*, 134–90.

18. Cf. Havel, *Open Letters*.

19. Badiou, *Ethics*, 25.

20. Ibid., 23.
21. Ibid., 24.
22. Ibid., 25.

Notes to Introduction to Part Two

1. Spinoza, *Theological-Political Treatise*, 131; Cf. *EI* 23–24.

Notes to Chapter 10, "Levinas, Judaism, and the Primacy of the Ethical"

1. Levinas was born on December 30, 1905, according to the Julian calendar then in effect in Lithuania.
2. See, Salomon Malka, *Monsieur Chouchani.*
3. *Sifre Deuteronomy, Berachah*, no. 355, 17.
4. I am deliberately using the dyad "perfect/imperfect," rather than such alternatives as "infinite/finite," "unconditioned/conditioned," or "absolute/relative," because the former *begins* with God while the latter begin with *creation.*
5. Nonetheless, there is a third alternative: to affirm a nonreligious irrationality, a subrationality that denies rationality, but at the same time also denies the perfection, that is to say, the existence of God. This is the position of sophism, skepticism or what Levinas calls a "pure humanism" (in contrast to "biblical humanism") that deny truth in the name of *extra-rational* power relations such as habit, good manners, force, equanimity, will, libido, the "nomadic" and the like. Influential and destructive though this third posture has been, and continues to be, it is essentially *pagan* and—except for a few allusions to Heidegger—is not the concern of the present paper on monotheism.
6. See, for example, Strauss, *Jewish Philosophy.*
7. Lingis translates "*se raminer à*" as "be reduced to." In this context, this is both wrong and misleading. It is made all the worse because in this sentence Levinas is articulating one of his most important thoughts. A religious signification can have several meanings and does not need to be *reduced* to only one meaning, even if that one meaning invokes an intersubjective relation. Nevertheless, all religious significations, so Levinas teaches, can be and should be *brought back* to their intersubjective significance for at this level one discovers their "superior" or highest significance, their ethical sense. For instance, in *EE, TO,* and *TI,* Levinas shows that the term "transcendence," while in a certain sesen applicable to death, only gains its full meaning from the absolute alterity of the other person, which is more other, more transcendent than death. Thus, Levinas is saying of religious significations that they gain their full, superior, or adult sense from the ethical intersubjective relations they express, and that other levels of meaning are, wittingly or not, derived from or dependent upon these. Other levels of meaning are therefore not to be reduced away in the sense of eliminated, but are (or can be) intensified and infused with transcendence through their ethical sense. This return of sense is, given the limitations Levinas discovered in the phenomenological method's commitment to "intentional analysis," the ultimate function of *ethical exegesis,* as one sees practiced in all of Levinas's talmudic readings.

8. While one usually associates the "to" of "to someone" with the dative, which refers to an indirect object, it is not always so easily distinguishable from the accusative, which refers to an immediate object. Beyond grammatical niceties, however, what Levinas is emphasizing is that signification originates in communicative speaking, and hence arises from a dimension of provocation or "accusation," of being accused or charged with a responsibility to and for the other person.

9. In a chapter entitled "Monotheism and Ethics" (74–119), from his book *Monotheism*, Goodman writes: "The emulation called for by the very contemplation of the concept of divine perfection—expressed biblically as the human pursuit of holiness (Lev. 19) and in Plato as the striving to become as like to God as lies in human capacity (*Theaetetus* 176)—means simply the pursuit of the highest conceivable moral standards" (86). See also a later revised version of this chapter in Goodman, *God of Abraham,* 79–114.

10. With some minor revisions of the Lingis translation.

11. Levinas, "The Meaning of Religious Practice," 285–89.

12. See, for instance, Levinas's close analyses of Husserlian phenomenology in *Discovering Existence with Husserl.*

13. The unity of Levinas's philosophical and confessional writings can hardly be better recognized than on the pages of his extraordinary essay of 1973, "God and Philosophy" (*CPP* 153–86); as well as in a second English translation (*GCM* 55–78).

14. Elsewhere, Levinas writes: "In certain very old prayers, fixed by ancient authorities, the faithful one begins by saying to God 'Thou' and finishes the proposition thus begun by saying 'He,' as if, in the course of this approach of the 'Thou' its transcendence into a 'He' supervened. It is what in my descriptions I have called the 'illeity' of the Infinite. Thus, in the 'Here I am!' of the approach of the Other [person], the Infinite does not show itself. How then does it take on meaning? I will say that the subject who says 'Here I am!' *testifies* to the Infinite. It is through this testimony, whose truth is not the truth of representation or perception, that the revelation of the Infinite occurs. It is through this testimony that the very glory of the Infinite glorifies *itself.* The term 'glory' does not belong to the language of contemplation" (*EI* 106–07). For a better understanding of what Levinas might mean by "a 'He' supervened," in the above citation, by means of a concise review of several classic Jewish commentators (Talmud, Abudraham, Riva, Rashba, Ramban, et al.) on the "You"-"He" syntax of Jewish blessings, see Jacobson, *Meditations on the Siddur,* 61–64.

15. That justice, *for Levinas*—which operates otherwise than morality—that is, in terms of equality rather than inequality—is required to rectify morality and is also regulated by morality has escaped critics of his politics, including Howard Caygill, Robert Bernasconi, and Asher Horowitz. See, for example, Horowitz, "Beyond Rational Peace," in *Difficult Justice,* 27–47.

16. For a more extended discussion of Levinas's appropriation of Rabbi Hayyim of Volozhyn, see "The Face of Truth and Jewish Mysticism" in Cohen, *Elevations,* 241–73 (especially 261–73).

17. *Pesikta Kahana,* 140a.

Notes for Chapter 11, "Emmanuel Levinas: Philosopher and Jew"

1. Hirsch, *Jewish Symbolism*, 60. More recently, and also in the name of halachic Judaism, Berkovits has also defended the primacy of ethics in critical dialogue with modern Jewish philosophers. See Berkovits, *Essential Essays on Judaism*. In the philosophical tradition one discovers the same primacy in Plato, in the very form of his discourse: dialogue. And one finds it again, to be sure, in Kant. Of course, Aristotle and Hegel, among many others, will defend the primacy of a purely theoretical virtue, or self-knowledge.

2. Cassirer, *The Philosophy of the Enlightenment*, 114–20.

3. *BV* 159, 160, 161, 162; Levinas also wrote a preface to the French translation of *Nefesh Ha'Hayyim*, vii–x.

4. While Levinas supports the "liberal state" (which he describes as "the modality according to which the conjunction of politics and ethics is intrinsically possible" (*OS* 123), he conceives it in terms of a socially responsible liberalism. Hence it would be closer to the liberalism of T. H. Green, as found in his *Lectures on the Principles of Political Obligation*, rather than the classical or individualistic laissez-faire liberalism of John Stuart Mill or of those who style themselves "neo-conservatives" in America today.

5. Václav Havel, address to the French Senate, March 3, 1999, Paris.

Notes to Chapter 12, "Uncovering the 'Difficult Universality' of the Face-to-Face"

1. For a radical critique of Kierkegaard's dictum that "Truth is subjectivity," see Kaufmann, *From Shakespeare to Existentialism*, 193–99.

2. Aristotle, *Poetics*, 1451b2–7. Here, and in the next long citation from the *Poetics*, I have slightly altered Bywater's translation, having substituted the term "particular" for "singular" to avoid confusion with Levinas's notion of singularity.

3. Aristotle, *Poetics*, 1451b8–10, 16–18.

4. Cf. Bergson, *Time and Free Will*.

5. Bergson, *The Two Sources of Morality*, 317.

6. Shelley, "A Defense of Poetry," 48. This is the final phrase of Shelley's essay, in which he also writes: "Poetry redeems from decay the visitations of the divinity in man" (40).

7. Marion, *In Excess*.

8. Cohen, *Elevations*, 274–86.

9. On the issue of the inherent "moralizing" of Levinas's ethics, see chapter five of this volume.

10. Aristotle, *Poetics*, 1451b15.

11. Cf. Schechter, *Aboth de Rabbi Nathan*, vers. I, xxxi, 45b, 46a, cited in Montefiore and Loewe, *A Rabbinic Anthology*, 182: "And him who commits one sin, desecrates one Sabbath, and destroys one human life, the Scripture regards as if he had destroyed the whole world" (182).

12. Let us only recall Stevens's dictum "that the style of a poem and the poem itself are one," and its consequence, "that, in considering style and its own

creations, that is to say, the relation between style and the unfamiliar, it may be, or become, that the poets who have little or nothing to say are, or will be, the poets that matter." Norman, *Poets on Poetry*, 364–65.

13. Massey, *Find You the Virtue*, 128. Massey locates "fiction" between the violence of myth and the peace of ethical life, hence in an ambivalent position, one that, as Levinas has said, requires the critic for its rescue. "Fiction," according to Massey, "is only a minor by-product thrown off by the victory of the ethical, a substitute for myth that remains beset by uncertainties, weaknesses, and distinctly unethical implications" (129).

14. Ozick, "The Pagan Rabbi," 1–37.

15. The five talmudic readings of this volume, along with the four found in Levinas's *Quatre lectures Talmudiques*, appear in English translation in *Nine Talmudic Readings*.

16. See, especially, the articles collected in Heidegger, *Poetry, Language, Thought*; Heidegger, *On the Way to Language*; and Heidegger, *Existence and Being*.

17. When books are burned because they are "Jewish," can the murder of real Jews be so far away?

18. By a somewhat different route, one which has perhaps traveled too far along the Heideggerian path of language, Gadamer also discovers the universal as the "dialogical" in the poetic word. For an explication of Gadamer on this point, see Di Cesare, *Utopia del comprendere*, 179–92.

19. Soloveitchik, *Halakhic Man*, 82.

20. Fishbane, *The Exegetical Imagination*.

21. Kant, *Foundations of the Metaphysics of Morals*, 55.

22. The mutuality so important to Buber's "I and Thou," is for Levinas an aspect of Eros rather than morality.

23. Cf. Derrida, "Violence and Metaphysics," *Writing and Difference*, 79–153.

24. *BV* 123. One assumes that Levinas's "master," in this citation, is Shoshani. In his article "A Religion for Adults," Levinas makes the same observation and connection between the universality of Judaism and moral election (*DF* 21).

25. It is well known that for the founder of modern biblical criticism, Baruch Spinoza, variant readings built on such otherwise inexplicable switches between the letters Vov and Yud, for example, far from being fruitful and giving rise to new and subtle layers of meaning, are merely "doubtful," based on nothing more than the "similarity" between the letters and a probable scribal error or editorial oversight. Cf. Spinoza, *Theological-Political Treatise*, 123–127.

26. Maimonides, *Mishnei Torah*, 10:7–15.

27. Newman, *Hasidic Anthology*, 321. I learned this teaching firsthand from Rabbi Shalom Friedman of Sanhedria, Jerusalem.

28 On the topic of holiness in Levinas, cf. Hansel, "Utopia and Reality," 168–75.

29. Is it just an idle dream that listening to the Hebrew, thinking of the Holy of Holies, or of the Holiest, one also still hears the hint of Moses' stammering voice?

Notes to Chapter 13, "Singularity: The Universality of Jewish Particularism"

1. Elijah Benamozegh is unfortunately still relatively unknown, even in Italy and Jewish intellectual circles. He was the rabbi of the important Italian Jewish community of Livorno and an intellectual leader of 19th century Italian Jewry. Although he wrote prolifically, for the most part in Italian and Hebrew, two of his works written and published in French have been translated and published in English: *Jewish and Christian Ethics* and *Israel and Humanity.* An excellent, recently translated book on his thought, is by Alessandro Guetta, *Philosophy and Kabbalah.* See also, Josue Jehouda, "Elie Benamozegh," in *Jewish Leaders;* David Novak, *The Image of the Non-Jew;* and Naor and Silvera, "Elia Benamozegh," in *La Rassegna Mensile.*

2. Although Levinas delivered many addresses published under the name of "talmudic readings," he was the first to admit that he was not a "talmudist." This title is reserved for those pious Jewish scholars whose authority derives from having mastered significant portions or all of the vast legal (*halachic*) dimension of the Talmud, something Levinas not only did not and never claimed to have accomplished, but an authority to which he several times publicly deferred. For example, at the start of his commentary to the talmudic tractate *Shabbat* 88a–88b, Levinas makes the following prefatory remarks: "Finally, I am a bit embarrassed that I always comment on the aggadic texts of the Talmud and never venture forth into the Halakhah. But what can I do? The Halakhah demands an intellectual muscle, which is not given to everyone. I cannot lay claim to it" (*NT* 32). Or, another example, Levinas's prefatory remarks to his commentary to tractate *Sanhedrin* 36b–27a: "As in all previous years—and this is not merely a formal excuse—I feel inadequate to the task entrusted to me. The public, responding to these commentaries so favorably as to intimidate me, has in its midst many people who know the Talmud infinitely better than I do" (71). Again, the opening sentence of his commentary to *Baba Metsia* 83a–83b: "As always when I begin my talmudic readings at this colloquium of intellectuals, I fear the presence in the room of people who know the Talmud better than I do. That is not a difficult feat but one which places me in a state of mortal sin, the sin of the student holding forth before his master" (96). These expressions are not false, misleading, or ironic gestures. And Levinas knew the Talmud quite well!

3. While much has been written on the topic of modernity and secularization, the *locus classicus* no doubt remains the debate between Hans Blumenberg (in *The Legitimacy of the Modern Age*) and Karl Löwith (in *Meaning in History*).

4. Thus Levinas and Benamozegh stand against both Blumenberg, who argues for the irreducible, secular character of modernity, and Löwith, who argues that the secularity of modernity remains a transfigured form of religion (Christianity), to which it is reducible. Blumenberg would be wrong to think that secularity is irreducibly independent of religion and Lowith would be mistaken to think that secularity can be reduced to religion. For Levinas and Benamozegh, in contrast, the "secular"—without reduction—is already religious. Of course this means conceiving religion differently than either Blumenberg or Löwith conceive it.

5. In his introduction, entitled "Les politiques du salut," to the recently republished book by Benamozegh, *Morale juive*, Shmuel Trigano comments on the pernicious effects of the divorce between religion and politics found in Christianity; 7–12.

6. Benamozegh, *Israel and Humanity*, 297.

7. Ibid., 326.

8. Ibid., 302.

9. Understanding Jewish universalism not only in terms of ethics but no less in terms of Talmud and Jewish tradition, Benamozegh and Levinas join and continue the earlier labors of Rabbi Samson Raphael Hirsch in opposing Liberal or Reform Judaism. I would also like to link the name Abraham Joshua Heschel to the traditionalist defense of Jewish ethical universalism that unites Hirsch, Benamozegh, and Levinas.

10. On Benamozegh and the German Reformation of Judaism, see Guetta, *Philosophy and Kabbalah*, 135–41.

11. Other types or mixed types of universalism might also exist. For example, the slogan sometimes heard in American "Conservative" (Masorti) Judaism: "Be a Jew at home and a citizen outside," might be seen as a hybrid of concrete universalism at home (and presumably at the synagogue, Mikvah, and Talmud Torah) and abstract universalism in the public sphere. Whether such a hybrid is faithful to either concrete universalism or to abstract universalism, however, is debatable.

12. Benamozegh, *Israel and Humanity*, 257 (citing *Megillah* 13a, and *Kiddushin* 40a).

13. See Samson, *Torat Eretz Yisrael*.

14. See Ravitzky, *Messianism, Zionism*, 181–206.

15. Benamozegh, *Israel and Humanity*, 128.

16. Ibid., 203.

17. On Paul and his transformation of Judaism, see the remarkable scholarly study by Maccoby, *The Mythmaker;* and, brilliantly emphasizing the literary strategies of Paul's abstract universality, see Boyarin, *A Radical Jew*.

18. Not only Reformers, however, have been defenders of an abstract universality in Judaism. I think a persuasive case can be made that the late Yeshayahu Leibowitz (1903–1995), and many of his present day disciples, defended an abstract universalism in the name of Jewish orthodoxy. Jewish law would be obeyed "for its own sake" and not for the self and social perfection it effects. It would thus be a form devoid of content, or, at least, a form whose peculiar content—whatever that might be, perhaps pure obedience?—would have to be supplemented by external considerations of morality and justice. The fact is not surprising, then, that Liebowitz's academic expertise was in chemistry and neurophysiology (though of course it must be said also that not all scientists who happen to be Jewish and orthodox share his beliefs about the abstract nature of orthodox Jewish law).

19. This defense, by the way, was also and precisely the point Moses Hess made against Karl Marx, namely, that nations are not simply ignorant obstacles

to a global proletarian, but rather an integral part of what it means to be human. See Marx, "On the Jewish Question" (1843); Hess, *Rome and Jerusalem* (1862); and, more generally, on the modern dissolution of intermediary groups between individuals and an allegedly more rational global humanity (which in fact means, the State), see Gehlen, *Man in the Age*. Bergson, interestingly enough, also admits "the requisite moral conformation for living in groups" between the solitary individual and humanity in general, in *The Two Sources of Morality*, 95. The defense of the singular also lies at the heart of Vico's *New Science* in contrast, say, to Hegel's *Science of Logic*.

20. Benamozegh, *Israel and Humanity*, 315.

21. Ibid., 315. Benamozegh invokes Symmachus (late second century), who said: " 'It is because the mystery is so great that it is impossible to reach it by a single path.' "

22. Ibid., 294–95.

23. For a fuller explanation of this phrase — "a difficult wisdom concerned with truths that correlate to virtues" — see my introduction to *NTR* (1–46); or my *Ethics, Exegesis and Philosophy*.

24. Benamozegh, *Israel and Humanity*, 198.

25. Ibid., 201.

26. Ibid., 151.

27. Ibid., 133; cf. 203.

28. Ibid., 206. This is also Benamozegh's perspective in *Jewish and Christian Ethics, with a Criticism of Mohamedism*.

29. Ibid., 315.

30. Because of space limitations, let me simply refer readers to one more of Levinas's shorter articles on Jewish universalism, "Israel and Universalism" (*DF* 175–77).

31. Benamozegh, *Israel and Humanity*, 237–38.

32. Ibid., 238.

33. Ibid., 239.

34. Ibid., 318.

Notes to Chapter 14, "Levinas and Rosenzweig"

1. Levinas published two pieces on Rosenzweig: one, originally published as the preface to Stephane Moses' *System and Revelation in Franz Rosenzweig*, appears in English as "The Philosophy of Franz Rosenzweig" (*ITN* 150–60); the other, entitled " 'Between Two Worlds' " (*DF* 181–201).

2. Rosenzweig, "The New Thinking," 110; my italics.

3. See chapter 7, in Cohen, *Elevations*, 162–72. "The central inspiration guiding Levinas's thought is at the same time the central inspiration guiding Rosenzweig's. The inspiration they share is the recognition that there is a mode of relation both *more concrete and more important* than the modes of relation that have hitherto constituted and concerned philosophical comprehension. This relation is the intersubjective relation" (162).

4. Rosenzweig, *The Star of Redemption*, 189; Rosenzweig, "The New Thinking," 122. The translators all translate Rosenzweig's German *Reihe* as "sequence," in preference to a more literal but less accurate rendition as "series."

5. "Representation is a pure present.... To be sure the I who conducts his thoughts *becomes* (or more exactly ages) in time, in which his successive thoughts, across which he thinks in the present, are spread forth. But this becoming in time does not appear on the plane of representation: representation involves no passivity" (*TI* 125; cf. 281–82).

6. Rosenzweig, *Star*, 125.

7. Ibid., 185.

8. Ibid., 178.

9. Ibid., 174.

10. See Baeck, *Judaism and Christianity.*

11. In "The New Thinking," Rosenzweig will explicitly acknowledge Feuerbach, Hermann Cohen, Eugen Rosenstock, Hans Ehrenberg, and several others as those also thinking language and dialogue as essential to meaning and truth (127–28).

12. Rosenzweig, *Star*, 175.

13. Rosenzweig, "The New Thinking," 126.

14. Levinas rejects the common view of an irreconcilable opposition between religion and philosophy, and all the more so his thought stands against the simplistic version of this opposition found in the writings of Leo Strauss. Nietzsche, especially in the third book of his *A Genealogy of Morals,* also rejects the fundamental status of the opposition between science and religion, but clearly for different reasons.

15. Levinas begins this article also with a paean to Rosenzweig: "I would like, in all simplicity, to say how, through the years, my personal attitude toward Christianity has gone through a certain change, precisely thanks to reading Franz Rosenzweig."

16. Rosenzweig, *Star*, 177.

17. "The patriarch Abraham heard the call of God and answers it with his 'Here I am,' and the individual only in Abraham's loins. Henceforth the individual is born a Jew" (ibid., 396). Levinas, speaking in an ecumenical setting, will say, as if commenting on Rosenzweig: "The authentically human is the being-Jewish in all men (may you not be shocked by this!) and its reflection in the singular and the particular" (*ITN* 164).

18. Rosenzweig, "The New Thinking," 120.

19. Rosenzweig, *Star*, 283.

20. Ibid., 78.

21. Ibid., 283.

22. Ibid., 286.

23. For this ambivalence in Schelling, see Habermas, "Dialectical Idealism in Transition." This article is also helpful to see to what extent some of the notions we have found in Rosenzweig (and then also in Levinas) have been borrowed from the later Schelling.

24. Rosenzweig, "The New Thinking," 125.

25. Ibid., 138.

26. See my article on this notion of justice, "Justice and the State."

Notes to Chapter 15, "Virtue Embodied"

1. Two other "signs" associated with Jewishness: *tefillin*, again worn only by males, and Sabbath. Two signs for men, one for all Jews.

2. For an extended discussion of the role of gender in Levinas's thought, see Cohen, *Elevations*, 195–219.

3. Benamozegh, *Israel and Humanity*, 162.

4. "The sight of the *tsitsit* should remind (again a reminder!) the Jew of his obligations. A sight that awakens obligation. A privileged sight, protecting the faithful from the temptations and seductions of sight itself, and from the supposed innocence of his uninformed heart" (*ITN* 79).

Notes to Chapter 16, "Against Theology"

1. Because Levinas does not aim to create a technical vocabulary (indeed, he aims at the reverse), there are many isolated exceptions in his use of the term "theology." For instance, he uses it in such specific forms as "negative theology" and "onto-theology," the former expression referring primarily to its medieval usage by Islamic, Jewish, and Christian religious thinkers, and the latter expression being a neologism of Martin Heidegger, invented in order to speak of and criticize the Western historical forgetfulness of Being—or rather of the "onto-logical difference"—by its reduction to an ontic entity, in this case "God," as was especially the case throughout the medieval period, though certainly not exclusively then. In the course of this chapter we will invoke Heidegger's term "onto-theology" and his critique of it in the name of "fundamental ontology."

2. However, one must beware of commentators mistaking Levinas's loose usage of the term "theology" for his strict usage. How does one tell the difference? It is a long story, a matter of integrity, but, very simply, one must know how to read, which is to say, to learn.

3. I am using the word "performative" here in the sense J. L. Austin gave to this term in his lectures delivered at Harvard University in 1955; see, Austin, *How to Do Things*. So, whether one is "sincere" or not (which one cannot measure—which is the problem, indeed the impossibility of verifying all religious "witnessing"), if at the appropriate moment in a wedding service, say, one pronounces the words "I do," then one *is* married (assuming that the other person in the marriage has also said "I do"!).

4. Monotheism is based on a paradox that is irrational to rationalists but suprarational to monotheists. Cf. chapter 10 of this volume and my "Levinas and the Paradox of Monotheism."

5. While Levinas opposes the "holy" to the "sacred," in English the term "sacred" is often used to mean precisely what Levinas means by the

"holy." Levinas is not instituting an artificial or technical language; the careful reader must attend to what he means—in this case by "sacred" in contrast to "holy"—rather than becoming attached to words, which invariably have several meanings.

6. The three-letter "root" of this word consists of the Hebrew letters *Kof, Dalet and Shin*. See, Schacter-Haham, *Compound of Hebrew*, 595–96, for a variety of related terms derived from this same root.

7. The loss of identity is also Socrates' critique of defining knowledge in terms of perception in the *Theatetus*—"that nothing *is* one thing just by itself, but is always in process of becoming for someone" (157a). Levinas refers to this dialogue, and its critique of Protagoras' claim that "man is the measure of all things" (cf. *TI* 59). "I am surprised," Socrates says in the *Theatetus,* "that he [Protagoras] did not begin his *Truth* with the words, 'The measure of all thing is the pig, or the baboon, or some sentient creature still more uncouth' (161c)."

8. This complex structure or movement, linking the universal work of justice and the exceptional exigencies of morality, which I call the "double dialectic" of Levinas's thought, is its most central and characteristic movement. It is a movement at once relative, dealing with the moral issues and options of today, and absolute, moved by what forever transcends today both in moral terms and in terms of justice or truth. To grasp this structure fully we would have to contrast what Levinas calls the intersubjective time of "diachrony," which is the ultimate structure/movement of time, with the derivative structures of the spatial time of representation and the ecstatic temporality of existence, Such an exposition, however, which I have entered into elsewhere, exceeds the limits of the present chapter.

9. Wyschogrod, "Interview with Emmanuel Levinas," 107.

10. In Matthew 25, Jesus says, referring to the neglect of the needs of the hungry, the thirsty, the stranger, the naked, the sick: "Truly I say to you, to the extent that you did not do it to one of the least of these, you did not do it to Me." (25:45; cf. 25:40).

11. In an interview with François Poirié, Levinas humorously comments on Pope John Paul II's historic visit to a synagogue in Rome at which time he referred to Judaism as the Church's "elder brother": "Of course," Levinas comments, "in the Bible the elder brothers are often those who turn out badly." On a more serious note, in the same answer Levinas notes "that the executioners of Auschwitz must have all done the catechism, and that did not prevent them from committing their crimes" (*IRB* 70).

12. The first statement of this is by Saint Cyprian of Carthage (d. 258), in his Letters, and reads: *Quia salus extra ecclesiuam non est.* The position has continued to be affirmed by the Catholic church including the Fourth Lateran Council (1215), the Dogmatic Constitution *Lumen gentium* 14 of the Second Vatican Council (1964), and by too many popes to enumerate including the present-day Pope Benedict.

13. The importance of this point can hardly be over-emphasized. No dialogue is possible between a religion that (whatever its surface good manners) must convert its interlocutors and one that needs not. One enables speech,

respects the unsurpassable conditions of communication that Levinas's entire philosophy strives to articulate, while the other does not. For this reason Judaism (and Levinas) conceives of universality in terms of *shalom*, the peace or harmony of differences, where a plurality of voices and perspectives are necessary for "the truth," and hence where tolerance is a sign of an ever growing conviction and truth. Merold Westphal has put the point nicely as follows: "[E]ach of us has good reason to think that we might learn something from the other, and this is the best rational for conversation that is not chatter but a serious meeting of the minds" (Westphal, "Whose Philosophy?," 28.) The "serious" alternative, however, and unfortunately, is not chatter, but the religion that must convert rather than converse. In the hubris of having nothing to learn, it prefers silencing others into submission rather than respecting different voices each of which has its own contribution to the communal search for salvation. Its spiritual error, as I consider it, derives from a fundamental categorical mistake: displacing the universality of the religions (properly *shalom*) with the allegedly accomplished ideal truth-values of mathematical science. Instead of celebrating differences, and in this way celebrating Creation, it would eradicate them. Because he thought Christian theology incapable of genuine conversation, Rabbi Joseph Soloveitchik, perhaps the preeminent "modern orthodox" rabbi of the twentieth century, argued that "interfaith" dialogue with Christianity was simply not possible (though he continued to endorse joint efforts for social causes). For more on these different forms of universality, see chapter 13 of this volume.

14. Heidegger, *The Piety of Thinking*, 9, 10, 11.

15. See Cohen, *Elevations*, 300–01. Cf. Richardson "Heidegger and God—and Professor Jonas," 13–40, in which he says, among other things, in defense of Heidegger's ontological thinking: "Because there is truth in Heidegger and wherever there is truth there is God" (40).

16. In 1944 Levinas wrote that onto-theology, in contrast to fundamental ontology, produces merely narratives and myth. Ontic "theology is essentially history and mythology. This is why, in the matter of theology, *authority* guarantees truth" (Wahl, *Existence humaine*, 136). He adds: "Heidegger therefore breaks with theology to the precise extent that he makes the distinction between the ontic and the ontological." (ibid., 137; my translation). Of course, Levinas rejects Heidegger's fundamental ontology for the same reason, ultimately, that he rejects so-called ontic theology: both remain disclosure.

17. Burggraeve, *The Wisdom of Love*.

18. Marion, *God Without Being*, 150–51.

19. See, for instance, Heidegger, *The Question of Being*.

20. Heidegger, "On the Essence of Truth," 114–41.

21. Levinas makes use of this reference to Dante for the title of section four of his essay, "God and Philosophy" (*CPP* 153–73).

22. Levinas's position is close to that of the "Social Gospel" vision of Christianity; see, Rauschenbusch, *A Theology for the Social Gospel*. I will cite only two of the many relevant claims made by Rauschenbusch: "The Church is primarily a fellowship for worship; the Kingdom [of God] is a fellowship of righteous-

ness. When the latter was neglected in theology, the ethical force of Christianity was weakened; when the former was emphasized in theology, the importance of worship was exaggerated" (134). "The establishment of a community of righteousness in mankind is just as much a saving act of God as the salvation of an individual from his natural selfishness and moral inability" (139–40). See also the recent book, Gordon, *Solitude and Compassion.*

Notes tso Chapter 17, "Theodicy After the Shoah"

1. "The passion of Israel in the sense in which one speaks of the passion of Christ—is the moment humanity begins to bleed from the wounds of Israel" (*IRB* 92). Cf., Littell, *The Crucifixion of the Jews.*

2. Rubenstein, *After Auschwitz.*

3. For these and more Jewish "explanations" of the Shoah, see, Cohn-Sherbok, *Holocaust Theology.*

4. "Why dost thou hide thy face, and forget our affliction and our oppression?" (Psalm 44:25). Berkovits, in *Faith After the Holocaust,* relies on this notion, that God hides his face (Hebrew: *hester panim*), to explain his "absence," or, positively, to explain the presence of human freedom, and hence human evil, during the Shoah.

5. Nietzsche, *On the Genealogy,* 25.

6. Cohen, *The Tremendum.*

7. Nietzsche, *On the Genealogy,* 162

8. Ibid., 162.

9. This article also appears in two short volumes pertinent to the themes of this chapter: van Beeck, *Loving the Torah More than God?;* Kolitz, *Yossel Rakover Speaks to God.*

10. Stone, "Emmanuel Levinas," paper given at the University of Oregon, May 6, 1996.

11. If the masochist, who voluntarily suffers and "enjoys" suffering, did not *suffer* he or she would not be a masochist.

12. Jean Amery, *At the Mind's Limits,* quoted in Roth and Berenbaum, eds., *Holocaust,* 189.

13. In Latin *malus,* "bad," and *male,* "ill," both derive from *mel,* "bad." In biblical Hebrew *mameer,* "malignant," "evil," (cf. *Leviticus* 13:51), suggests *to cause pain.*

14. Levinas's strong claim finds a fainter echo in the normative Jewish code of Law, *Shulchan Aruch, Choshen Mishpat* 228:4–5.

15. Recently, from within an explicitly Christian standpoint, and primarily regarding the suffering of children with terminal illnesses, Hauerwas, in *God, Medicine, and Suffering,* touchingly recognizes many of the themes in Levinas: that suffering has "no point" (78–79), the link between suffering and medicine, the crucial difference between others suffering and "my suffering as service" (89), and the wrong committed when forcing the other's suffering into an explanation, including traditional theodicy.

16. Genesis 18:27. See Levinas's talmudic reading on this topic, "Who is One-Self?" (*NTR* 109–26).

17. Here, in the solidarity of suffering, in compassion, lies the path to the ethical theory of "animal rights" that certain commentators have found lacking in Levinas's thought (see Llewelyn, "Am I Obsessed by Bobby?," 234–45). More broadly, it opens the path to the entire dimension of an ethical rather than a naturalistic environmentalism. Alphonso Lingis, for instance, writes: "But to turn away from the intrinsic importance of the fragile and endangered earth, the air, the skies, the lakes and the mountains, and flood plains of rivers and the rain forests, the insects and the fish is also an injustice done to human voices" (Lingis, "Practical Necessity," 82).

18. Levinas, "The State of Caesar and the State of David" (*LR* 268–77).

19. See Fackenheim, *The Jewish Return into History.*

20. Cf., *Jerusalem Talmud*, tractate *Hagigah* 1:7, commenting on Jeremiah 16:11: "Better that they [Israel] abandon Me [God] and continue to observe My laws."

21. Isaiah 63:9: "In all their affliction He was afflicted, and the angel of His presence saved them: in His love and in His pity He redeemed them; and He bore them, and carried them all the days of old." Of course, long before Isaiah, the Jews already understood God to be "compassionate" (*rachoum*) and "long-suffering" (*erek apayim*) (cf. Exod. 34:6–7).

22. Cf. Cohen, *Religion of Reason*, 216–35. Cohen also rejects interpreting another's suffering (226), "unless the sufferer is considered as suffering for the sake of others" (227), which compassion is a "means" toward redemption, for "redemption is also liberation from suffering" (230). All this, encapsulated in Cohen's formula: "Without suffering—no redemption" (235), invites comparison with Levinas on suffering and evil.

23. In stark contrast to the inaugural story of the Jewish nation leaving Egypt for Israel in Exodus, the story of Esther in Persia, told on Purim, contains no overt miracles or divine interventions. Jewish sages have often noted that in this biblical text, unlike any other, the name of God does not appear. Precisely for this reason, too, it is said that when in the messianic era all the other holidays become outmoded, only Purim—a "minor" holiday today—will remain (cf. Midrash to Prov. 9). But was there no miracle—precisely the "miracle" of ethical suffering—in the three day fast of Esther, Mordechai, and the Jews of ancient Shushan?

24. For a comparison of morality without compensation in Levinas and Spinoza, see my "To Love God for Nothing, 339–52.

BIBLIOGRAPHY

Amery, Jean. *At the Mind's Limits.* Trans. Sidney Rosenfeld and Stella P. Rosenfeld. New York: Schocken Books, 1986.

Aristotle. *Organon.* In *The Basic Works of Aristotle,* ed. Richard McKeon. New York: Random House, 1968.

———. *Poetics.* In *Rhetoric and Poetics,* trans. Ingram Bywater. New York: Random House, 1954.

Aron, Raymond. *Marxism and the Existentialists.* New York: Simon and Schuster, 1969.

Aronson, Ronald. *Sartre's Second Critique.* Chicago: University of Chicago Press, 1987.

Austin, J. L. *How to Do Things with Words.* Ed. J. O. Urmson. New York: Oxford University Press, 1962.

Badiou, Alain. *Ethics: An Essay on the Understanding of Evil.* Trans. Peter Hallward. London: Verso, 2001.

Baeck, Leo. *Judaism and Christianity.* Trans. Walter Kaufmann. New York: Jewish Publication Society, 1958.

Beauvoir, Simone de. *The Second Sex.* Trans. H. M. Parshley. New York: Alfred A. Knopf, 1952.

Benamozegh, Elijah. *Israel and Humanity.* Ed. Aime Pallier and Emile Touati, trans. Maxwell Luria. New York: Paulist Press, 1995.

———. *Jewish and Christian Ethics, with a Criticism of Mohamedism.* Trans. Emmanuel Blochman. San Francisco: Emmanuel Blochman, 1867.

———. *Morale juive et morale chretienne.* Paris: In Press Editions, 2000.

Bergson, Henri. *Creative Evolution.* Trans. Arthur Mitchell. New York: Random House, 1944.

———. *Time and Free Will: An Essay on the Immediate Date of Consciousness.* Trans. Frank L. Pogson. New York: Harper Torchbooks, 1960.

———. *The Two Sources of Morality and Religion.* Trans. R. Ashley Audra and Cloudesley Brereton. Garden City, N.J.: Doubleday, n.d.

Berkovits, Eliezer. *Essential Essays on Judaism.* Ed. D. Hazony. Jerusalem: Shalem Press, 2002.

———. *Faith after the Holocaust.* New York: KTAV Publishing House, 1973.

Bloom, Harold. *Shakespeare: The Invention of the Human.* New York: Riverhead Books, 1998.

Blumenberg, Hans. *The Legitimacy of the Modern Age.* Trans. Robert M. Wallace. Cambridge, Mass.: MIT Press, 1985.

Boyarin, Daniel. *A Radical Jew: Paul and the Politics of Identity.* Berkeley and Los Angeles: University of California Press, 1994.

Buber, Martin. *Between Man and Man.* Trans. Ronald Gregor Smith. London and New York: Routledge, 2002.

———. *I and Thou.* Trans. Walter Kaufmann. New York: Charles Scribner's, 1970.

———. *Eclipse of God.* Trans. Maurice Friedman, et al. Atlantic Highlands, N. J.: Humanities Press, 1988.

———. *Paths and Utopia.* Trans. R. F. C. Hull. New York: Macmillan, 1988.

———. *The Way of Man: According to the Teachings of Hasidism.* New Jersey: Citadel Press, 1966.

Buchler, Justus. *Metaphysics of Natural Complexes.* New York: Columbia University Press, 1966.

Buck-Morss, Susan. *The Origin of Negative Dialectics.* New York: Free Press, 1979.

Burggraeve, Roger. *The Wisdom of Love in the Service of Love: Emmanuel Levinas on Justice, Peace, and Human Rights.* Trans. Jeffrey Bloechl. Milwaukee: Marquette University Press, 2002.

Camus, Albert. *Notebooks, 1942–1951.* Trans. Justin O'Brien. New York: Alfred A. Knopf, 1965.

———. "The Philosophy of the Century." In *Youthful Writings* [*Cahiers II*], trans. Ellen Conroy Kennedy. New York: Random House, 1976.

———. *The Rebel.* Trans. Anthony Bower. New York: Alfred A. Knoft, 1956.

Cassirer, Ernst. *The Philosophy of the Enlightenment.* Trans. Fritz C. A. Koellin and James P. Pettegrove. Princeton: Princeton University Press, 1968.

Cohen, Arthur A. *The Tremendum.* New York: Crosswords, 1981.

Cohen, Hermann. *Religion of Reason: Out of the Sources of Judaism.* Translated by. Simon Kaplan. Atlanta: Scholars Press, 1995.

Cohen, Richard A. *Elevations: The Height of the Good in Rosenzweig and Levinas.* Chicago: University of Chicago Press, 1994.

———. *Ethics, Philosophy and Exegesis.* Cambridge: Cambridge University Press, 2001.

———. "Justice and the State in Spinoza and Levinas." *Epoche* 4 (1996): 55–70.

———. "Levinas and the Paradox of Monotheism." *Cahiers d'Etudes Levinassienes* 1 (2003): 61–67; reprinted in *Emmanuel Levinas: Critical Assessments of Leading Philosophers,* vol. 3, ed. Claire Katz, 59–71. London: Routledge, 2005.

———. "To Love God for Nothing: Levinas and Spinoza." *Graduate Faculty Philosophy Journal* 20.2–21.1 (1998): 339–52.

Cohen, Richard A., and James L. Marsh. *Ricoeur as Another: The Ethics of Subjectivity.* Albany: State University of New York Press, 2002.

Cohn-Sherbok, Dan. *Holocaust Theology.* London: Marshall Morgan and Scott, 1989.

Conrad, Joseph. *Youth, a Narrative: and Two Other Stories. Memorial Edition: Collected Works of Joseph Conrad.* Vol. 6. New York: Doubleday, 1925.

de Boer, Theodore. *The Rationality of Transcendence: Studies in the Philosophy of Emmanuel Levinas.* Amsterdam: J. C. Gieben, 1997.

Derrida, Jacques. *Writing and Difference.* Chicago: University of Chicago, 1976.

Desan, Wilfrid. *The Marxism of Jean-Paul Sartre.* Garden City, N.Y.: Doubleday, 1965.

———. *The Tragic Finale: An Essay on the Philosophy of Jean-Paul Sartre.* New York: Harper and Row, 1960.

Dostoyevsky, Fyodor. *The Brothers Karamazov.* Trans. Constance Garnett. New York: New American Library, 1957.

Fackenheim, Emil. *God's Presence in History.* New York: New York University Press, 1970.

————. *The Jewish Return into History: Reflections in the Age of Auschwitz and a New Jerusalem.* New York: Schocken Books, 1978.

Farias, Victor. *Heidegger and Nazism.* Trans. Paul Burrell and Gabriel Ricci. Philadelphia: Temple University Press, 1989.

Faye, Emmanuel. *Heidegger: The Introduction to Nazism into Philosophy.* Trans. Michael B. Smith. New Haven: Yale University Press, 2009.

Frankl, Viktor. *From Death-Camp to Existentialism.* Trans. Ilse Lasch. Boston: Beacon Press, 1959.

Fromm, Erich. *Escape from Freedom.* New York: Avon Books, 1969.

Gehlen, Arnold. *Man in the Age of Technology.* Trans. Patricia Lipscomb. New York: Columbia University Press, 1980.

Gibbs, Robert. *Correlations in Rosenzweig and Levinas.* Princeton: Princeton University Press, 1992.

Goodman, Lenn. *God of Abraham.* New York: Oxford University Press, 1996.

————. *Monotheism: A Philosophic Inquiry into the Foundations of Theology and Ethics.* Totawa, N.J.: Allanheld, Osmun & Co., 1981.

Gordon, Gus. *Solitude and Compassion.* Maryknoll, NY: Orbis Books, 2009.

Green, T. H. *Lectures on the Principles of Political Obligation.* Ed. Paul Harris and John Morrow. Cambridge: Cambridge University Press, 1986.

Guetta, Alessandro. *Philosophy and Kabbalah.* Trans. Helena Kahan. Albany: State University of New York Press, 2009.

Habermas, Jurgen. "Dialectical Idealism in Transition to Materialism: Schelling's Idea of a Contraction of God and Its Consequences for the Philosophy of History." In *The New Schelling,* ed., J. Norman and A. S. Welchman, 43–89. New York: Continuum, 2004.

Halliday, F. E. *Shakespeare and His Critics.* New York: Schocken Books, 1963.

Hansel, Joelle. "Utopia and Reality: The Concept of Sanctity in Kant and Levinas." *Philosophy Today* 43, no. 2 (1990): 168–75.

Harbage, Alfred. *Conceptions of Shakespeare.* New York: Schocken Books, 1968.

Hauerwas, Stanley. *God, Medicine, and Suffering.* Grand Rapids, Mich.: Eerdmans, 1990.

Havel, Václav. Address to the French Senate. Paris, France. March 3, 1999.

——. *Open Letters: Selected Writings 1965–1990*. Ed. Paul Wilson. New York: Random House, 1992.

Hayyim of Volozhin, Rabbi. *Nefesh Ha'Hayyim*. LaGrasse: Verdier, 1986.

Heidegger, Martin. *Being and Time*. Trans. John Macquarrie and Edward Robinson. New York: Harper and Row, 1962.

——. *Kant and the Problem of Metaphysics*. Trans. James S. Churchill. Bloomington: Indiana University Press, 1962.

——. "On the Essence of Truth." Trans. John Sallis. In *Basic Writings*, ed. David Krell, 114–41. New York: Harper and Row, 1977.

——. " 'Only a God Can Save Us': The *Spiegel* Interview" (1966). Trans. William J. Richardson. In *Heidegger: The Man and the Thinker*, ed. Thomas Sheehan. Chicago: Precedent Publishing, 1981.

——. *The Piety of Thinking: Essays by Martin Heidegger*. Ed. and trans. J. G. Hart and J. C. Maraldo. Bloomington: Indiana University Press, 1976.

——. "The Question concerning Technology." In *The Question concerning Technology and Other Essays*, trans. W. Lovitt, 3–35. New York: Harper and Row, 1977.

——. *The Question of Being*. Trans. Jean T. Wilde and William Kluback. New Haven, Conn.: College and University Press, 1958.

——. *Schelling's Treatise on the "Essence of Human Freedom."* Trans. Joan Stambaugh. Athens, Ohio: Ohio University Press, 1985.

——. *What Is a Thing?* Trans. W. B. Barton Jr. and V. Deutsch. Chicago: Henry Regnery, 1967.

Hertz, J. H., trans. *Sayings of the Fathers*. New York: Behrman House, 1945.

Hirsch, Samson Raphael. *Jewish Symbolism: The Collected Writings*. Vol. 3. Trans. Paul Forchheimer and Isaac Levy. New York: Philip Feldheim, 1984.

Höffe, Otfried. *Immanuel Kant*. Trans. M. Farrier. Albany: State University of New York Press, 1994.

Horowitz, Asher. "Beyond Rational Peace." In *Difficult Justice: Commentaries on Levinas and Politics*, ed. Asher Horowitz and Gad Horowitz, 27–47. Toronto: University of Toronto Press, 2006.

Husserl, Edmund. *Cartesian Meditations: An Introduction to Phenomenology.* Trans. Dorion Cairns. The Hague: Martinus Nijhoff, 1970.

———. *Phenomenology and the Crisis of Philosophy.* Trans. Quentin Lauer. New York: Harper and Row, 1965.

Hyde, Michael J. *The Call of Conscience: Heidegger and Levinas, Rhetoric and the Euthanasia Debate.* Columbia: University of South Carolina Press, 2001.

Irigaray, Luce. "Questions to Emmanuel Levinas: On the Divinity of Love," in *The Irigaray Reader,* ed. and trans. M. Whitford, 178–89. Oxford: Basil Blackwell, 1991.

Jacobson, B. S. *Meditations on the Siddur.* Trans. Leonard Oschry. Tel-Aviv: Mtzuda Press, 1966.

Jameson, Fredric. *Marxism and Form.* Princeton: Princeton University Press, 1971.

Jehouda, Josue. "Elie Benamozegh." Trans. A. Propp. In *Jewish Leaders (1750–1940),* ed. Leo Jung, 233–46. New York: Bloch, 1953.

Kandinsky, Wassily. *Concerning the Spiritual in Art.* Trans. M. T. H. Sadler. New York: Dover, 1977.

Kant, Immanuel. *Critique of Pure Reason.* Trans. N. K. Smith. New York: Macmillan, 1965.

———. *Foundations of the Metaphysics of Morals.* Trans. L. W. Beck. Indianapolis: Bobbs-Merrill, 1980.

———. *Religion within the Limits of Reason Alone.* Trans. T. M. Greene and H. H. Hudson. New York: Harper and Row, 1960.

Kaufmann, Walter. *From Shakespeare to Existentialism.* Garden City, N.Y.: Doubleday, 1960.

Keenan, Dennis King, *Death and Responsibility: The "Work" of Levinas.* Albany: State University of New York Press, 1999.

Kirk, G. S., J. E. Raven, and M. Schofield, eds. *The Presocratic Philosophers.* Cambridge: Cambridge University Press, 1983.

Kisiel, Theodore. *Heidegger's Way of Thought.* Ed. Alfred Denker and Marion Heinz. New York: Continuum, 2002.

Kohn, Hans. *Martin Buber: Sein Werke und seine Zeit.* Koln: Jacob Meltzner, 1961.

Kolitz, Zvi. *Yossel Rakover Speaks to God: Holocaust Challenges to Religious Faith.* Hoboken, N.J.: KTAV Publishing House, 1995.

Laing, R. D., and David. G. Cooper. *Reason and Violence: A Decade of Sartre's Philosophy 1950–1960.* New York: Random House, 1964.

Lawlor, Leonard. *Thinking through French Philosophy.* Bloomington and Indianapolis: Indiana University Press, 2003.

Levinas, Emmanuel. *Alterity and Transcendence.* Trans. Michael B. Smith. New York: Columbia University Press, 1999.

———. *Basic Philosophical Writings.* Ed. Adriaan T. Peperzak, Simon Critchley, and Robert Bernasconi. Bloomington: Indiana University Press, 1996.

———. *Beyond the Verse: Talmudic Readings and Lectures.* Trans. Gary D. Mole. Bloomington: Indiana University Press, 1994.

———. *Collected Philosophical Papers.* Ed. and trans. Alphonso Lingis. Pittsburgh: Duquesne University Press, 1998.

———. *Difficult Freedom.* Trans. Sean Hand. Baltimore: Johns Hopkins University Press, 1990.

———. *Discovering Existence with Husserl.* Ed. and trans. Richard A. Cohen and Michael B. Smith. Evanston: Indiana University Press, 1998.

———. *Entre Nous: Thinking-of-the-Other.* Trans. Michael B. Smith. New York: Columbia University Press, 1998.

———. *Ethics and Infinity.* Trans. Richard A. Cohen. Pittsburgh: Duquesne University Press, 1985.

———. *Existence and Existents.* Trans. Alphonso Lingis. The Hague: Martinus Nijhoff, 1978.

———. *God, Death, and Time.* Trans. Bettina Bergo, ed. Jacques Rolland. Stanford, Calif.: Stanford University Press, 2000.

———. *Humanism of the Other.* Trans. Nidra Poller. Urbana: University of Illinois Press, 2003.

———. *In the Time of the Nations.* Trans. Michael B. Smith Bloomington: Indiana University Press, 1994.

———. *Is It Righteous to Be? Interview with Emmanuel Levinas.* Edited by Jill Robbins. Stanford, Calif.: Stanford University Press, 2001.

———. *Otherwise Than Being or Beyond Essence.* Trans. Alphonso Lingis. Pittsburgh: Duquesne University Press, 1998.

———. *The Levinas Reader.* Ed. Sean Hand. Oxford: Basil Blackwell, 1989.

———. "The Meaning of Religious Practice." Trans. Peter Atterton, Matthew Calarco, and Joelle Hansel. *Judaism* 25, no. 3 (2005): 285–89.

———. *New Talmudic Readings*. Trans. Richard A. Cohen. Pittsburgh: Duquesne University Press, 1999.

———. *Nine Talmudic Readings*. Trans. Annette Aronowicz. Bloomington: Indiana University Press, 1990.

———. *Of God Who Comes to Mind*. Trans. Bettina Bergo. Stanford, Calif.: Stanford University Press, 1998.

———. *On Escape*. Trans. Bettina Bergo. Stanford, Calif.: Stanford University Press, 2003.

———. *Outside the Subject*. Trans. Michael B. Smith. Stanford, Calif.: Stanford University Press, 1995.

———. "The Primacy of Pure Practical Reason." Trans. B. Billings. *Man and World* 27 (1994): 445–53.

———. *Proper Names*. Trans. Michael B. Smith. Stanford, Calif.: Stanford University Press, 1996.

———. *"Quelques Reflexions sur la philosophie de l'hitlerisme." Les imprevus de l'histoire*. Montpellier: Fata Morgana, 1994.

———. "Le scandale du mal: Catastrophes naturelles et crimes de l'homme." *Les Nouveaux Cahiers* 85 (1986): 15–17.

———. *The Theory of Intuition in Husserl's Phenomenology*. Trans. Andre Orianne. Evanston, Ill.: Northwestern University Press, 1973.

———. *Time and the Other [and Additional Essays]*. Trans. Richard A. Cohen. Pittsburgh: Duquesne University Press, 1987.

———. *Totality and Infinity*. Trans. Alphonso Lingis. Pittsburgh: Duquesne University Press, 1969.

———. *Unforeseen History*. Trans. Nidra Poller. Urbana: University of Illinois Press, 2004.

———. "Useless Suffering." Trans. Richard A. Cohen. In *The Provocation of Levinas*, ed. Robert Bernasconi and David Wood, 156–67. London: Routledge, 1988.

Lingis, Alphonso. "Practical Necessity." *Graduate Faculty Philosophy Journal* 20.2–21.1 (1998): 71–82.

Littell, Franklin H. *The Crucifixion of the Jews: The Failure of Christians to Understand the Jewish Experience*. Macon, Ga.: Mercer University Press, 1986.

Llewelyn, John. "Am I Obsessed by Bobby?" In *Re-Reading Levinas,* ed. Robert Bernasconi and Simon Criticley, 234–45. Bloomington: Indiana University Press, 1991.

Löwith, Karl. *Meaning in History.* Chicago: University of Chicago Press, 1957.

Lyotard, Jean-François. *The Postmodern Condition.* Trans. Geoffrey Bennington and Brian Massumi. Minneapolis: University of Minnesota Press, 1984.

Maccoby, Hyam. *The Mythmaker: Paul and the Invention of Christianity.* New York: Harper and Row, 1987.

Maimonides, Moses. *The Guide of the Perplexed.* Vol. 1. Trans. Shlomo Pines. Chicago: University of Chicago Press, 1963.

———. *Mishnei Torah, Hilchot Mat'not Ani'im (Laws of Gifts to the Poor).*

Malka, Salomon. *Monsieur Chouchani: L'enigme d'un maitre du XXC siecle.* Paris: Jean-Claude Lattes, 1994.

Marcel, Gabriel. *The Philosophy of Existentialism.* Trans. Manya Harrari. New York: Citadel Press, 1956.

Marion, Jean-Luc. *God without Being.* Trans. T. A. Carlson. Chicago: University of Chicago Press, 1991.

———. *In Excess: Studies of Saturated Phenomena.* Trans. Robyn Horner and Vincent Berraud. New York: Fordham University Press, 2002.

Mendes-Flohr, Paul. *From Mysticism to Dialogue.* Detroit: Wayne State University Press, 1989.

Montefiore, C. G., and R. H. Loewe, eds. *A Rabbinic Anthology.* New York: Schocken Books, 1974.

Munster, Arno. "De la pensée Buberienne du je-tu vers la pensée de l'autre dans la philosophie d'Emmanuel Levinas." In *Le principe dialogique: de la refiexion monologique vers la pro-fiexion intersubjective.* Paris: Editions Kime, 1997.

Naor, Luisa Franchetti, and Myriam Silvera, eds. "Elia Benamozegh, Livorno 1822–1900: Un maestro in eta moderna, " special issue of *La Rassegna Mensile di Israel* 43, no. 3 (1997).

Nemo, Philippe. *Job and the Excess of Evil.* Trans. Michael Kigel. Pittsburgh: Duquesne University Press, 1998.

Newman, Louis I., ed. and trans. *Hasidic Anthology: Tales and Teachings of the Hasidim.* New York: Schocken Books, 1963.

Nietzsche, Friedrich. *The Anti-Christ.* In *Twilight of the Idols and The Anti-Christ,* trans. R. J. Hollingdale, 113–87. London: Penguin Books, 1968.

———. *On the Genealogy of Morals and Ecce Homo.* Trans. Walter Kaufmann and R. J. Hollingdale. New York: Random House, 1969.

Norman, Charles, ed. *Poets on Poetry.* New York: Collier Books, 1962.

Novak, David. *The Image of the Non-Jew in Judaism.* Lampeter: Edwin Mellen Press, 1983.

Nussbaum, Martha C. *The Fragility of Goodness: Luck and Ethics in Greek Tragedy and Philosophy.* Cambridge: Cambridge University Press, 1986.

Perpich, Diane. *The Ethics of Emmanuel Levinas.* Stanford: Stanford University Press, 2008.

Plato. *Phaedrus and Letters VII and VII.* Trans. Walter Hamilton. Middlesex: Penguin Books, 1973.

———. *Symposium.* Trans. Alexander Nehamas and Paul Woodruff. Indianapolis: Hackett, 1989.

Plotinus. *The Enneads.* Trans., Stephen MacKenna London: Penguin Books, 1991.

Prada, Manuel Gonzalez. "Catholic Education." *Free Pages and Hard Times.* Trans. F. H. Fornoff. Oxford: Oxford University Press, 2003.

Proctor, Robert. *Defining the Humanities.* Bloomington: Indiana University Press, 1998.

Rauschenbusch, Walter. *A Theology for the Social Gospel.* Nashville: Abingdon Press, 1978.

Ravitzky, Aviezer. *Messianism, Zionism, and Jewish Religious Radicalism.* Trans. Michael Swirsky. Chicago: University of Chicago Press, 1996.

Richardson, William. "Heidegger and God—and Professor Jonas." *Thought: Fordham University Quarterly* 40 (1965): 13–40.

Ricoeur, Paul. *Oneself as Another.* Trans. Kathleen Blamey. Chicago: Chicago University Press, 1992.

Rosenzweig, Franz. "The New Thinking." In *Philosophical and Theological Writings,* ed. and trans. Paul W. Franks and Michael L. Morgan. Indianapolis: Hackett, 2000.

———. *The Star of Redemption.* Trans. William W. Hallo. Boston: Beacon Press, 1972.

Roth, John K., and Michael Berenbaum, eds. *Holocaust: Religious and Philosophical Implications*. New York: Paragon House, 1989.

Rubenstein, Richard L. *After Auschwitz: Radical Theology and Contemporary Judaism*. Indianapolis: Bobbs-Merrill, 1966.

Samson, David. *Torat Eretz Yisrael: The Teachings of HaRav Tzvi Yehuda HaCohen Kook*. Jerusalem: Torat Eretz Yisrael Publications, 1991.

Sartre, Jean-Paul. *Being and Nothingness: A Phenomenological Essay on Ontology*. Trans. Hazel E. Barnes. New York: Washington Square Press, 1966.

———. *Critique of Dialectical Reason: Theory of Practical Ensembles*. Trans. Alan Sheridan-Smith. Atlantic Highlands, N.J.: Humanities Press, 1976.

———. "Existentialism Is a Humanism." Trans. Philip Mairet. In *The Existentialist Tradition*, ed. Nino Langiulli, 391–419. Garden City, N.Y.: Doubleday, 1971.

———. "The Humanism of Existentialism." In *Essays in Existentialism*, ed. Wade Baskin, 31–62. New York: Citadel Press, 1967.

———. *Nausea*. Trans. Lloyd Alexander. New York: New Directions, 1964.

———. *No Exit and Three Other Plays*. Trans. Stuart Gilbert. New York: Random House, 1949.

Schacter-Haham, H. *Compound of Hebrew*. Jerusalem: Kiryat-Sefer, 1989.

Schechter, Solomon, ed. *Aboth de Rabbi Nathan*. London, 1887.

Scheler, Max. "Lived Body, Environment, and Ego." Trans. Manfred S. Frings. In *The Philosophy of the Body: Rjections of Cartesian Dualism*, ed. Stuart F. Spicker, 159–86. Chicago: Quadrangle Books, 1970.

Schlipp, Paul Arthur, ed. *The Philosophy of Jean-Paul Sartre*. La Salle, Ill.: Open Court, 1981.

Shelley, Percy Bysshe. "A Defense of Poetry." In *English Essays: Sidney to Macaulay* Vol. 26, ed. Charles W. Eliot, 329–62. New York: Collier and Son, 1910.

Shestov, Lev. *In Job's Balance*. Trans. Camilla Coventry and C. A. Macartney. Athens: Ohio University Press, 1975.

Sluga, Hans. *Heidegger's Crisis: Philosophy and Politics in Nazi Germany*. Cambridge, Mass.: Harvard University Press, 1993.

Spinoza, Baruch Spinoza. *The Ethics*. Trans. Samuel Shirley. Indianapolis: Hackett, 1992.

———. *Theological-Political Treatise*. Trans. Samuel Shirley. Indianapolis: Hackett, 1998.

Stone, Ira F. "Emmanuel Levinas, the Musar Movement and the Future of Jewish Ethical Living." Paper presented at the "Ethics after the Holocaust" conference, University of Oregon, May 6, 1996.

Strauss, Leo. "An Introduction to Heideggerian Existentialism." In *The Rebirth of Classical Political Rationalism: An Introduction to the Thought of Leo Strauss,* ed. Thomas L. Pangle. Chicago: University of Chicago Press, 1989.

———. *Jewish Philosophy and the Crisis of Modernity: Essays and Lectures in Modern Jewish Thought*. Ed. Kenneth Hart Green. Albany: State University of New York Press, 1997.

Taylor, John F. A. *The Masks of Society: An Inquiry into the Covenant of Civilization*. New York: Meredith Publishing Company, 1966.

Tönnies, Ferdinand. *Community and Society*. Trans. Charles P. Loomis. New York: Harper and Row, 1963.

Trilling, Lionel. *A Gathering of Fugitives*. Boston: Beacon Books, 1955.

van Beeck, Franz Jozef, S.J. *Loving the Torah More than God?: Towards an Ethical Appreciation of Judaism*. Chicago: Loyola University Press, 1989.

Vlastos, Gregory. *Platonic Studies*. Princeton: Princeton University Press, 1973.

Wahl, Jean. *Existence humaine et transcendence*. Neuchâtel: Editions de la Baconnier, 1944.

Westphal, Merold. "Whose Philosophy? Which Religion?" In *Transcendence in Philosophy and Religion,* ed. James E. Faulconer, 13–34. Bloomington: Indiana University Press, 2003.

Wolfe, Cary. "In the Shadow of Wittgenstein's Lion," in *Zoontologies: The Question of the Animal,* ed., Cary Wolfe, 1–58. Minneapolis: University of Minnesota Press, 2003.

Wolin, Richard. *The Politics of Being: The Political Thought of Martin Heidegger*. New York: Columbia University Press, 1993.

Wyschogrod, Edith. "Interview with Emmanuel Levinas: December 31, 1982." *Philosophy and Theology* 4, no. 2 (1989): 105–18.

Žižek, Slavoj. "Neighbors and Other Monsters: A Plea for Ethical Violence," in *The Neighbor: Three Inquiries in Political Theology,* Slavoj Žižek, Eric L. Santner, and Kenneth Reinhard. Chicago: University of Chicago Press, 2005.

INDEX

Abraham, 221, 288, 324
abstract universality, 261, 266–68, 349n18
accusative dimension of meaning, 13, 217–18, 345n8
Adam, 74, 339n32
aestheticism: Bergson and, 48, 301; dangers of, 153, 157; Heidegger and, 28, 48, 95, 107, 215, 245–46; Nietzsche and, 95, 301; religion and, 215; Rosenzweig and, 284–86; and value, 231
aesthetics: art for art's sake, 154, 157, 244; ethics in relation to, 3–4; Levinas and, 153; science in relation to, 3–4. *See also* art; poetry
agnosticism, 315–16
Althusser, Louis, 193
Amery, Jean, 320
animals, 187–91, 324, 338n13, 356n17
anxiety *(angst)*, 46, 60, 87, 89
appearance, 21, 146–48
Aquinas, Thomas, 298
Aristophanes, 20
Aristotle, 5, 10, 17; *Nicomachean Ethics*, 125; *Organon*, 42; *Poetics*, 238–43
art: Heidegger on, 340n2; Levinas on, 153–54, 156–57, 159–60, 244, 340n2; morality and, 157–58, 244–45; as myth, 154, 245; Nietzsche on, 154, 341n6; philosophy and, 153, 156. *See also* aesthetics; literature; poetry
art for art's sake, 154, 157, 244
atheism, 131, 133–34, 279–81, 315–16. *See also* God
Athens and Jerusalem, 94, 104, 112, 174, 201, 235, 288
Austin, J. L., 218
autonomy, 21, 145

bad faith, 145
Badiou, Alain, 193–96
Baeck, Leo, 276; *Judaism and Christianity*, 203
Baudrillard, Jean, 192
Beauvoir, Simone de, 185–86
being: adequacy of, 20; better than, 37, 38; beyond, 140, 340n34; of the body, 37; in classical philosophy, 38–39; in contemporary philosophy, 39–40; death and, 59; disruption of, 49; as entrapment, 72; God and, 212; Heidegger and, 17–20, 82–83, 215, 268, 310, 331n4; history and, 48; infinity and, 112; *logos* and, 42; otherwise than, 20; and the right to be, 51, 158; time and, 41–43. *See also* ontology; otherwise than being
being-toward-death, 46–47, 50, 59–61, 68–69, 163
belief, 191, 213
Benamozegh, Elijah, 203, 257–72, 294, 348n1; *Israel and Humanity*, 263
Bergson, Henri, 230; Buber and, 92; contemporary philosophy and, 11; and death, 331n6; influence of, 176; and time, 44–46, 48, 49–50, 239, 274; *Time and Free Will*, 44, 176
Bernasconi, Robert, 171
"Between Two Worlds" (Levinas), 286
beyond being, 140, 340n34
Beyond the Verse (Levinas), 242
Bible, 33, 35, 55, 163, 202, 223, 232, 254, 263, 353n11
biblical humanism, 179, 202, 225, 253, 260, 269, 287
Blanchot, Maurice, 153, 165, 169
Bloom, Harold, 156, 341n8

philosophy and, 8; responsibility for the other and, 8, 63, 236
humanism: biblical, 179, 202, 225, 253, 260, 269, 287; critics of, 193; and particularity, 267
Humanism of the Other (Levinas), 166
humility, 251–54
Husserl, Edmund, 53, 54, 59, 230; abstractness of, 268; *Cartesian Meditations,* 136; contemporary philosophy and, 11; *The Crisis of the European Sciences,* 118–19; and doubt, 121; *Ideas,* 164; and intersubjectivity, 136; and phenomenology, 46, 175, 283, 301; "Philosophy and the Crisis of European Man," 118–19; "Philosophy as Rigorous Science," 4; and representation, 300–01; and science, 4, 5, 7, 118; and signification, 216–17; students of, 107, 174, 207; and time, 274; and totality, 110; and truth, 15, 178
hyper-reality, 192

"Ideology and Idealism" (Levinas), 172
Ihde, Don, 172
il y a. See "there is"
imagination: and Cartesian dualism, 329n9; and happiness, 23; poetry and, 240
immanence, 91, 192, 193, 219, 245, 278
immemorial past, 52, 275
individuality, 108–10, 126
infinity: ethics and, 115; and finitude, 109–11; Kant and, 116–17; morality and, 4, 7, 105, 113, 125, 241; of responsibility, 9, 135; science and, 118–19; as surplus, 111–12, 114–15; totality vs., 111–14, 126
in-itself, 128, 132–34, 146–47
interhumanity, 293
intersubjectivity: asymmetry of, 136–37; Confucianism and, 179–80; death and, 50, 73–74, 320–21; Levinas and, 137; meaning and, 13, 217–18; morality and, 270, 311; as nonepistemological relation, 86–87; Sartre and, 136–37; time and, 53–54, 71
"*In the Image of God,* according to Rabbi Hayyim Volozhiner" (Levinas), 222
Irigaray, Luce, 169, 185–86

irrationality, 199–200. *See also* nonrationality
Isaac, Solomon ben (Rashi), 210, 299
Isaiah, 228, 312, 326, 356n21
Islam: and ethics, 224; and paradox of monotheism, 212; Rosenzweig on, 278; and tolerance, 307; Wahabi, 307
Israel, 272, 295, 324, 325
I-Thou relation, ii, 81, 84, 87, 90–91, 136

Jacob, 250
Jacobi, Friedrich Heinrich, 6
Jeremiah, 312–13
Jerusalem. *See* Athens and Jerusalem
Jesus, 264, 267, 296, 297, 353n10
Judaism: and animals, 189–90; and the Bible, 55; and *bris mila,* 288–95; concrete universality of, 268–72; and ethics, 221–24; forms of, 173–74; God in, 32–33, 236; and history, 17; infinity and multiplicity in, 108–09; and justice, 31–32, 257–58, 286–87; Kant on, 26, 29, 329n10; Levinas and, 29, 160–61, 173–74, 200–03, 207–09, 220–35, 257–72, 279, 348n2; and morality, 257–58; nature of, 255–56; and paradox of monotheism, 212, 224; and particularity, 259–62; and pleasure, 33; and purpose, 19; ritual in, 221; and sanctification, 269, 293; and Talmud, 294; and tolerance, 258, 353n13; universality of, 202–03, 228–29, 246, 256–72, 279; as way of life, 259; *Wissenschaft,* 260. *See also* Talmud; Torah
"Judaism and Kenosis" (Levinas), 251
Jung, Karl, 82, 83
justice: death and, 76–78; as end, 30; God and, 78, 312–13; Judaism and, 31–32, 257–58, 286–87; and mercy, 220, 234; morality in relation to, 14, 30, 55, 201–02, 233; philosophy and, 15; religion and, 225; science and, 13–15, 233, 282; time and, 54–55; and utopia, 92

Kandinsky, Wassily, 46
Kant, Immanuel, 53, 82, 207; Christianity of, 203; *Critique of Judgment,* 21; *Critique of Practical Reason,* 6, 21, 29; *Critique*

"A Religion for Adults" (Levinas), 286–87
representation: theology as, 300–06; of the
world, 30
resoluteness, 68, 84
responsibility: art and, 157–58, 244;
freedom and, 28; and the human, 8,
63, 236; infinity of, 9, 135; Levinas
and, 135–36; nature of, 8; for the other,
234–35; Sartre on, 134–36; and the self,
149, 187; after the Shoah, 326–27; and
signification, 219; subjectivity and, 52–
53; suffering and, 324; vulnerability and,
103, 112, 125. *See also* ethics; morality;
obligation
revelation, reason and, 290
"Revelation in the Jewish Tradition"
(Levinas), 222–24
Revillon, Bertrand, 296
Richardson, William, 309
Ricoeur, Paul, 161, 208; *Oneself as Another,*
184–85
righteousness, hierarchy of, 251–53
right to be, 51, 158
ritual, 221
Roman Catholicism, 264
Rosenstock-Huessy, Eugen, 276
Rosenzweig, Franz, 58, 273–87; *The Star of
Redemption,* 131, 273–77, 280, 282–83,
285
Rubenstein, Richard, 315

sacred, the, 299–300
sacred history, 51, 154. *See also* history; holy
history
Sade, Marquis de, 188–89, 342n11
said, the: dangers of, 184; saying in relation
to, 12, 35, 111, 177, 277
Salanter, Israel, 38, 290
sanctification, 269, 293
Sanhedrin, 295
Sartre, Jean-Paul, 82, 83; *Anti-Semite
and Jew,* 129; and atheism, 133; and
being, 109; *Being and Nothingness,* 107,
109, 112–13, 128, 132, 134–35, 140,
336n1; criticisms of, 138–48; *Critique
of Dialectical Reason,* 128, 338n9;
"Existentialism Is a Humanism," 135,
145, 338n12; and the for-itself, 66,

128, 132–34, 140, 142, 145–47; and
freedom, 66, 109, 128–33, 141–44, 149;
and intersubjectivity, 136–37; Levinas
and, 128–49, 336n1, 336n2, 337n7;
and literature, 159; *Nausea,* 147; *No
Exit,* 137, 164–65; on the other, 144; on
responsibility, 134–36; on subjectivity,
132, 140, 145
saying: ethics and, 218, 304; the said in
relation to, 12, 35, 111, 177, 277
"*Le Scandale du mal*" (Levinas), 317
Schelling, Friedrich Wilhelm Joseph von, 6,
27, 273, 277, 283, 284
Schleiermacher, Friedrich Ernst Daniel, 27
Schopenhauer, Arthur, 46, 100
science: and abstract universalism, 266;
aesthetics in relation to, 3–4; ethics in
relation to, 3–7, 9–10, 13–15, 27, 118; as
first philosophy, 14; infinity and, 118–19;
justice and, 13–15, 233, 282; Kant and,
117–18; Levinas and, 4, 117–18, 282,
284; modern, 4–5; nature and meaning
of, 9–10, 15; Nietzsche on, 123; religion
in relation to, 214, 230; Rosenzweig
on, 282; and scientism, 118, 231; and
totality, 4, 7; and values, 230. *See also*
knowledge
scientism, 118, 231
secular modernity, 259
self, the: atheism/paganism and, 280–81;
ethics and, 304; the other in relation
to, 8–9, 13, 54, 224, 234–35, 249–50,
302–03; responsibility and, 149, 187. *See
also* subjectivity
self-sacrifice, 52, 75
sensibility, 22–23, 65, 78, 134, 176, 177
Shakespeare, William, 70, 150–68, 279,
341n8; *Hamlet,* 151, 167; *King Lear,* 166;
Macbeth, 163, 164, 167. *See also* literature
shalom (peace), 123, 225, 234, 354n13
Shoah, 314–27. *See also* Holocaust
Shoshani, Professor, 32, 208
signification, 182, 216–19, 344n7. *See also*
meaning
simulation, 192
singularity: morality and, 8, 194, 249,
253–54; of the other, 8, 194–95, 243;
particularity vs., 243; truth and, 151–52;